BIBI

BIBI

The Turbulent Life and Times
of Benjamin Netanyahu

ANSHEL PFEFFER

HURST & COMPANY, LONDON

First published in hardback in the United Kingdom by

C. Hurst & Co. (Publishers) Ltd. in 2018
41 Great Russell Street, London, WC1B 3PL
© Anshel Pfeffer, 2018
All rights reserved.

Printed in the United Kingdom by Bell and Bain Ltd, Glasgow

First published in the United States by Basic Books, Hachette Book Group, 1290 Avenue of the Americas, New York, NY 10104, www.basicbooks.com
This edition published by arrangement with Basic Books.

The right of Anshel Pfeffer to be identified as the author of this publication is asserted by him in accordance with the Copyright, Designs and Patents Act, 1988.

A Cataloguing-in-Publication data record for this book is available from the British Library.

ISBN: 978-1-84904-988-7

This book is printed using paper from registered sustainable and managed sources.

www.hurstpublishers.com

Print book interior design by Linda Mark.

For David Landau ז״ל

Contents

Prologue
Netanyahu's Israel

Benjamin Netanyahu sat back on the narrow bench, the tired puffiness beneath his eyes still visible under the perpetual television makeup. The Sikorsky Sea Stallion clattered off the Hadassah hospital helipad and headed south over the Judean Desert. Wearing the rectangular reading glasses he is rarely seen with in public, he perused his daily intelligence briefing papers. But for most of the hour-long journey, he seemed lost in his own thoughts.

Forty years earlier, as a young special forces lieutenant, he would fly in such a helicopter as he led his team of commandos on missions deep within enemy territory, most of them still classified. Today's trip was public: his first visit to the construction site of the new border fence between Israel and Egypt.

It was September 2011, midway through his second term. Netanyahu had been back in power for over two years and was now facing his most significant challenge since reelection. That summer, a grassroots protest movement had begun in Tel Aviv, out of the Facebook page of a young woman. Enraged at the raising of her rent, Daphni Leef had set up a tent on Rothschild Boulevard. Thousands of young people and families had joined in, setting up their own tents in Tel Aviv and other cities.

The public anger focused on one of Netanyahu's weakest points—the growing gap between a thin layer of businesspeople and entrepreneurs, making millions from Israel's high-tech-fueled economic success, on the one hand, and, on the other, the majority, those who were struggling with rising housing and consumer prices.

Israel had weathered the global financial crisis of 2008–2010 relatively unscathed. Unemployment was down, gross domestic product (GDP) was up, and headlines announcing yet another sale of an Israeli start-up, for hundreds of millions or even billions of dollars, was an almost weekly occurrence. But the complaints of young middle-class Israelis, who were unable to buy their own homes and live a comfortable life without incurring crushing debt, made Netanyahu vulnerable.

The government's derisory attempts to deflect criticism, announcing housing reforms and appointing a special commission to examine the problems of the middle class, failed to arrest the plummeting popularity of Netanyahu and his right-wing party, Likud, in public opinion surveys. At least one senior minister warned that "if this continues, we can say goodbye to power in the next elections."

Netanyahu was loath to change his economic policies. He believed that the economic reforms he had made in 2003–2005, while serving as finance minister, had saved the country's economy during the worldwide recession. After winning the 2009 elections, he had awarded himself the title of "Supreme Minister for Economic Affairs." A group of activists, dangerous left-wing anarchists funded by foreign money, in his view, would not blow his economy off-course. Netanyahu would change the national agenda instead of engaging with them.

The chopper flight south was a thinly veiled attempt to wrest back control of the news agenda. Work on the new border fence had been in progress for years, but in the wake of a terror attack launched from Egypt, in which eight Israelis were killed, Netanyahu pushed through a decision to immediately add another 1 billion shekels of funding for the 250-kilometer-long, 5-meter-high reinforced steel barrier and prioritize its construction. On his first visit to one of the completed sections, Netanyahu was taking along defense correspondents from the main media organizations, who would be less likely than other journalists to press for his response to the protests. Their presence would lend a suitable military atmosphere to the visit.

Landing in a small desert wadi hidden from the sight of any snipers who might be lurking across the border, he was taken in a convoy of bulletproof jeeps to an observation post prepared nearby. An air-conditioned tent with refreshments had been erected. Dozens of senior officers had been brought in to provide a backdrop for the prime minister's viewing of the fence. The camera crews were taken closer in to get a good view of the barrier, so they could impress their audiences with footage of the impregnable fortification. After hearing the briefings and seeing for himself the long fence snaking away to the desert's horizon, Netanyahu stood at a podium to deliver a few carefully prepared sentences and swat away the reporters' softball questions.

He was in such a good mood that on the flight back to Jerusalem, he sat up front in the crew chief's jump seat, between the two pilots, animated by the spectacular view of the Negev Desert and Israel's heartland beyond. Netanyahu obviously felt that the visit to the border fence had been a success; he returned there with reporters in tow twice more over the next sixteen months.

The fence has become Netanyahu's signature project, his physical version of the metaphorical "Iron Wall" that Ze'ev Jabotinsky, the spiritual father of Israel's right wing, had called for in 1923 to protect the Jews from their hostile Arab neighbors.

The fence was not only meant to block terror attacks—it would have the additional benefit, in Netanyahu's eyes, of keeping out African migrants fleeing the impoverished and war-torn Horn of Africa. Tens of thousands had crossed the old ramshackle fence. Most had made their way to the run-down neighborhoods of South Tel Aviv, their illegal status allowing them only to scrabble a meager existence.

At the final cabinet meeting before the 2013 election, Netanyahu proudly announced that "as a result of building the fence, we have totally stopped the entry of infiltrators to Israel's cities. Over the past seven months, zero infiltrators have entered our cities." It was "one of the greatest engineering feats ever achieved in the state of Israel."[1] To those who accused Israel of mistreating refugees, he responded, "There is no asylum seeker problem in Israel—they are illegal job immigrants."[2] Israel, he said, had the right to control its borders—seemingly unaware of the irony that he had spent his entire political career trying to ensure that Israel did not have clearly defined or internationally recognized borders.

Western countries have not had a particularly stellar record of dealing with the influx of migrants escaping war and poverty in recent years. But most countries prefer keeping the waves of immigration at bay by following the measures already in place. In Netanyahu's Israel, the Iron Fence, for many, is a source of pride. With the election of US president Donald

Trump, justification for the fence seemed even more solid—it became a model for what the United States might erect on its border with Mexico.

Netanyahu had spent much of his career telling Americans how much they had in common with Israel, and trying to convince Israelis that despite living in a "tough neighborhood," they could have a smaller version of America, complete with their own Wall Street and Silicon Valley on the banks of the Jordan.

Netanyahu was convinced that just like America, which has sent its superior military forces across the globe to neutralize any threat to its security and interests, real or perceived, Israel could not allow threats to exist. He has done little to find solutions to the conundrum of Israel's occupation of the Palestinians. Instead, he has done everything in his power to create a bubble in which the majority of Israelis believe they are enjoying a Western lifestyle and the benefits of democracy. A short drive away, their beloved army maintains its rule over a population not much smaller than their own, keeping out infiltrators who would seek to swamp the Jewish paradise.

Jabotinsky's Iron Wall was aimed at creating military deterrence that would ultimately allow Jews and Arabs to coexist in mutual respect. Netanyahu has scant faith in such an outcome—certainly not in his lifetime. Instead, he believes that his wall, perched between Africa and Asia and surrounded by enemies, keeping the Arabs and Africans out, can safeguard the state.

THIS BOOK TELLS the story of a man. It also tells the story of a nation. Benjamin Netanyahu was born seventeen months after the State of Israel was born. He was the first leader of Israel—and at the time of this writing, its only leader—to have been born in the new state.

Israel's story has been told over the years chiefly from the perspective of its founding generation. It has been the story of David Ben-Gurion, Golda Meir, Moshe Dayan, and their contemporaries, the pioneering generation of Israelis who came from Eastern Europe, founded the kibbutzim, and built and commanded the army. But there was always an alternative narrative to the Israeli story.

The underdogs of the Zionist enterprise—the members of the right-wing Revisionist movement, religious Jews, the Mizrahim emigrating from Arab lands, the petite bourgeoisie of the new towns and cities—all were to be melted into the crucible of the "new Jew" and airbrushed out of official Israeli history. It didn't work. The other Israel has dominated the second half of Israel's history thus far, and Benjamin Netanyahu has been its champion.

Netanyahu belongs to both Israels—its old "serving elite" and the seething underdogs. He is also a product of the United States, where he spent much of his early life and career. He believes that he understands and connects with America better even than some American presidents, and when he thinks it's necessary, he challenges them on their own turf.

Netanyahu doesn't seek, as some have facetiously suggested, to make Israel the fifty-first state of the union. He is a staunch believer in Jewish sovereignty and in his own personal role in history as the man ensuring its survival, endurance, and prosperity. This has engendered in him a sense of entitlement that in recent years has evolved into an autocratic style. But he fervently believes that Israel shares in the exceptional destiny of the United States—that together they are the world's indispensable nations. He sees an even greater bond between the two countries than what Winston Churchill described as "the Special Relationship" between the United States and Great Britain. And while to many these notions may seem risible, there is no lack of influential people in America who are prepared to accept and reinforce his view.

Netanyahu's Israel enjoys an American-style standard of living while keeping its immediate neighbors under military occupation, shutting out the Middle East behind high walls and communicating with its soulmate six thousand miles away. It is a hybrid society of ancient phobias and high-tech hope, a combination of tribalism and globalism—just like Netanyahu himself. It is impossible to understand Israel without first understanding the man who leads it.

PART ONE

Frustrated Lovers of Zion

1879–1948

I

An Orator of the Highest Grace

The Netanyahus could have been one of Israel's founding dynasties, like the Dayans, the Weizmans, or the Herzogs, if the first two men of that name had been less ideological and more pragmatic. Benjamin Netanyahu's father and grandfather were learned men—writers and orators, men of many words but much less action. They shared many of the ideals and beliefs of the founders, but were not themselves cut out to be pioneers, fighters, or politicians.

Nathan Mileikowsky was born in 1879 in the small town of Kreva, in today's Belarus, not far from the Lithuanian border. At the time, Kreva and its ethnic Lithuanian and Jewish inhabitants were subjects of the Russian Empire. Like most of the 5 million other Jews living across the Pale of Settlement, the area where Jews were allowed to reside, the Mileikowsky family was impoverished. Nathan's father was an agricultural laborer scraping a living off a tiny plot of land leased from local gentry.

For gifted boys like Nathan there was only one way out of the bleak subsistence of the shtetl. Family mythology maintains that at the age of ten he was sent to Volozhin to study at the famous yeshiva there.

Though many students began studying in Volozhin in their early teens, a ten-year-old student like Nathan was rare. Zvi Mileikowsky would not have had the funds to finance his son's travel twenty-two miles away, let alone his lodging and meals. A group of families in Kreva would have to contribute, or a wealthy relative might serve as his patron. Either way, being spared from working alongside his father would have marked him out early as a particularly pious and studious youth, the kind of boy who was capable of sitting in the yeshiva's study hall to pore over arcane tractates of the Talmud. Volozhin wasn't for beginners. Students were expected to arrive already capable of deciphering the unpunctuated jumble of ancient Hebrew and Aramaic sentences and reams of commentaries.

Although for teenagers like Mileikowsky, the yeshiva was light-years away from the miserable drudgery back home, they were still keenly aware of their limited prospects. They were being prepared for a rabbinical career, and other types of knowledge or skills would not have been taught. Students were forbidden books on mathematics, philosophy, the sciences, and foreign languages, and even those who studied them surreptitiously in their spare time knew their chances of attending a university were slim. A *numerus clausus*—or "closed number" in Latin, a "Jew quota" act—limited the proportion of Jewish students in Russian universities. Just 3 percent of the students in the top institutes of Moscow and St Petersburg could be Jewish.

Many of the best students chafed at the rabbis' edict that only the Talmud and other religious texts be allowed in the yeshiva. Some of them studied secular subjects in their rooms at night and were members of secret societies that exposed them to the new ideas fermenting in the decaying tsarist empire. Some were attracted to the tracts of Russian Narodnik revolutionaries. Others were reading anarchist, socialist, and Marxist pamphlets. Adherence to these ideologies usually led to the abandonment of traditional Jewish life and even to assimilation. There was one revolutionary ideology, however, that shared roots with the Talmud in the sacred biblical texts.

The wave of murderous pogroms that swept the Russian Empire in 1881–1882 caused many Jews to seriously consider their future. For secular assimilationists, who had believed there was hope for emancipation and full equality, it was a rude awakening. For religious Jews, who had continued to believe in the Messiah who would return them to a rebuilt temple in Jerusalem, there was a growing realization that the Messiah was taking too long. The solution, for many, was emigration. By the outbreak of World War I in 1914, over 2 million Jews had left Russia, the great majority of them crossing the Atlantic to the United States. Some, however, among them both secular intellectuals and yeshiva students, began planning a return to the ancient homeland.

Hovevei Zion—the Lovers of Zion—were the precursors of the Zionists. Local groups sprang up spontaneously in towns across Eastern Europe. They became forums for discussion and raised funds for emigration to Eretz Yisrael, the historic land of Israel, which at the time was divided among four districts of the Ottoman Empire. Its members founded and supported the first Jewish agricultural settlements there in many centuries. Hovevei Zion became the first international movement dedicated to Jewish nationalism.

By the time Nathan Mileikowsky arrived in Volozhin, the yeshiva was already a hotbed of Hovevei Zion activism, though most of the rabbis disapproved of such dangerous ideas. He was swept up by this new vision of Jewish destiny. It would dominate his life, as well as the lives of his oldest son and his grandsons.

Hovevei Zion preceded Theodor Herzl's Jewish awakening. As a young journalist, Herzl covered the Dreyfus Affair in Paris in 1894, and the conviction of the Jewish officer on trumped-up espionage charges, along with the anti-Jewish passions whipped up by the Parisian mob, disturbed him. Soon after that experience, the people of Herzl's hometown of Vienna elected a rabble-rousing anti-Semite, Karl Lueger, as mayor. Herzl concluded that Jews needed a sovereign state of their own.

Herzl became the founder of political Zionism. He was an "assimilated" Jew from a secular family, with little knowledge of Judaism. But many of his earliest followers had grown up in traditional environments and were still in a gray zone landing somewhere between the parochial Yiddishkeit of the shtetl and what would soon become a global initiative for Jewish statehood. Mileikowsky was an early acolyte of the leaders of Russian Zionism, Yehiel Chlenov and Rabbi Yaakov Mazeh.

Despite being ordained before leaving Volozhin, however, Mileikowsky never served as a rabbi. Instead he made his living as an educator and Zionist orator, traveling by rail throughout the Russian Empire to spread the word among the persecuted Jews. Using the ancient rhetorical methods of itinerant rabbinical preachers, speaking to his audiences in folksy scripture-laden Yiddish, he acquired a reputation as a spellbinding firebrand.

The Russian Zionists admired Herzl but nevertheless staunchly opposed him over the "Uganda Plan," a British proposal in 1903 to establish a Jewish homeland in East Africa. Herzl supported the plan reluctantly, partly on account of his horror over a new wave of pogroms in Russia and the refusal of the Ottoman rulers to discuss any form of Jewish autonomy in the ancient homeland. But an overwhelming number of Russian delegates to the Sixth Zionist Congress in August 1903, representing the very communities under attack, along with the representatives of the pioneers in Palestine, were emphatically opposed to even considering a Jewish state anywhere but in Zion. The movement was acrimoniously split, and it would remain so until Herzl's death a year later.

Mileikowsky would later explain to his son Benzion that he had opposed the Uganda Plan, but not because he thought it was unviable. "It was precisely because we believed that the project could be carried out that we were all the more opposed to it. For so many centuries the Jewish people had made so many sacrifices for this land, had shed their blood for it, had prayed for a thousand years to return to it, had tied their most intimate hopes to its revival—we considered it inconceivable that we would now betray the generations of Jews who had fought and died for this end."[1]

Britain, under the pressure of its own colonialists in Africa, quickly backed down from the proposal, and at the Seventh Zionist Congress in 1905, the first without Herzl, the Uganda Plan was officially laid to rest. The rift within the movement, however, was far from healed.

The supporters of "political Zionism," mainly delegates from Central and Western Europe who had been close to Herzl, believed that the overall priority must be to continue diplomatic efforts to obtain an international charter from the great powers for a Jewish commonwealth in Palestine. In sharp disagreement were the Russian delegates and those from Palestine. The "practical Zionists" demanded that every resource be directed toward encouraging Jewish immigration to Zion and building new settlements there, even without international approval.

Passions ran high. Nathan Mileikowsky, who attended the Eighth Zionist Congress in 1907, accused fellow delegates who had been in favor of the Uganda Plan of "betraying all the generations."[2] Benjamin Netanyahu keeps a photograph of his grandfather speaking at the congress.

At the age of twenty-nine, Mileikowsky married Sarah Lurie, who, like him, was a Lithuanian and a supporter of Hovevei Zion. The couple settled in Warsaw, where he became a teacher of Hebrew at a local Jewish gymnasium. In 1910, their first son, Benzion ("son of Zion"), was born. Over the next decade of unrest and war, Mileikowsky traveled much less, instead channeling his activism into writing polemics in the Jewish newspapers of Eastern Europe. At home, with a growing family, he took the unorthodox step, even for Zionists of the era, of speaking Hebrew with his children. He began writing his newspaper columns under the pseudonym "Netanyahu" ("given by God"), a name of minor figures in the Old Testament during the period of the First Temple. Over the ensuing decades, some of his children would adopt Netanyahu as their family name.

In 1920, following the breakup of the Ottoman Empire, the League of Nations awarded Britain a "mandate" over Palestine, bringing four centuries of Turkish rule to an end. Mileikowsky decided to embark on the path he had been advocating for two decades, emigrating with Sarah and their family of seven children to Zion. The voyage, first overland to Trieste, and then by sea, was arduous. The arrival was hardly easier. With a large family to feed and not cut out for life as a pioneering farmer, Mileikowsky accepted the job of school principal in the northern town of Safed.

The Galilee in those days was isolated, and its Jewish population had dwindled as a result of financial hardship and pestilential conditions. Safed, then a mixed Jewish-Arab town, its Jewish community long past its heyday as a center of Jewish learning and mysticism, consisted mainly of the impoverished descendants of the Jewish families who had settled there following the Spanish Expulsion of 1492. Less than two years after settling there, Mileikowsky jumped at the opportunity to move to Jerusalem, where Keren Hayesod, the newly founded financial arm of the Zionist movement, offered him a position.

Mileikowsky didn't remain in Jerusalem for long. Keren Hayesod soon sent him to the United States, where millions of Jews from the old country had resettled. Once again his rhetorical skills were enlisted in the service of the Zionist cause. For four years he traveled among Jewish communities, speaking in Yiddish at synagogues and small halls and calling upon those who had found a comfortable life in the New World to help establish the ancient homeland. During his long absence, part of it with Sarah joining him, their by now nine children were deposited in boarding schools.

Mileikowsky's speeches were rich with Jewish history, drawing upon stories from the Bible and the Talmud, invoking ancient Jewish martyrs and rabbis, and painting an attractive picture of the life of the modern pioneers who were rebuilding Eretz Yisrael. In 1926, in New York, he exhorted his listeners to look eastward. "As long as one Jew remains, even just one, the land of Israel has hope and opportunity. A small or large settlement, rich or poor, in the land of the fathers, is where the Jewish people will be reborn and become a great nation." He mocked the prosperity they had found in America, which he said ranked among the "foreign impure lands."[3]

"In exile, a house filled with riches encourages the neighbors to thieve and steal the house of Israel. Today we know what prosperity in exile is worth. Where are our millionaires in Russia? They were the richest men and nothing is left of them. All the riches of exile are finished, the money remains in the hands of those who became Christians and assimilated." His listeners opened their pockets, donated to Keren Hayesod, and remained in America.[4]

Back in Palestine, Mileikowsky fell out with the executives of Keren Hayesod and moved to a farm he bought in Herzliya, then an agricultural settlement north of Tel Aviv. In the accounts of his children, Mileikowsky comes across as a cantankerous figure, frustrated at his lack of influence within the movement to which he had given his life. The ascendant groups within Zionism were increasingly secular and socialist-oriented, and Mileikowsky found himself identifying with the religious and Zionist Mizrahi (or Merkaz Ruhani, "Spiritual Center") movement, forerunner of the National Religious Party and Jewish Home, and the nationalist Revisionist movement, which was becoming an embattled opposition.

NATHAN MILEIKOWSKY DIED in February 1935 at the age of fifty-five. He was eulogized by Chief Rabbi Abraham Isaac Kook as "an orator of the highest grace" and as having possessed "a heart filled with the love of Torah, love of the people of Israel, love of the land of Israel."[5] Most of his children, however, were to live secular lives, far away from Israel.

Though glorified by his descendants as a leading Zionist of his era, Nathan Mileikowsky-Netanyahu remained barely a footnote in Zionist history, his grandiloquent speeches yellowing in the archives of the Yiddish press. And yet more than eighty years after his death, the brand of Zionism he advocated, integrating Jewish nationalism and religious tradition, is one of the dominant ideologies in Israel.

Mileikowsky's grandsons never met him, but they were nevertheless strongly influenced by him. One apocryphal anecdote from his life features repeatedly in Benjamin Netanyahu's political rhetoric. It has served as part of his stump speech for twenty years across numerous campaigns:

> My grandfather Nathan Netanyahu Mileikowsky stood at a train station in the heart of Europe at the end of the nineteenth century, together with his younger brother Yehuda, two yeshiva students. They were suddenly spotted by a mob of anti-Semitic ruffians, waving clubs, shouting "death to the Jews." My grandfather said to his brother, "run away Yehuda, run." He tried to delay the mob, to save his brother, and they beat him senseless, leaving him for dead. Before he lost consciousness, lying bleeding, he said to himself, "The shame. The shame that a descendant of the Maccabees is lying here in the mud, helpless." And he promised himself that should he survive the night, he would move with his family to the land of Israel and help to build a new future for the people of Israel in its land. I am here today as prime minister of Israel due to the promise my grandfather made.[6]

As in other parts of the Netanyahu family mythology, it's not clear whether this ever happened. But it has become a chapter in the narrative putting Benjamin Netanyahu and his dynasty at the center of Zionist history.

2

Propaganda, Propaganda, and Propaganda

Benzion Netanyahu had an itinerant adolescence. The eldest child of Nathan and Sarah, he was born in Warsaw, and after the family's arrival in Palestine, he lived in Jaffa, Tel Aviv, Safed, and then Jerusalem, where he studied in a succession of boarding schools.

The family settled in 1924 in the new middle-class neighborhood of Beit Hakerem, amid spacious pine groves north of the teeming Old City. The house had been built for them with money from a cousin who had emigrated to the United States. It was a period of intensive Jewish building and the foundation of new institutions for the state-on-the-way. The Zionist leaders were enthused by the declaration of British foreign secretary Arthur James Balfour in November 1917 that the British government would "favour the establishment in Palestine of a national home for the Jewish people."

Nathan Mileikowsky was an absent parent, busy with his Zionist work. Two years after the family moved to Jerusalem, he embarked on a prolonged fundraising tour of the United States. Their home filled with relatives recently arrived in Palestine. For the teenager Benzion, his studies at the nearby Beit Hakerem Seminar—the most advanced Hebrew high school at the time in Palestine, dedicated to training a new generation of Zionist educators—were a welcome respite from an unsettled family life. To symbolize his coming of age in a new country, he jettisoned his father's Polish family name, adopting instead his literary pseudonym, Netanyahu.

The summer of 1929, when Benzion Netanyahu graduated, brought a rude awakening for the burgeoning Jewish community in Palestine. A wave of religious violence swept the land, leaving in its wake 133 dead Jews and 116 dead Arabs; in addition, 339 Jews and 232 Arabs were wounded. Nearly all the Jewish casualties were families and passersby hacked to death by angry mobs.

A long-standing dispute over prayer arrangements at the Western Wall, the sole standing remnant of the Jewish temple in Jerusalem—and, by Muslim tradition, the spot where the Prophet Muhammad tied his winged steed on the night journey from Mecca—had ostensibly sparked the rioting. The narrow alleyway by the two-thousand-year-old wall was owned by the Jerusalem Islamic Waqf, an Islamic religious trust, and under the Ottomans Jews had been allowed to pray there on the condition that they made no changes to the site. Attempts by Jewish philanthropists to buy the site had failed, and by the late 1920s groups of Zionist nationalists were trying to challenge the status quo, demanding a more permanent presence at the wall in the form of benches and a traditional partition between men and women.

It was of course much more than a religious argument or a local dispute over real estate. The rows over the Western Wall and accusations by radical Arab leaders, such as the mufti of Jerusalem, Amin al-Husseini, that the Jews were planning to destroy the Haram al-Sharif mosques on the other side of the wall and rebuild the temple inflamed the passions that had first been unleashed by the Balfour Declaration twelve years earlier. The events of August 1929 brought into sharp focus the Jewish-Arab struggle for ownership of the land. To many Jews, they were clear evidence that the Balfour Declaration, or any other form of international recognition of Jewish statehood, would not be enough.

Each side told its own narrative. As far as the Jews were concerned, they were finally returning home, with the blessing of the civilized nations of the world. The Arabs saw themselves as a native community being usurped by European colonists backed by the British Empire. Very few Jews had fully realized how their growing presence impacted the local Arabs.

August 1929 drove home the reality that two nations were competing for the same piece of land. Before then, the Arabs living there had not factored into Zionist thinking. The main question had been how to convince the great powers carving up the Middle East to grant the Jews sovereignty. The realization that the Arabs were going to fight, and that the British, despite Lord Balfour's grand promises, weren't going to automatically fulfill the Balfour Declaration, tore the Zionist movement apart once again.

For the next two decades an acrimonious debate would rage over whether the Zionist movement should continue to seek the support of Great Britain and other powers, while at the same trying to reach an accommodation with its Arab neighbors, or forge its own independent path in seeking sovereignty, if necessary confronting the Arabs with force. There were many gradations of opinion between the two poles. There were not just strategic questions of diplomacy but also practical considerations. Should the Yishuv, the body of Jewish residents, put its emphasis on building agricultural settlements and a collective economy, or on establishing an independent Jewish fighting force, despite Britain's opposition?

The emerging factions reflected the competing global ideologies of the early twentieth century, ranging from the capitalist powers, Britain and the United States, to the radical socialism of the Soviet Union, a new revolutionary power, to nationalist Polish militarism and Italian fascism. There was ample inspiration for every faction of the Zionist movement. During the early 1930s, the fault lines of what would become Israeli politics emerged.

I N AUGUST 1929, as the isolated Beit Hakerem came under attack by villagers from nearby Deir Yassin, Benzion Netanyahu, along with his family and their neighbors, sheltered in the new building of the nearby teachers' college, from where he had just graduated. At nineteen, he was already a member of the one political faction that had decided not to take the Arab claims to the land into consideration and not to be deterred by the policies of the British Mandate.

Netanyahu had joined Hatzohar, the World Union of Zionist Revisionists, an opposition group within the Zionist Organization, in 1928. Becoming a member of the new faction was an act of defiance by the young Benzion, not only toward the Yishuv establishment, but also toward his absent rabbi-father. Revisionist Zionism was a secular movement built around the compelling figure of one man, Ze'ev Jabotinsky, who had founded Hatzohar three years earlier.

Jabotinsky and Nathan Mileikowsky were Russian Zionists of the same generation. But while Rabbi Mileikowsky's Zionism was based on ancient Jewish texts and legends, Jabotinsky's was secular and sought inspiration in European nationalism, particularly that of the Italian revolutionary Giuseppe Garibaldi and Poland's Marshal Józef Piłsudski. While their political beliefs were similar, Benzion's departure from religion was his rebellion against his rabbi-father. He would bring up his sons as staunchly secular Zionists like him.

The pragmatic Zionist leaders of their generation emphasized the importance of establishing agricultural settlements throughout the land as a foundation for an autonomous state. Although they founded a small Jewish militia, they relied mainly on the British for protection. Jabotinsky tried to create an independent Jewish fighting force. He was much more forthright than the cautious Zionist diplomats in confronting the British.

When Jabotinsky founded the Revisionist Hatzohar group in 1925, it was officially part of the wider Zionist movement, but later it became his independent platform. He angered his Zionist colleagues in his headstrong attempts to form armed groups and build alliances with other European governments besides that of Great Britain. The British saw him as an agitator, and following a particularly fiery speech in 1929, where he accused the Mandate government of being anti-Semitic and serving Arab interests, he was declared persona non grata in Palestine and expelled. He spent the rest of his life outside Palestine, though he continued to actively speak and write on behalf of Revisionist Zionism.

Jabotinsky was a man of many contradictions. A romantic ideologue, a poet and novelist, and an impassioned leader with militant tendencies, he was drawn to the radical politics of early twentieth-century Italy, including, initially, fascism. At the same time, he tried to infuse his writings with rationalism. His outlook was in some respects Hobbesian: he wrote that for a nation to survive it must "keep apart, untrusting, perpetually on guard, a club at all times the only way to survive in this wolves' fight." He warned his followers away from mystic nationalism and believed the Jews must earn the respect of other nations. He demanded resolute opposition to any Arab enemy—an "Iron Wall of Jewish bayonets"—but at the same time dreamt of a future when on both banks of the Jordan, "from the wealth of our land, there shall prosper the Arab, the Christian, and the Jew."[1]

Jabotinsky preached in favor of democracy and against leadership cults, but the Revisionist movement accepted its leader by acclamation. He was to be its undisputed leader until his death. His successor, Menachem Begin, would lead the movement for four decades. Benjamin Netanyahu is their successor, the fourth leader of the movement following Yitzhak Shamir, who succeeded Begin in 1983.

UNLIKE THE PRAGMATIC Zionists, Jabotinsky had been clear-eyed from the beginning; he realized that the local Arab community would put up a strong resistance to Zionism as early as 1923, when he wrote, in his "Iron Wall" essay, that "any indigenous people will fight the settlers as long as there is a spark of hope to be rid of the foreign settlement. That is what the Arabs of the land of Israel are doing and will continue to do, as long as a spark of hope lingers in their heart that they can prevent 'Palestine' becoming the Land of Israel."[2]

Jabotinsky's greatest political foe was David Ben-Gurion, the young leader of Mapai, the Workers' Party of Eretz Yisrael. Like Jabotinsky, Ben-Gurion rejected the early Zionist reliance on the goodwill of Britain and the rest of the world. "We won't receive a land from congresses. We won't receive land as a gift—a homeland is created and built by the power of the people," he wrote. Neither did Ben-Gurion believe that compromise with the Arabs was possible, or even desirable. As early as 1924, he announced at a political meeting that the only path to sovereignty was "multiplying national settlements, towns and villages." With them "our national autonomy will grow, be reinforced and overcome, and the Jews' state will be built."[3]

Ben-Gurion had arrived in Palestine as a pioneering agricultural laborer. He rose to prominence as an organizer and leader of workers' unions and believed that collectivized labor, both on kibbutzim and in the cities, would form the foundation for the new state. Young laborers would become the nucleus of the Haganah (Defense), the Yishuv's militia under the British Mandate. Jabotinsky was repelled by Ben-Gurion's socialism and instead espoused a militarist approach to achieving statehood.

Ben-Gurion's new Jew was a spartan pioneer-farmer, whereas Jabotinsky's was a disciplined soldier. Ben-Gurion called Jabotinsky a fascist; Jabotinsky believed Ben-Gurion was an uncultured defeatist.

Ben-Gurion's young comrades worked in the fields of the kibbutzim or in the factories and workshops of the new Zionist industry. Jabotinsky's followers were petit bourgeois who studied at university and spent much of their time parading in uniform and undergoing paramilitary training. Benzion Netanyahu's decision to join the Revisionists was not just an act of youthful radicalism. It was a clear ideological choice with lifelong implications for himself and his sons. It meant, above all, spending the next half-century as an outsider to mainstream Zionism.

Nathan Mileikowsky had tried his entire life to be part of the Zionist establishment. His son chose Jabotinsky instead.

BENZION NETANYAHU DETESTED his alma mater and would reject nearly everything it stood for.

The Hebrew University, one of the flagships of the Zionist enterprise, had opened in 1925, only four years before Benzion arrived there. It represented the political view furthest from Netanyahu's thinking. The chairman of its board of trustees was Chaim Weizmann, the president of the Zionist Organization, who steadfastly believed in working under the auspices of the British Empire. The chancellor was Professor Judah Leon Magnes, a Reform rabbi who had emigrated from the United States; Magnes was also a founder of the short-lived Brit Shalom movement, which called for the establishment of binational Jewish-Arab autonomy under British rule. Many among the faculty were active in Brit Shalom. The group disbanded in 1933 having failed to find Arab interlocutors interested in exploring the idea of a shared homeland.

The majority of the student body in the early 1930s did not share their professors' views, and most of them belonged to more activist Zionist parties, socialist or Revisionist.

Benzion, who was studying history, literature, and philosophy, found himself among fellow Revisionists, many of whom would go on to leadership positions within the movement. They had one ally within the faculty—Professor Joseph Klausner, a brilliant and controversial historian. Klausner was a staunch nationalist who advocated the idea that Jews should reclaim Jesus as their own national hero, rather than him being the Christian messiah. His political views were the opposite of his reserved, liberal, German-educated colleagues.

Klausner enjoyed leading campaigns. He fiercely opposed the teaching of Yiddish, the Jewish jargon of the Diaspora, at the university, and led the Committee for the Western Wall. He was a natural mentor for Benzion and deeply influenced his career. The professor, whose book on Jesus scandalized the rabbis of Jerusalem, was, like Jabotinsky, a model secular Jewish nationalist, and, also like Jabotinsky, was very different from Netanyahu's father, the rabbi.

B ENZION'S TIME AT Hebrew University included the only recorded instance when his political activism strayed from writing and lobbying to action.

The Revisionist students, who chafed under what they saw as the stuffy and repressive atmosphere enforced by the faculty, were eager to make their mark. They chose as their target the ceremony for the installation of Professor Norman Bentwich as the university's chair of international relations—or, as it was grandly called by Chancellor Magnes, "Chair of World Peace." Bentwich, a British Zionist who had arrived in Palestine to serve as the Mandate government's attorney general, had lost his job following the 1929 riots, when the authorities had tried to demonstrate a more even-handed approach by removing him as the Mandate's senior Zionist official. But many Jews were also critical of Bentwich for being too "neutral," and the Revisionists in particular reviled him. His appointment as professor thus became the perfect target.

Benzion was one of the ringleaders of the protest. He wrote a notice posted around campus that read, "It is not us, the defenseless, who are denied even the right of self-defense, who need lectures on international peace." He accused the members of Brit Shalom, Bentwich among them, of being "one of the main causes of Zionism's ideological and political crisis," and castigated the university for appointing "a professor who aspires to constrain it in anti-Semitic boundaries." "The national student cannot agree with this and therefore expresses his protest with every force," he fulminated.[4]

Benzion's younger brother, Elisha Netanyahu, a mathematics student, was tasked with making a stink bomb in Benzion's room. It was thrown into the hall where the ceremony was taking place as one of the students cried, "Take your international chair to the Mufti!" Pandemonium broke out as the hall was cleared.

It wasn't just a stunt, and it wasn't treated as such. The great and good of the Yishuv had all gathered there and police were at hand to arrest protesters. The incident was covered widely by the Jewish media, most of which was furious at the perpetrators. Fourteen of the protesters were expelled, though Benzion wasn't even one of the suspects.

Benzion himself certainly didn't regard the protest against Bentwich as merely a youthful prank. Seventy years later he still regarded it as one of his proudest moments.[5]

A T TWENTY-TWO, BENZION became one of the editors of the new Revisionist newspaper *Ha'Yarden* (The Jordan), named for the Revisionist belief that the Jewish state should be established on both sides of the Jordan River. In 1921, over the protests of the Zionists, Britain had given the Hashemite dynasty the East Bank. What Zionists believed had been intended as part of the Jewish homeland, promised in the Balfour Declaration, became part of the Kingdom of Jordan.

Ha'Yarden was founded in April 1934 in the wake of a political event that deeply affected the young Benzion Netanyahu. With the rise of the Nazi Party in Germany, most, but not all, of the Revisionists turned their backs on fascism and demanded that the Zionist movement join with other Jewish organizations in boycotting the Third Reich. They broke into the German consulate in Jerusalem and burned the swastika flag flying from its roof. The Jewish Agency, the organization that has been responsible for the Aliyah, the immigration of Jews from the Diaspora, since 1948, and had served as the Jewish government-in-waiting, running all the Yishuv's affairs, before 1948, instead entered negotiations with the Nazi German government to enable the emigration of German Jews to Palestine. The Revisionists focused their anger on the man who signed the controversial Ha'avara (Transfer) Agreement, Haim Arlozorov.

Under the agreement, German Jews, who were forbidden to take their money out of the country, could instead invest in a special fund that financed the purchase of German goods to be exported to Palestine and elsewhere. The fund helped some sixty thousand German Jews emigrate before the war with some financial security and gave a major boost to the Jewish economy in Palestine. However, it also helped the Nazis overcome international boycotts.

In vicious newspaper articles, some Revisionists suggested that Arlozorov was a traitor to his people, or not even Jewish. In June 1933, two days after returning from talks in Germany, Arlozorov was shot dead on one of the beaches of Tel Aviv.

Many assumed the brilliant young socialist economist, who had been appointed as the Jewish Agency's political director at the age of thirty-two, had been murdered by Revisionists. Arlozorov had brokered a deal between Ben-Gurion's Mapai workers' party and Weizmann's pragmatists at the Zionist Congress in 1931, and that agreement had effectively shut the Revisionists out of the Zionist leadership. He symbolized for them not only the Jewish Agency's dealings with Germany but also the growing hegemony of Mapai.

The suspicion fell on the members of a hardline Revisionist group—Brit Ha'Biryonim, literally, The Alliance of Thugs. They had pushed Jabotinsky's militaristic teachings to the extreme, eschewing democracy and calling for the violent overthrow of the British and their Jewish "collaborators." The Biryonim leader, Abba Ahimeir, a university friend of Benzion Netanyahu's who had been expelled following the Bentwich protest, wrote a regular column in one of the Revisionist newspapers called "From a Fascist's Notebook." Ahimeir and three other members of the Biryonim were arrested and charged with having planned and carried out Arlozorov's assassination.

Although many of the members of Mapai were certain that Revisionists had been the assassins, many others in the Yishuv couldn't believe Jews could murder one of their brothers for political motives. Nathan Mileikowsky, who by then was ill, and who had become embittered against the new generation of activists—including Arlozorov, who he felt had usurped his rightful place in the leadership—was one of the Biryonim's main defenders. He visited them in prison and together with Benzion mobilized senior academics and rabbis, including Chief Rabbi Kook, in their defense. This was the first and only time he worked with his son on a political mission. Some of his admirers believed that Mileikowsky's anguish at what he saw as a grave injustice committed against patriotic young Jews hastened his early death a year later.

The four defendants were eventually acquitted, though many remained convinced of their guilt. As far as the Revisionists were concerned, the indictment was a "blood libel," just like the murderous accusations that had been leveled against the Jews of the Diaspora. The episode left

Benzion convinced that there was nothing the left wing would not do to cast the Revisionists out of the Zionist camp.

Benzion Netanyahu saw journalism as part of the "political battle" and lectured his fellow Revisionists that "the first condition for our total victory is a combination of three factors: propaganda, propaganda and propaganda."[6] Together with his mentor, Professor Klausner, he was one of the founders of *Beitar*, a right-wing monthly focusing on "questions of life, science and literature." *Beitar* published original Hebrew poetry and short stories along with translations of the Western canon, from Shakespeare to Goethe, and, of course, political polemics. Its first issue included a rather admiring essay on the merits of fascism, though the editors were careful not to actually endorse any foreign ideology.

Beitar lasted a year before folding for lack of funds. Benzion Netanyahu then became editor of *Ha'Yarden*. The newspaper was originally founded to report on the Arlozorov case, to support the Biryonim members, and, more generally, to provide the Revisionists with a semi-respectable mouthpiece. At the top of its masthead were the names of Professor Klausner and the exiled Jabotinsky.

Ha'Yarden was less radical than previous Revisionist publications, which had regularly compared their Mapai rivals to the Nazis. Netanyahu, who wrote columns both under his own name and under a variety of pseudonyms, never made such comparisons—nor did he express admiration for fascism—but he was scathing on the dangers of combining Zionism with socialism. "It seems that the blue-white flag, the symbol of kinship and national unity, planted by Herzl, our divine captain, is in the 1930s being shaded by a foreign color, the color of the flag of the class-warfare ideology."[7]

Netanyahu accused Weizmann and other political rivals of "warping Zionism" and of leading "a politics of Zionist liquidation." "A nice end they are preparing for us," he wrote in June 1934. "That end is an Arab state in the land of Israel." In the name of democracy, he accused Weizmann, who was never a socialist, of "fighting every Jew who is not subservient to him. Any Jew who desires to live in the land of Israel without the oppression of leftist dictatorship." He castigated the Revisionists' rivals for appeasing the Arabs, writing that "the only criteria for Zionism's moral legitimacy in their eyes is its degree of usefulness to the Arab masses."[8]

In June 1934, the paper was closed for over a month after the British objected to the tone of its coverage of the Arlozorov case. A year after its founding, *Ha'Yarden*, which was based in Jerusalem, could no longer cover its debts. Rather than close voluntarily, Netanyahu and his fellow editors wrote pieces accusing the British of being accomplices in the murder of a member of Beitar, a Revisionist youth movement, in Jerusalem. They were promptly shut down. Three months later, *Ha'Yarden* relaunched in Tel Aviv, this time without Netanyahu, who remained in Jerusalem, still hopeful of continuing his academic career.

Revisionists like Benzion Netanyahu faced a cruel dilemma: with Jabotinsky in exile and his movement shut out of the establishment, many put their youthful radicalism aside. Some moved abroad to seek their fortunes elsewhere. Among them were two of Netanyahu's closest friends, Noach Ben Tovim and Tzila Segal, who emigrated to Britain. Netanyahu and Ben Tovim had spent their teens together in Jerusalem. At university, they were both attracted to the statuesque and vivacious Tzila, who had moved from the coastal town of Petach Tikva to become one of the first female students in Jerusalem. The three of them shared the same politics. Tzila married Ben Tovim, a son of one of the wealthiest families in Jerusalem, and left Palestine with him, first traveling to Finland and then to London. In London, Tzila studied law while her husband worked with the exiled Jabotinsky.

The most resolute of the young Revisionists went underground.

THE IRGUN ZVAI Leumi (IZL), a Zionist paramilitary group, was founded in 1931 by Haganah commanders who broke away from the Yishuv's main security organization in protest over its official policy of "restraint" in the face of Arab attacks.

Jabotinsky was officially the IZL's supreme commander, appointing its military commanders in Palestine from afar, but he often failed to impose his will. He opposed the IZL's decision to carry out reprisals against Arab civilians and was skeptical about its ties with Poland's ultranationalist and anti-Semitic government. In the late 1930s, the Poles secretly agreed to train and equip IZL fighters as part of their ambition to encourage the emigration of Poland's large Jewish community. Benzion Netanyahu never joined the IZL. He believed that as an ideologue, academic, and writer, he had more to give the movement as a propagandist than as a fighter.

As the threat to Europe's Jews from Nazi Germany became clearer from the mid-1930s onward, Jabotinsky threw himself into efforts to organize their emigration to Palestine. In 1936 he published his "evacuation plan" to facilitate the emigration of a million and a half Jews from Europe, mainly from Poland, over the next decade. While the Zionist movement stuck to the policy of working with the British government, IZL organized illegal emigration by sea, bringing around twenty thousand Jews across the Mediterranean before 1939—a drop in the ocean.

In April 1936 a wave of concerted Arab protests broke out against the Jews and the British Mandate. There were violent attacks and economic boycotts. This would be the last major pre-independence attempt by the nationalist Arab leadership in Palestine to prevent Jewish statehood. The Arabs' objective was to convince the British government to officially rescind the Balfour Declaration, prohibit Jewish emigration and purchase of land, and hand greater political control to representatives of the Arab majority.

But the Arab revolt failed and the Yishuv pursued economic self-reliance, including the establishment of an autonomous Tel Aviv port, replacing the ancient one in Jaffa where Arab boatmen had transported Jewish immigrants to shore during the first fifty years of Zionism. The British Army cooperated with the Haganah, allowing the nascent Jewish army to greatly improve its military training, organization, and intelligence-gathering capabilities. As a result, while in further conflicts over the next three years the British lost 262 men and around 300 Jews were killed, 5,000 Arabs died.

The IZL clamored for reprisals against Arab citizens. Jabotinsky opposed such actions from his exile in London, but a younger generation of commanders was now in control. The murder of Arab civilians was popular among some in the Yishuv who were angry at what they saw as a weak response to Arab attacks by the British and by their own leadership. In 1939, even David Ben-Gurion authorized the formation of a special operations unit to carry out a number of reprisals. But many of his colleagues were resolutely against such actions, both for moral reasons and in the interest of preserving the alliance with the British.

By early 1939, as the Arab revolt was dying out, the British government began reappraising its official policy toward Zionism. The resulting

"White Paper," a statement of policy on Palestine published in May 1939, was rejected by Jews and Arabs alike. Rather than rescinding the Balfour Declaration, the British government reinterpreted its promise of establishing a Jewish homeland to mean some form of Jewish self-autonomy in a binational state in which the Jews would remain a perpetual minority. The British refused to stop Jewish emigration to Palestine altogether, but capped it at seventy-five thousand over the next five years and placed severe restrictions on the sale of land to Jews.

The Arabs opposed any continuation of Jewish emigration and the affirmation of even the most limited Jewish autonomy. But the Jews felt the White Paper's edicts—which had been approved by the Parliament in London despite protests by many members of the Parliament that Britain was betraying the Balfour promises—represented an existential threat. With Jewish refugees fleeing Germany, Austria, Czechoslovakia, and other countries soon to fall under the Third Reich, most nations were shutting their gates. Now even the Promised Land was to be closed to them.

For the Revisionists, the White Paper vindicated Jabotinsky's dire predictions. The IZL began carrying out attacks on British military bases, intensified its reprisals against the Arabs, and made plans to prepare a Jewish fighting force in Poland. The plan was for this force to set out for Palestine within months and launch an armed rebellion to eject the British and reopen the land to Jewish emigration.

Zionism was once again thrown into an ideological and diplomatic crisis. Over three decades of cooperation with the British had ended in failure. The Haganah launched its own illegal emigration operation, which Ben-Gurion urged his colleagues to expand and defend, if necessary, if it faced a direct armed confrontation with British troops. But a majority still believed the Yishuv was dependent on British goodwill. The argument would be decided by the outbreak of World War II.

THE PREWAR YEARS represented a long period of frustration for Benzion Netanyahu. He had scaled back his journalistic writing in the hope of launching his academic career. But the still small Hebrew University had few posts for young researchers, and Professor Klausner was not an influential patron. Netanyahu vented his frustration in a *Ha'Yarden* column titled "'Our' University." In it he described the university's hall as being "cold [since] the burning wind of the national liberation movement does not blow within its walls . . . [with] most of the professors and faculty boasting they are not national, but instead pure scientists. Their 'pure science' doesn't prevent them from intervening when necessary in favor of the Marxist parties within Zionism."[9]

Seven decades later, Netanyahu would deny that he had ever sought to continue his career at Hebrew University. But over many years, friends and relatives spoke of how he had been blocked by his alma mater for political reasons.

During the late 1930s, Netanyahu spent most of his time on "The Political Library," a collection of the writings of early Zionist ideologues that he translated and edited. The authors included Theodor Herzl, Max Nordau (who coined the phrase "muscular Judaism"), and Israel Zangwill, an early supporter of "cultural Zionism." These three founders of political Zionism were all formerly assimilated Jews who had converted to Zionism, resolutely secular proponents of a Jewish nationalism untainted by socialism.

Before becoming a Zionist, Nordau had written a homophobic book attacking the degeneration of Western culture. Zangwill popularized the saying "Palestine is a country without a people; the Jews are a people without a country," which has continued to this day to serve as the fundamental belief of many right-wing Zionists, who see the Palestinians as an "invented nation" with no legitimate claim to the land. These were among the sources of inspiration for Netanyahu's Zionist beliefs.

The books brought Netanyahu to the attention of Jabotinsky. In a letter to Professor Klausner in March 1939, Jabotinsky praised him as "a young man with excellent talents." Netanyahu planned a second series of selected writings on "the merit and nature of the most important phenomenon in the history of human society—the nation-state, which has been hidden from the Jewish people during many centuries of ghetto life." Despite the idea being "very interesting," wrote Jabotinsky, "to my deep regret, we cannot finance it."[10]

A few weeks later, Netanyahu visited Jabotinsky in London. Nursing a secret heart disease, the father figure of Revisionist Zionism was demoralized by his failure to warn the world of the coming storm. By the time Netanyahu first met Jabotinsky, it was clear that Europe was on the brink of a war that would be calamitous to European Jewry and quite likely also to the Zionist enterprise, which still recruited most of its members in Europe. Jabotinsky thanked him for the latest volume of Zangwill's writings, promising to read it during his upcoming visit to Poland. But reading political tomes was no longer a priority for him.

The ailing fifty-eight-year-old leader appointed the twenty-nine-year-old Netanyahu to represent the Revisionists in the United States in the following year. He predicted that that was where the fate of the Jewish people would be determined. Jabotinsky promised to join the representatives of the Revisionist movement in the United States to lobby American Jews and politicians in the hope of saving the endangered Jews of Europe.[11]

NETANYAHU RETURNED TO Jerusalem to prepare for his journey to America. His plans were postponed by the start of the war in September. Although Palestine was not within the war zone, the conflict had immediate implications for the Yishuv. For the great majority of Jews in Palestine, it was clear that the confrontation with Britain was over for as long as Britain was at war with Nazi Germany.

"We will fight the White Paper as if there is no war, and fight the war as if there is no White Paper," announced Ben-Gurion at a Mapai meeting on September 12. Jabotinsky had already pledged the Revisionists' support for Britain, and the IZL officially suspended all its operations against the Mandate. Tens of thousands of the Yishuv's men and women were lining up to volunteer to fight Germany in the ranks of the British Army.

There was no dilemma, yet it wasn't a simple decision. That very same British Army was still forcefully preventing the arrival of ships carrying Jewish refugees. Arrests of Haganah and IZL fighters were still taking place. But the Zionist leadership had no choice but to make the Yishuv's interests secondary to the greater war effort. In October 1939, the IZL's commander, David Raziel, and most of its members in prison, who agreed to cooperate with Britain, were released. Not all the Revisionists, though, were on board.

Avraham Stern was the IZL commander charged with training a force in Poland to fight an insurrection against the British in Palestine. He defied Jabotinsky and Raziel and refused to lay down his arms. The Polish officers who had helped train and equip his men had been killed or captured by the German Wehrmacht, but that didn't deter Stern from trying to ally himself with the Third Reich. Like the more radical Revisionists who had admired fascism back in the 1920s and 1930s, Stern believed that despite the Nazis' anti-Semitism, their interests could be aligned in the war against the British. His attempts to communicate with Berlin were ignored, but Stern stuck to his anti-British policy. Officially breaking with the IZL in August 1940, he formed Lohamei Herut Yisrael (Fighters for the Freedom of Israel), dismissively known by the British and many mainstream Zionists as the Stern Gang.

Benzion Netanyahu was not involved in these events. He had his own mission. Leaving Palestine also held the prospect of pursuing an academic career across the Atlantic. He would spend the next eight years living in New York, occasionally traveling around the country like his father before him, to speak before Jewish audiences and lobby politicians for the cause. It was the first in a series of long sojourns in America that would ultimately constitute the bulk of his career.

3

On the Sidelines of History

Before he left for New York in March 1940, Benzion Netanyahu had one last meeting with his old university friend. David Raziel, the IZL commander, wanted Netanyahu to be part of a group traveling to the United States on behalf of the IZL. Netanyahu refused. He agreed with Raziel on all the objectives, but Jabotinsky had already appointed him to work on the political side of the equation. As far as he was concerned, politics stood supreme above the Revisionists' armed wing. This was a failure on Netanyahu's part to perceive that the IZL was about to become the main vehicle of the Revisionist movement, both in Palestine and abroad. With the establishment of the Jewish state, those who had fought underground would emerge as the leaders of the Revisionists. Ultimately, this decision would marginalize and isolate him from any real influence.

The IZL's dominance within the movement would soon be reflected in the standing of its own representatives in the United States, a group that eclipsed the official Revisionists. Netanyahu would also lose his own personal connection to the IZL's leadership. Raziel was killed in May 1941 in a German Luftwaffe bombardment during a secret mission with the British Army in Iraq. Raziel's eventual replacement as IZL commander would be a man whom Netanyahu had never met, and he would have little respect for him once he did. But another death was about to affect him much more deeply than Raziel's.

Jabotinsky arrived in New York shortly after Netanyahu. His followers were shocked by his harrowed visage. Jabotinsky was terminally ill, and exhausted by his failed efforts to lead a great awakening and military insurrection that would have established a safe haven in Zion before the war broke.

The Netanyahu family and its supporters have long sought to portray Benzion during those days as Jabotinsky's secretary, but he was, at most, a peripheral figure in the leader's entourage, struggling to improve his English at the delegation's small office on Forty-second Street quickly enough to be of use. His boss at the time was Benjamin Akzin, the man who actually served as Jabotinsky's secretary. Akzin was also the director of the political department of Jabotinsky's New Zionist Organization.

Benzion wasn't among the small group of friends who traveled with Jabotinsky on August 4, 1940, to a Beitar summer camp in the Catskills, where he was to address young acolytes, and who were with him there when his heart failed.

With Jabotinsky gone, the Revisionists were leaderless, and the group that had traveled to New York was adrift. Akzin moved to Washington, where he became a lobbyist for Jewish war refugees, leaving Netanyahu alone for the most part in the New York office. The IZL group that had come to the United States, led by Hillel Kook, who went by a pseudonym, Peter Bergson, was much larger. It was well funded, dynamic, and had the support of prominent figures among American Jewry. Jabotinsky's son Eri was one of its members. The natural thing for Benzion Netanyahu would have been to join what became known as "the Bergson Group," but he remained aloof, lonely and largely irrelevant as the United States became the main hub of Zionist activism during the war.

In October 1940, Ben-Gurion also arrived in the United States, where he was to spend long periods during the war working with influential Jew-ish American leaders. The political arguments that had divided Jews in Palestine and Europe were now to be replicated in Washington and New York. In what was the darkest hour for the Jews, with the "Final Solution" of the Nazis being put into motion in the lands that had fallen to the Wehrmacht, the secure and prosperous Jewish American community be-came what it has remained ever since—a parallel arena for Israeli politics.

When he returned to Jerusalem, Ben-Gurion told the leadership of the Jewish Agency that "the way to acquire the American administration is acquiring the people, the public opinion."[1] Zionists should find allies in the American media, in Congress, in the churches, in the workers unions, and among intellectuals: "When they will be with us—the administration will be with us." Moving the emphasis to the United States wasn't just a geographical shift—it meant a departure from discreet Zionist diplomacy, which had engaged with cabinet ministers and heads of state, to public relations and advocacy.

It was the birth of the Zionist strategy of *hasbara*—literally, "explanation," the conduct of public diplomacy to explain the case for a Jewish state. It operated on every level, from the grass roots all the way to the White House. Public opinion and the political and financial power of the Jewish community were to be mobilized as a lever of pressure on the Roosevelt administration. If Ben-Gurion invented the concept, over forty years later Benjamin Netanyahu would become its most talented and controversial practitioner—the great explainer and ultimate *hasbarist*.

Both Ben-Gurion's mainstream Zionists and the raucous Revisionists scandalized the more staid leaders of American Jewry, who felt that overt Jewish activism, especially at a time of war, could stoke anti-Semitic sentiment. The Bergson Group was relentless in trying to draw public attention to the wholesale slaughter of Jews in Europe, using everything from full-page ads in the *New York Times* to a massive musical pageant commemorating the memory of the Jewish martyrs at Madison Square Garden in March 1943.

As the opposing wings of Zionism fought for the support of American Jews, the man responsible for promoting Revisionism became increasingly irrelevant. Occasionally Benzion Netanyahu appended his name to a petition or addressed a group of Jewish students. Eventually he had to swallow his pride and cooperate with his rivals, the representatives of the IZL, as he didn't have the resources to launch his own lobbying campaign. But though he failed, like his father before him, to become anything more than a bit-player in the Zionist enterprise during his American mission, there were two sources of comfort during those bleak years.

The marriage of Benzion's university friends, Noach Ben Tovim and Tzila Segal, had been short and miserable. Tzila, the daughter of a Minneapolis scrap dealer who had spent part of her childhood in the United States, had found work as a secretary at the Emergency Committee for the Rescue of European Jewry, one of the organizations set up by the Bergson Group, when she returned to the United States early in the war. Benzion had been in love with her for a decade, ever since they had met in Jerusalem. This time around, Tzila was drawn to the reserved intellectual whose radical politics she shared. Both were lonely and homesick in New York. They were married in 1944. Tzila had received degrees in Jerusalem and London and was an extremely resourceful woman who could make her own way in life. Yet, from the time of their marriage in the Radio City Synagogue, she dedicated her life to her husband's career. Unlike Benzion, she had an outgoing character—she maintained contact throughout her life with a wide range of friends. But she believed in his talents and would do everything in her power to provide him with the space and peace of mind to pursue his research.

Tzila also encouraged Benzion to resume his studies. Failing to secure a grant to write his PhD at Columbia University, he applied successfully to the small Dropsie College of Hebrew and Cognate Learning in Philadelphia and began commuting there on a regular basis. His choice of historical focus—the Spanish Inquisition and the expulsion of Jews in 1492—was closely related to more current affairs. After seeing how Jabotinsky had failed in his attempts to avert a Jewish genocide in the 1930s, Netanyahu sought to understand similar failures in Jewish history. His dissertation was on Don Isaac Abravanel, the fifteenth-century Portuguese-born scholar and financier who had tried and failed to intercede with King Ferdinand and Queen Isabella to prevent them from signing the Alhambra Decree expelling the Jews.

F OR DECADES, BEN-GURION and his colleagues in the Zionist leadership would be accused of having not done enough to save more Jews during the Holocaust and pursuing narrower political objectives. These accusations would come from all quarters—from non-Zionist Jewish groups and the ultra-Orthodox community as well as from Revisionists and others within the Zionist movement. In many ways this debate was a continuation of the dispute over the Ha'avara Agreement in 1933. It would continue to occupy a large place in national politics during Israel's early decades.

It wasn't just a political or historical debate, but went to the heart of the Zionist enterprise. Was its sole objective to build a state that would serve as a haven for Jews who would choose to live there? Or did the Zionist movement and the Jewish state have a wider responsibility for all Jews in peril?

The Revisionist-Mapai divide tainted even the remembrance of the Holocaust. The Warsaw Ghetto Uprising would be exalted in the new state as the greatest story of Jewish bravery and sacrifice—but only the fighters of the Warsaw Jewish underground, which was composed of members of left-wing Zionist and Communist groups, were celebrated and commemorated. A separate underground, consisting of Revisionists, and in particular the members of Beitar who had fought the Germans in Warsaw, was for many years airbrushed out of Israeli history. It was only through the research and efforts of Moshe Arens—who during the war years had been a young Beitar activist in New York, and would go on to become Israel's defense minister and the young Benjamin Netanyahu's political patron—that the members of Beitar received belated recognition nearly seven decades after they died in the burning ghetto.

Just as during the 1930s Jabotinsky accused his political rivals both of collaborating with the Nazis and then of ignoring the gathering storm, so in the 1950s the Holocaust would overshadow much of Israeli politics. It would become pivotal both to Benzion Netanyahu's historical outlook and to his son's political ideology.

T HE 1944 US presidential election saw for the first time lobbying by Zionist organizations to influence the parties' platforms. This lobbying was conducted in the hope that the postwar administration would force Britain to fulfill the Mandate by granting Jewish statehood in Palestine. In June, Benzion Netanyahu was one of many activists, led by the most prominent of American Zionist leaders, Rabbi Abba Hillel Silver, who descended on the Republican National Convention in Chicago. They secured a pro-Zionist plank in the party platform when the Republicans called to "give refuge to millions of distressed Jewish men, women and children driven from their homes by tyranny," and for "the opening of Palestine to their unrestricted immigration and land ownership" so that "Palestine may be constituted as a free and democratic Commonwealth."

It was the first time a major party platform had taken up the subject of Zionism. The Republicans even went a step further in condemning "the failure of the President to insist that the mandatory of Palestine carry out the provision of the Balfour Declaration and of the mandate while he pretends to support them." Support for the Jewish State became a partisan issue in US politics even before the establishment of Israel in 1948.

The Republicans' position put pressure on the Democrats to adopt a similar policy at their national convention three weeks later. In their platform, they declared, "We favor the opening of Palestine to unrestricted

Jewish immigration and colonization, and such a policy as to result in the establishment there of a free and democratic Jewish commonwealth."

Playing off the two parties against each other in this way was unprecedented in American Jewish life. It was also a rare instance of joint action by the rival Zionist factions at a time when, back in Palestine, they were literally at each other's throats.

Months earlier, the wartime truce between the Revisionists and the British Mandate had collapsed. Menachem Begin, the newly appointed IZL commander, had published his "Call for Revolt" accusing the British government of doing nothing to save the Jews of Europe, while at the same time in Palestine the White Paper restrictions on Jewish immigration were still being enforced.

The IZL at first made a point of attacking only nonmilitary British targets, including empty tax and immigration offices, although the revolt quickly escalated to assaults on police stations and firefights with British police officers.

Despite the anger toward the Mandate's policies, most of the Yishuv was scandalized by the renewed conflict with the British while the war was still being fought in Europe. For the Mapai-dominated Jewish Agency, this was not just a question of endangering their own uneasy cooperation with the British at a crucial moment, when they hoped that the White Paper could be canceled at the end of the war; it was also a direct challenge to their monopoly on the Yishuv's security policy.

"THERE IS NO choice, we will have to respond in force to force," said David Ben-Gurion. "It will be a tragedy, but a smaller tragedy than the danger of a small group trying to take over the entire Yishuv in this way."[2]

The anti-IZL operation would be called "the Hunting Season," or "the *Saison*," and was not publicly acknowledged by Mapai. Ben-Gurion gave secret orders to the Haganah to arrest IZL members. Hundreds were rounded up and held incommunicado on kibbutzim, some brutally interrogated to give up the location of their comrades. Many who were known to be affiliated with the Revisionists were fired from their jobs or even expelled from high schools and colleges. Names and addresses of other members were handed over to the British, who exiled hundreds to detention camps in Africa.

The Saison was discontinued after three months, but in that short time it deepened the rift and enmity that would last within Israeli society for decades to come. Begin refused his followers' entreaties to respond violently or retaliate by kidnapping Haganah leaders. He used rhetoric instead, warning his opponents, "If you harm the IZL's fighters, your children will spit on your graves!" He explained to his commanders that they could not afford a civil war with the Haganah because in the not-too-distant future they would be fighting side by side with Haganah soldiers in the Jewish state's War of Independence. He was prepared to fight the British, not his fellow Jews.

By refusing to escalate to civil war in 1945, or afterward, Begin in effect was accepting Ben-Gurion and Mapai's long-held dominance and the rules of the democratic system. Ben-Gurion's party would rule Israel for decades. Begin would have to wait until 1977 to assume national leadership. "The Saison" would remain a byword among Israeli right-wingers, a reminder of left-wing perfidy and proof that it was they, and not their opponents, who were the true democrats.

I N THE PARALLEL universe of Zionist activism in the United States, a more genteel version of the Saison had been inaugurated. The established American-Jewish and Zionist organizations there, together with the British government, had tried to curb the influence and growing popularity of the Revisionists, urging the Roosevelt administration to deport Hillel Kook and other members of the Bergson Group, launch IRS investigations into their fundraising operations, or have them drafted into the military for service overseas. There is no record of Benzion Netanyahu, who would eventually be naturalized on the basis of Tzila's American citizenship, also being targeted. He was probably too minor a figure to draw attention, and he wasn't directly involved in the IZL's American operations. In any case, the Roosevelt administration wasn't inclined to get involved in the internal wars of the Jews. By the end of World War II, the mainstream Zionist movement had established itself as the administration's main interlocutors, just as it had at the end of World War I with the British Empire.

The United States was to prove Zionism's true ally, although the one central lesson the Jews had taken from three decades of dealing with the British was that they could never fully trust any ally.

4

The End of the Great Zionist Dream

The Allied victory in Europe brought an end to the slaughter but little joy for the Jews as the enormity of the Holocaust began to sink in. Benzion Netanyahu had almost lost hope.

Over fifty years later, he said in an interview that "until the Second World War I was very optimistic. I believed that the founding of the Jews' state was undoubtable." He had no faith in the Zionist leadership, which he saw as defeatist and beholden to its socialist principles. Neither did he have much faith in the new leaders of his own movement who had replaced Jabotinsky and Raziel. He saw Menachem Begin and Hillel Kook and their acolytes as charlatans devoid of intellectual depth or ideological backbone. Before the war he had subscribed to Jabotinsky's grand design—that two million Jews would arrive from Eastern Europe and conquer the land. Those Jews were now dead, and after five years in New York, Benzion had no illusions that the soft and ineffectual American Jews would take up the fight. "Our real national core had been destroyed; ceased to exist. That made me very pessimistic and deeply worried already in the 1940s," he told his interviewer.[1]

There were still over ten million Jews in the world, including over four million in America, two and a half million in the Soviet Union, over a million Holocaust survivors in Europe, and a similar number living in Muslim countries in North Africa and the Middle East, as well as over half a million by then in Palestine. They were not up to the task in Benzion's estimation.

Even without the advantage of historical hindsight, Benzion Net-anyahu's pessimism in 1945 seems rather short-sighted. But his political outlook and historical writing over the years would always blend a deep pride in his Jewish identity with a lack of faith in the political wisdom and resilience of the Jews themselves. As far as Netanyahu was concerned, the Jews had been blessed with the genius of a few individuals, such as Herzl and Jabotinsky, but others had not followed in their footsteps. Even in the following years, when the Jewish state quickly became a reality, he never fully regained faith in its viability. He would bequeath his insecurities to his son Benjamin.

If other Zionist ideologues and leaders had shared Benzion Netanya-hu's defeatism in 1945, Israel would never have been brought into being only three years later. But both Ben-Gurion and Begin believed other-wise and reenergized their supporters. And although Zionism had been largely relegated to the sidelines during the war, the conflict had momen-tous implications for the movement.

In 1917, as they had witnessed the British general Edmund Allenby capture Jerusalem, ending six and a half centuries of Muslim rule, and Lord Balfour pen his declaration, the Zionists had believed that sover-eignty would be granted by the British Empire. However, it would take Britain's relegation to second-class power status and the US-USSR ri-valry of the Cold War to create the framework for Israel's establishment.

The Revisionists had been fundraising for arms in the United States since the late 1930s, while the Haganah still largely depended on the British. In late 1945, Ben-Gurion, who now focused his organizational skills on military matters, set up a network of Jewish American donors who would secretly give millions of dollars for arms for what would be-come the Israel Defense Forces. Here was yet another pattern that would persist for decades to come. The number of Jews emigrating from Amer-ica to Zion would always be relatively tiny, but they would provide a major proportion of the necessary funds.

With the war over, the United States was dismantling the massive military machine that had vanquished Germany and Japan. Jewish money was spent on surplus aircraft, tanks, and dismantled weapons fac-tories for a Jewish army that had yet to be raised. Ben-Gurion's repre-sentatives were doing this on a much larger scale than the Revisionists, and alone engaged with the new Truman administration and the other world powers. For all intents and purposes, Ben-Gurion was now at the head of a government-in-waiting.

BENZION AND TZILA's first son, Jonathan (Yonatan), was born in March 1946 at Sydenham Hospital in Harlem.

As the battle for statehood entered its crucial final stage, the Netanyahus settled down to family and academic life in their tiny apartment in the Narragansett Hotel, on the southeast corner of Broadway and Ninety-fourth Street, with Benzion writing his dissertation and Tzila nursing Yoni and typing her husband's words. Officially Benzion was still head of the Revisionists in the United States, but aside from editing a biweekly magazine and the occasional lecture or meeting, the group had been totally eclipsed by the Bergson Group and the much larger Jewish Agency operation, which was gearing up for a great diplomatic battle at the United Nations.

The new Labour government of Clement Attlee in Great Britain had abandoned its pro-Zionist positions from the 1930s and continued to enforce the White Paper. British foreign secretary Ernest Bevin opposed the Truman administration's demand that one hundred thousand Holocaust survivors, languishing in displaced persons camps in Europe, be allowed to emigrate to Palestine. The British position remained that an influx of Jews would alter the delicate balance and provoke another outbreak of Arab violence.

At the end of 1945, with the British refusing to rethink their policy, Ben-Gurion directed the Haganah to cooperate with the Revisionist IZL and Lohamei Herut Yisrael (LHY, known as the Stern Gang). For the first time in their history, the Yishuv's paramilitary organizations began operating together under a joint command, launching an unprecedented campaign of sabotage against the British.

The armed insurgency within Palestine tied down tens of thousands of war-weary troops. Meanwhile, a global public relations campaign attempted to appeal to the conscience of the world, highlighting the plight of the Holocaust refugees in Europe and those bobbing in leaky ships on the Mediterranean, who were desperately trying to evade the British blockade and reach the Promised Land. A concerted diplomatic campaign in the United States lobbied the Truman administration in Washington and used New York as a base for lobbying other governments around the world. The United Nations temporary headquarters at Lake Success on Long Island became a hub of activity.

The cooperation ended following an IZL attack on the British administrative headquarters in the south wing of the King David Hotel in Jerusalem. On July 22, 1946, ninety-one people, including many British, Arab, and Jewish civilians, were killed when milk cans filled with explosives demolished the wing. The IZL and the LHY continued their attacks on the Mandate's security forces, while the Haganah from then on targeted only British installations and equipment directly involved in enforcing the marine blockade preventing Jewish refugees from arriving.

The joint resistance movement had been short-lived and certainly hadn't been enough to heal the rift between the Zionist parties, but the experience of fighting together strengthened the recognition of the rival organizations that they were ultimately fighting for a common cause. It would help them overcome their differences less than two years later when all the armed groups were disbanded and their members joined the new Israeli army. The bombing campaign would also enhance the dawning realization of the British government that it could not continue the Mandate for long.

At the Zionist Congress in late 1946 in Basel, Switzerland, the first to be held after the war, the Revisionists returned to the fold. It was a tacit admission by the Revisionists that in the future state they would have to work within the confines of democratic rules. For the foreseeable future, at least, they would have little choice but to accept the dominance of Mapai and David Ben-Gurion.

HARRY TRUMAN'S STATEMENT on October 4, 1946, in which he publicly supported the establishment of a "viable Jewish state in an adequate area of Palestine," deserves to be remembered in history as a much more significant event than the Balfour Declaration twenty-nine years earlier. Britain had spent most of the intervening period trying to get out of its foreign secretary's commitment, and still was.

Truman expressed his support for a Jewish state on the eve of Yom Kippur in the knowledge that the message would reverberate throughout Jewish synagogues across America. Exactly a month later, he faced his first nationwide electoral test in the 1946 midterms. While the Zionist and American Jewish narrative has highlighted shared values and instinctive support and sympathy for the Jews, these have always been underpinned by pragmatic political calculations.

Furious Zionist lobbying that played on the Democrats' fear of losing the Jewish vote (and donors), and concern that the Soviet Union would exploit any American hesitation to assert its own influence, forced Truman's hand. He made the decision in the face of a majority view among the highest echelons of the US State Department and the Pentagon that the establishment of a Jewish state would destabilize the Middle East and jeopardize America's relations with the Arabs.

On February 14, 1947, Britain formally referred Palestine's future to the United Nations. The United Nations Special Committee on Palestine (UNSCOP) delivered its report on September 3, 1947, favoring an end to the Mandate and the partition of Palestine into two states. The Jewish Agency endorsed the report. The Arabs rejected it. But they were not alone in rejecting partition.

In a lead-up to the final showdown at Lake Success, where an ad hoc committee was to prepare the resolution that would be voted upon by the General Assembly, the United Zionists–Revisionists of America published a full-page ad in the *New York Times* titled "Partition Will Not Solve the Palestine Problem!" The ad, drafted by one of its signatories—Dr. B. Netanyahu, executive director—claimed that partition would rob the Jews of their historic homelands of Judea, the Galilee, and Jerusalem, "the cradle of the Jewish race," and "would spell the end of the great Zionist dream."[2] The objections were also practical. As Menachem Begin wrote in a separate article, with the Jews receiving only 12,000 square kilometers (about 4,500 square miles), there would not be sufficient space for the millions of Jews expected to arrive. Partition, he wrote, meant "giving up on the redemption hope of 90 percent of the Jewish people."

Benzion Netanyahu had little time for politics in those days. Besides drafting the ad in the *New York Times*, he was busy commuting to Dropsie, completing his dissertation on Don Isaac Abravanel. Netanyahu believed that Ben-Gurion and the other Zionist leaders who had come after Herzl had failed, just like Abravanel. They had not heeded Jabotinsky's warnings of impending destruction. With such weak and misguided leaders, and without the millions who had been lost in the Holocaust, they were about to fail again with their plans to found a Jewish state on a sliver of the Promised Land.

The Revisionists were deluding themselves in thinking that the Jews could reject partition, defying both the Arabs and the world powers, and conquer the entire land by force of arms. Ben-Gurion, the ruthless pragmatist, realized that partition was the only option available.

On November 29, 1947, the partition plan was approved by the United Nations 33–13. That night, thousands of Jews danced in the square in front of the Jewish Agency headquarters in Jerusalem.

Ben-Gurion's lack of dogmatism and his political adaptability were a key factor in Israel's foundation and the reason he became its founder. The Revisionists' ideological rigidity was to keep them for long decades in the wilderness of opposition. And few of them were as rigid as Benzion Netanyahu.

On May 14, 1948, when Ben-Gurion stood up in the Tel Aviv Museum of Art to announce the establishment of the State of Israel, Netanyahu was still in New York. The Revisionists had not been invited to the party. Ben-Gurion had appointed representatives of the other Zionist groups, and even of the ultra-Orthodox, non-Zionist Agudat Yisrael, as members of the Minhelet HaAm (People's Administration), which would become the provisional national government upon independence, but no Revisionists. Two days earlier, the Minhelet HaAm had voted to declare independence the moment the British left (the Mandate was set to expire at midnight on May 14). Three Revisionist representatives had served on the Jewish National Council, the body that had helped organize the provisional government, and were among the thirty-seven signatories of the Israeli Declaration of Independence, but they were to have no say on policy.

The members of the Minhelet HaAm heard at that fateful meeting on May 12 a report from Moshe Sharett, the director of the Jewish Agency's political department, who had just returned from Washington. He was carrying a warning from Secretary of State George Marshall that Israel was at risk of losing its war with the Arab nations and the United States would not come to its aid. The administration was urging Israel to postpone its declaration of independence as part of an appeal for international mediation.

Haganah commander Yigael Yadin admitted at the meeting that he couldn't promise anything better than a fifty-fifty chance of staving off the Arab attack. Ben-Gurion pushed for a vote in favor of independence and narrowly won, 6–4.

B EN-GURION WAS TAKING a gamble with the lives of the six hundred thousand Jews of the Yishuv and the hopes of millions of Jews in the Diaspora. He had prepared for this moment for years, but now five Arab armies were about to invade the new state. Tens of thousands of local Palestinian fighters and volunteers from around the Arab world had already been fighting the Jewish forces inside Palestine in the six months since the UN vote. The Haganah had the upper hand in these local battles, but it was about to face regular armies and expected to be vastly outnumbered.

Ultimately, it would be superior organization and mobilization on the Israeli side that would decide the war. But on May 15, Ben-Gurion could not have known for certain that the invading Arab armies would be poorly coordinated, suspicious of each other, and willing to commit only relatively small forces to "liberating" Palestine. Despite initial advances by the Arab armies and the loss of the Jewish Quarter in Jerusalem's Old City, by the end of 1948 the tide had turned decisively in Israel's favor. The new state's borders greatly exceeded those marked on the map of UN Resolution 181.

The founding of the new state was Ben-Gurion's personal triumph and that of Mapai. It was their Haganah which served as the foundation for the new Israel Defense Forces. IZL members who were fighting the Arab forces were also to come under the command of Ben-Gurion's officers.

The seeds of the resentment that would one day grow to become the Likud coalition of perpetual outsiders, Benjamin Netanyahu's power base, had already been sown. The historical argument within the Zionist movement was not resolved by independence.

Throughout its history, political Zionism has remained divided between those believing in cooperation with the international community and seeking an accommodation with the Arabs, on the one side, and, on the other, those who are convinced that the Jews must pursue their national interests forcefully and not be deterred by local opposition or international opinion. This issue has remained the main fault line of Israel's politics to this day. No major Israeli leader could ever lead from one of the extreme poles. Ben-Gurion, ostensibly from the left, would defy the world powers at critical moments, and in 1955 he famously said that "our future depends not on what the *goyim* [gentiles] say, but on what the Jews do."[3] Begin, who spent most of his political career accusing Ben-Gurion and his allies of kowtowing to the goyim, would be forced to make his own compromises with them upon coming to power. As would Benjamin Netanyahu.

B ENZION NEVER BELIEVED in Zionist pragmatism. He was certain that Ben-Gurion's gamble would fail. Half a century after the War of Independence had been won, he admitted that "with all the faults and weaknesses it was a wonder in my eyes that with the human material at our disposal, which was not ideal, we succeeded in building a viable state."[4]

The Netanyahu family mythology has constantly tried to place itself at the center of the Zionist narrative. In reality, the father and grandfather were at most bit-players. Yoni Netanyahu's death as a hero in 1976 would be the first time the family gained national and international recognition. Political influence would come only a decade later, when Benjamin joined Likud in 1987. But the roots of Netanyahu's Israel are in Nathan Mileikowsky's days in the Volozhin yeshiva in late nineteenth-century Lithuania. The grandfather was the first Netanyahu Zionist outsider, frustrated by his inability to become part of the establishment.

Benzion was just as peripheral a figure as Nathan, a failed politician who never once failed to bet on the wrong horse. Bibi is the exact opposite—a politician with near-flawless timing. He transformed his father's ideology into political capital. In the space Benzion occupied outside the Zionist mainstream, Netanyahu's Israel was built.

PART TWO

Outsiders in the New State

1949–1976

5

Life Within Sharp Borders

Benjamin Netanyahu was born on October 23, 1949, in Tel Aviv. He was registered as a citizen of the new state of Israel and, like his mother, a citizen of the United States of America as well. The Netanyahu family had returned from New York eleven months earlier. Named after his maternal grandfather, Benjamin Segal, he swiftly became known as "Bibi" to differentiate him from older cousins of the same name.

Tzila had been the main force behind the move. Benzion still had scant faith in the new state's prospects of survival and prosperity. He preferred the more secure course, which would have been to focus on his academic career in America. For the first year in Israel they lived in Tzila's mother's house in Petach Tikva, near Tel Aviv.

By the end of 1948, when the family arrived, Israel's War of Independence was almost over and the nation was gearing up for its first elections. It was a disorientating time. Over 6,000 Jews had been killed, 1 percent of Palestine's pre-independence Jewish population. For its Arab community the results were much more devastating. Around two-thirds of that community, some 750,000 people, had fled their homes, at the advice of Arab leaders, for fear of the fighting and Jewish reprisals, or had been forcibly banished by the new Israeli army.

From a territorial perspective, Israel had won decisively. Despite the efforts of the local Arabs and the five Arab nations surrounding Israel to strangle it at birth, the Jewish state, which had been allocated by the United Nations 55 percent of the land east of the Jordan River, now controlled nearly 80 percent. The remaining 20 percent—the West Bank, the eastern part of Jerusalem, and the Gaza Strip—were now occupied by the Jordanian and Egyptian armies.

The armistice agreements signed between Israel and its neighbors in 1949 left around 160,000 Arabs within the new state's borders, and for the first time in nearly 1,900 years there was a Jewish majority in the land. This population was soon bolstered by hundreds of thousands of Holocaust refugees and Sephardi Jews fleeing Arab countries. Israel's population would double in its first five years.

As the new state struggled to deal with the flood of newcomers, the government introduced harsh austerity and rationing measures, some of which were to remain in effect until 1959. The Segal home in Petach Tikva, then still a farming community, suffered less than the rest of the country, but the tins of corned beef that Benzion and Tzila had brought with them were a welcome addition to the family diet. In their first few months in the new homeland, Benzion tried to reestablish his political career. It wasn't going to be easy. The movement he had belonged to for over two decades was now firmly sidelined.

With the Jewish state established and secured, its founder-in-chief, David Ben-Gurion, and his party, Mapai, reigned supreme. Twelve days after the declaration of independence, the temporary government ordered the establishment of the Israel Defense Forces (IDF) and the disbandment of all other armed groups within the new state. The Revisionist militias, Irgun Zvai Leumi (IZL) and Lohamei Herut Yisrael (LHY), were to be disbanded, their arms handed over to the IDF.

Ben-Gurion drove his message home ruthlessly three weeks later when he ordered the new army's coastal battery to fire on the *Altalena*, an arms ship brought by IZL from the United States. The IZL had agreed to disband, but demanded that they be allowed to keep some of the weapons for their men, who were still fighting under IZL's banner in Jerusalem, which at the time was not yet recognized as part of Israel. Sixteen IZL members and three IDF soldiers were killed in the skirmish off the coast of Tel Aviv.

Ben-Gurion and the Mapai press accused the IZL of trying to launch a coup against the young state. Menachem Begin, the IZL leader, who had been on the *Altalena* during the battle, accused Ben-Gurion's men of trying to assassinate him. Yet he once again refused the entreaties of some of his comrades to oppose their rivals by force and launch an armed grab for the Yishuv's leadership. Not only would such a path have been futile, as the IZL was hopelessly outnumbered, but Begin had already decided that the Revisionist movement would play by the rules of democracy. He knew that subsequent generations would never forgive him for splitting the Yishuv at a time of war.

It was a low point for Begin. In the years leading up to independence, he had been hiding from the British, a mythical and invisible leader of resistance. Emerging into the light of day, marginalized from any decision making, with his men now fighting as soldiers in the new IDF beyond his control, the short-statured, Polish-accented lawyer with a Charlie Chaplin mustache (which he soon shaved) seemed an inconsequential figure. As he began rebuilding the movement as a political party—Herut (Freedom), the forerunner of Likud—many Revisionists doubted he could ever take on Ben-Gurion and Mapai.

Benzion Netanyahu, arriving in Tel Aviv in November 1948, was prepared to join Herut, but he expected a leading role as one of its ideologues, and at the very least to be offered a spot on the party's list of candidates for the Knesset, Israel's new parliament.

Neither offer materialized. Begin, aware of his internal opposition, was reserving most of the leadership positions for those who had fought by his side in the underground. Netanyahu was seen as an obscure figure whose contribution and influence didn't warrant a place within the party's cramped hierarchy.

To say that Netanyahu and Begin had a tense relationship would be an exaggeration. They had no real relationship to speak of. Netanyahu was not alone among Jabotinsky's followers in despising the Polish lawyer. Some IZL veterans thought he was an unworthy successor to David Raziel because he had not fought himself, but instead had only sent others to their deaths on dangerous operations. At the same time, and more significantly, many among the intellectual wing of the party considered Begin a lightweight. Revisionist philosopher and biblical scholar Israel Eldad derided Begin and his acolytes as "half-intelligent" and refused to join Herut.[1]

For the majority of the Revisionists, however, after the five years he had spent as an underground leader hiding from the British, forever one step ahead of his pursuers, who had put a price on his head, Begin was an icon. He may not have had Jabotinsky's intellectual brilliance, and it would take decades for him to command a similar slavish loyalty within the movement, but he would persevere. Begin painstakingly built an enduring coalition of secular Ashkenazi right-wingers and younger traditional Sephardi immigrants, people who had been marginalized by Mapai, which would come to power in 1977. Benjamin Netanyahu's power base is Begin's creation.

Benzion Netanyahu, however, would never change his views or curry favor just to gain a job or political advancement. Others in the movement, including his own son, moderated their views with time, especially upon entering government. Begin himself would prove much more pragmatic as prime minister. Not Benzion.

In the first Knesset elections on January 25, 1949, the Revisionists split into three separate parties. Begin's Herut performed well below its expectations, receiving only 11.5 percent of the vote. Few Israelis seemed to credit Begin for wresting independence from the British. The breakaway factions fared even worse. Netanyahu had supported Brit Hatzohar, the party of Revisionists who refused to accept Begin's leadership, which received only a pitiful 2,892 votes and failed to enter the Knesset. Brit Hatzohar accepted its fate and soon merged with Herut.

Benzion Netanyahu didn't join Herut; nor did he join Likud later on. At the age of thirty-nine, he gave up politics once and for all. With the exception of a rare letter to the newspapers, from that point on he focused solely on his academic career.

I N EARLY 1950, a few months after Benjamin's birth, the family moved to Jerusalem.

The Israeli capital, though officially not recognized as such even by the country's closest allies, was very much a frontier town at the time. The Jordanians remained in control of the ancient highway leading up to Jerusalem from the coastal plain. Access to the city was by a narrow winding road on which trucks, buses, and private cars crawled for hours. The old Ottoman train line was no faster.

The city itself was split down the middle by a barbed wire fence and snipers' nests. The Old City, the eastern and northern neighborhoods, were in the hands of the Jordanians, whereas west and south Jerusalem were under Israeli control.

Toward the end of the Independence War, Ben-Gurion had decided not to pursue the IDF's advantage and capture the West Bank. He believed Israel would be better off without its large Arab towns and hundreds of thousands of hostile citizens.

In the armistice talks with Israel's Arab neighbors in early 1949, he agreed on "ceasefire lines," not recognized international borders. He feared that pressure from the United Nations and the US and British governments could force Israel to retreat to the original lines of the partition plan, and he wanted to preserve the possibility of further enlarging Israel's territory in the future. Just like Benjamin Netanyahu over six decades later, Ben-Gurion had an aversion to making concessions and reaching permanent solutions.

In December 1949, Ben-Gurion ordered the newly elected Knesset and most of the main government offices to move from Tel Aviv to Jerusalem. Tel Aviv, a coastal city, and the "first Hebrew city" in the Zionist narrative, was by then the main financial and cultural hub of the country. Many of Ben-Gurion's party colleagues were enraged at the prospect of having to move—or make the arduous commute—for what they saw as an empty political gesture.

For the Netanyahu boys, Jonathan and Benjamin, known to family and friends by their nicknames Yoni and Bibi, the divided unrecognized capital of Ben-Gurion's borderless Israel was a childhood paradise. Twelve years later, a homesick Yoni would reminisce in a letter from Philadelphia of "hiding in giant fields, covered nearly totally by grass, searching for ladybird bugs and looking at the world as the most wonderful thing."[2]

Even small boys could not fail to notice that at one end of the fields was an army base, the Allenby Barracks, filled with soldiers on alert, and at the other, the barbed wire and minefields of no-man's-land. In an interview later in life, Bibi recalled how his mother would take him by the hand and "mark out the boundaries" where he was permitted to go. They lived "not feeling a siege, but life within sharp borders."[3]

When Tzila took the boys to explore the world outside their small rented bungalow in Talpiyot, Benzion remained in his study, working. The closed door behind which their father read and wrote, and the general quiet required from the boys while in the house, would be the abiding memory of their childhood home.

The one advantage that Jerusalem had in those days over Tel Aviv, and the reason for the family's move there, was that it was still the only university town in Israel. But Hebrew University was in disarray, having been forced to move from its Mount Scopus campus, which had become a tiny Israeli-held enclave in Jordanian-occupied territory. The faculty had been forced to relocate to cramped quarters in a building rented from the Catholic Church in central Jerusalem.

The Israeli writer Amos Oz, whose father, a researcher of Hebrew literature, failed to find a post at the university more senior than junior librarian, recalled in his memoir, *A Tale of Love and Darkness*, that Jerusalem was then "filled with the refugees of Poland and Russia and refugees of Hitler, among them leading lights of famed universities. There were in those days many more lecturers than pupils, many more researchers and intellectuals than students."[4]

Oz's father, Yehuda Klausner, had something else in common with Benzion Netanyahu: both were regular guests at the home of Klausner's uncle, Benzion's early mentor, Professor Joseph Klausner. Oz describes magical Saturday afternoons as he roamed his great uncle's home and garden in Talpiyot, while the grown-ups in the dining room discussed Jewish history and the new state's politics over tea and cakes. He had one dim recollection of the Netanyahu boys: "I kicked one of them once, when I was about thirteen, with the full force of my shoe, because he was crawling beneath the table and opening my laces and pulling at the hems of my trousers (to this day I don't know whether I kicked the hero brother or the nimble brother)."[5]

Since Yoni at the time would have been around five, the child crawling under the table whom Oz kicked was almost certainly the young Bibi.

For decades, the Netanyahu family has propagated the myth that Benzion's prospects in Israeli academia were blocked on account of his political views. In reality, his failure to secure a post was probably due to other issues. Although it is undoubtedly true that a majority of senior professors at Hebrew University and the new Israeli universities were and remain on the left in their politics, there was no shortage of upcoming academics on the right.

Benzion's younger brother, Elisha Netanyahu, his coconspirator in the Bentwich stink bomb incident, was already a celebrated mathematician and lecturer at Haifa's Technion Institute, where he would go on to become a professor and dean. Other prominent Revisionists in Israeli academia included the Orientalist and linguist Yossef Rivlin, the father of the current president of Israel, Reuven Rivlin, and the classicist Raanana Meridor, the wife of the IZL commander Eliyahu Meridor and the mother of the Likud finance minister under Benjamin Netanyahu, Dan Meridor.

Benjamin Akzin, who had been Benzion's boss during the Revisionist efforts in New York, was a law professor and the founder of Hebrew University's law school, as well as the first rector of Haifa University.

The position coveted by Benzion—researcher and lecturer on the history of Spanish Jews and the Inquisition—went to a younger academic, Haim Beinart, who had not only been a member of the IZL, but was kidnapped and interrogated by Haganah members during the Saison, refusing to disclose the locations of weapon stores and of his commander, Begin. Beinart's Revisionist background didn't prevent him from becoming the protégé and successor of Professor Yitzhak Baer, the doyen of medieval Jewish history and founder and head of the Department of Jewish History at Hebrew University.

Most mainstream historians were of the opinion that the Jews of medieval Spain had been forced to convert to Christianity, but remained practicing Jews in hiding, and that the Inquisition had aimed to root out these crypto-Jews. Benzion had a much dimmer view of the *conversos*. He believed they had converted for social advancement and were not prepared to sacrifice their lives for their religious beliefs. Professor Netanyahu's conclusion was that the persecution of Jews by the Spanish Inquisition, the expulsion and massacres, were racially motivated. He saw a clear line connecting the attitude of the medieval Roman Catholic Church to modern anti-Semitism and even the Holocaust.

Nearly sixty years later, Benzion admitted in an interview that his differences with Baer were personal, not political. He bluntly described Baer as "a not successful lecturer with no variety in his discourse." He added: "I opposed his views. In essays on subjects he suggested, I would always write against his views. 'In my humble opinion,' I wrote, 'you are mistaken.' He gave me very good grades and always wrote 'interesting, but wrong.' He did not recommend me as his successor."[6]

With Benzion unable to secure a post, the young Netanyahu family relied on the support of his siblings, who were making money in the United States, and of Tzila's family. This was not where a man of Benzion's talent and ambition had pictured himself being in his early forties. Incapable of conforming or hiding his contrarian views, it seemed that not only had this outsider's political career come to an end, but his academic career, too.

6

A Terrible Dislocation

Bibi Netanyahu's childhood was overshadowed by his parents' dilemma—Should they build their family's future in Israel, or in the United States?

Denied an academic post in Jerusalem, Benzion's preference was to return to America, where he believed his talents were more appreciated. Tzila had already devoted her life to her husband's career, but by 1952, with the birth of a third son, Iddo, she wanted to remain close to her own support base of family and friends. Another argument for staying in Jerusalem was Benzion's new and lucrative job.

Benzion's mentor, Professor Klausner, had hired him to serve as deputy editor of the new *Encyclopaedia Hebraica*. The encyclopaedia was a commercial success, quickly establishing itself as a flagship of Jewish and Zionist learning. Its entries were a Who's Who of the new state, with politicians and cultural figures vying for a mention in its pages. Celebrated academics in Israel and abroad had been lined up to write the entries. Klausner, who was editor-in-chief, left much of the work to his protégé.

Benzion had proved himself a capable editor in his postgraduate years, and he was a perfect fit for the job. For over a decade he cranked out a volume each year, and in 1957 he replaced Klausner as editor-in-chief, a role he had effectively filled for the prior five years. He worked from home and kept his own hours. A fast reader and an efficient editor, he now had abundant time and ample funds to pursue his own research, setting off on long annual research trips, occasionally with Tzila, to Spain and the United States. But engaging with the encyclopaedia's contributors, the leading Jewish academics of the age, was a constant and frustrating reminder of what he had been denied.

In 1953 they moved into a home of their own. The six-room villa, close to central Jerusalem, was a palace by Israeli standards of the time. The hand-painted floor tiles gave it the nickname "The Armenian House," though no one knew who the previous Arab owners had been.

Katamon had been a neighborhood of middle- and upper-class Christian Arabs situated between mainly Jewish areas. Its residents fled the fighting between the Haganah and the local Arab militias in early 1948. Most of the buildings were expropriated by the Israeli government under a law passed in 1950 nationalizing the land and buildings belonging to absentee owners.

Benzion Netanyahu purchased the house at well below its market value. The only vestige of the previous occupants was a lone bullet hole by the door that intrigued the boys. But like the rest of the 750,000 Palestinians uprooted during Israel's War of Independence, the anonymous previous owners of the Netanyahu home had been erased from Israeli memory.

Visitors to the house remember an echo effect between its walls. Childhood friends of the boys had to remain silent so as not to disturb Benzion when he was working in his study, which was behind a door with an opaque pane of glass. Tzila ran the house and tended to the boys' needs. Schooldays were short, from eight in the morning until just after noon. Yoni and Bibi walked to school together and were back home for lunch.

Friends were not allowed in the house between two and four in the afternoon, the time reserved for homework and reading. It was also the only time of the day in which the boys had their father's attention. Bibi remembers his father tutoring him, especially in history. But most of the time, he said, Tzila "was the axis of our family." She would say, "I'm married to a genius but even a genius needs his socks put away." For all his admiration for his father, Bibi later made clear that "our mother raised us." Their father did at least teach them chess.[1]

Few Israelis had the time or money to travel abroad. Benzion, as a result of his new job, had both. As a toddler, Bibi would spend his summers with the Segal family in Petach Tikva. While Benzion traveled, Tzila went there with the boys, and Bibi played with his cousins, who gave him the nickname that would stick throughout his life. She is still remembered by Petach Tikva old-timers as "the kind of lady who would get up at five to help milk the cows and in the afternoon was in high-heels." President Reuven Rivlin, a decade older than Netanyahu, whose grandmother was also from an old Petach Tikva family, once recalled a summer get-together in one of the homes there where the two-year-old Bibi took his first hesitant steps in the living room.

Tzila would join Benzion occasionally on his travels, leaving the young boys with her family. The novelist Yehudit (Judith) Katzir, a descendant of another of the founding families of Petach Tikva, recorded in a memoir how her great-grandmother, who ran a small kindergarten, would take care of them during the long summer days. "Yoni was six, I think, and Bibi three. There was a large veranda where they ate at a long table with benches. Morning and evening there was semolina porridge, or oats, with raisins and sugar and cinnamon. I remember Yoni hated that porridge, and Bibi was crazy for it and always asked for seconds. When Tzila and Benzi returned after a few weeks, they discovered that Yoni was as thin as a stick and Bibi fat like a ball."[2] From childhood, Yoni was lean and austere like his father, while the thickset Bibi inherited his mother's more rounded looks.

Many of the children the Netanyahu boys knew were sons and daughters of parents who held influential posts in the young state's hierarchy. All around them in the small-town Jerusalem of the 1950s there were constant reminders of their father's outsider status. Benzion was closeted in his study most of his waking hours, his social life consisting mainly of a weekly game of canasta with Tzila and another couple.

MEANWHILE, BEN-GURION'S ISRAEL was building its economy and military apparatus. Dashing paratrooper officers, commanded by Ariel Sharon, led cross-border commando raids against the bases of the Fedayun, the Palestinian refugees sent by Egyptian colonels to attack Israeli towns and villages. As the Israeli and Arab armies eyed each other across the temporary borders, another war was just a question of time.

The diplomatic front also remained fluid. The Soviet Union had initially supported the establishment of Israel and allowed its proxy, Czechoslovakia, to sell arms to the nascent army. But the good relations did not last long. In his last paranoid years, Joseph Stalin saw the Soviet Jews as dangerous "Zionist agents," and show-trials took place in Moscow and Prague. The communist bloc began to support the new revolutionary Arab governments in Egypt, and later on in Syria and Iraq, supplying them with advanced weapons. Ben-Gurion in any case preferred building Western alliances, although the United States, which had been the first nation to recognize the new state, competed with the Soviets for influence with the emerging Arab nations.

Israel had no choice but to turn to France, which for the next fifteen years would become its main source of modern weaponry, along with West Germany, which in 1952 had signed a Reparations Agreement with Israel for the Holocaust. The reparations boosted the economy, allowing the government to finance arms deals, build dozens of new towns, and absorb a million new immigrants. They also boosted Menachem Begin's moribund political career, as he led the principled opposition to the deal with Germany in often violent demonstrations.

Hebrew University's elite left-leaning faculty members were scandalized by the start of secret nuclear research, run by physicist Ernst David Bergmann and Ben-Gurion's young aide Shimon Peres, in the mid-1950s, and the building of a new French-designed reactor near Dimona in the Negev Desert. They became the unofficial opposition to what their ringleader, the philosopher Yeshayahu Leibowitz, called the secret "state within a state," warning of a nuclear holocaust.

Leibowitz and Benzion Netanyahu were bitter rivals. Leibowitz was editor of the natural science entries in the *Encyclopaedia Hebraica*, working directly with the publishers. He had strident political views and was a critic of Ben-Gurion from the left. But he was also a pillar of the local academic establishment. Had Netanyahu been privy to the debate on the nuclear program, he would certainly, for once, have sided with Ben-Gurion.

In October 1956, Israel joined France and Britain in a secret pact to attack Egypt. For Israel, the Sinai Campaign was an attempt to defeat and discredit Egypt's new president, Gamal Abdel Nasser. The emerging leader of Arab nationalism was trying to impose a siege on Israel by closing the Straits of Tiran, blocking shipping to Israel's southern port at Eilat, sending the Fedayun from the Gaza Strip, and creating a joint military command with Syria and Jordan. The French and the British were enraged by Nasser's nationalization of the company managing the Suez Canal, which they had jointly owned, and feared his firebrand nationalism, which threatened their interests in the region.

Israel decimated the Egyptian Army, taking control of the Sinai Peninsula in six days. But the wider political objective that Israel shared with Britain and France—of removing Nasser and changing the regional balance of power—failed.

Ben-Gurion, momentarily swept away by military triumph, promised in a victory speech that parts of Sinai would "resume being part of the third kingdom of Israel."[3] He was forced back to his customary pragmatism only twenty-four hours later by a letter from Soviet leader Nikolai Bulganin, who threatened to join the war against Israel and even use nuclear weapons. To make things worse, the Eisenhower administration joined the Soviets in their demand that Israel, France, and Britain pull back from Sinai and Suez. Israel became a partisan issue in American politics as Dwight Eisenhower and his secretary of state, John Foster Dulles, threatened to cut off US civilian aid to Israel, despite pressure from the Democratic majority in the Senate to keep it.

Ben-Gurion backed down and announced that Israel would be pulling out of Sinai. A UN peacekeeping force entered the region, and Israeli ships were assured passage through the Straits of Tiran (though not the Suez Canal). Nasser's image in the Arab world as the man who had stood up to the former colonial powers, Britain and France, was enhanced. With Soviet support, Egypt swiftly reconstituted its army. The Fedayun attacks ceased, and a fragile truce, valuable for Israel in terms of building up its economy and military, held for a decade. But the stage was already set for a much larger and more fateful Israeli-Arab war.

In his book *A Place Among the Nations*, Benjamin Netanyahu wrote that his memories as a seven-year-old during the Sinai Campaign "are sharp, but not traumatic."[4] He mentions sticking strips of tape on his room's windows, in case of a bombardment of Jerusalem that never happened (the tape was meant to keep the glass from shattering and injuring anyone nearby). But his main memory is of the father of a neighboring family returning from the Sinai battlefield in a dusty jeep, distributing chocolate bars to the children. He had bought them in the Egyptian town of El Arish. The sight of someone else's father, who, like nearly all the other fathers of his friends, was contributing to the war effort, in this case in uniform, while his own father remained home, must have rankled. Growing up with an admired but painfully civilian father in the young, spartan Israel would motivate all three Netanyahu boys to serve in the most elite of combat units.

Before they reached those battlefields, the brothers got into trouble closer to home. Yoni was the leader of a gang of neighborhood boys, with Bibi always in tow. Dressed in clothes sent by Benzion's brothers from America, they stood out among their more carefree friends, who often wore shorts and sandals. "You felt with Yoni and Bibi, that they were sent out from home with an instruction manual," said Eli Hershkowitz, a classmate of Bibi's. From their childhood friends' recollections, it is clear that the boys chafed under the strict discipline of their household. Friends would sometimes sneak through the window of the bedroom at the back of the house shared by Bibi and Iddo. Headstrong Yoni was forever testing the boundaries. Friends remember Tzila slapping him when she discovered that as a prank he had purloined a stamp collection that belonged to one of the neighbors. Bibi was always more obedient and was less likely than his older brother to break the rules.

One of Yoni's gang's favorite pastimes was exploring locked-up abandoned homes and gardens. One such house stood at the edge of Moon Grove, a wild, wooded area near the neighborhood. On an incursion into its garden, ten-year-old Yoni climbed to the top of the fence and then hoisted up the rest of the gang. Bibi, already then heavier than most of his friends, slipped from his grasp, fell, and split his upper lip. To this day Benjamin Netanyahu is self-conscious of the scar, tilting his head slightly sideways in photographs, and obscuring it with makeup. Officially, the family blames the scar on an electric burn at the age of two. The very idea of Yoni dropping his younger brother is a heresy against the cult they have built around the eldest son's memory since his death.

Bibi's world was turned upside down in 1958, when Benzion convinced Tzila to move back to New York so he could accept a fellowship at Dropsie College. It was a disorientating two years for the eight-year-old, who left sleepy, small-town Jerusalem for a cramped apartment in the Cameron Hotel on West Eighty-sixth Street. Bibi's memories from that period are dominated by going to school without knowing a word of English. At home, Tzila tutored him for hours, trying to help him master the foreign "th" sound, while at school he sat next to a girl who helped with "Spot the Dog" reading cards. The second year in the United States, the family moved to a more rural setting on Long Island where the children had room to run around, but for once, the homesickness that Tzila and the boys felt trumped Benzion's career, and they moved back to Jerusalem in 1960.

Back in Jerusalem, Benzion continued to feel ostracized and isolated as he began quarreling with the publishers and the other editors of the *Encyclopaedia Hebraica* over money and editorial control. Eventually, Professor Leibowitz would usurp him as editor-in-chief.

In 1961, Bibi began high school at Gymnasia Rehavia, then the most elitist school in Jerusalem. Being among the children of the leading politicians and senior officials of the young state was another stark reminder of his father's permanent outsider status.

For Bibi, high school meant being once again under his elder brother's shadow. Yoni was the president of the gymnasia's student council and leader of the local Scout troop. Being accepted by the establishment was a new experience for the brothers. While Benzion remained detached and aloof from Israeli society, his sons were joining Israel's elite already in their early teens.

Bibi's group of friends from his first year in the gymnasia would remain his main social circle for years to come, even when he would be thousands of miles away in America and during his intensive military career. Like him, they had been born to the new state and felt confident of their future role leading it. When his parents announced in late 1962 that they were going back to Philadelphia, the prospect of leaving these friends behind was "very traumatic," he would say over fifty years later. "A terrible dislocation. It was awful, very hard."[5]

The impending departure was particularly difficult for Yoni, who at sixteen was already looking forward to joining the IDF. He had a series of explosive arguments with his parents, and they usually ended with him closing himself in his room for hours.

For Benzion, the move was necessary. Past fifty, he was still stymied in his academic career. America offered the prospect of tenure and uninterrupted time to research the origins of the Spanish Inquisition (his book on it would be published over three decades later). He also wanted his sons to have the kind of education in the United States that he believed was unobtainable at the Hebrew University that had rejected him. Benzion's decisions to move his family to the United States were always motivated by career opportunities he did not have in Israel. On a subconscious level, however, it seems that life in the Jewish state, which he had worked and yearned for, but under a socialist government that he abhorred and was convinced could not save the state from ultimate destruction, was unbearable. He would return to live in Israel permanently only under a Likud government. Benzion was incapable of identifying with his sons, who felt that by leaving Israel, they were abandoning the Zionist enterprise that was central to their self-identity.

Most of Benzion's siblings had already moved to the United States in the 1930s and 1940s, and Tzila also had extensive family in the United States. In the early decades of Zionism, it was clear that the austere life in the Promised Land wasn't for everyone.

After independence, the new self-confidence born from the early achievements of the young state resulted in the stigmatization of the act of leaving Israel. In Jewish tradition, emigration to Zion has always been known by the biblical term *Aliyah*, which means ascent, going upward. The immigrants themselves are called *Olim*—those who have risen. In the new Israel, those who left were awarded the derogatory term *yordim*— those who went down.

Netanyahu has always insisted that his family's move to Philadelphia was temporary, that they were no different from anyone else who had spent a few years abroad serving the state as diplomats or finishing a PhD. But you can still hear that deep scorn in the voice of veteran members of Likud who have been sidelined by Netanyahu, those whose parents remained in Israel, unlike Benzion, when they say that "they were a family of yordim!"

Benzion lived in his detached bubble of Jewish history. He still had little faith that Israel would survive for long, and he would go through life with a foreboding sense of impending doom. But as far as Yoni and Bibi were concerned, he wasn't just taking them away from their friends, but snatching them out of the Israeli narrative. Unlike their father, they envisioned themselves building Israel's future. For Benzion and Tzila it would be the start of a long period of living mainly abroad, but all three sons would soon insist on returning without them.

7

American Ben, Israeli Bibi

The Netanyahus arrived in snowy Philadelphia in January 1963 and settled in a two-story house in Elkins Park. For the next year and a half, the brothers were a unit of two, neither of them making much effort to make friends or create a lasting impression at Cheltenham High. The younger brother's grasp of English was swifter, though both were already relatively fluent from their two years in New York. Both were voracious readers—Bibi carried around a small notebook in which he jotted down any new word he read or heard, a system Yoni eventually adopted as well.

It wasn't just the foreign surroundings that knitted the brothers together. It was also their silent but defiant opposition to their father. The narrative told by the family years later was that there was no question that upon graduation they would both immediately return for military service in Israel. Any other version of the family history would have marked them in the eyes of ordinary Israelis as deserters and shirkers. But from the collection of Yoni's letters published in Israel in 1978, a year after his death, it is clear that as far as Benzion was concerned, his sons should take advantage of the opportunity to enjoy a superior academic education and remain in the United States. For all the talk of how Benzion influenced his sons' views of the world, their most formative years were marked by a resentment of their father for uprooting them from Jerusalem and for resisting their determination to return to join the army.

Neither Yoni nor Bibi found the standards of Cheltenham High difficult, and language was not a barrier to either of them becoming honors students.

Success in class didn't extend to social life. Yoni encapsulated the brothers' feelings toward their American classmates in an April 1963 letter to a friend back in Jerusalem. "People here talk about cars and girls. Life revolves around one subject—sex, and I believe Freud would have rich ground here to seed and pick his fruit. Slowly I am being convinced that I live among monkeys, not humans."[1]

The Netanyahu brothers were eager to proselytize for Israel. In another letter from that period, Yoni wrote,

> I've adopted a new role in the U.S.—making propaganda for Israel. A month ago they interviewed me for the student newspaper. It seems the interview was very successful and has caused invitations to homes, parties etc., since 'the parents want to get to know me.' Yesterday I sat until one in the morning with four girls and preached Zionism. Etc. I'm happy to note, that I've discovered here a few humans, with brains and wisdom of a high order. The problem with the young people here is that their lives are so poor in substance and are passed as if in a dream or game.[2]

The two teenagers were anxious to remain untainted by the host culture. "It is a terrible world, there is nothing to do here, everything is stunted, without any real life," grumbled Yoni.[3]

There were a few aspects of their new lives that appealed to them. Yoni discovered that Cheltenham High offered well-taught courses in mathematics and physics, and found himself warming to his science teachers, much more than to his classmates. Bibi was drawn to American history, which remains among his favorite subjects for reading in his spare time. In the prime minister's office he still often whiles away hours with a biography of an American statesman or general.

Yoni spent his only summer vacation in the United States as a counselor at a Young Judea camp in New Hampshire, where he ended up teaching rudimentary Hebrew to his young Jewish charges and lecturing them on the wonders of Israel. By July 1964, both brothers were back in Jerusalem: Bibi for a summer's reunion with his school friends, Yoni for the draft.

Joining the IDF in early August, Yoni volunteered for the Paratroopers Brigade. While the twenty-first-century Israeli army abounds with crack infantry and special forces units, in the 1960s the paratroopers were the sole undisputed elite. The brigade had been created in the mid-1950s when the legendary Unit 101, which had carried out the first cross-border retribution raids against Fedayun bases, had been merged with an earlier paratrooper battalion. Led by their first battalion commander, Ariel Sharon, the paratrooper battalions bore the main brunt of IDF ground operations. Paratroopers worked under extremely strenuous and physically demanding conditions. Attrition was high: over 50 percent of recruits didn't make it through the seven months of basic and advanced training.

Yoni had promised his parents that at the end of the mandatory two-year period of service he would return to the United States to attend college, but it was not a promise he intended to keep. A year into his service, he was selected for officer training. He assured Benzion, who in his letters continued to badger Yoni about college applications, that it would only mean an additional four months of service. In January 1966, he completed the training as the outstanding cadet of his company, receiving his officer's badge from the IDF chief of staff, Lieutenant General Yitzhak Rabin. He was commissioned back to the paratroopers as a new platoon commander.

M EANWHILE, BACK IN Philadelphia, his brother pined for him. Although Bibi's letters from that period have never been published, it's clear from Yoni's that the bond between them only intensified during their period apart. In a letter Yoni wrote to his girlfriend, he described Bibi as "the person I love more than anyone else in the world" and "who knows me better than anyone."[4] He relied on Bibi to give him an accurate picture of the family's life back in the United States. They supported each other through letters in their joint determination to serve in Israel against their father's wishes.

Not that Bibi and Yoni were alike in every way. Bibi spent four and a half years in Philadelphia; Yoni had spent only eighteen months there. The younger brother was shaped by America to a much greater degree than his older sibling was, though in unexpected ways.

Bibi (*left*) and Iddo arrive from Philadelphia for vacation in Israel with paratrooper Yoni (*in uniform*).

Benjamin Netanyahu still enjoys recounting how he would work evenings and weekends washing dishes in local restaurants. He says that he didn't want to take any money from his parents, though they were willing to give it. The real reason was that he was saving up for airfare. With the exception of 1963, he spent his high school summers alone in Israel. During their first four and a half years in America, the entire family visited Israel together only once.

At the age of fourteen, not only was Bibi much more independent than his peers, with his own travel plans and finances, but he was also developing the dual persona that would characterize him for life. There emerged the American Netanyahu and the Israeli Netanyahu, which were so distinct from each other that they had different names, and he toggled between them depending on the season. At Cheltenham High he was Ben, a studious and rather detached teenager. Outside of class, the only extracurricular activities he participated in were those that fit his competitive personality and that were familiar to him from back in Israel. He played on the school's soccer team and was a member of the chess society. At home and during the two summer months of each year that he spent in Israel, he was more gregarious and outgoing, though he kept mainly to the close-knit circle of friends he had made before leaving in 1963. To them he would always be Bibi.

Without Yoni, who never felt at ease in America and never lost his Hebrew accent, Bibi became a chameleon. His Israeli friends began to detect a man-of-the-world swagger about him. He affected an urban cosmopolitanism among his Israeli friends, wearing American clothes and talking about pop culture and television, which at the time were all but nonexistent in provincial Jerusalem. It helped that despite his soft life in Philadelphia he kept physically fit on the soccer field. By his mid-teens he had grown into the bulky, muscular physique of his adulthood, and he never lagged behind his friends on the desert hikes and weeks of agricultural work on kibbutzim.

America was also informing his political outlook. Growing up in the post-Kennedy years, amid the intensifying civil rights struggle, doesn't seem to have made much of a lasting impression on the young Netanyahu. This was due partly to the Manichean worldview he inherited from Benzion and partly to his disdain for the liberal-leaning, Democrat-voting American Jews he was encountering. What he did appreciate was American capitalism, which he contrasted favorably with Israel's centralized and collectivist economy under Mapai. In the summers, when they visited kibbutzim, where all property and income was shared among the members, Netanyahu would lecture his friends on the evils of socialism.

An early influence was a book he read on Yoni's recommendation—*The Fountainhead*, by Ayn Rand. Bibi was taken with its hero, the architect Howard Roark, and his struggle as an independent thinker against the conformism and socialism dominating his profession. Rand's muscular blend of capitalism and individualism appealed to Netanyahu and has influenced his political and economic thinking ever since. Roark, Rand's "ideal man," was also one of his inspirations to utilize his talent for sketching and studying architecture.

Netanyahu has never publicly acknowledged any ideological debt to Rand, preferring to refer to more mainstream thinkers. The antireligious elements of her philosophy would constitute electoral suicide for an Israeli politician dependent on religious votes. But the leading lights of the small community of Rand admirers in Israel are by and large also secular supporters of Netanyahu, seeing in him an iron-willed and nonconformist Israeli exemplar of the classic Randian hero.

Toward the end of his high school years, it seemed that Bibi had given in to Benzion and was resigned to going to college before returning to Israel for his military service. Bibi had applied and been accepted to Yale, but a few months later, Yoni was already sending him advice for his upcoming return and enlistment. Israeli Bibi had prevailed over American Ben, for now.

Netanyahu rarely speaks of his American adolescence. In his book *A Place Among the Nations*, he summed up in one short paragraph the "three years I spent in high school in Philadelphia,"[5] though he was actually there for over four years. He claimed to have moved up his departure on account of the winds of war that were blowing once again in the Middle East, although Yoni had already advised him to spend a few months back in Israel before enlisting. Bibi's real incentive for returning as early as possible was to spend time with his brother.

Yoni had been discharged from the IDF at the end of January 1967 after two and a half years of service. He had turned down the entreaties of his battalion commander to sign up for another year or two and take command of a company. He had received a scholarship to Harvard, but despite his plans to start college in the fall, and the fact that he had seen his father only once over the previous three years, he seemed in no hurry to fly back to the United States. Instead he rented a room in Jerusalem and worked as a gardener.

A FTER A RELATIVELY lengthy period of calm on Israel's borders, tension had arisen with Syria over attempts by Israeli farmers to work on land in contested areas of the demilitarized zone between the two countries, and, more crucially, over a joint Syrian-Lebanese plan to divert water from the rivers feeding into the Jordan—and Israel's main water source, the Sea of Galilee—for their own use.

In 1964 the Arab states held two special summits in Egypt at which they endorsed the plan to divert the Jordan waters. They also made a joint decision to set up a unified Arab military command and establish the Palestine Liberation Organization (PLO). The security situation deteriorated as Israel launched a series of ground and air strikes against the heavy machinery the Syrians planned to use to divert the Banias River, a tributary of the Jordan. Palestinian guerrillas, mainly from the Fatah movement, which had been founded in 1959 by a group of students at Cairo University, and was led by Yasser Arafat, began launching raids against Israeli targets from Syria and Jordan.

As a soldier and officer in the IDF's busiest combat unit, in between exercises and training Yoni was often in the thick of action. In the Samu raid of November 13, 1966, or, as the IDF called it, Operation Shredder, the paratroopers blew up dozens of buildings in the village Fatah was using as a base. When Jordan's Arab Legion unexpectedly counterattacked, they beat them off, killing at least fifteen Jordanian soldiers.

The devastating raid brought international condemnation and was another step in the escalation toward inevitable war. The mild-mannered Israeli prime minister, Levi Eshkol, was particularly concerned about the effect it could have on Israel's rapidly improving ties with the United States.

Throughout the early 1960s, France had remained Israel's main strategic partner and arms supplier. Meanwhile, the Kennedy administration was still considering the possibility of an alliance with the Arab states and was concerned about reports on Israel's nuclear reactor in the Negev Desert. In a series of meetings in Washington, Israel and the United States agreed to nonintrusive American inspections of the reactor, and in 1963, Israel's deputy defense minister, Shimon Peres, assured John F. Kennedy that "we shall not introduce atomic weapons to the region. We certainly shall not be the first to do so." Israel maintains this policy of "nuclear opacity," of neither acknowledging nor denying that the country has nuclear weapons, to this day.

Kennedy gave the green light for the first sale of an American weapons system to Israel—Hawk antiaircraft missiles, which were classified as "defensive." The relationship continued to improve under President Lyndon Johnson, who invited Eshkol for the first official visit of an Israeli prime minister to the White House. In 1965, Johnson authorized the first sale of military aircraft to Israel—A-4 Skyhawk light attack jets, although a number of "offensive" capabilities were removed from the plane.

The rapid escalation to war in 1967 was caused by a combination of factors, including Syria's bombardment of the kibbutzim in northern Israel, its support of Fatah, Israel's tough response, the even tougher rhetoric by Chief of Staff Rabin and Prime Minister Eshkol warning the Syrian regime of dire consequences, and the Soviet Union's support for its client-state in Damascus. In mid-May 1967, the Soviets passed on false reports to Egyptian president Gamal Abdel Nasser claiming that Israel was amassing troops in the north to attack Syria. Egypt was ill-prepared for war and suspected that the Soviets were lying, but Nasser had presented himself as the leader of the Arab nation for over a decade, and Egypt had a defense treaty with Syria. In the space of a week he embarked on three fateful acts of brinkmanship.

American Ben, in his high
school yearbook.

Was Nasser seriously contemplating going to war on May 15, when he
ordered his army into Sinai and expelled the United Nations observers who
had been there since 1956? Many historians today claim that he was only
bluffing. But as far as Israel was concerned, the massing of troops on its
borders—not just with Egypt, but in Jordan and Syria as well—along with
the rhetoric about destroying the "Zionist entity" coming from Arab capi-
tals, was an existential threat . Nasser's announcement, on May 22, that he
was closing the Straits of Tiran, a crucial waterway for Israel's oil supplies
from Iran (which was then still a friendly state), was a closing gauntlet.

The next two and a half weeks would become known as "the waiting
period." Israelis were starkly split between those who were petrified of
a second Holocaust and those who were confident of an Israeli victory.
The IDF's reserves, including Yoni, who was assigned to Reserve Brigade
80, were mobilized, and then they were sent to cool their heels in staging
areas. Eshkol's cabinet dithered while the generals demanded immediate
action. Once again, the drama played out not only in the Middle East,
but also in Washington.

Eshkol was adamant about not going to war without some form of
backing from the US administration. Israeli foreign minister Abba Eban
traveled to Washington, but succeeded in receiving only vague promises
that the United States would send a flotilla to ensure Israel's maritime
rights in Tiran. The more forthright Mossad (Israeli intelligence agency)
chief, former major general Meir Amit, flew out for meetings at CIA
headquarters and with the US secretary of defense, Robert McNamara.

Two months later, Israeli Bibi, in his IDF induction ID photo.

He returned with the tacit understanding that as long as it appeared that Israel hadn't fired the first shot, and that it could achieve a swift victory without US military support, it could proceed.

As Eban and Amit were shuttling between Washington and Israel, Bibi was about to board one of the same flights. He returned to Israel a week before war broke out. He later wrote, "My parents didn't try to talk me out of it. 'Are you sure there will be a war?' they asked. 'Sure,' I answered. 'And besides, I want to see Yoni before it breaks out.' That was it."[6]

It was the end of Netanyahu family life as they had known it for twenty-one years. Along with Bibi, the fifteen-year-old Iddo was also to return to Israel. Unlike his older brothers, he would be allowed to finish high school back in Jerusalem. Benzion and Tzila, however, had no intention of returning. Benzion soon became a professor of Jewish history and Hebrew literature at the University of Denver, and he wasn't about to give up on his career. At the age of fifty-seven he was finally beginning to prosper. The three Netanyahu boys would never live with their parents again.

There are only two photographs of "Ben Netanyahu" in the Cheltenham High School yearbook for 1967—his graduation picture, in a dark suit and tie, and another of him playing soccer. In both photos he looks a fair bit older and more mature than his classmates. He was also listed among the students in his class who received a National Merit Letter of Commendation. In the school's archives there is a note saying that he did not attend the graduation ceremony. By then, he was back in wartime Israel.

8

You Have to Kill Arabs

L anding at Lod Airport on the night of June 1, 1967, Bibi encountered a blacked-out terminal in a country bracing for war. Foreign nationals, as well as some well-to-do Israeli families, were scurrying for tickets on the few departing flights. Bibi made his way to Jerusalem, and with his bags stowed at his friend Uzi Beller's home, set out searching for Yoni, who had been summoned to his reserve unit.

A quarter of a million reservists had been called up over the previous two weeks. Once in uniform, they awaited the government's decision or an Arab attack. The paratroopers camped in the citrus groves south of Tel Aviv.

Three days before war broke, Bibi found Yoni drinking coffee with a group of older officers under an orange tree. Not far away, in Tel Aviv and other Israeli cities, they were digging thousands of graves, preparing makeshift mortuaries and burial grounds for the expected casualties. As Yoni and his fellow officers greeted the admiring younger brother, their quiet confidence was unmistakable. This was a war they had spent years training and preparing for. "We'll win, we have no choice," said Yoni.[1]

After his coffee with Yoni, Bibi returned to Jerusalem and spent the next two days with his friend Uzi, cleaning out the air raid shelter beneath the Bellers' apartment building in Jerusalem. Bibi later claimed to have been woken on the morning of June 5 by explosions.[2] He had overslept the beginning of the Six-Day War, which had begun two hours earlier with a preemptive air strike on Egypt's airfields, wiping out most of the Egyptian Air Force. Half an hour later, ground forces were on the move toward the Sinai border. Israel sent repeated messages to Jordan's King Hussein not to intervene in its war with Egypt. Hussein was misinformed by the Egyptians, who told him they were gaining an advantage on Israel. Having already put his troops under the command of an Egyptian general, he gave the fateful order to attack.

At 9:40 a.m., Jordanian soldiers opened fire across the border in Jerusalem, followed a quarter of an hour later by a massive artillery barrage on civilian targets. Netanyahu recalled watching from the Bellers' rooftop as shells impacted the city. A mobile company of the Jerusalem Brigade swiftly repulsed a Jordanian incursion and went on the counter-attack. Thus started the Battle for Jerusalem and the West Bank and the beginning of the Israeli occupation of territories, which lasts to this day.

Yoni's brigade was on the Egyptian front, part of the division commanded by Ariel Sharon, which was breaking its way into the central sector of the peninsula. On the first night of the war, he was in an airborne force helicoptered to the rear of the fortified Egyptian division formation to take out its artillery batteries on the Umm Katef plateau. By dawn, the battle of Umm Katef was over. The decimation of its Second Division led the Egyptian high command to order all units to retreat eastward across the Suez Canal.

Three days later, with war against Egypt and Jordan won, Yoni's battalion was transported two hundred miles northward. Israeli defense minister Moshe Dayan, who had initially opposed broadening the ground war in the north, gave the order to capture the Golan Heights in the time left until the United Nations imposed a ceasefire.

Late on the afternoon of June 10, hours before the ceasefire was set to begin, Yoni led a small squad flanking the Jalabina outpost, the point from which the Israeli villages of Mishmar Ha'Yarden and Gadot had been shelled for years. A machine gun opened fire, killing the soldier standing next to Yoni. As Yoni dove to the ground, another burst hit him in the arm, smashing his elbow. Yoni dragged himself back over the battlefield to a dressing-station. He ended the war in Safed Hospital. Bibi was by his bedside the next day. "You see, I told you we would win," grinned Yoni.[3]

T HE IMMEDIATE AFTERMATH of the Six-Day War was a euphoric and bewildering period for most Israelis. Many Israelis believed it was the last war they would fight. The Arabs would surely understand now that the Jewish state was a permanent reality. But Israel had half-planned, half-blundered into the war. Now it would approach a long military occupation of another nation in the same manner.

Dazed, Israelis flocked to the Western Wall in Jerusalem's newly liberated Old City and toured the biblical homeland of Judea and Samaria. The local Palestinians were picturesque extras in their home movies. Israel annexed eastern Jerusalem days after the war, but the rest of the territories captured remained under military governance, ostensibly as bargaining chips. As Dayan said, Israel "waits for a phone call from Hussein." Since 1937, the Zionist mainstream had in principle accepted the partition of the land to separate Jewish and Arab states. In 1967, they suddenly found themselves in possession of the entire land of Israel, but without a strategy to deal with it.

A million and a half stateless Arabs now lived under Israeli rule in East Jerusalem, the West Bank, and the Gaza Strip. A week after the war, Eshkol said in a cabinet meeting, "Sooner or later, everyone will ask: Tell us clearly, what do you want to do with the Arabs?"[4] Over fifty years later, Israel still hasn't come up with an answer.

Netanyahu claims not to have shared in the postwar euphoria. A quarter of a century later, he wrote, "I remember that even as an eighteen-year-old I found inanely childish this notion that the Arab leaders would pick up the phone and call the whole thing off any moment now. Yet it is remarkable how many in Israel actually believed this at the time, making no allowance for the possibility that the Arabs would pursue the war against Israel by other means until they were ready for the next military round."[5]

Meanwhile, there was family business to attend to. Recovering in the hospital, Yoni had proposed to his girlfriend, Tirza. Still only twenty-one, he was fully aware that he could have been one of the 779 Israeli soldiers killed in the war, and now he wanted to grab all that life had to offer. Other parents may have been expected to fly immediately to attend their wounded son, but Benzion was on his annual visit to the medieval archives in Spain, and Tzila was ill back in Philadelphia.

The first member of the family to arrive in Israel was fifteen-year-old Iddo, who had returned to high school in Jerusalem alone. It was left to the two older brothers to find Iddo a school and lodgings, organize Yoni's wedding and the young couple's departure for the United States, and prepare for Bibi's upcoming military service.

The small ceremony on August 17 took place at the Mount Scopus amphitheater at the Hebrew University campus. For nineteen years it had remained empty, lying in a tiny Israeli enclave within Jordanian-occupied territory. Bibi's role for most of the ceremony was keeping away tourists at the site, which overlooked the newly conquered Judean Desert. Although Benzion and Tzila had not been able to come visit Yoni in the hospital, they did come to the wedding. Benzion, back at his alma mater, gloomily predicted that a weak Israeli leadership would soon relinquish the territories.

The week after Yoni's wedding, Bibi joined up.

P RIVATE BINYAMIN NETANYAHU enlisted with the intention of fol-
lowing in Yoni's footsteps and serving in the Paratroopers Brigade. Those reporting for duty in August 1967 donned uniforms feeling they had "missed the war." Bibi, however, believed there would still be plenty of soldiering to come.

Hovering around the new conscripts who had just passed the strenuous physical tests to join the brigade were two young officers. They approached the well-built Netanyahu, who had just been accepted to the elite corps, and asked if he would be interested in joining a special unit.

Israel's most secretive special operations unit was undergoing a transformation. The Six-Day War had ended with Israel controlling greatly expanded borders. Its intelligence services had to lay down new surveillance networks.

From Israel's earliest days, its intelligence community had made great efforts to penetrate its enemies' communications. This meant developing both the necessary technology and the expertise to operate deep behind enemy lines. In 1957, a new unit had been formed within the IDF's intelligence branch specializing in covert penetration missions.

To hide its true purpose, it was called Sayeret Matkal—General Staff Reconnaissance Unit. For thirty-five years, its existence remained an official secret, military censorship allowing it to be revealed only in late 1992. Its members wore uniforms similar to those of the paratroopers, including red berets and boots, but with no insignia. Even within the army it was usually referred to as "Ha'Yechida"—The Unit, or by its number, 269. In the rare cases when its operations came to the public's attention, they were attributed to "an elite unit," or "special paratroopers."

In the years leading up to the Six-Day War, Matkal carried out a series of intelligence-gathering missions, painting a detailed picture of the Egyptian, Syrian, and Jordanian forces it would face in 1967. During the war itself, the unit played only a minor role, as it was being kept in reserve for a raid on Egypt's air bases, should the opening strike of the war fail.

The details of one contingency mission were revealed only fifty years later. A Matkal team was to be flown deep into Sinai, where it would lay an "object" at the top of a remote mountain. The "object," a small nuclear device, would be detonated as a warning to the Egyptians in the event they used chemical or biological weapons, bombarded Israeli cities, or simply seemed to be winning the war. Shimon Peres, then a backbench Knesset member, but until recently the deputy defense minister in charge of nuclear development, had advocated Israel carrying out a nuclear test to prevent the war's outbreak. Ultimately, Eshkol trusted that Israel's conventional forces would be sufficient, and the operation went no further than the planning stage.

In its first decade, Matkal had accepted its soldiers and officers mainly on referrals. The new postwar missions called for enlarging the unit, however, and its commanders arrived at the induction center to draft two new teams. Many of the men Netanyahu met in his early days as a soldier would go on to fill the most senior posts in Israel's security establishment. The first officer to interview him for the unit was Danny Yatom, who was just a lieutenant at that time. Twenty-nine years later, when Netanyahu became prime minister, Yatom was head of Mossad.

Out of over 150 candidates, 30 were selected. Once accepted, they were sent for four months of basic training and a parachutist course with the Paratroopers Brigade. Basic infantry training in the IDF has barely changed in six decades, although reforms have been made to reduce the number of dropouts due to stress fractures. Conscripts are now given six hours of sleep and the physical demands are scaled up more gradually, but the basic framework remains the same. The first month is dedicated to rifleman's proficiency. In 1967, recruits used a Belgian FN FAL rifle, though once in Matkal they would use AK-47s and Uzis. The next month was mainly devoted to developing field skills. Training is taken off-base, and from this point the soldiers live almost

Netanyahu demonstrated
a near-fanatical level of
physical fitness while in
the IDF.

entirely in tiny two-men tents. In the third and fourth month they learn open-fire tactics, first as individual riflemen, and then as part of three-man fire teams and larger squads. Throughout basic training the soldiers go on weekly pack marches, often carrying stretchers.

During his basic training Netanyahu was noted for his near-fanatic level of physical fitness—he often got up early for an extra run—and for his ability to carry heavy loads, due to which he was assigned the platoon's machine gun. Similarly to his scruffy childhood friends from Jerusalem, who remembered an always neatly dressed boy, Bibi's basic training comrades recalled how the private always seemed to keep his combat fatigues immaculate. He was also known for spending his rare free moments reading magazines and books in English. For the next five years, these would be his main connection to the United States and its current affairs.

Only twenty of the original thirty candidates made it to the morning in January 1968 when, outside Haifa, they were met by their new Matkal officers and split into two teams. Led by Second Lieutenant Amiram Levin, Bibi and his fellow team members began the traditional twenty-four-hour, 120-kilometer march to the unit's base at Sirkin, near Petach Tikva, where there had been a British air base during the Mandate.

Most of Netanyahu's actions over the next four and a half years remain classified. The new teams were trained for Matkal's cross-border core mission. Much of the training consisted of long and grueling navigation treks.

Much of this training took place in the West Bank and used populated Palestinian villages as mock-up enemy targets. Twenty-five years later, musing on the historical memories evoked by ancient Jewish sites in Judea and Samaria, Netanyahu waxed lyrical about Mount Shiloh, the site of the Tabernacle, or Tent of Meeting, during the biblical period of the judges; Bet Horon, where the Maccabees fought the Greeks in the second century BCE; and Beitar Fortress, the scene of the last revolt against the Romans in the second century CE. "We stood there," Netanyahu later wrote. "A handful of nineteen-year-old boys, breathing the night air and drinking from our canteens—silent. Because what we felt didn't need to be put into words: we were back, for all the generations of the Jewish people who had dared to dream from the depths of humiliation and persecution that we would return to this land."[6]

The IDF's operational workload increased in the wake of the Six-Day War. Clashes with the Egyptian Army on the Suez Canal resumed in late 1967; meanwhile, the Palestinian armed groups, particularly the PLO's Fatah and the Popular Front for the Liberation of Palestine (PFLP), emerged as independent entities, no longer just proxies of Egypt and Syria. Using Jordan and Lebanon as staging grounds, they unleashed a series of attacks against military and civilian targets within the West Bank and the Gaza Strip as well as against sovereign Israel. The PFLP, a Marxist-Leninist-inspired organization, cooperating with like-minded groups outside the Middle East, began expanding its operations and attacked Israeli targets abroad, especially the aircraft of the national El Al Israel Airlines.

Within the IDF there was increasing pressure on Matkal to commit its considerable resources and highly skilled operators to battle on these new fronts. Eventually this period would lead to a broadening of the unit's portfolio and an increasing emphasis on counterterrorism. Initially there was reluctance at Sirkin to deviate from the core deep-penetration missions, and often it was the younger soldiers who were sent on the more conventional operations—which is how, after seven months in the army, Netanyahu found himself in Jordan, at the Battle of Karameh.

THE JORDAN VALLEY town of Karameh, north of the Dead Sea, had been taken over by Fatah as its main headquarters. Operation Inferno, launched against Karameh on March 21, 1968, did not go to plan. Armored units that were to secure the main approaches were bogged down in difficult terrain. The airborne force could not take off on account of the weather. Leaflets warning civilians to evacuate were dropped on schedule, however, and this gave Fatah time to prepare for the attack and Yasser Arafat time to escape.

Israel lost 33 soldiers in Karameh. Enemy casualties were much heavier, with the Jordanians losing 61 soldiers and Fatah over 100 of its fighters, with another 150 taken prisoner.

Netanyahu's team had only a minor role in the battle, manning one of the roadblocks out of town and then helping evacuate wounded tank crews. Twenty-eight years later, when he met Arafat as prime minister, he remarked that they had both been there. It was Bibi's first taste of war and death.

Death would come again soon, and much closer to home. Only four days after the Karameh operation, on a training exercise, a mortar shell exploded while being launched, fatally wounding two members of the team—Zohar Linik and David Ben Hamo. Bibi cradled Ben Hamo's head in the evacuation vehicle on the way to the hospital. The next day, immediately after the funerals, Levin took the team north to continue training. The meticulous planning of Matkal's operations often stood in stark contrast to the cavalier approach to safety in the unit. Sudden, arbitrary death, whether in training accidents or on operational duty, was all around. Bibi would soon become accustomed to it, but the first deaths of his comrades shook him. Normally an extremely circumspect letter writer, he wrote a detailed account of the incidents to Yoni, but sent it to his parents by mistake.

Along with carrying out secret intelligence-gathering missions, Matkal was engaging in more offensive operations during that period. One of the biggest was the attack on Beirut Airport on December 28, 1968, in retaliation for attacks on El Al planes. The decision to target the largest airport in the Middle East sent a message to the government of Lebanon, which was becoming a base for terrorist activity. It was Matkal's largest operation to date, deploying forty-four of its soldiers, Netanyahu among them, as well as twenty-two paratroopers in three large helicopters. Within twenty-nine minutes they had lain explosives on fourteen Lebanese airliners, in some cases firing in the air and emptying them of passengers. They took off back toward Israel before the charges blew up the planes.

Prime Minister Eshkol responded angrily upon receiving the initial report. "We spoke of three, four, five planes. How did we destroy so many?" Israel's Beirut operation was condemned by an emergency session at the United Nations, but the more lasting effect was to effectively end Israel's military ties with France, the source of much of its advanced weapons systems over the previous fifteen years.

French president Charles de Gaulle, who had already imposed a temporary arms embargo on the eve of the Six-Day War, was enraged by the attack—the Israeli commandos had landed in Beirut in French-made helicopters, and most of the airliners destroyed belonged to Middle East Airlines, in which French shareholders had a large stake. He declared the arms embargo permanent.

The end of French arms sales to Israel would spur two major developments. First, it would seal Israel's reliance on its by then flourishing strategic ties with the United States. Israel had already signed the first contracts for the American F-4 Phantom fighter-bomber, which was more capable than the French Mirage 5 fighter-bombers that had been ordered but not received due to the embargo. Israel was well on its way to becoming a main customer for advanced US weaponry, much of which would be financed by American taxpayers under the Foreign Military Financing (FMF) program. Second, the cancelation of arms deals with France gave a major impetus to Israel's indigenous arms industry, which over the next few years would build its own local versions of the French Mirage 5: the Nesher (Vulture), and the upgraded Kfir (Lion Cub) fighter jets. The investments in an indigenous advanced arms industry would give rise, decades later, to Israel's civilian high-tech sector.

YONI AND BIBI had now both fought in Israel's main battles and operations. Defying Benzion's wishes that they remain effectively bystanders and academic observers, they had chosen to join the mainstream and become members of Israel's military elite. At Samu and Karameh, on the battlefields of the Six-Day War and in the attack on Beirut, the two brothers had taken part in the events that would influence the trajectory of Israel and the region for decades hence. After two semesters studying philosophy, mathematics, and physics at Harvard, Yoni was coming back for more.

In a letter to Bibi from the United States, Yoni complained of the weak response of Israel's politicians to the Palestinian attacks. "I'm getting the impression that the civilian sector in Israel has despaired of solving [the problem] and even of military solutions to terror operations. It's clear that this is the only way to fight them. All this campaign of tiny terrorists just reinforces the Israeli consciousness within me." He concluded, "I just have to return to Israel—and live there. Now more than ever."[7]

In another letter, to Iddo, he wrote, "I find it hard to understand the Israelis who live [in the US] year after year." He could have been describing their parents. Benzion tried to convince him to remain in Boston, arguing, "If you want to serve Israel the best thing you can do is finish Harvard. The Foreign Ministry needs Harvard graduates."[8]

After only ten months in the United States, Yoni and Tirza returned to Jerusalem. "I belong to Israel, Abba, as Israel belongs to me and every Jew," Yoni wrote Benzion. "I belong to her now, at this moment, as things are about to blow up again." Even at that point, Benzion's sons were incapable of fully confronting the contradictions between their father's Zionist ideals and his living in America. Yoni tried to mollify him. "You dedicated more years of life than I have to Israel," he said to justify his move.[9]

Benzion could hardly have been mollified by his son passing up on a Harvard education to study at Hebrew University instead. But as it turned out, Yoni didn't spend much time there either. "I'm finding it hard to concentrate on studying," he wrote in January 1969 to his parents, who had just moved to Denver, where Benzion had been made professor.[10] In another letter he predicted, "We are getting close to war—gradually and inexorably. The Arab world will not agree to see us living within it." He couldn't remain at the university. "I find it hard to bear the thought that I am living thanks to others, who protect me with their bodies, while I have to 'play' the role of civilian."[11]

Despite running five miles every day in Boston and undergoing an operation on his elbow at Walter Reed in Washington, Yoni was hardly fit to return to combat service. In early 1969, facing increasing warfare on the Suez Canal with the Egyptians as well as nearly daily incursions by Palestinian fighters from Jordan, the IDF was anxious for experienced officers to return to service. Yoni had little trouble in getting a medical board to declare him fit for combat. But he didn't just want to go back to the Paratroopers Brigade. For the first time in their lives, Bibi, serving in a more elite unit, had an advantage over him.

By then, Bibi had completed a year in the unit, and Matkal's commanders were pressuring him to attend an officers' course, return to the unit as a team commander, and sign up for an extra year's service. He recommended they take his older brother instead. Over the years, Netanyahu has told interviewers that at that point he had no intention of remaining in the army; he had planned to return to the United States to study architecture at Yale, and it had been his idea to recommend Yoni. But Iddo, in his 1991 hagiography of his oldest brother, *Yoni's Last Battle*, told a different story, portraying Bibi as unwilling to offer his spot to Yoni.[12] Iddo describes walking in on a conversation between his two brothers in Jerusalem, where Yoni was telling a reluctant Bibi what to say to his commanding officers. It seems that Bibi at first wasn't eager to see Yoni take his place as one of Matkal's new officers.

In any event, the plan worked. In February 1969, Yoni returned to active service. Lieutenant Jonathan Netanyahu was in uniform again for what would be a meteoric seven-year military career. The Matkal commanders were initially skeptical that the twenty-three-year-old who could have taken command of an entire infantry company would "go backwards" and fit in as team commander of a handful of conscripts, but once they interviewed him, they were convinced that he was motivated to do so. In April, he became a Sayeret Matkal team commander. The natural order was reestablished: Yoni was serving with Bibi in the same unit, but in a more senior role. Whatever his original intention, Bibi wasn't prepared to return to the United States just yet, and a month later he left for officers' school. He almost never made it.

F OR THREE YEARS, until a US-brokered ceasefire was reached in August 1970, there was almost constant artillery fire exchanges between the Israelis and the Egyptians, escalating to sea battles, commando raids, and air strikes deep within Egyptian territory. For the Israeli troops taking cover under fire in fortified positions overlooking the Suez Canal, it would become known as the "War of Attrition." Matkal and other special forces were called in to do their bit. Or, as the IDF's southern commander, Major General Ariel Sharon, bluntly told Amiram Levin, "You have to kill Arabs."[13]

The two depleted teams that had begun training fourteen months earlier had been amalgamated under Levin's command. Their mission was to cross the canal—on the rubber dinghies of Flotilla 13, the naval commando unit—and wreak havoc on Egyptian positions. The joint raids by the two elite and extremely competitive units were dubbed Operation Frenzy. On May 11, 1969, in Frenzy 3, Levin's team crossed over undetected, destroyed an Egyptian truck, killing two soldiers, and returned without casualties. Bibi, the team's heavy-machine-gunner, put down the covering fire.

Two nights later, they launched Frenzy 4, and this time, the Egyptians were waiting. The force was detected while still in the water and the boats came under fire. Chaim Ben Yona, the first member of Bibi's original team to have graduated from an officers' course, was killed on the spot. Taking hits, the next boat listed, and Netanyahu fell into the canal. Weighed down by his machine gun and boxes of ammunition, he began to sink into the dark water. His life was saved when one of the naval commandos reached down and grabbed his hair, while another Matkal soldier took hold of his combat webbing. The two men dragged him back to the edge of the canal, where, oblivious to the explosions all around them, Bibi was able to catch his breath.

Despite the failure of Frenzy 4, the raids continued. On July 19, in Frenzy 6, Flotilla 13 and Matkal forces stormed a large fortified island at the canal's southern exit, near Suez Port. Six Israeli and eighty Egyptian soldiers were killed in the raid. The War of Attrition was rapidly escalating. Bibi wasn't on that operation—by then he was in an officers' course, which, like Yoni, he would complete as the outstanding cadet of his company. By January 1970 he was back in Matkal commanding a team.

For a short while Yoni and Bibi were back together. Yoni was already a captain, while Bibi was just a second lieutenant. Yoni by that point intended to pursue a long-term military career. An IDF psychologist who worked with Matkal officers during the period later recalled seeing the brothers arriving together at the army's headquarters. "Yoni had a meeting at the operations branch, Bibi waited for him outside. I still remember the look of complete and utter admiration on Bibi's face, watching Yoni going in. It wasn't the kind of look you see on an adult. It was completely astonishing."

Prime Minister Eshkol and some of his colleagues had sent out half-hearted feelers, particularly to Jordan's King Hussein and local leaders of the West Bank Palestinians, offering a limited autonomy. Both engagements were nonstarters. The Jordanians and Egyptians were prepared to negotiate only with the precondition that Israel retreat from all the territories it had captured in the Six-Day War. The local Palestinian leadership wouldn't dare enter formal talks with their own younger revolutionary generation pledging "armed struggle until the liberation of all Palestine." Meanwhile, in September 1967 in Khartoum, the Arab leaders delivered their "three no's"—no recognition, no negotiation, and no peace with Israel. For the Israelis, this was reason enough to stop even trying to hold talks.

In November, the United Nations Security Council passed Resolution 242 calling for "respect and acknowledgement of the sovereignty, territorial integrity and political independence of every State in the area and their right to live in peace," and for the "withdrawal of Israeli armed forces from territories occupied in the recent conflict." The wording of the resolution, which passed unanimously in the council, allowed both sides to cling to their positions. The Arabs demanded Israeli withdrawal, while Israel demanded recognition. The fact that Resolution 242 mentioned "territories," not "*the* territories," enabled Israel to stick to the interpretation that it didn't mean "*all the* territories," and that they shouldn't be expected to withdraw all the way to the pre-1967 war frontier. No other country accepted this interpretation, not even the United States.

Although the alliance between the two countries intensified over the years, the United States continued to refuse to accept Israel's perpetual control of the occupied territories. Israel has received over $100 billion in military and financial assistance from the United States since 1962, but has never received diplomatic backing for its conquests.

On February 26, 1969, the day Yoni returned to serve in the IDF, Levi Eshkol died. He was replaced by Golda Meir, who, like him, was an old and ailing member of Ben-Gurion's founding generation. Unlike Eshkol, Meir was suspicious of any attempt at reaching a peace agreement with the Arabs, and she rarely challenged the generals. Born in Russia, her family moved when she was eight to Milwaukee; from there she emigrated to Palestine at the age of nineteen. She was the first Israeli prime minister to have spent her formative years in the United States, and until

Netanyahu, the only one. And, like him, she was prepared to challenge America openly.

In December 1969, the US secretary of state under President Richard Nixon, William Rogers, presented a plan whereby Israel would retreat to its prewar borders, with a few modifications, and enter talks toward solving the Palestinian refugee problem. Israel had legitimate reservations about the plan, as it didn't include any commitment by the Arab nations to recognize Israel or make peace with it. But instead of treating it as a starting point for negotiations, Meir attacked it publicly as "a disaster for Israel" and launched a political campaign against it in Washington. This was the administration that was supplying fifty advanced F-4 Phantom fighter jets to Israel. Over the misgivings of her "dovish" foreign minister, Abba Eban, Israel's new ambassador to the United States, the former IDF chief of staff Yitzhak Rabin, promised Meir that Israel had sufficient support in Washington to call the administration's bluff.

Rabin also assured Meir that she could go ahead and approve the IDF's plan to escalate the War of Attrition by launching a campaign of air strikes deep within Egypt against power plants, factories, and military bases. Not for the first time, Israel succeeded in influencing the US administration and Congress by playing one off against the other.

While the State Department remained in favor of an "even-handed" policy in the Middle East, there were those in Washington who saw Israel's attacks on Egypt as an extension of the global contest with the Soviet Union being fought in Vietnam. The Soviets certainly saw it as such and in response to Israel's deep strikes deployed an airborne division, fighter squadrons, and advanced antiaircraft missiles to Egypt. Soon Israeli and Soviet pilots were engaging in dogfights over Egypt. In June 1970, Secretary Rogers proposed a new plan. This one called for a ceasefire and disengagement of forces between Israel and Egypt and an agreement from both countries, along with Jordan, to enter UN-brokered negotiations based on Resolution 242.

Meir initially rejected this "Rogers Plan" as well, but after receiving a personal letter from Nixon promising that nothing would be imposed on Israel—including final borders and any solution to the Palestinian issue—and that the United States would continue its military and financial assistance to Israel, she agreed. The administration also silently acquiesced to Israel's nuclear ambitions.

The ceasefire ending the War of Attrition between Israel and Egypt went into effect on August 7, 1970. Both sides immediately broke the agreement—Egypt by moving its antiaircraft missiles to the banks of the Suez Canal, and Israel by refusing to join negotiations. Nevertheless, a period of wary calm began on the southern frontier.

Not everyone in Israel's security establishment had supported escalation against Egypt. Some generals even dared to say, in private, that while Egypt had suffered far worse casualties, as well as massive damage to its civilian economy, Israel had not won the War of Attrition.

Many Matkal officers were dovish kibbutz members. Bibi enjoyed taking them on. "He would hold forth at length that more than Israel needs America, America needs Israel as its ally against global communism," one officer later remembered. Netanyahu "understood" America and was convinced that if only Israel held to its guns, it would continue to have Washington's support and respect. The Netanyahus had no sympathy for the Palestinians. In one of his letters, Yoni described them as "a rabble of cave-dwellers, fighting for 'liberty and progress etc.,'"[14] and in another he wrote, "My national identity is much stronger than theirs."[15] In March 1972, he described an operation against Fatah in Lebanon dismissively as "nearly a friendly hike."[16]

Yoni had been seconded in late 1970 to command a company of Sayeret Haruv, a reconnaissance group carrying out ambushes against Palestinian fighters infiltrating the border with Jordan and in the West Bank. He returned in mid-1971, when he was put in charge of Matkal training. Bibi, meanwhile, had been planning to leave military service, but the new Matkal commander, Lieutenant Colonel Ehud Barak, prevailed upon him to sign on for another year; in return, he promised he would get to plan and lead more complex missions.

Colonel Yossi Langotzky, a senior intelligence officer who was involved during that period in directing Matkal's special operations, and who later on was no fan of Prime Minister Netanyahu's policies, remembered him well. "The system was that I set the Matkal officers a target and they had to come up with the method," he said. "I was very impressed by Bibi, not that it should come as a surprise, but he was part of the crème de la crème of the IDF. He was extremely professional and achieved a very high operational level. He planned and carried out two operations, deep in enemy territory, in extremely difficult conditions, one of them at high altitude in the snow. He dealt with changing circumstances very well."

By then all three Netanyahu brothers were serving in the unit. Iddo, who was less militarily inclined than Yoni and Bibi, never became an officer, but the ethos his older brothers had created, in defiance of Benzion, pushed him to overcome the physical and mental obstacles and become a special forces operator as well.

In June 1972, Lieutenant Colonel Barak appointed Yoni as his deputy. The older officer had become by then Yoni's closest friend as well as something of a mentor to Bibi. Yoni and Barak shared a keen intelligence and wide interests in the world outside the army. They both loved classical music but held a deep disdain for generals and politicians. Barak, who had been selected originally for Matkal because he was a "natural navigator" and had a passion for taking apart clocks, was one of the first officers to "grow up" within Matkal, and he personified the unit's unorthodox spirit. The Matkal officers witnessed him disobeying orders in the field and cutting off radio communications when senior commanders ordered him to abort missions. He was capable of shouting at generals when they disagreed with his aggressive plans. Bibi believed then that Ehud and Yoni would in the future serve as Israel's prime minister and the IDF chief of staff, respectively. He still saw himself as an iconoclastic architect.

Barak insisted on deploying Matkal in every high-risk situation, even when it had no special advantage or expertise. One such case nearly got Bibi killed: Operation Isotope, Matkal's first hostage rescue operation.

On May 8, 1972, a cell of "Black September," a Palestinian terrorist group formed on Arafat's orders, hijacked a Sabena Boeing 707 airliner on its flight from Brussels to Tel Aviv. The hijackers ordered the plane to land at the intended destination, Lod Airport in Tel Aviv, and demanded the release of 315 Palestinian prisoners in exchange for the passengers and crew. The four hijackers, two men and two women, placed explosive charges throughout the aircraft.

Hundreds of security personnel descended on Lod Airport. Following the first attacks on Israeli airliners in 1968, Israel's Shin Bet security service had formed a specialist unit to combat hijackers. As the experts, its agents expected to be sent in, but Barak convinced Defense Minister Moshe Dayan, who was on the scene, to give the operation to Matkal. Barak quickly requisitioned a nearby hangar and began training on a similar Boeing. He assembled a team that included a number of Matkal reservists who had recently served in Shin Bet. It also included Bibi Netanyahu.

Shortly before the operation was to get under way, Yoni arrived at the airport and asked to be placed on the team. Bibi, who feared that an explosion could kill everyone who boarded the plane, tried to dissuade him. "Are you crazy? Think of our parents, what would happen if both of us are killed?" Yoni snapped back, saying, "My life is mine alone and so is my death."[17] He argued that as the more experienced officer, he should replace Bibi. For once Bibi stood up to his brother, insisting that he would be leading soldiers from the team he had trained. It was left to Barak to rule that Yoni had arrived too late—he would not change the team.

The plan was for the team members to approach the aircraft wearing white overalls in order to pose as technicians, with handguns hidden in their belts. The hijackers would be led to believe that their demands were about to be met and that the plane was being prepared for takeoff with the released prisoners. The team would enter the plane through different entrances in five groups, coordinated by Barak, and attempt to overcome the terrorists in just seconds. It was a reckless operation, based on the assumption that even though they had prepared explosives, the hijackers did not intend to commit suicide. Matkal had accumulated valuable experience in conducting secret operations behind enemy lines and in commando raids, but had not dealt until then with a hostage situation. Twenty-five years later, Netanyahu admitted in an interview that, like most other members of the team, he had never even held a handgun before that day, only rifles and machine guns.[18]

This attitude was to cost twenty-two lives in May 1974, when Matkal was sent into a school in the northern town of Maalot, where Popular Front for the Liberation of Palestine members held 102 students and 10 teachers hostage. The botched assault was detected in advance by the terrorists, who opened fire on the children. The Maalot tragedy led to drastic changes in Matkal's counterterrorism training and the formation of a new elite antiterror police unit.

Despite the lack of experience, the Sabena raid worked just as planned. Within ninety seconds of the team entering the plane, Operation Isotope was over. The two male hijackers, who had been holding guns, were shot dead, and the female hijackers, who were holding grenades and detonators, were overwhelmed. One hostage was killed in the cross fire and two others injured. Bibi, who had led his squad through the emergency door above the left wing, had run to the back of the plane, where passengers had pointed out one of the female hijackers. He had grabbed her hair, and

Lieutenant Netanyahu receiving
a citation from President Zalman
Shazar for his actions in the
Sabena operation.

her wig had come off in his hand. Grabbing her again, he demanded to
know where the explosives were. Another soldier joined him, pistol-
whipping her face. His gun went off, and the bullet passed through the
hijacker, wounding her, and then hit Bibi's arm. For years, until the full
details of the operation were published, the story told in Israel was that
one of Bibi's soldiers had shot him in the ass.

Bibi was carried down to the tarmac, and Yoni rushed over as he was
administered morphine. When Yoni realized the wound was not serious,
he grinned. "You see? I told you not to go," he joked. On the Boeing's
wing, a press photographer captured a picture of Ehud Barak, still in his
white overalls and holding a gun, shepherding the hostages off the plane.[19]
Twenty-eight years later this image would feature heavily in Barak's campaign to oust Prime Minister Netanyahu in the 1999 elections.

9

I've Reached My Target

The friendly-fire wound from the Sabena operation was superficial, and Benjamin Netanyahu was back on operational duty within a couple of weeks. It was nearly the end of his five years of service. Throughout, Bibi had remained ambivalent toward his military career, keeping up correspondence with Yale's admissions office. He had signed on for two additional years when there was the prospect of commanding a team and planning and leading complex operations. Staying on would mean promotion but also leaving Matkal, at least for a year or two, to command an infantry or armored company in one of the less "special" parts of the army. There was some desultory talk of moving to a tank battalion, but Bibi's heart wasn't in it. Having spent his entire military service in the most elite of units, he shared the dismissive attitude of fellow officers like Ehud Barak to the "big and stupid" IDF.

In the end, it was his relationship with Miki Weizmann, whom he had been dating on and off since high school, that sealed his decision to leave military life and Israel. Bibi and Miki were the same age. Their lives had run on parallel lines. She had been in Bibi's year at the gymnasia in Jerusalem, though they hadn't known each other before the Netanyahus had left for Philadelphia. Introduced during one of Bibi's summer vacations in Israel, they remained an intermittent couple throughout his long absences and while both served in the IDF, though Miki became exasperated by Bibi's reluctance to commit to a long-term relationship. During his military service, Bibi never had a fixed abode off-base. He lived in Jerusalem's Rehavia neighborhood, alternately with Miki in her parents' home, during the periods when they were dating, and with his brothers Yoni and Iddo, or with his friend Uzi Beller's family, when they were less close.

Miki, or Miriam Haran, as she is more commonly known today, was not about to wait around for Bibi. After completing her military service as a training officer in 1969, she studied chemistry at Hebrew University. In 1972 she was about to leave for Boston, where she had received a scholarship to pursue a master's degree in organic chemistry at Brandeis. Miki's departure caused Bibi to abandon any thought of remaining in the IDF, as well as his Yale plans.

On June 19, he took part in Operation Crate, led by Ehud Barak inside Lebanon, to capture a group of senior Syrian intelligence officers. When Lebanese gendarmes came close to the location where Netanyahu's team was waiting in the underbrush, the operation was aborted. The next day Bibi was discharged back to civilian life. In July, he flew to Boston, and the next month he and Miki were married in a small ceremony at his uncle's house in Westchester County. Benzion and Tzila were there, but Miki's parents remained in Jerusalem, as did Yoni and Iddo, who hadn't even been notified in advance. Yoni was hurt. It took him another month to send the couple a letter of congratulations, in which, rather undiplomatically, he chose to notify them of his upcoming divorce.

For the first time Bibi's life began to revolve around someone other than Yoni. Unlike his second and third wives, the fiercely ambitious and intelligent Miki was not someone who would be content to support her husband's career. The only concession she made was to agree to living half an hour from Brandeis, in the dorms of the Massachusetts Institute of Technology, where Bibi had enrolled at the School of Architecture and Planning. The plan was for Miki to complete her doctorate and Bibi to become an architect before returning to Israel. For the next four years, it went nearly as planned.

From the first day of the semester in September 1972, the twenty-three-year-old freshman insisted he wasn't prepared to abide by the normal academic schedule. He demanded that his faculty adviser, the professor Leon Groisser, sign off on a double-load of courses. "He made it clear that he didn't have four years to get an undergraduate degree," Groisser recalled in interviews twenty-four years later, when Netanyahu was first elected prime minister. He argued that having spent five years as an officer in the high-stress environment of special operations, he could deal with the double-load. "He didn't say it with bravado," said Professor Groisser. "He said it as fact."[1] The Jewish (and Zionist) professor, skeptical but sympathetic, agreed to a semester's trial period.

"He proceeded to overload and he did very well," Groisser said. "He did superbly. He was very bright. Organized. Strong. Powerful. He knew what he wanted to do and how to get it done. He's not the flippant, superficial person I keep reading about in the newspapers. He was organized and committed."[2]

Early on, Netanyahu reverted to the name he had gone by at high school in Philadelphia—Ben. He would also change his family name to Nitay, as he and Miki quickly grew tired of the way Americans failed to pronounce Netanyahu. Years later, his critics in Israeli media would use the new name, "Ben Nitay," as proof of his having rejected his Israeli roots and becoming a *yored* in America. These charges were baseless. Ben Nitay was the Hebrew pseudonym that Benzion had used during the 1930s and a name appearing in the Bible and in the Talmud.

But there is something to the charges that have dogged Netanyahu over the years that he is more American than Israeli. From the time he left Israel in 1963 at the age of thirteen, he would never spend a prolonged period living there as a private citizen. His army years were spent in a secret cocoon. Besides during officers' course, he rarely had much to do with other ranks and corps. When he finally returned to Israel in the late 1970s, he was already a public figure, the brother of a fallen war hero. Soon after he again left for the United States, he returned as a senior diplomat and then became a prominent politician. Netanyahu had never lived as an ordinary grown-up civilian in Israel.

As a consequence of spending most of his formative years as a teenager, student, and rising diplomatic star in the United States, Bibi developed a chameleon-like ability to adopt an Israeli or American persona at will. In many ways he prefers American culture and American ideas, particularly conservative ones, to Israeli ideology. He has scant appreciation for much of Israeli society or its academia (at least in the fields not connected to technological research), and little interest in the nation's diverse communities, save for the need to appeal to them for votes. As much as Israel has changed over the decades, it remains a much more egalitarian society than America. In this sense, Netanyahu is an American.

Even as the son of an outsider to the establishment, Netanyahu always lived among the Israeli elite in central Jerusalem. Accusations of him spurning his Israeli identity during the 1970s in Boston are particularly hollow. Most of the students in his social circle were Israelis studying in neighboring universities. Those were the friends Miki invited to meals at their tiny dorm apartment. When he was-required to present a paper with a fellow student, it would invariably be another Israeli. Of course, Israelis studying in the United States were themselves another Israeli elite. And just like many of them, when the Yom Kippur War broke out in October 1973, Netanyahu rushed to return home and fight.

In the early 1970s, Israel's main borders were relatively calm. Despite the Egyptian Army moving antiaircraft missile batteries to the Suez Canal Zone, the ceasefire agreed upon in August 1970 held for over three years. The Syrian border remained quiet as well—Israel's control of the Golan Heights preventing shelling or incursions into Israeli territory.

Since the end of the Six-Day War, Jordan had become the main base for Palestinian attacks on Israel, but tension between the Hashemite Kingdom and the Palestine Liberation Organization, which had been accused of establishing "a state within a state," was growing.

Hussein's perceived impotence in his kingdom was too much and he declared martial law, sending troops into Palestinian bases and neighborhoods. Thousands were killed in the operation, which the Palestinians named "Black September." Syria threatened to invade Jordan in support of the Palestinians, and Hussein secretly appealed to Israel. The IDF mobilized troops near the Israel-Jordan-Syria border triangle, and its aircraft flew menacingly over the Syrian tanks. US Marines and airborne troops were also preparing to come to Jordan's aid. The invasion was averted while Jordan's army continued mowing down Palestinian fighters. By the end of October, PLO leader Yasser Arafat was forced to sign an agreement dismantling his bases in Jordan.

Now based in Lebanon, Arafat ordered the establishment of the Black September group, which would carry out "deniable" operations against Jordanian and Israeli targets. For the next three years, Israel contended with terrorist organizations rather than with conventional Arab armies. It was a campaign waged in the Middle East and Europe, with the Palestinians enlisting the assistance of radical groups from around the globe.

In September 1972, at the Olympic Games in Munich, Black September carried out its most daring attack, infiltrating the Olympic Village and taking eleven members of the Israeli team hostage. Two of the hostages were killed in their sleeping quarters and nine during a botched rescue attempt by German police. In response to the Munich massacre, Prime Minister Golda Meir launched Operation Wrath of God to track down and eliminate Black September operatives. The operation would continue into the 1980s, long after Arafat had disbanded the group in late 1973. It consisted mainly of assassinations carried out by Mossad, but the IDF also played a role.

On the evening of April 9, 1973, teams of Matkal, paratroopers, and naval commandos landed on the Lebanese coast, where they were met by Mossad agents who drove them to their targets. As many as a hundred Fatah members were killed in the operation. Yoni Netanyahu was among those who killed, at close-quarters, Muhammad Yousef al-Najjar, one of Arafat's deputies, who doubled as Black September's chief of operations. Al-Najjar's wife, who tried to defend him, was also killed.

A few months earlier, Yoni had divorced his wife after a miserable four and a half years of marriage. Except for the ten months at Harvard, he and Tirza had spent little time together. In his increasingly infrequent letters to his parents, he continued to promise that he would return to Harvard, but by mid-1973, the only studies he was seriously contemplating were at IDF staff officers' college.

Yoni made it back to the country of his birth one last time in 1973, spending a rare vacation on a summer semester at Harvard that had been arranged by Bibi. It was also the last significant period of time the two brothers would spend together. They ran along the Charles River, attended lectures and concerts, and had long philosophical conversations, smoking cigars. Years later, Bibi would often describe it as "a magical summer."[3] In many ways it was the end of their youth together. Yoni enjoyed Harvard, but he left with mixed feelings about what he called, in one of his letters to a friend, "the decadent, naïve and destructive American society." The brothers shared a low view of many of the young Americans they met, along with an appreciation of America's merits. "Young people here seem to be in constant frustration, incapable of emerging from the infantile stage," he added in the same letter.[4]

"Everyone is educated to be antiestablishment and everyone slanders the administration," he continued. "The most radical are the Jews. They seem to have long ago ceased being objective. A pity for America, because these crazies will destroy it. On the other hand, there's no limit to my amazement. This is an incredible country! Technically, in its achievements, efficiency, politeness, order, comfort and more. They are ten levels above the rest of the world (and fifty above Israel)."[5]

Yoni and Bibi parted in August, not expecting to see each other for a long while. They weren't the only ones not expecting war in October.

ON SEPTEMBER 28, 1970, Egypt's president, Nasser, died of a heart attack at the age of fifty-two. His admirers believed he had never recovered from the defeat of 1967. With him, aspirations of pan-Arab nationalism were laid to rest. His successor, Vice President Anwar al-Sadat, was initially viewed by many observers as a political lightweight.

In 1971, through UN and US intermediaries, Sadat passed on to the Israeli government proposals for entering a comprehensive peace process and an interim disengagement agreement between Israeli and Egyptian forces on the Suez Canal.

Israel's political and military leaderships were split over whether to take Sadat at face value. Golda Meir was firmly in the skeptic camp and relayed wary answers to Sadat, insisting that Israel would not retreat from all the territories captured in 1967 and demanding that Egypt commit to non-belligerence with Israel from the start. Messages were relayed back and forth for months, but by early 1972, Sadat had seemed to lose interest.

The annual intelligence assessment for 1973 set the prospect of war at "low probability." A few midlevel analysts argued that Sadat was preparing for war, and in the summer the IDF General Staff put the army on high alert for three months. By mid-August, the "concept" that Egypt would not go to war without the necessary air power for carrying out strikes deep within Israel reestablished itself. The belief that the Arabs would not risk a second humiliation was so deeply entrenched that even when, by early October, reports accumulated that mass mobilization by Egypt and Syria exhibited a clear preparation to attack, Israel's generals still convinced themselves that the Arabs were just carrying out exercises.

Sayeret Matkal, the intelligence branch's most elite unit, was not preparing for all-out war. Since his return from Harvard, Yoni had been training a special team to carry out a rescue operation of Israeli servicemen from Cairo's Abbasiya Prison. On the morning of October 6, 1973, Yom Kippur, the Jewish Day of Atonement, he was summoned to Sirkin. The IDF was convinced that war would start in a matter of hours, and Meir had given the go-ahead for full mobilization. But once again, fearful of drastic actions, whether in war or peace, Israel's inflexible prime minister would not authorize a preemptive strike.

For the next twenty-four hours, frustrated Matkal officers waited on base, as no mission orders arrived from the high command. Three years earlier, under Ehud Barak's command, they had carried out a complex operation planting "special devices"—surveillance instruments capable of monitoring communications between Egyptian command posts. This was Israel's insurance policy, to be used in time of emergency for clear indication that the enemy was on a war footing. Two days earlier, the special devices had been activated for nine hours and shut down. No irregular signals had been recorded, but the instruments were deemed too valuable to be used for long. Matkal's efforts were to prove useless.

Bibi heard the news in the early afternoon of Yom Kippur in Boston. War had broken out seven hours earlier, at 1:55 p.m. local time, with simultaneous Egyptian and Syrian artillery barrages on Israeli forces. Within hours he bade Miki farewell and was on a train to New York. El Al, the only airline still flying to Israel, was about to dispatch its first Jumbo Jet, filled with students like him rushing back to their units. Bibi missed the flight and wasn't assured of a place on the next one. The terminal at JFK was filled with hundreds of reservists. The priority was for members of armored units to be transported so they could help relieve the tank crews, which were barely holding on by the Suez Canal and on the Golan Heights. It took urgent phone calls to the military attaché's office at the Israeli embassy in Washington, in which Bibi notified them that he was a Sayeret Matkal officer, to secure a seat. Another passenger on those first flights back to Israel was his old commander, Lieutenant Colonel Ehud Barak, who had just started a master's degree at Stanford. For the second time in just over six years, Netanyahu landed at a blacked-out terminal in Lod Airport without a clear idea of his role in the war.

Israelis who lived through those days remember it as the country's darkest hour. The lowest point was on the night of October 8, when, after sixty hours of hearing encircled soldiers crying for help on the radio from isolated outposts, and reports of air force jets being shot out of the sky by elusive surface-to-air (SAM) missiles, the generals in "the pit," the IDF's underground central command post in Tel Aviv, feared that Israel's strategic reserves were exhausted.

A despondent defense minister, Moshe Dayan, joined the IDF chief of staff, David "Dado" Elazar, as news arrived of the failure of Israel's counteroffensive in Sinai. Only hours earlier, Dado had confidently promised at a press conference, "We will break their bones." Dayan, the warlord of 1967, began talking darkly of drafting high school students, discharged veterans, and even Jewish hippies from America ("We'll cut their hair") to protect the approaches to Tel Aviv.[6] The "spirit of Masada" spread through the headquarters as Dayan predicted a "destruction of the Third Temple,"[7] and Israel's strategic forces were put on alert as a last resort. As morning broke, fresh reports arrived of the start of an Israeli counterattack on the Golan and the air force's first successes in taking out SAM missile sites. Spirits rose as plans were finalized to intensify the offensive against Syria, while holding the line in Sinai and preparing to cross the canal, taking the battle to the enemy's territory later in the week.

As Bibi arrived in Sirkin, he was unaware of any of these developments. With no time to prepare special operations, Matkal had split into crack infantry companies, deployed as emergency reinforcements to both fronts. The base was nearly empty, and he joined a group of reservists who were heading south with the mission to protect exhausted tank crews in Sinai, while they slept at night, from marauding Egyptian commandos. It was a frustrating war for Bibi, who had returned from the United States anxious to do his part. A week later he was transferred to the Golan front.

Although he has movingly described flying back on a plane with a group of his comrades, "for some of whom, it was their last journey," Netanyahu has never spoken of the last period of the war. Forty years later, when asked to recount his Yom Kippur experiences to an Israeli website, he wrote simply, "I went north to command a special operation."[8] Details of that operation are yet to emerge.

On October 24, when a ceasefire was agreed upon, Israeli troops controlled 1,600 square kilometers (618 square miles) of Egyptian territory west of the canal and on the Syrian front were shelling the suburbs of Damascus. Three weeks later, after a brief visit with Yoni, Bibi was back in Boston, resuming the grueling pace he had set for himself. He was allowed to make up his missing coursework during the January break.

ON THE BATTLEFIELD, Syria and Egypt suffered over eight times the number of casualties as Israel. But with more than 2,200 Israeli dead, it was still a heavy blow for a population numbering barely 3 million. Egyptians celebrate the "October War" each year as a great victory. They had removed the shame of 1967, crossed back over the Suez Canal, and forced the Israelis to realize that they could not hold Sinai for perpetuity. Israelis mark the war each year, on the day after Yom Kippur, with solemn ceremonies at military cemeteries. It is a victory tainted with the bitter failure of intelligence and chaos on the front lines during the first days of fighting.

A national commission of inquiry headed by the president of the Israeli Supreme Court issued a series of scathing reports on the military leadership that had been captured by "the concept" that the Arabs would not dare attack. Chief of Staff Elazar was forced to resign, along with the commanders of the intelligence branch and the Southern Command. The politicians escaped the commission's censure, as they had been following the assessments of the generals, but Meir bowed to public pressure. Ten days after the commission delivered its initial report, she resigned. It was the end of an era. Meir was the last of Israel's leaders to have served in government from the time of independence.

THERE WERE THOSE who had acquitted themselves well in the war. Major Jonathan Netanyahu was one. On the second day of the war he had led a Matkal company up to the Golan. Upon arrival, he and his men had fought off a Syrian airborne raid on divisional headquarters, wiping out forty-one enemy commandos. They had then joined the frantic armor battles on the front line, rescuing crews from burning tanks. For one of these missions, where Yoni and a small team extricated a wounded battalion commander from behind enemy lines, he was awarded the Medal of Distinguished Service, Israel's third-highest military decoration.

Entire echelons of the armored corps had been decimated in the war. Yoni's original plan to attend staff officers' college was scrapped. Instead, he transitioned to tanks, undergoing a crash course in armored warfare and taking command of a company of tanks that were involved in ongoing skirmishes with the Syrian Army within the enclave captured by Israel at the end of the war. He was on the fast track to rapid promotion with a promise to be a candidate for the next Matkal commander. Within four months he was promoted to battalion commander.

A FTER YOM KIPPUR, Israel was a nation suffering collectively and individually from posttraumatic stress disorder. The Israeli economy would grind to a standstill for months, as most of the able-bodied men remained on reserve duty, on high alert at the front. Over the next two years, defense expenditures, which have always been much higher proportionally in Israel than in the West, jumped to a crippling 30 percent of GDP. Arsenals were replenished and new weapons systems developed to deal with the Soviet-made antitank and antiaircraft missiles that had caused so many casualties. Israel's finances were tipped into a downward spiral that would become nearly catastrophic within a decade. It was a period of growing bitterness and recrimination. Yoni, at the age of twenty-nine, now promoted to lieutenant colonel, and Bibi, at MIT, were largely isolated from the economic problems. But generals always prepare to fight the previous war, and Israelis failed to realize at the end of 1973 was that they had just fought their last war in which they had been outnumbered. In all the subsequent rounds of conflict, Israel would unquestionably be the numerically superior force. They were about to transition from David to Goliath, and with that transformation, new challenges and opportunities would be created for them. They have been grappling with them ever since.

It was Bibi's generation—those who had enlisted after the Six-Day War, who had borne the main brunt of the war. The majority of those who had been killed and wounded, or were suffering from posttraumatic stress disorder, were men in their early twenties. Like Bibi, they had been born after Israel's War of Independence, and had missed out on the glory of 1967. Instead, they shared in the frustration of the War of Attrition and the anger over the failures of 1973. They were to emerge as a bitter and jaded generation, many of them driven by disillusionment with the old leaders to the extreme edges of politics on right and left. The war would have much less of an effect on Netanyahu, who had been brought up since childhood to have little faith in the Mapai leadership.

Of the members of the small team that had joined up with Bibi in August 1967, three had been killed near him in those early years. One more, Ilan Shapira, would die in the Yom Kipper war on the bank of the Suez

Canal as a reserve paratrooper officer. Two of the officers, Rafi Bar-Lev and Amit Ben-Horin, were killed as well. Bibi's first team commander, Amiram Levin, was severely wounded at the end of the war, though he returned to the unit six months later.

There was some rancor toward Bibi for rushing back to MIT, while most reservists, including his younger brother, Iddo, who had completed his service the previous year and was about to start medical school, remained for months, and would continue doing lengthy reserve stints for years. But Netanyahu was at the end of the military chapter in his life. The three Netanyahu brothers had defied their father, leaving America to serve in the IDF's most demanding unit. Now Yoni alone remained in service, on what was expected to be a long army career. He supported Bibi's early return to the US. "From your point of view, you were very clever," Yoni wrote him from the bombarded enclave in Syria. "It's good you're back studying, instead of wasting time."[9]

Colonel Omer Bar-Lev, who in the second half of the 1970s was in command of the Matkal reservists, later remembered Bibi returning only once to take part in an operation. "It was the first operation I commanded in 1975, and Bibi, who was back in Israel on vacation, commanded the rescue team. But that was a one-off. We barely ever saw him in uniform [again]."

Many Matkal officers who served with Netanyahu became political opponents over the ensuing years. Bar-Lev would go on to become the unit's commander and a member of the Knesset for the Israeli Labor Party. Together with other Matkal alumni, in 1978 he was among the founders of Peace Now, a movement that has continuously urged the Israeli government to make concessions for peace and strenuously opposed the West Bank settlements. Danny Yatom, one of the officers who selected Bibi for the Matkal unit, would also be elected a Labor MK. In 2017, both Bar-Lev and Bibi's first commander, Amiram Levin, ran unsuccessfully in Labor's leadership primaries, seeking to lead the parliamentary opposition to Netanyahu. And then, of course, there was Ehud Barak, perhaps the only person closer to Yoni than Bibi, who would unseat Netanyahu at the end of his first term as prime minister in 1999.

Early in his political career, Netanyahu would make very little use of his Matkal past. Until 1992, the unit's name could not even be mentioned in the Israeli media. Besides, when compared to his iconic brother, Yoni, and later on, his rival, Barak, it was a relatively minor record. In the first edition of his book *A Place Among the Nations*, published in 1993, there are only very brief references to his military service, and Sayeret Matkal is not mentioned, just "an elite unit." Later on, however, as the unit was slowly and very partially dragged out of the shadows, he began speaking of his days there more often, gradually verging on the boastful.

In March 2016, during a cabinet argument, Netanyahu slapped down his young challenger for leadership of the right wing, Education Minister Naftali Bennett, saying, "Don't preach to me on backing IDF soldiers. I've led more soldiers than you into battle."[10] Beyond the childishness of his remark, it wasn't even true. Bennett, who also served in Matkal, had commanded an entire special forces company and had continued to serve as a reserve officer for many more years than Netanyahu.

An even more bizarre boast came in January 2006, days after Prime Minister Ariel Sharon slipped into a coma. Netanyahu had just regained leadership of Likud after Sharon had split with the party and founded the centrist Kadima. Bibi was contemplating a three-headed election against Kadima and Labor, which was headed by his nemesis, Barak. One evening on a television talk show he told a story from the war about meeting Major General Sharon, who had commanded the crossing of the Suez Canal, the crucial turning point on the Egyptian front. He later repeated it in an interview with the *New York Times*. In the talk-show interview, he put it this way:

> I knew him in the Yom Kippur War. It was the third or the fourth day of the war. It was a makeshift force of Sayeret Matkal and we arrived there on the bank of the Canal, to help Arik, the IDF. The Egyptians had destroyed there some 200 tanks in the day or two before. We got into his command vehicle. There were three of us: Ariel Sharon; Ehud Barak, who commanded the unit; and your servant. It was interesting, because no one knew we had been there, three prime ministers. But you know, today we all belong to different parties. There we were in the same party. That is the greatness of this nation, in critical moments we are all in the same party.[11]

It was the perfect anecdote, putting him in the same company as his illustrious rivals. However, Barak and other officers on Sharon's staff had no recollection of the meeting ever taking place. It was highly unlikely that a junior reserve officer would have joined such a gathering with the

divisional commander. Neither does it tally with what is known of the
three men's whereabouts in those fateful days. But Netanyahu, when subsequently asked about the episode, insisted it happened and that he had
been "on the first plane" from the United States. In his own book, which
he had written thirteen years earlier, he had missed the first plane.[12]

Why did he need to puff up his already impressive military record
with an unlikely story? Just as he has spent decades creating a greatly
exaggerated narrative of his grandfather, father, and older brother at the
heart of the Zionist endeavor, it seems Netanyahu must also place himself at the heart of Israel's historic events.

S AYERET MATKAL LEFT an indelible mark on Benjamin Netanyahu,
beyond political posturing. It could hardly have been otherwise for
a young officer in his early twenties, sitting in front of large-scale maps,
planning strategic operations, with the Middle East his oyster. He has remained for his entire career a "big picture" politician, with little patience
for detail or consideration of obstacles. The small elite and secluded unit
instilled in him a hostility to large organizations, including the IDF itself,
which Bibi sees as cumbersome and obdurate. Managing Israel's strategic
affairs, he will always prefer using small special forces over larger regular
formations. He is more likely to engage in back-channel talks through
trusted confidential intermediaries than to use the services of the professional diplomatic corps, and more likely to appoint experts from the
private sector to ad hoc task forces than to work with the civil service.

In an interview in 1997, he explained that

the main thing you learn in the unit is to set a target and achieve
it. . . . The entire work process is captive to achieving one specific
mission. There's no routine. There are missions defined by periods
of time; months, sometimes even a year or two. And there is a certain destination which you home in on and dedicate all your mental
resources and everything else to reaching. That destination is almost
always reached and if it isn't, you try again. . . . You learn what you
can make of yourself. You learn the essential need of the people working around you to reach the destination. And afterwards, when you
achieve the goal, you say: here, I've reached my target, I'll go on to
the next thing.[13]

But the philosophy of a small elite unit is not always the best practice for running a country. "When things get fucked up in his chaotic office," says one long-suffering Netanyahu aide, "Bibi will shoot at you—'This couldn't have happened in 269,'" using the code number of Matkal. "Or he'll say—'This couldn't have happened at BCG,'" meaning Boston Consulting Group, the next self-perceived elite stop on Netanyahu's trajectory. "But he won't actually give you any idea of how to prevent the chaos he creates around himself."

10

Trying to Save the State

Netanyahu has always insisted that back in his twenties, he had no intention of going into politics in 1976. He certainly had little time then, with his double-load of courses, for student activism. But from the day in 1974 when he met a fellow student handing out pro-Israel leaflets on campus, he was hooked.

This is what his grandfather had done in the 1920s, and his father back in the 1940s. This is what Bibi wanted to do. His military service over, Netanyahu was about to embark on his next crusade.

Early on during his university days in the United States, Netanyahu still believed that public opinion in America and across the Western world would be broadly in favor of Israel. In September 1972, as news was broadcast of the murder of eleven members of the Israeli team at the Olympic Games in Munich, he was with Israeli friends at the home of an Israeli professor at Brandeis. The sentiment was that "at least now everyone will know who these people are."[1] The world would have a better understanding of what Israel was up against.

It was a pivotal period for Israel's supporters in the United States. For the first two decades of Israel's existence, most of the American Jewish community was relatively ambivalent toward Israel. While there were, of course, many Jewish supporters of Israel and Zionism, as well as some opponents, for the most part American Jews were much more ambivalent and inward-looking than they became after 1967. The postwar era was a time in which many of the barriers to the widespread acceptance and inclusion of Jews in the highest echelons of American society came down. Most American Jews were more concerned in those days with their own social advancement.

The fears of Israel's imminent annihilation in the weeks leading up to the Six-Day War and the subsequent lightning victory caused a sea change within American Jewry. Following the war, there was a feeling that they had also played their part. "All American Jews, it seemed, now basked in the pride of victory," wrote historian Melvin I. Urofsky, in *We Are One! American Jewry and Israel*.[2] They had gone in the space of weeks from suddenly fearing a second Holocaust in the Jewish state to taking vicarious pride in its military prowess. From then on Israel would play a central role in the self-identity of American Jews.

For many young American Jews who had no clear Jewish identity, and no longer faced discrimination or hostility in their own daily lives, support for Israel was a way of outsourcing that undefined identity to those glorious and triumphant Israelis.

The foreign policy of the Johnson and Nixon administrations mirrored this development as the United States began to openly identify itself as Israel's strategic ally. It reflected the worldview of those who, like Henry Kissinger, saw Israel as a pro-American bulwark in a Middle East that was in danger of coming under the aegis of the Soviet Union, as well as the growing influence of American Jews in the corridors of power. But the increasing intimacy between Jerusalem and Washington would cost Israel friends in other places.

THROUGHOUT THE 1950s and much of the 1960s, Israel—a state that had been created by refugees in defiance of colonial Britain, and with staunch socialist foundations that were expressed by the kibbutz movement—was widely seen by large sections of the American left as a progressive enterprise. This attitude was epitomized in Martin Luther King Jr.'s remarks in 1968: "I see Israel, and never mind saying it, as one of the great outposts of democracy in the world, and a marvelous example of what can be done, how desert land almost can be transformed into an oasis of brotherhood and democracy. Peace for Israel means security and that security must be a reality."[3]

But Dr. King's opinion of the Jewish state would soon become a minority view on the ideological left as the works of radical thinkers, such as Frantz Fanon, who identified the Palestinian cause as an "anti-colonialist" struggle, gained wider currency.

For most Jews around the world, Israel's astonishing triumph in 1967 was a source of pride. Even Noam Chomsky, a stalwart of the MIT faculty and a fierce critic of Israel, who had spent a few months in the 1950s living on a kibbutz, said that in the days before the Six-Day War he "did have concerns about Israel's possible fate, and didn't anticipate the quick and overwhelming victory."[4] But the emergence of Israel as a military power, and worse, one aligned with the United States, during a period of the Vietnam War in which many young Americans saw their own nation as being engaged in an unjust and bloody colonial war, swiftly pushed the Jewish state out of the progressive camp.

As the grand causes of the progressive left in previous decades—Cuba, Algeria, and, with the American military withdrawal in early 1973, also Vietnam—receded, new ones came to the forefront. Apartheid in South Africa was one. The Israel-Palestine conflict was another. By the time Benjamin Netanyahu returned to MIT in November 1973, the issue was firmly entrenched in the consciousness of many American students and professors. And while Israelis on campus believed that, like the athletes at the Munich Games, they were the victims of the conflict, some of their contemporaries saw Yasser Arafat, who had been directing Black September behind the scenes, as a brave freedom fighter—Che Guevara with a *keffiyeh*.

Bibi's first months back at MIT passed in a blur of studying as he made up for lost time. Miki was mostly preoccupied with her own studies and her part-time job at Brandeis. But as the New England winter began to thaw, he started paying more attention to what was happening around him. The fellow Israeli he had met handing out leaflets was Uzi Landau, a doctoral engineering student, who, like Bibi, had returned to fight in the Yom Kippur War as a paratrooper officer.

Uzi's father, Chaim Landau, was a Knesset member of the new party that had been formed around Menachem Begin's Herut a few months earlier. It was called Ha'Likud—"The Consolidation." Landau Sr. had been one of Begin's chief lieutenants in the IZL underground, serving as its last chief of staff before independence and as a Herut MK from 1949 onward.

Uzi Landau was one of a group of second-generation Herutniks, sons of the underground commanders, who would themselves go on to become prominent Likud politicians. From the mid-1980s onward, in

Israeli politics they would be called, often dismissively, "the princes." There are those who have sought to portray Netanyahu as one of the princes, by virtue of his Revisionist roots, but this characterization is groundless. Benzion never had anything to do with the Herut elite, which he despised. Throughout his political career, Bibi would fight the princes for control over the party, eventually driving nearly all of them out of Likud. Even Landau, a future minister, would in 2005 run against him for the party leadership, and three years later he left Likud for a more right-wing alternative, accusing Netanyahu of having led Likud "astray."

In those days, however, Landau welcomed Netanyahu to the fold. Bibi wasn't interested in handing out leaflets on campus. He had much grander ideas of fighting for Israel's cause statewide. He urged the members of the Israeli students association to find larger venues and to set up meetings with local politicians, members of Congress, and the governor. They were all in their early twenties, and unlike Bibi, lacked the polish or sophistication for public speaking and political lobbying. He would be their spokesman, with his perfect accent and preppy suit and tie. To add gravitas, he would sometimes invite Benzion, who was by then a professor at Cornell, to the important meetings. They were impressed. Landau had no illusions regarding Netanyahu's future: "It was clear to me that he would become a major political figure," he later said.[5]

The first mentions of Netanyahu—or Ben Nitay—in the media are laconic accounts in local Jewish newspapers of lectures he gave in Massachusetts and Philadelphia synagogues and Jewish federations on Israeli current affairs. Benzion, who had known little and understood even less of what his sons were doing back home in the army, finally approved, telling Bibi that he saw shades of his own father's rhetoric in him. Yoni wrote from the Golan praising him for "trying to save the state" and "working hard for our joint interest—continuing our existence."[6]

ISRAEL'S FOUNDER, DAVID Ben-Gurion, died on December 1, 1973. Upon resigning as prime minister ten years earlier, he had taunted the Revisionists in his farewell speech, saying, "I wasn't your partner when you praised Hitler." The next day he explained himself in a letter: "I have no doubt that Begin hates Hitler—but this hatred doesn't mean he's any different. When I first heard a Begin speech on the radio—I heard the voice and the screaming of Hitler." Ben-Gurion treated Begin as a pariah throughout his political career, but in the last decade of his life, relations between the two political rivals eased somewhat. During the 1967 crisis, Begin actually suggested that Ben-Gurion come back to lead the country. In 1969, Ben-Gurion wrote him that while he opposed him politically, "I never personally bore you a grudge and the more I've known in you in recent years—the more I've admired you."[7]

Ben-Gurion's successor, Levi Eshkol, allowed Jabotinsky's coffin to be brought to Israel for a state burial in 1964, and on the eve of the Six-Day War, he requested that Begin join a unity government. For the first time, the Revisionists were brought in from the cold. They were still far from power, but they were slowly gaining legitimacy.

In 1965, Herut and the Liberal Party set up a joint electoral bloc called Gahal, for Gush Herut-Liberalim (Herut-Liberals Bloc). The plan, pushed by the influential columnists of *Haaretz*, was to build a viable alternative to Mapai. The new party was to adopt the Liberals' market-orientated economic policies and Herut's hawkish positions on security and diplomacy. Begin agreed to one significant concession, dropping from the party's platform the demand that in the future Israel encompass the eastern bank of the Jordan.

By the early 1970s, they were beginning to look for the first time like a government-in-waiting. Ambitious young generals retiring from service, such as Dayan and Rabin, had in the past routinely joined Mapai on the fast track to a cabinet post. In 1972, former air force commander Ezer Weizman joined Herut. The next year, the Paratroopers Brigade founder, General Ariel Sharon, resigned from the army and set about trying to unite the parties of the center-right. Both Weizman and Sharon believed they would soon oust Begin and lead the party to power. Sharon aggressively brokered an alliance between Herut, the Liberals, and smaller parties from the center and the right.

On September 13, 1973, the Likud party came into being. In addition to Begin's Herut and the Liberals, it included the Free Center, a party of the rebels who had broken with Herut eight years earlier; the State List, which had been Ben-Gurion's last political vehicle, before his final retirement from politics in 1970; and the far right Greater Eretz Yisrael List. Likud was now poised to replace Mapai, which had rebranded itself as the Israeli Labor Party. Sharon was to be the campaign manager for the election scheduled for October 21. Four weeks later, however, he was back in uniform commanding a reserved armored division. His soldiers would cross the Suez Canal, finally turning the tide of the Yom Kippur War in Israel's favor.

The election, postponed by the war to December 31, proved a disappointment. Likud did far better than Begin's Herut ever had, receiving nearly a third of the votes and thirty-nine Knesset seats. But despite the public anger over the war's results, Golda Meir's Labor Party, running as "The Alignment" in an alliance with the socialist Mapam (Mifleget HaPoalim HaMeuhedet, or United Workers Party), held on with a plurality of fifty-one seats, enough to form a coalition. Begin encouraged his crestfallen colleagues. "Even though Labor won this election, after what happened in the Yom Kippur War to the nation and the government, they must lose power," he said. "It's just a question of time."[8]

Not everyone was convinced. Earlier that year, the editor of the newspaper *Maariv*, Shmuel Shnitzer, had written that even though Israel was ripe for a change in government, Begin's party, with its extreme baggage, was incapable of delivering. "There is a psychological barrier stopping many people going over to Herut," he observed. "What can be done when between an opposition seeking a party and the only party which can serve as opposition there are a thousand memories of old arguments that Herut gleefully renews whenever it seems there's a risk they may be forgotten."[9]

The Netanyahu family had certainly never believed in Begin as a viable leader. In a letter before the election to his parents, Yoni wrote, "No doubt, Israel needs a new leadership."[10] But he knew better than to mention Begin as a candidate. After the election, he wrote to them, "The alternative to Alignment [Labor] in Israel is so weak, and we are stuck in the middle. On the one side, we want change, on the other, we can't find the body that can bring it."[11]

For the time being, the alternative was a new generation of Labor leaders. Following Meir's resignation in April 1974, Yitzhak Rabin and Shimon Peres fought each other for the party leadership: the army's commander in the Six-Day War against Ben-Gurion's protégé. It was a bitter political rivalry; they were to battle over the party's leadership for the next two decades. This time, Rabin won narrowly, 298–254, in the Central Committee vote. He became Israel's fifth prime minister and its first born in the twentieth century. Grudgingly, he appointed Peres as his defense minister.

Rabin was an inexperienced politician, in his first Knesset term (it was Peres's fifth). He had been elevated to the premiership after only three months of serving as minister of labor. Before that he had been Israel's ambassador to the United States (1968–1973), and while in Washington he had built a personal relationship with Nixon, departing from diplomatic conventions by lobbying on the Republican president's behalf among Jewish leaders. Nixon saw the majority of American Jews as part of the East Coast liberal establishment controlling the media and implacably opposed to his administration. In private he was given to anti-Semitic remarks. Nevertheless, he developed an admiration for Israel and its military and intelligence capabilities. It was a dynamic that would be replicated in relationships between future Israeli governments and Republican administrations, which shared a conservatism alien to mainstream American Jews.

Early in the Yom Kippur War, Nixon had given the orders for a massive airlift of arms to Israel to replenish the arsenals depleted on the Egyptian and Syrian fronts. It was left to Kissinger, who had recently been promoted to secretary of state, to implement the airlift, which he did while fighting opposition in other parts of the administration, mainly from Defense Secretary James Schlesinger. The American arms arrived too late in the war to have any impact on its outcome, but the knowledge that they were on the way increased Israeli confidence as the counter-offensives were launched with existing resources. The delay did feed Israeli accusations that Kissinger had been willing "to let Israel bleed a while" to pressure it back to negotiations after the war.

In 1974, Kissinger embarked on a series of "shuttle diplomacy" missions between Jerusalem, Cairo, and Damascus to help broker disengagement agreements made on the front lines. The United States was rattled by the Soviet intervention at the end of the Yom Kippur War, when the Kremlin had threatened using its own military might, perhaps even nuclear weapons, if Israel continued to pursue its advantage against Syria and Egypt. For the first time US forces were placed on DEFCON 3, a defense readiness condition alert. The Arab oil boycott, in response to the arms airlift, had damaged the US economy and was felt by ordinary citizens at the gas pump. Achieving a comprehensive Israeli-Arab peace became a strategic interest of US foreign policy, and shuttle diplomacy between Israel and the Arabs, the norm for US envoys.

On June 16, 1974, Nixon landed at the recently renamed Ben Gurion Airport on the first presidential visit ever to Israel. He also visited Egypt,

Syria, and Jordan. Fifty-three days after leaving Israel, he resigned over the Watergate scandal. Under President Gerald Ford, Kissinger continued his shuttle diplomacy, pressuring Israel to make further withdrawals. Many in Israel criticized Kissinger for what they saw as his cavalier attitude toward Israel's security so soon after it had been jeopardized in war. Worse, he was seen as a traitor to his Jewish roots. In right-wing rallies he was routinely called "the "Jew-boy" (a nickname Nixon had in the past used for him) and "the husband of the gentile." In a Knesset speech, Begin castigated him: "Be careful Dr. Kissinger," he said. "You are a Jew. You are not the first to have reached high office in the country where you dwell. Remember the past. There were Jews who out of a complex of fear that people would say they are acting on behalf of their people because of their Judaism, did the opposite."[12]

The Netanyahus were deeply suspicious of the American moves. In Jerusalem, Yoni and Iddo joined thousands of Israelis in demonstrations against Kissinger. In a conversation with Bibi, Yoni dismissed the agreement that Kissinger had brokered with North Vietnam on ending America's military presence in Vietnam. "Is this the peace they are planning for us as well?"[13] In one letter, he referred to the administration as "friends" in quotation marks.

In March 1975, following Rabin's rejection of yet another disengagement plan, Ford and Kissinger openly blamed Israel for the failure of the initiative. The president announced a "reassessment" of US ties with Israel, including a freeze on arms sales. Rabin set out to overturn the president's decision, mobilizing support in the Democratic Congress. On May 22, seventy-six senators (fifty-one Democrats and twenty-five Republicans) signed a letter condemning Ford's decision.

Ultimately, a compromise was reached. Israel agreed to sign a disengagement agreement with Egypt whereby its forces would retreat nearly forty kilometers (twenty-five miles) in Sinai, leaving a buffer zone between the two armies. To compensate Israel, Rabin and Ford agreed on a secret deal that included the supply of advanced weaponry, including F-15 and F-16 fighter jets; an emergency plan for resupplying Israel in case of war; American guarantees for Israel's oil supplies; and the assurance that the United States would not recognize the PLO as long as the PLO refused to recognize Israel. The "reassessment" was over, but it had left Israelis with the realization that safeguarding the strategic relationship would take more than just a friendly president in the White House. It would mean continuous maintenance of all levels of support:

Congress, statehouses, and Jewish organizations and federations as well as the American media.

T HE ISRAELI STUDENTS group at MIT and neighboring universities sought the help of Israel's consulate in Boston in setting up meetings and coordinating their work. At first they were disappointed by the professional diplomats' lack of interest in their grassroots work. Israel's foreign service in its early decades had been built on the statesmanship ethos of its British-educated founders, men like Abba Eban, who were skilled diplomats and fine orators, but had little understanding or interest in the mass media and in the necessity of taking the message to wider audiences.

In early 1975, a new Israeli consul arrived in Boston. Colette Avital, one of the few women in the male-dominated diplomatic corps, had been relegated in her first postings to media and PR roles and understood their importance. She was the first Israeli diplomat to see the potential in the twenty-five-year-old Netanyahu, with his combination of special forces experience, an American accent, and a polished appearance. She sent Netanyahu on his first official speaking engagements and appearances on local television stations on behalf of Israel, for which he was paid twenty-five dollars a lecture. She couldn't foresee then that twenty-two years later, by then a veteran ambassador and avid supporter of the Oslo process, she would be forced out of the foreign service by the first Netanyahu government.

For Netanyahu, it was clear from the start that the campuses were only the lowest level of an all-out campaign on all fronts. For decades he has insisted that the strategic flaw in Israel's policy was not dedicating major resources and professional efforts to explaining its actions to the world. He has claimed that this PR project was the "third pillar" of Jabotinsky's vision for ensuring the nation's security, along with building its military might and settling the land of Israel.

There was nothing new about this observation. Ben-Gurion said in the early 1940s that "the way to acquire the American administration is acquiring the people, the public opinion."[14] But those in Ben-Gurion's camp, the center-left mainstream of Zionism, always saw propaganda as something the right wing was best at; while they focused on physically building a new state, the Revisionists could just talk.

In the mid-1970s in Boston, Netanyahu's enthusiasm for becoming an architect was waning. Over the years he has said that he felt he lacked the creative instincts to succeed in the field of architecture and was becoming more attracted by the world of business. In 1975, close to completing his second degree in architecture, he began a master's degree at MIT's Sloan School of Management and took four courses in the Department of Political Science doctoral program. By this point in the last year of his studies, he was handling a triple course load. Despite Bibi's consistent denials that he harbored any thoughts of a public career at that point, it is hard to escape the impression that he was already finding his métier.

Netanyahu's first experiences of advocating for Israel in the United States had certainly left him with an appetite for more. It was clear that at some stage, not far off, there would be a change of government in Israel, to one more fitting to his political inclinations. But even if we are to believe Netanyahu's protestations that he had no plans then of going into politics, the events of July 1976 would launch him on an unstoppable trajectory.

PART THREE

Breaking the Elite
1976–1996

I I

Stop the World!

The Israeli military goes to great lengths, including instituting media blackouts, to ensure that close family members of a fallen soldier are notified personally by authorized personnel of their loss. It's relatively straightforward in a small country like Israel, where experienced teams of military doctors and psychologists are on call to visit families quickly. It's more difficult when the family is scattered across continents.

"Yoni's dead" was the first thing Colonel Ehud Barak, waiting for the arrival of the four C-130 Hercules transports carrying the rescued hostages from Entebbe in Uganda, was told by the commander of the mission, Brigadier General Dan Shomron, as they landed to refuel in Nairobi. It was in the early hours of July 4, 1976, in Africa. Barak went forward to where the body of Jonathan Netanyahu had been lain behind the cockpit and bade farewell to his old friend. Three hostages who were killed in the cross fire lay beside him. He then went to phone his wife. The Baraks lived in the same apartment building as Yoni and his partner, Brurya Shaked. They weren't married, and Barak feared that she wouldn't be formally notified. It fell to Nava Barak to go downstairs and break the news to her.

As morning dawned in Jerusalem, officers knocked on Iddo Netanyahu's door. He had been up all night, listening on the radio as news of the successful rescue operation came through. A Matkal veteran himself, he had called the unit and been told to remain at home. He called Bibi. It was still nighttime in Boston.

Colonel Yossi Langotzky, the newly appointed military attaché for intelligence affairs, was woken with the news and instructed to inform the Netanyahu family and organize their flight back to Israel for the funeral. "I called Bibi, who told me he already knew and that he was on his way to tell his parents. I said I would take care of the tickets and meet them in New York," Langotzky later recalled.

The seven-hour drive west from Boston to Ithaca, New York, where Benzion was a professor at Cornell, was the worst experience of Bibi's life. He took Tzvika Livne, a former Matkal officer who was also at MIT, and they took turns driving. Miki and Tzvika's wife, Ruth, sat in the back. Halfway there, Bibi called ahead to ensure that a doctor was waiting near the house. Bibi had preceded Yoni in joining Matkal. He knew the risks and arbitrariness of death in a special operations unit. He had feared not coming out alive from the Sabena rescue four years earlier and insisted that Yoni not join the team in order to avoid risking two brothers being killed together. Although he was not overly surprised by Yoni's death, that didn't in any way soften the devastating blow of losing the person he had been closest to since earliest childhood. Entebbe would irrevocably change his life.

They arrived in Ithaca at eleven in the morning. His parents had already heard of the Entebbe operation on the news. Tzila was worried, Benzion oblivious. He had never fully grasped the danger of his sons' military service. When they saw Bibi and the doctor walking toward the house from the window, Benzion finally understood.

Langotzky met them at a New York City hotel, where they waited for twelve hours before going to JFK. "I knew them from Jerusalem, where my family had lived only a few streets away in the fifties," Langotzky later said. "My mother was a nurse at the children's clinic and had treated the Netanyahu boys. I spoke with them for hours—with Tzila about my mother and with Benzion about his research. They were incredibly composed. No crying or screaming." Langotzky had known Yoni well. Before leaving for Washington, he had been in charge of directing Matkal's "core missions." He didn't tell the family that only three weeks earlier, one of his last decisions as head of intelligence-gathering had been to recommend that Lieutenant Colonel Netanyahu be relieved of his command. Removing the commander of Sayeret Matkal would have been an unprecedented move, and it had to be authorized at the highest levels. Before Langotzky's recommendation was acted upon, Yoni was killed leading his men at Entebbe.

So much has been made of the Entebbe raid over the years that it's hard to grasp today just how daring Prime Minister Yitzhak Rabin's decision was to send a small military force over 3,000 kilometers (1,864 miles) from Israel's borders to rescue 106 hostages held in a hostile country. Benjamin Netanyahu later described it as "the decisive battle against international terrorism. Following it, security forces of Western countries began a series of daring counterattacks against terror."[1] For once, Netanyahu wasn't exaggerating. Admiral Bill McRaven, the Navy SEAL officer who commanded Joint Special Operations Command (JSOC), has written that Entebbe was "the best illustration of the theory of special operations yet presented."[2]

Air France Flight 139 from Tel Aviv to Paris was hijacked on June 27, 1976, by four members of a Palestinian-German cell of the Popular Front for the Liberation of Palestine, boarding during a stopover at Athens. Six days of intelligence-gathering, operational planning, and training culminated in fifty-eight minutes on the ground at Entebbe Airport in Uganda. The captors, who had demanded the release of forty prisoners held by Israel and thirteen in other countries, were killed in the raid, along with around forty-five Ugandan soldiers who were aiding the hijackers under the orders of President Idi Amin.

Yoni had a relatively minor role in the planning. At Entebbe, he commanded one of the units. Matkal's role in storming the old terminal where the hostages were held and taking out the hijackers was crucial. Yoni was the IDF's only fatal casualty in the operation, and since the names of most of the officers involved remained secret for years, in his death he became the public face of the operation.

Yoni's heroic death obscured the fact that he had been going through a deeply troubled time in the months leading up to Entebbe. He had not been the universal choice for Matkal commander. He lacked the irreverent charm of Ehud Barak, or the endearing, down-to-earth gruffness of his immediate predecessor, Giora Zorea. There were two candidates—Amiram Levin and Yoni. Many within the unit were rooting for Levin, a legendary warrior who had begun his career in Matkal. Yoni, who got the job partly because the chief of staff, Mordechai Gur, admired his intellectualism, was seen by many as an aloof stickler. Iddo remembers angrily leaving the ceremony for Yoni's appointment on August 1, 1975, after he heard Matkal officers bad-mouthing Yoni.[3]

At first Yoni set even higher standards for the unit, especially on physical resilience. Like any other commander, he had his fair share of operational successes and failures. But at some point his officers began to feel Yoni's heart wasn't in it. In the last months of his life, officers couldn't help noticing Yoni's increasing absences and lack of attention during briefings.

As chief of intelligence-gathering, Langotzky was a rank above Yoni. "I can't pinpoint where I noticed it, but in operational meetings, he just wasn't there," he later recounted. "He didn't listen, was writing things to himself, detached. A couple of times I asked him to stay behind and tell me if anything was wrong. He said everything was fine. But then officers from within the unit, at different levels, came and asked to meet. They said Yoni was unfocused and losing control."

Those who knew Yoni at the time later believed he was suffering from depression, or perhaps posttraumatic stress disorder. His situation may have been exacerbated by the years of living alone, far from his parents in the United States, as a young divorcé, incapable of forming lasting relationships with women. Despite his shining military career, at thirty Yoni still felt shiftless and without a clear direction in life. In his letters he would repeat his plans for returning to Harvard, but he never completed the degree he had started there eight years earlier.

The last letter to Brurya, which he left in their apartment five days before his death when he was back for an overnight break from an operation in Sinai, discloses something of his anguish: "I am at a critical juncture in the saga of my life and facing a deep internal crisis that has been shaking for a while the chain of my concepts."[4] Describing his feelings, he quoted the title of a musical he had seen years ago in America: "Stop the world! I want to get off!"

His admiring brother Bibi, who had only seen him briefly in the last years of his life, since that golden summer of 1973 in Boston, predicted blithely that "Yoni will be the IDF chief of staff one day." But the elder brother had none of Bibi's political instincts, which he would have needed to climb the greasy pole of IDF General Staff politics.

UNSURPRISINGLY, NONE OF Yoni's shortcomings were brought up during the *shiva*, the seven days of mourning. Israel's entire leadership attended the military funeral at Mount Herzl. Bibi stood between Benzion and Prime Minister Rabin while Defense Minister Peres gave the eulogy. The family sat shiva in Iddo's small apartment in Jerusalem. As senior officers and Matkal comrades visited, Yoni's praises were sung. Those who had been central to the planning and execution of the operation downplayed their own roles, creating the impression that Yoni's part was much larger than it actually was.

The first stage in the mythologization of Yoni as the peerless commander of the Entebbe raid was constructed in those days, out of sincere consideration for his family. Benzion, who had never had a clear idea of what Yoni did during all those years far away, eagerly grasped for every detail. Incapable of seeing his son as a vulnerable human being, he began building the posthumous image of a warrior-philosopher and leader-in-waiting.

Moshe Arens, a Likud Knesset member and veteran Revisionist, who had met Benzion in New York back in the 1940s and would soon play a pivotal role in Bibi's career, later recalled being surprised by Benzion's tone at the shiva. "I expected the father to say how much he loved his son and missed him," he said. "Instead Benzion said, 'The Arabs don't know yet what a loss they have inflicted on the Jews. He was the best general who could lead the Jewish people and now he's gone.'"

As the shiva ended, Bibi and Iddo set about collecting every letter and note Yoni had ever written and interviewing those who had known him over the years. The project quickly expanded way beyond the norm for even the most conscientious of families anxious to reserve a bit of enduring glory for their sons in a country that does not lack for dead heroes. Bibi automatically became the family's spokesman and was soon in demand to speak to visiting delegations of Jewish Diaspora leaders eager for their own vicarious basking in the Entebbe glory.

Israel devotes great resources to preserving the memory of fallen IDF soldiers. Yet no other Israeli soldier has ever been accorded anything like the praise and commemoration that Yoni Netanyahu has received. Over the decades, the Yoni project intensified as his brother Bibi became a powerful politician. Local council leaders discovered that the way to his heart was naming a street or school after his fallen brother. Even visiting statesmen from overseas have learned that adding a visit to Yoni's grave on Mount Herzl to their itinerary is a means of gaining face-time with the prime minister.

But the Entebbe operation took place less than three years after the debacle of the Yom Kippur War, and many wanted to share in its success. The Netanyahu family's insistence on making it all about Yoni would soon irk others who had been involved. Over the decades, an entire industry of books, movies, and research was built around Entebbe, with the Netanyahus and others sparring for their place in the front row.

The debate over the raid is still ongoing. Over two hundred men took off in the four C-130s on July 3. They included an aircrew, paratroopers, soldiers from the Golani Brigade (a renowned infantry brigade), and doctors along with the Matkal team. The operations commander on the ground was the IDF's chief infantry officer, Brigadier General Dan Shomron, whose team had done most of the planning alongside the air force and the intelligence services. For most of the week leading up to the operation, Yoni had been busy in Sinai, while his subordinates in Sirkin had planned and trained for Matkal's part. He joined them forty-eight hours before takeoff and until the last moment was skeptical that the government would give the green light.

Officers, including Shomron; the pilots who executed the complex logistical feat of bringing the force to Entebbe; military intelligence and Mossad operatives, who had obtained crucial details; and commanders of other units in the Entebbe force have all clashed with the Netanyahus over the years. Even within Matkal, a group of former officers coalesced around one of Yoni's deputies, Muki Betzer, who had done most of the planning and led the storming of the terminal, in opposition to the Netanyahus' version of events. Yoni has been accused of acting against orders by opening fire on Ugandan soldiers and exposing himself to the control tower, from which the shots that killed him were likely fired. Yoni's loyalists, in turn, accuse Betzer of hesitating at the entrance to the terminal.

Even the most successful military operation includes its share of errors. The firefight that began as the Matkal commandos sped toward the terminal jeopardized the crucial element of surprise. Twenty-five men rushed for the entrances, abandoning the original plan. Yoni was hit then. On his orders, the storming of the terminal was completed before casualties were tended to. Whatever mistakes he made in the last minute of his life should pale beside the sheer bravery needed to enter a dark building held by an invisible enemy. If it wasn't for the way the Netanyahu family tried to marginalize the role of others in the operation, Yoni's missteps would probably have never been mentioned.

Iddo wrote the family's version in his book *Yoni's Last Battle*, which differs from the IDF's official account of the operation on key points. Iddo indicated that Yoni was actually killed by the German commander of the hijackers, rather than by a Ugandan soldier, suggesting to some that the family felt that being felled by an "inferior" African soldier was somehow a lesser way to die. Even some people closest to the family despaired. "When I became defense minister, Bibi spoke to me about it," said Moshe Arens. "He was convinced Dan Shomron and others were trying to steal Yoni's glory. It's paranoid. Shomron wasn't like that."

The next stage was commissioning a biography of Yoni—a tall order for a subject who had died at the age of thirty, made much more difficult by the family's aspirations to produce a weighty tome. The British publisher George Weidenfeld, an ardent Zionist, set about finding a suitable foreign writer. The choice fell on Max Hastings, a British war correspondent who was beginning to make a name for himself as an author of military histories. Twenty years later, in his memoirs, Hastings would describe the association with the Netanyahus as "one of the sorriest episodes of my own career."[5]

Hastings was granted, on orders of the defense minister, unprecedented access for a journalist, let alone a non-Israeli, to Yoni's former units, including Matkal and its officers. He spent time with Benzion, who impressed upon him "that his son had been both a soldier and an intellectual, an important thinker as well as a man of action." Having interviewed dozens of Yoni's contemporaries, Hastings reached the conclusion that Yoni was a "troubled young man of moderate intelligence, striving to come to terms with intellectual concepts beyond his grasp," who had been "actively disliked by more than a few of his men."[6]

The Netanyahus hated his manuscript. To make matters worse, Weidenfeld had given the Israeli government copy-approval as well. Hastings was not to even mention the existence of Sayeret Matkal. After an angry exchange of letters, he was forced to agree to a massively bowdlerized version of his manuscript, or else lose the money he had been promised.

Hastings never visited Israel again and became a fierce critic of its policies. He finally got his revenge on the Netanyahus in his memoirs over two decades later. He dedicated a chapter to his months with the family, describing Benzion mercilessly as a dogmatic and "emotional old man" who had helped to destroy his eldest son's life with unrealistic expectations. Bibi, he wrote, was a slick, humorless "marketing man." One passage included damning quotes from his conversations with Bibi:

> "In the next war, if we do it right we'll have a chance to get all the Arabs out," he said. "We can clear the West Bank, sort out Jerusalem." He joked about the Golani Brigade, the Israeli infantry force in which so many men were North African or Yemenite Jews. "They're okay as long as they're led by white officers." He grinned.[7]

Support for the ethnic cleansing of Arabs—and what would have been worse for many Israelis, overt racism toward Mizrahi Jews and the IDF's oldest brigade—could have been deeply damaging for a mainstream Israeli politician. However, by the time Hastings's memoirs came out in 2000, Netanyahu was already an ex–prime minister, and so much mud had already been slung at him that the quotes, which Netanyahu, of course, denied ever saying, barely caused a stir.

OVER THE YEARS, the argument has continued to rage over Yoni Netanyahu's record, with all manner of personal and political implications. Former officers who sided with the Shomron and Betzer camps found themselves ostracized from events by Prime Minister Netanyahu, and formal invitation lists were limited to those who praised Yoni. Meanwhile, journalists who hoped to keep an open channel to Netanyahu have been careful to dismiss the criticism of Yoni.

In 1994, a critical profile of Yoni was published in the newspaper *Maariv*.[8] For the first time, the details of Yoni's last months in command of Matkal and his impending removal from command were revealed in public. A group of former Matkal officers wrote *Maariv* an open letter praising Yoni. Another group of officers, still in uniform and therefore prohibited from writing openly, endorsed the letter. Four years later, under Prime Minister Netanyahu, one of them, Shaul Mofaz, was appointed IDF chief of staff. Thirteen years later, during Netanyahu's second term, another, Tamir Pardo, was appointed chief of Mossad. Notably, for some, while both men were suitable candidates, both had

volunteered to posthumously support Yoni and were chosen by Bibi over
a more likely candidate.

T HE MYTH OF Yoni would go on to serve as a political platform for
Yoni's brother. But Bibi wasn't the first to use Yoni for his political
ends. That would be Shimon Peres.

Rabin and Peres were both deeply involved in the plans to send the
men to Entebbe, but the final decision and ultimate responsibility were
the prime minister's. Rabin even prepared a letter of resignation should
the operation end in disaster. With the hostages back safely in Israel, a
rancorous battle over the credit broke out between the two men that
continued for years. In conversations with friendly journalists, Peres
pushed the narrative whereby he had argued for the operation, while
Rabin was skeptical. Rabin, in retaliation, omitted Peres's name from
official accounts of the operation, and in his memoirs branded Peres a
"tireless underminer," an epithet that would stick for decades.

The Rabin-Peres rivalry would extend to the silver screen. Three
full-length movies were made on the Entebbe operation, and in the
Oscar-nominated version, produced by Israeli director Menachem Golan, Rabin and Peres even had cameos. The film featured the original
Hercules aircraft that flew to Entebbe. Both politicians subjected Golan
to intense pressure to ensure they got sufficient screen-time.

Peres had one asset in his grab for glory. He had befriended the Netanyahus, eulogizing Yoni at the funeral and subsequently presenting himself as an old friend of the family, an outright lie. In interviews, Peres told
of how he had been extensively briefed by Yoni before the operation, and
of how it was Yoni who had assured him that the hostage rescue could
be pulled off. Peres pushed for the posthumous renaming of Operation
Thunderbolt as Operation Yonatan.

In the eulogy, Peres said, "I saw him a few nights before [the opera-
tion], at the head of his men." In 1978, he published a book containing
seven portraits of men he had worked with, beginning with his mentor David Ben-Gurion and ending with Yoni. He pretended to know
the Netanyahu family well, writing that "his grandfather, Willikovsky,
authored an important book on biblical research,"[9] getting not only
Nathan Mileikowsky's name but also his profession wrong. Of Yoni he
wrote that his appointment as Matkal commander had been "natural and

unchallenged," and added detailed descriptions of his conversations with Yoni before the operation.

The problem was that these briefings had never taken place. Defense Minister Peres had been briefed by Major Betzer. It was Betzer who had been in charge of the planning and training for Matkal in the Entebbe mission, while Yoni had been in Sinai. Peres's version enraged Matkal's officers; years later, he wrote a letter apologizing to Betzer, though he never set the public record straight. Peres needed the myth of Yoni and their invented meetings before Entebbe to put himself at the center of the operation, on level with Rabin.

There was no way Peres could have foreseen then that in constructing the Yoni myth, he was helping to build the political platform that would bring Yoni's brother to power. Bibi would cause Peres his most painful political defeat, worse than any inflicted on him by Rabin.

E VEN WITH RABIN and Peres dead, the bitter dispute continues. Amiram Levin, Bibi's first commander, who replaced Yoni in 1976 as Matkal commander, launched a failed bid for the Labor Party leadership in 2017 and gave a blunt, no-holds-barred interview to Israel's Channel 10 describing how many Matkal veterans see the Netanyahus: "You don't question a legendary warrior's bravery. For that there's no forgiveness. I expect Bibi and his brother Iddo who were in the unit [Matkal] to understand that. It's not done, to build Yoni's glory at the expense of Muki's bravery. With us, in the unit, with warriors and commanders, it doesn't pass."[10]

Benzion and Tzila, Bibi and Iddo, remained convinced that there were those intent on stealing Yoni's glory and denying his greatness. On his final briefing to the Matkal team, before boarding the Hercules on July 3, Yoni had said, "We cannot compromise with terrorists." As decades passed and successive Israeli prime ministers, including Netanyahu, agreed to release thousands of Palestinian prisoners in exchange for captured Israeli soldiers, his sacrifice began to seem futile.

In 1997, in a rare interview with the *Washington Post* a year after her second son was elected prime minister, Tzila admitted she was angry. "What for? Thousands of prisoners are released today. For that Yoni had to be killed! It wasn't worth it."[11]

12

Why Aren't You in Uniform?

In the fall of 1976, Bibi Netanyahu returned to the United States. On his passport it still said he was Ben Nitay, but he had spent the past few months as Binyamin, brother of Yoni Netanyahu, and his American name would soon fall out of use. Just before Yoni's death, Bibi had landed a lucrative new job, and he was still working on a doctorate in political science. He would not stick with either for very long. The next few years would be a frustrating period as Bibi struggled to adjust to life in Yoni's shadow. It would take him nearly six years to achieve some stability.

In June 1976, after a grueling series of tests and interviews, he had been hired by the Boston Consulting Group (BCG). In many ways it was his dream job. BCG, founded only thirteen years earlier, was well on its way to becoming one of the leading consulting firms. It had developed a reputation for its swashbuckling yet cerebral approach to management. Its consultants placed corporations in matrices of profitability and competitiveness, no matter what their core business was. This method fit Bibi, who employs broad-picture analysis in just about every conversation he has. What better place to work than in a company that not only dealt in those sweeping generalizations, but also rewarded the select few it hired with a handsome wage?

The plan was to work at BCG for two years, until Miki finished her doctorate at Brandeis, and then figure out their next step. But Yoni's death had placed new responsibilities upon him and opened up new opportunities. There was growing demand for him to speak in Jewish communities across America. Benzion, who had returned to Cornell, was anxious not only to see a biography and collection of Yoni's letters in print, but to found a think tank in his son's name. Most of the organizing and fund-raising would fall to Bibi.

Bibi enjoyed being the center of attention, with wealthy American Jews inviting him to meetings and lectures. Work at BCG may have appealed to his intellectual sensibilities, but he was merely another team member there, and the firm's brainiacs regularly outshone him, as if he were an officer demoted to foot soldier.

Twenty-six years later, Republican presidential candidate Mitt Romney, who had overlapped with him at BCG, made a great deal of the time they had spent there together. Eager for Netanyahu's support in the election, he told an interviewer that "we share common experiences and have a perspective and underpinning which is similar."[1] Netanyahu reciprocated, saying they enjoyed "easy communication" as a result of "B.C.G.'s intellectually rigorous boot camp," and that they "employ similar methods in analyzing problems and coming up with solutions for them."[2]

In 2012, Netanyahu was torn between his desire to see Romney beat Barack Obama and the need as prime minister of Israel to appear neutral. In a subsequent interview he downplayed their BCG relationship, saying, "We did not know each other that well. [Romney] was the whiz kid. I was just in the back of the room."[3] This was the more accurate depiction. The two never worked on the same team at BCG, and Romney left in 1977 for competitors Bain & Company, where he would make his millions. Netanyahu stayed on another year, but his career as a management consultant never took off, at least not until he was a former prime minister.

His time at BCG did leave a mark on him, or at least strengthen his tendency to regard issues from the widest possible perspective with scant regard for detail. He worked on a team advising national governments on how to overhaul their economies, including Sweden and Ireland (the team would also advise Israel, but by then Netanyahu had left). The team was led by Ira Magaziner, who would much later become a central policy adviser to President Bill Clinton. Their prior acquaintance would not help make Netanyahu more popular in the Clinton White House. Netanyahu speaks to this day of the influence BCG's founder Bruce

Henderson's philosophy of competitive advantage had on him and how
he has applied it in his management of Israel's economy. But when he
actually worked there, he lacked the drive and focus to endure.

MEANWHILE, A MOMENTOUS shift occurred back in Israel. On May
17, 1977, after eight successive defeats, Menachem Begin won an
election. Likud's share of the vote had barely increased, but Begin was the
beneficiary of a gradual erosion of trust in the Labor Party, leading to a
collapse in its support.

Infighting, lingering trauma from the Yom Kippur War, a sharp turn
to the right of the once moderate religious community, and a series of
high-profile corruption cases had all combined to end Labor's uninterrupted run in office since Israel's founding.

Forty days before the election, Rabin had announced his resignation.
An illegal bank account in his wife Leah's name had been revealed by
Haaretz. Rabin had to choose between leaving office or having criminal charges brought. Israelis at the time were forbidden to hold foreign
bank accounts. Diplomats were allowed to have them only when posted
abroad. The account had been opened when Rabin served as ambassador
in Washington, but they kept it when they returned to Israel in 1973.

Rabin has been lionized as a "Mr. Clean" leader who insisted on resigning just because his wife was accused of a technicality. In reality, the
money in the account had been paid by American Jewish organizations
for speaking engagements. As ambassador, he was forbidden to receive
such payments, and they had not been declared to the tax authorities.
Rabin's misdemeanors paled beside the allegations of corruption that
would be leveled at some of his successors, who clung onto office despite
being the subject of police investigations. Nevertheless, he was the first
Israeli prime minister to be tainted by Jewish American money.

Almost by default, Peres led Labor in the election. Likud's campaign
portrayed him as a shifty and corrupt figure who had "risen to the top
climbing over his colleague's body," and downplayed Begin's ideological
positions, in the hope of allaying the voters' fears. Instead, they highlighted his frugal lifestyle. Labor warned of an apocalypse for Israel if the
voters ditched its tried and true leadership.

For the first time in Israel, a televised debate was held. Both Peres
and Begin gave measured performances, without drawing each other into

fierce arguments. It was judged a draw and a huge achievement for Begin, who finally appeared as Peres's equal, a legitimate prime minister.

Twenty-nine years of Labor rule in Israel had come to an end, along with nearly half a century during which Mapai had been the dominant force within the Zionist movement. The disciples of Jabotinsky had finally fulfilled the words of his poem: "God, you chose us to rule."

Begin was determined not to rule in the same manner as his Mapai rivals, who had kept the Revisionists out of the establishment. He shocked both his own camp and his rivals by insisting on not replacing senior officials of the previous government. Asked to stay on, Rabin's diplomatic adviser, Yehuda Avner, answered, "But Mr Begin, I'm not a member of your party." To which the prime minister responded, "This is the first time there has been a change of political administration in Israel and we have no intention of plundering power. There has to be continuity. This is a democratic transition. The world must see this; the nation must see this."[4]

The old hawk was determined to prove to the world that he was no extremist. Begin's insistence on not replacing the "old elites" with loyal Likudniks, however, would breed a bitterness within the right wing from its implication that its own leaders "don't know how to rule." It was a sentiment that would serve Netanyahu well in time as he convinced Likud members he had no such limitations.

In 1977, Begin's victory did not bode well for Bibi's budding political aspirations. Most of the appointments Begin did make were from the IZL veterans, the "fighting family," and their sons, "the princes." The close-knit group that had held together through the long years in the wilderness viewed Benzion as a pompous windbag who had preferred a comfortable life in the United States. With Labor's defeat, the Netanyahus also lost their benefactor, as Peres languished in opposition.

WITH HIS PROSPECTS diminishing back in Israel, Netanyahu's life in Boston was also starting to disintegrate. For the first four years of their marriage, Bibi and Miki had been close partners, as both focused on their studies together. Miki had a part-time research job at Brandeis, and Bibi had support from various wealthy Mileikowsky relatives. It was sufficient for a lifestyle comfortable by the spartan standards they had known back in Jerusalem. They expected to complete their PhDs in about six years and return together to Israel. Whether it was Yoni's death that changed Bibi's focus, or the temptations of life in the fast lane at BCG—or, what's more likely, a combination of both—by the five-year mark of their marriage it was no longer a partnership.

Bibi's absences became more frequent. He flew off to give lectures in other cities, and he returned to Israel to tend to Yoni's commemoration. There were also distractions close to home. In early 1978, Miki, who was by then pregnant with their first child, discovered that he was having an affair. If their relationship had been stronger, she may have felt that it was worth fighting for, but they had already grown distant, and she insisted that he leave.

Distraught at the thought of losing his young family, Bibi tried to convince Miki to take him back, but at the same time he continued seeing his new girlfriend. He had always been dependent in some distant way on his family—his parents, Yoni, Miki. After losing Yoni, the thought of being cut off from Miki and his unborn child as well was unbearable. Miki, however, was adamant. She had decided to continue with her plans without Bibi.

Of Netanyahu's three wives, Miki is the only one who seemed to be "perfect for Bibi"—at least that was the consensus among all those who knew them at the time. They shared the same background and similar political beliefs, they were at ease in each other's company, and they were both highly intelligent and ambitious. Miki made up for any social awkwardness on Bibi's part and had made their home a hub for the Israeli students in Boston. She had shared in the crushing blow of Yoni's death and knew how to handle his parents. But as forceful and driven as he was in his political career, Netanyahu has always been much more passive in his private life, especially in his relationships with women, where he was rarely the initiator. It was Miki who had pressed him to finally get married, and she was the one who decided to end the relationship. Netanyahu has over the years frozen out hundreds of former friends and associates, but he always tried to cling to the women in his life.

Much has been made of his relationship with Fleur Cates, the other woman who would become his second wife, but neither ex-wife has ever given an interview on their years with Bibi. In a way they have come to symbolize his separate Israeli and American sides. This is, of course, a crude oversimplification of both relationships, not least because Miki lived with Bibi for over five years in the United States, and Fleur was prepared to follow him back to Israel.

They met studying in Harvard Business School's Baker Library. The British-German Fleur had graduated from Cambridge University in England and went on to her master's in business administration at Harvard as a Baker Scholar. The socially accomplished and attractive Fleur represented a different world from Miki's, a world Netanyahu aspired to belong to as well. One friend of Netanyahu's who knows all three of his wives observed that, while "both Miki and Fleur are highly educated, Miki was always going to be her own woman and put her career first. Fleur could have been the perfect politician's wife."

Fleur initiated their relationship, and Bibi could not end it, even when it threatened his marriage to Miki. He continued to hanker after Miki and tried to dissuade her from divorce. On April 29, 1978, their daughter Noa was born in a Boston hospital. Miki allowed him to visit a few hours later, and in the years since never tried to prevent him from seeing his daughter. But there was no way back. Three months later, her PhD completed, Miki returned to Jerusalem. Once again Miki Weizmann, she was soon to remarry, and she went on to become one of the few women to serve as a director-general of a ministry. Their relations remained cordial; nearly forty years after they separated, Netanyahu appointed Miki, by now a respected scientist, to the prestigious and sensitive position of head of Israel's nuclear safety board.

Bibi spent the next four years between Boston and Jerusalem. Drifting between denial over the end of his first marriage and indecision over the relationship with Fleur, he left BCG and searched for work in Israel. He continued to tend to the ever-expanding commemoration of Yoni. In 1978, a collection of Yoni's letters was published. The book, which included letters from the time Yoni was sixteen and the family left for Philadelphia until just before his death, became an immediate bestseller, and it remains in print to this day. A staple of Zionist youth groups, it has endured in the age of social media as an inexhaustible source of motivational quotes on love of the Jewish state and the importance of service.

In June 1978, Netanyahu took part in a televised panel on Boston's WGBH station's *Advocates* show. In response to the question, "Should the United States support 'self-determination' for Palestinians in a Middle East peace settlement?," he said no. In ten minutes of serving as a "witness," he put forward what would become over the decades his classical arguments against the establishment of a Palestinian state, or, as he called it, "a PLO state."[5] He was presented as Benjamin Nitay, an economic consultant and an Israeli, not an American. In the recording, Bibi can be seen coming into his own as a public speaker, not just as Yoni's brother.

At twenty-eight, he spoke with the authority of a man much more senior in years, and his core argument was the same as it is today. The only obstacles to peace in the Middle East, he said, were the Arabs' determination to destroy Israel and the lack of democracy in the Arab world. He came furnished with a long list of well-rehearsed quotes proving this proposition and spoke with all the self-confidence—though not yet the swagger—that he would bring over the years to hundreds of similar appearances. Not yet tutored in the art of television, his movements are a bit jerky; he fails to hold the camera's eye and most of the time remains scowling. But he was already the emphatic and fluent performer. Comfortable in his skin, he didn't seem to feel out of place in the grand Faneuil Hall. Interestingly, he stressed his Israeli identity a number of times. For all intents and purposes, he was speaking on behalf of Israel. The topic of the discussion was Prime Minister Menachem Begin's policy toward the Palestinians, but he didn't mention Begin even once.

A T THE TIME of his return, the Israeli private sector wasn't a particularly welcoming job market for an applicant with a master's degree in business management but no real experience in management. Likud, with its more free-market-orientated approach, had been in power for over a year, but most of the national economy was still dominated by state-owned corporations, or those controlled by the Histadrut, a trade union federation. Privately owned companies were relatively small and mostly managed by the families who founded them. Friends and relatives helped set up job interviews for Bibi, but despite doing his research on prospective employers, most were looking for candidates with specific knowledge of their line of business.

Bibi experienced long and fruitless months searching for work. Benzion had recently reached retirement and finally returned with Tzila to Jerusalem. Bibi lived with them for a while, back in his small childhood house. His parents went through the same routines—Benzion closed in his study, working on his great book on the Spanish Inquisition, Tzila diligently typing his handwriting. Over the house hung the heavy air of Yoni's absence. A large bronze bust in his likeness dominated the living room. It was a claustrophobic and gloomy atmosphere and no way for a man nearly thirty to live. But his old friends still living in Jerusalem had families of their own by then, and he lacked the social graces to make new acquaintances. With Miki working long hours at Hebrew University, he spent many of his days taking care of baby Noa, in the forlorn hope of a reconciliation.

At meals in the Netanyahu home and when guests arrived, the main topic was criticism of Begin.

L IKUD's VICTORY DISMAYED the Carter administration. Jimmy Carter had already clashed with Begin's predecessor when he had departed from the assurances that Ford had given Rabin in 1975 that the United States would not pressure Israel into negotiating with the PLO or coordinate peace proposals in advance. Carter was the first US president to put the establishment of a Palestinian state at the center of his Middle East policy. Begin's election could only mean further clashes.

Begin was committed to "integrity of the homeland" and the Jewish people's inherent right to Judea and Samaria. A year before his election, during a tour of the West Bank, he had promised "there will be many Elon Mores," referring to one of the first settlements that the Labor government had initially tried to prevent but eventually authorized. "The new government will call upon young people to come and settle the land."[6]

There were also signs of pragmatism. Begin had given up his demand for the East Bank of the Jordan in 1965, as part of Herut's joint platform with the Liberals, in order to present a more moderate image. Likud's 1977 platform included a commitment to United Nations Resolutions 242 and 338, which spoke of Israeli pullbacks. To the two most senior posts in his new cabinet, instead of veteran hardliners he appointed Labor's Moshe Dayan as foreign minister and, as defense minister, Ezer Weizman, who was always more of a pragmatic opportunist than an ideologue.

As Begin arrived in Washington for his first meeting with Carter, both sides launched charm offensives. The two leaders in their public speeches praised each other as men of faith. Flattering Begin's sense of Jewish pride, the first-ever fully kosher state dinner was held at the White House in his honor. But beneath the bonhomie of their first meeting, the differences between Carter and Begin were deep. The sole ray of light was Carter's insistence that in return for Israeli pullbacks, the Arabs would have to agree to peace and full diplomatic relations.

Before heading to Washington, Begin had sent Dayan on a secret mission to meet Egypt's vice president in Morocco, in part to avoid Carter's Palestinian initiative. Begin was not prepared to make concessions on historic Eretz Yisrael. Sinai was another matter. The secret messages had a positive result. In the Egyptian parliament in November, Egyptian president Anwar al-Sadat said he was "ready to go to the ends of the earth, and even to [the Israelis'] home, to the Knesset itself, to argue with them, in order to prevent one Egyptian soldier from being wounded." Begin issued an invitation, and ten days later Sadat landed at Ben Gurion Airport.

After thirty years of bitter enmity and four bloody wars, the leader of the largest Arab nation had arrived in the Jewish state, and it was a prime minister from the nationalist Revisionist wing of Israeli politics who was making peace. It would take another difficult eighteen months, including seventeen dramatic days of negotiations at Camp David, until the peace agreement was signed on the White House lawn on March 29, 1979.

Carter and Sadat's joint insistence that the peace agreement also include a deal on the Palestinians almost scuppered the talks. In the end, Begin agreed at Camp David to "a framework for peace in the Middle East," a general outline for future talks with the Palestinians and Israeli concessions that was much less specific than the framework for the Israeli-Egyptian agreement. That part of the deal was meaningless. Ultimately, both sides got what they wanted: Sadat restored Egyptian sovereignty to the entire Sinai Peninsula, including the dismantlement of Begin's cherished settlements there, and Begin got a full peace deal with Egypt, separate from the empty promises on the Palestinian issue. It was a "cold peace," but Israel no longer faced a powerful enemy on its southern border. Egypt became another American ally in the Middle East.

Many Likudniks saw Begin's decision as an ideological betrayal, and only 29 out of the party's 43 MKs voted in favor of the Camp David Accords; the overall vote was 84 in favor and 13 opposed. Some Likud members broke away to form the far-right Tehiya (Revival) party.

Since the Netanyahus had never joined Likud under Begin, they had no option to leave, but they certainly were not in favor of the agreement with Egypt. Benzion had feared since 1967 that the Labor government would squander the territorial gains of the Six-Day War. Now, in doing so, Begin had proved himself an unworthy successor to Jabotinsky.

Moshe Arens, who remained in Likud, was an opponent as well. An occasional visitor to the Netanyahu home, he later remembered that they agreed that "Israel should have held out for a compromise on Sinai," adding, "It was clear that Egypt could not fight another war and there was no need for Begin to give up every grain of sand. Benzion believed that and Bibi shared his beliefs."

Netanyahu has always been wary of either endorsing or criticizing the agreement with Egypt in public. By the time he entered politics it was consensus. In his book *A Place Among the Nations* he tiptoes around the subject, merely observing that "no winning side in history" had ever retreated from all the territory it captured in war.[7] Twenty years later, Benzion still could not abide Begin, blaming him in an interview of "losing all this massive territory and massive power we had without receiving anything substantial in return. They don't want a real peace with us. Egypt hasn't yet changed its fundamental position. Today they still don't want a strong Jewish state here and are trying to obstruct us in every possible way. So the peace with Egypt is an incomplete peace."[8]

Neither Netanyahu, father or son, lent their names to the movement opposing withdrawal from Sinai. At the time, they needed the endorsement of the country's leadership for the first international conference of the "Jonathan Institute." Remaining quiet paid off. In July 1979, the Israeli establishment gathered at the Jerusalem Hilton, not just the Likud government, but also Labor luminaries—President Efraim Katzir, Peres, Rabin. Begin came, too, for once putting aside his differences with Benzion. In his speech at the conference's opening session, he called him "the father of our nation's and mankind's hero."[9]

High-level international conferences were a rare occurrence in Israel at the time. It was a stellar lineup of politicians, academics, pundits, and military and intelligence veterans. The star speaker was former CIA director George H. W. Bush, who had dropped out of the Republican presidential primaries a few weeks earlier and would soon be selected as Ronald Reagan's running mate. Bush lectured on "The U.S. and the Fight Against International Terrorism." A majority of the speakers were on the right politically, including both Republicans from the United States and members of conservative parties in Europe. The few Democrats who attended from the United States were "Cold War liberals," such as Senator Henry Jackson, who spoke on "Terrorism as a Weapon in International Politics."

The message of the conference was clear. Terrorists were on no account to be regarded as "freedom fighters," or as representing any form of legitimate cause. Neither were they acting on their own accord. Speaker after speaker claimed that the Palestinian organizations were part of a global network orchestrated by the Soviet Union, which assisted them with arms and training. The commander of Israeli military intelligence, Major General Shlomo Gazit, claimed the existence of terrorist training camps on Soviet territory. The message generated headlines in major American newspapers at a time when many in both American political camps were criticizing the Carter administration for going soft on the Soviet threat.

The conference was a harbinger of themes that would serve Netanyahu well ideologically and politically throughout his career. He has always had a tendency to see security threats to Isreal as part of a wider campaign, and to draw every conflict into very stark sides of good and evil. The conference brought together those who shared these views, not only from Israel, but also from America and Europe. There were no dissenting or alternative views, no Muslims or other non-Western voices.

Bibi, at twenty-nine, didn't yet have an impressive enough CV to be one of the speakers. But as executive director of the conference, he was everywhere, meeting and greeting the VIPs. A childhood friend who had been hired to work on the conference staff later remembered bumping into him. "Don't call me Bibi," he was warned sternly. "I'm Binyamin."

It was an impressive event, furnishing Bibi with contacts that would come in use over the years. In the minds of a small band of Netanyahu loyalists, it was "a turning point" in the struggle against terror. Conspiracy theorists reference it online as an early coming together of the devious cabal of neo-con warmongers. Both views, of course, are highly exaggerated. The Jonathan Institute did not become the prestigious think tank that Benzion envisioned. The conference's lectures and papers were collected in a book, with an introduction by Bibi, and over the years he has referred to it as "my book," but there was no follow-up for another five years, until the second and last conference. Perhaps if Netanyahu had thrown himself into fundraising, it could have become the sort of institution his father dreamed of; but as the illustrious guests departed, Bibi was focused elsewhere. He had finally found a job: he would be marketing director of a furniture manufacturer. To make things better, Fleur had agreed to move to Israel, where she had found a job at a high-tech firm.

The first few months of the 1980s were promising. Bibi threw himself into his new job, computerizing the company's distribution system and launching an American-style incentives scheme for the sales reps. With a live-in girlfriend, who had few acquaintances or distractions in a new country, he was also enjoying life with Fleur at his side. Had the timing been a bit different, or Netanyahu more inclined to "civilian" life, thirty could have been his age of settling down to a business executive's career, making a success of marriage, and we may never have heard of Benjamin Netanyahu the politician.

But 1980s Israel still wasn't that place. Israelis were skeptical of cheap, mass-produced furniture. It wasn't just the old-fashioned customers. Israel was still paying for massive rearmament after the Yom Kippur War, and the first Likud government was hapless in its attempts to transition from the socialist economy its predecessors had built. Inflation sky-rocketed. By 1979, it stood at an annual rate of 111 percent; in 1980, it was 133 percent. Israelis, if they were purchasing furniture at all, were buying it to last. Instead of expanding his efficient distribution system, Netanyahu found himself dealing with irate customers who demanded to speak to the manager when their new cupboards fell apart. Private companies in Israel were permanently on the brink.

Israeli life remained spartan. For anyone moving there from a Western country in the early 1980s, the dip in the material quality of life was immediately noticeable. Israelis lived in hot, cramped apartments without air-conditioning. On television there was one black-and-white channel, and a years-long waiting list for telephone lines. In the fetid grocery markets you could choose white or yellow cheese. In Jerusalem and Tel Aviv, there were only a handful of semi-decent restaurants, and the department stores were still making a brisk trade in kibbutz-style khaki. Israel was no place for anyone who was used to the basic creature comforts of Western middle-class existence.

Fleur didn't last long, and Bibi wasn't prepared to commit. By 1981, she was back in Boston. His CEO was sympathetic, allowing him to spend a week each month overseas, but Bibi's enthusiasm for the job was waning. After a few months of flying back and forth, he finally broke down. In May 1981, Fleur and Bibi married and returned to Jerusalem together. For a while calm was restored, but Netanyahu soon began searching for a job that would allow them to live in the United States. When the offer came in early 1982, he didn't think twice.

Oⁿ June 6, 1982, Israel embarked on Operation Peace for Galilee, a major invasion of Lebanon and offensive against the Palestinian and Syrian forces there. It would be known as Israel's First Lebanon War. As in the Yom Kippur War, Sayeret Matkal temporarily shifted from its special operations role, and teams of its officers and soldiers, along with hundreds of Matkal's reservists, joined the armored columns as infantry units. Captain Binyamin Netanyahu didn't join them this time.

Major Omer Bar-Lev was at Matkal's temporary base in Damour, by the makeshift landing strip south of Beirut, as a helicopter landed. "Bibi got off the chopper with two Americans, wearing suits. He saw me and grinned, 'Hi Omer.' I shouted back, 'What hi? Why aren't you in uniform? Why haven't you signed out a gun and kit?'"

Netanyahu wasn't reporting for duty. Unexpectedly, he had been offered a role that would allow him to do what he did best: he would be an Israeli on the American stage. He had already gone on to a new phase allowing him to utilize his skills in the service of Israel while pursuing his own aspirations.

13

Prime Minister in Ten Years' Time

After making peace with Egypt, Menachem Begin took a sharp right turn. Having given up the last grain of Sinai sand, perhaps he just couldn't contemplate further concessions. Or perhaps his capitulation to Egypt's demands in Sinai had been planned in advance so that he could avoid any retreat from the West Bank. In any case, Begin's new nationalist stance shaped legislation, policy, and his cabinet.

In October 1979, ill and exhausted, Moshe Dayan left his post as foreign minister. The Speaker of the Knesset, Yitzhak Shamir, a hardliner who had opposed the peace agreement with Egypt, was appointed foreign minister in his place. In May 1980, Ezer Weizman resigned as defense minister in protest over new settlements being built in the West Bank. Agriculture Minister Ariel Sharon, who had pushed for the new settlements, demanded the post, but Begin hesitated. He remarked to a colleague, "If Sharon were defense minister, he might well send tanks to surround the prime minister's office."[1] Eventually he relented and named Sharon to the post in August 1981.

In June 1980, the Knesset passed the Jerusalem Law, spelling out that all of Jerusalem was a united city under Israeli sovereignty. It was a declarative act that only underlined the situation that had existed in Jerusalem since the Six-Day War, but it was also a message to the world.

A much more explosive message came eleven months later, when eight Israeli Air Force F-16 jets bombed "Osirak," an Iraqi nuclear reactor ten miles southeast of Baghdad. Begin had lived his entire political career traumatized by the Holocaust, and his fear of a nuclear weapon in the hands of Israel's enemies was deep-rooted. Under the "Begin Doctrine," no Arab country was to be allowed to develop an atomic bomb.

On June 30, 1981, Likud scraped past the Labor Alignment to achieve a second election victory for Begin. Israel's politics had truly shifted. Begin formed a narrow coalition of right-wing, religious, and Mizrahi parties, with Sharon and Shamir as senior ministers.

The Reagan administration in the United States was furious over the Iraqi reactor bombing, accusing Israel of using weapons supplied for "self-defense" in an operation far from its borders and going behind the back of its ally. The administration froze the supply of further F-16s— the standard punishment over the next couple of years whenever Israel stepped out of line.

Begin had high hopes for the new president and a more favorable attitude after Carter's censoriousness. Ronald Reagan was instinctively pro-Israel and remained so throughout his presidency, though his friendship was severely tried. During the US presidential campaign, he said that the 1979 Islamic Revolution in Iran had "increased Israel's value as perhaps the only remaining strategic asset in the region on which the United States can truly rely."[2]

But Reagan had decided to sell Saudi Arabia five Airborne Warning and Control System (AWACS) aircraft. The administration insisted that selling AWACS to the Saudis would bolster their ally as a bulwark against both Iranian and Soviet influence in the region. Israel claimed that the advanced technology would render its air force transparent to the Arabs. Begin mobilized Israel's supporters on Capitol Hill as well as American Jewish organizations.

On September 9, 1981, he arrived in Washington for his first meeting with Reagan. The new president surprised the Israelis by agreeing immediately to Begin's request for the countries to sign a strategic cooperation agreement. Reagan's disposition quickly soured, however, when news filtered back of Begin lobbying against the AWACS deal in his meetings in Congress. In the run-up to the Senate vote, Reagan sternly warned, "It is not the business of other nations to make United States foreign policy."[3]

In December 1981, in another nationalist gesture, the Knesset passed the Golan Heights Law, extending Israeli sovereignty to the territory captured from Syria in 1967. The Reagan administration, infuriated by the unilateral move, suspended the strategic alliance in retribution. When the US ambassador to Israel, Sam Lewis, went to deliver the message to Begin, Begin was furious. "What kind of language is this—punishing Israel?" Begin demanded. "Are we a vassal state? Are we a banana republic? Are we fourteen-year-old boys that have to have our knuckles slapped if we misbehave?"[4]

Making matters worse, before Lewis could relay Begin's message to the White House, the media was reporting it. "Boy, that guy Begin sure does make it hard to be his friend," Reagan observed.[5]

Israel's chief supporter in the US administration was Secretary of State Al Haig. Major critics included Secretary of Defense Caspar Weinberger, White House Chief of Staff James Baker, and Vice President George H. W. Bush, whose invitation as guest speaker to the Jonathan Institute conference in 1979 hadn't made him a fan of Likud. To counter their influence on Reagan's Middle East policy, Begin departed from his policy of leaving diplomacy to professional diplomats of the old Labor establishment and appointed his own man as ambassador in Washington.

PROFESSOR MOSHE ARENS was an old-school Revisionist, embodying the Jabotinskean values of *hadar*—decorum and Jewish nationalism. He had been active in the movement since his teens in New York. He moved to Israel in 1957 after completing his engineering studies at MIT and the California Institute of Technology, becoming a professor of aeronautics at Technion in Haifa and then chief engineer at the Israel Aircraft Industry. He became a Likud MK in 1973, and Begin offered him the Defense Ministry after Weizman's resignation. Arens, who always lacked burning political ambition, turned down the second most powerful position in Israel because he opposed the agreement with Egypt. He didn't want to be the minister in charge of dismantling the Sinai settlements. In early 1982, Begin asked him to go to Washington.

Arens was the first former US citizen to be appointed Israel's ambassador in Washington. Begin wanted him there with his American accent and connections, rallying support for Likud policies in a way that a professional diplomat couldn't. Beneath his unflappable and always courteous exterior, Arens was an unrelenting hawk. He was to be not only Israel's ambassador but also Begin's personal envoy.

Before leaving for the United States, Arens needed a deputy head of mission as his number two in Washington. His first choice turned him down. Then he remembered Benzion Netanyahu's son who had made such an impression three years ago organizing the Jonathan Institute conference. The job interview, which took place in the lobby of a Jerusalem hotel, was short and conducted in English. Arens believed that diplomacy in Reagan's America "didn't call for a Metternich, but public-relations expertise. I saw how our interlocutors in Washington were more impressed when we gave good performances on television." Arens wasn't looking for a wingman in the corridors of the White House and Congress. He wanted a number-two man who could tour the TV studios and charm the pundits.

Netanyahu didn't hesitate, saying yes the moment Arens made the offer without waiting to notify the furniture company. He'd had enough of civilian life as a sales executive. Deputy chief of mission (DCM) at the Washington embassy was a dream job. It would allow him to live with Fleur in the country she preferred while at the same time serving his country.

Arens left for Washington in April, arriving at what he described as "a low point in the US-Israeli relationship." Bibi had to first clear his bureaucratic hurdles. The Foreign Ministry's union objected to outside hires filling professional diplomatic posts. Netanyahu's appointment had been approved by Foreign Minister Shamir and they couldn't block it forever, but they could delay the employment and accreditation process. Bibi's already low opinion of Israeli diplomats from his Boston *hasbara* days hardened. It would take three months for his affairs to be settled.

On June 24, he gave up his US citizenship, as required by all Israeli diplomats. War had broken out, and he was needed to face the American media onslaught.

THE RABIN GOVERNMENT had supplied arms to the Christian militias fighting the Palestinians in Lebanon in 1976. In 1981, as fighting intensified, Begin took Israel's involvement up a notch, ordering air strikes to help the embattled Christians. The Palestinians bombarded Israeli towns in the Galilee. In May 1982, Sharon traveled to Washington to brief Haig and the Pentagon. He left them with little doubt of his plans to invade Lebanon. Haig urged restraint, but Sharon and Begin were just looking for the right opportunity.

On June 4, following the attempted assassination of Israel's ambassador in London, the cabinet authorized Operation Peace for Galilee.

The operation was presented as limited to forty kilometers (twenty-five miles) from Israel's border and focused on destroying the Palestinians' military infrastructure. The Israeli cabinet and the White House were assured that the IDF would not enter Beirut and that it would avoid confrontation with the Syrians. But Sharon and Begin had much grander plans. The IDF exceeded the forty-kilometer line in the first days of the Lebanon war, not only mopping up PLO fighters but also engaging the Syrians on the ground and in the air.

Arens was fighting his own battle in Washington. Reagan and Haig were in Europe, meeting North Atlantic Treaty Organization (NATO) allies. Bush and Baker were running the show, threatening sanctions against Israel. Jeane Kirkpatrick, the US ambassador to the United Nations, one of Israel's staunchest allies in Reagan's cabinet, met with Arens secretly. "Bush has taken charge and only God knows what he's going to do," she warned.[6]

On June 11, Reagan and Haig returned to Washington. All talk of punishing Israel was put on hold until Begin arrived for a crucial meeting ten days later.

The exchange between the two leaders in private was testy. But Haig, who was becoming increasingly isolated in the administration, won that day. Publicly at least, the administration was supporting Israel. To the reporters outside Reagan said, "All of us share a common understanding." The headline the next morning in the *Washington Post* was "REAGAN BACKS ISRAEL."

With the IDF closing its siege on Beirut, Sharon and Begin ignored entreaties from the Reagan administration and its senior envoys on the ground, Philip Habib and Morris Draper, who were frantically trying to achieve a ceasefire.

On July 25, Haig, who had been frozen out of decision making by a cabal of senior aides led by Baker, tendered his resignation. The accusation that he had somehow "greenlighted" Israel's invasion was one of the reasons they pushed him out. The previous evening, he had warned Arens that Reagan was "under massive pressure" to act against Israel. With Haig's departure, Israel had lost its chief backer in the administration. His replacement, George Shultz, was an unknown quantity. But the fact that he had been president of the Bechtel Group, which did a lot of business in Saudi Arabia, was not encouraging.

Netanyahu arrived in Washington in July, immediately joining Arens's efforts to stem the tide. The Israeli embassy was largely out of the loop.

Sharon was directing the army's moves, only partially updating Begin and the cabinet. In August, Begin complained, "I know about all the operations, sometimes before, sometimes after."[7]

Often their first indication of developments on the battlefield came when Arens was summoned to the State Department to respond to reports from Habib and Draper. Arens strenuously defended Israel's latest action before rushing back to the embassy to try to gather, over the phone, what had happened and why. In some cases he came under friendly fire from Jerusalem for acting on his own initiative. "We'd thank you if you would send your thoughts to us first," cabled Begin after Arens discussed possible ceasefire terms.[8]

In this tense period in US-Israeli relations, the two men in charge of the embassy had between them just three months of diplomatic experience. What Arens and Netanyahu did have was their sense of Israeli and American identity and a burning desire to prove that they were equals to their administration interlocutors.

Israel's bombardment of Palestinian-controlled neighborhoods in Beirut intensified. Habib, inside the city, tried to broker an agreement for the departure of Palestinian fighters. On July 19, after an angry conversation with Sharon, who refused to allow supplies in, Habib was taken ill. Arens was summoned, but he was out of town. Netanyahu went instead. It was his first high-level diplomatic meeting. "Sharon behaved like a bull in a china shop," rumbled Undersecretary of State Lawrence Eagleburger. He told Netanyahu that the Israelis must treat Habib with the respect the president's envoy deserved. Netanyahu, the novice diplomat, was a messenger-boy being reprimanded by a man two decades his senior.[9]

As the bloody summer in Lebanon wore on, it seemed American diplomacy had achieved a breakthrough. Yasser Arafat agreed to the departure of his fighters from Beirut. On August 25, eight hundred US Marines arrived as part of an international force overseeing the evacuation of fifteen thousand Palestinians, led by Yasser Arafat, into further exile. For a moment it seemed that Israel had achieved its objectives—the PLO was denied its last base in a country bordering Israel. Bashir Gemayel, the leader of the Lebanese Phalanges Party and Israel's ally, was elected as Lebanon's new president. It was a brief illusion.

On September 1, Begin was taking a belated vacation when Ambassador Lewis arrived at his hotel with an urgent message. Reagan was about to launch his own peace plan: Israel would withdraw from Lebanon and enter talks with Jordan and the Palestinians, resulting in full autonomy for the Palestinians in the West Bank and Gaza Strip as part of a Jordanian federation. Begin was stunned. His intention had been to push the Palestinians far away and off the international agenda.

For the Israeli embassy in the United States it was an embarrassment. They had failed to detect a plan in the offing. Arens had returned to Israel for consultations two days earlier, assuring the media that all was well in the relationship. Netanyahu was left to prepare an assessment of the new plan. He had been in Washington for less than two months, and was still without reliable sources in the administration. He counseled waiting for the latest American initiative to blow over, just as like the previous ones. It proved to be a shrewd assessment, but Begin totally disregarded it. Instead he lost no time in angrily rejecting the Reagan Plan.

Arens returned to Washington with orders to nip the Reagan Plan in the bud. They were soon overtaken by events. On September 14, the newly elected president of Lebanon, Gemayel, was killed by a bomb planted by a Syrian agent at Phalangist headquarters. Israel defied Washington's exhortations and sent the IDF into West Beirut, where Palestinian fighters remained in breach of the evacuation deal. The job of going after these fighters, who were sheltering in Palestinian refugee camps, was given to the Phalangists.

On September 16, Arens and Netanyahu were summoned for another dressing-down by Eagleburger. The undersecretary accused the Israelis of having misled the administration, saying, "Israel's credibility has been severely damaged here in Washington." Arens responded bluntly. "I'm not sure you guys know what you're doing," he said. The administration's claim that Israel had been untruthful, he said, was "fabricated." Following his lead, Netanyahu urged Eagleburger to take the claim that Israel's actions were "contrary to assurances" out of the State Department's daily briefing. "If there's still time, I would suggest you delete this, particularly the Draper business. Otherwise you'll give us no choice but to defend our credibility by setting the record straight. We'll end up in a shooting war with each other, and that's not good for either of us," Netanyahu said.[10]

Arens was pleased with his number two's forceful interjection, adding that Israel could reveal the transcript of the conversation between Begin and Draper. "You may leave us no choice."

Unbeknownst to them, as they were meeting in Washington, Phalangist fighters were entering the Sabra and Shatila refugee camps in Lebanon. A thirty-six-hour killing spree, in which at least seven hundred Palestinians (some estimates go as high as three thousand) were brutally murdered, had begun. As news of the massacre began filtering out of Beirut, and photographs of piles of corpses were screened around the world, a shocked Reagan said, "All people of decency must share our outrage and revulsion."[11] He stopped short of directly blaming Israel.

Arens and Netanyahu were called to meet a shocked Shultz, who relayed the administration's "demand" that "you get your forces out of West Beirut!" It was Rosh Hashanah, the Jewish new year, and under any other circumstance, summoning an Israeli diplomat on that day would have been unthinkable. Arens responded that he was "horrified, moved and touched by this event just as you are. If anything, even more so because of our proximity to the event." He blamed the Lebanese Army for not controlling West Beirut and said the massacre had been carried out by Phalangists who had "entered the camps from the east." He added: "At 2 o'clock we became aware of what was happening and immediately moved in and got the Phalangists out."[12]

What Arens may not have known when he met with Shultz was that the Phalangists had gone into the camps at Israel's urging to "mop up" Palestinian fighters, and that from its early hours, Israeli officers and journalists had been receiving news of the ongoing carnage and updating senior generals and ministers. It took a day and a half for the IDF to order the Phalangists out. Netanyahu remained silent throughout the meeting.

Eleven days after the massacre, the Marines returned to Beirut as part of a multinational peacekeeping force that included France and Italy. It was an ill-fated mission. On April 18, 1983, an explosion tore apart the US embassy, killing 63, including 17 Americans. On October 23, an explosives-laden truck smashed into the Marines barracks. A simultaneous attack was carried out on the French base. Altogether, 241 Americans, 58 French, and 6 Lebanese were killed. The attacks were carried out on orders of the Iranian regime. The perpetrators were operatives of a shadowy new Shi'a organization, Hezbollah. Four months later, Reagan ordered the Marines to leave Beirut.

Relations between Washington and Jerusalem were on the mend. The targeting of US troops in Beirut had convinced many Americans that they were essentially on the same side as Israel. A key figure in the rapidly improving relationship was Shultz, whom Arens had subjected to a personal charm offensive. Shultz proved amenable not only to frequent meetings with Arens, but also to social get-togethers. Shultz and his wife, Helena, frequently met with Moshe and Muriel Arens outside office hours. Many in the administration believed the mild-mannered Arens to be a likely successor to Begin and were interested in getting to know him. Sending Israeli American diplomats to Washington had proved an effective strategy, even before Bibi captivated the capital's media elite.

I N HIS FIRST days in Washington, Netanyahu, with the help of the embassy's press officer, had compiled a detailed list of the main movers in the town's punditocracy—the senior White House and State Department correspondents, bureau chiefs, and foreign policy commentators. Within weeks he had met all of them and had begun compiling a similar list of New York's media elite, whom he cultivated on frequent trips there. Israel was rarely out of the headlines, and Bibi was always available for a quote, or some intriguing insight from "a senior Israeli official." Young, personable, and oozing self-confidence, he quickly became a fixture on news shows.

Ever a perfectionist, he worked assiduously on his televisual skills, taking lessons from professional coaches and spending weekends rehearsing at home with Fleur using hired video cameras. He learned how to keep his eye fixed on the lens while presenting the left side of his face, the side without the scarred lip. He practiced his delivery of terse and soundbite-heavy sentences and memorized the leading anchors' first names. He even learned the mystery of male makeup. His favorite venue was ABC's *Nightline*. The late-news show, presented by Ted Koppel, had started three years earlier during the Iran hostage crisis. America's latest Middle East disaster in Lebanon was a natural subject for extensive coverage. Bibi established a close relationship with Koppel and his producers. One media monitoring organization keeping count of interviewees claimed that in the 1980s Netanyahu was *Nightline*'s most-interviewed "terrorism expert."[13]

Bibi's practice of making frequent appearances on the kinds of shows that were watched within the Capital Beltway, including *The MacNeil/ Lehrer Report* (later *NewsHour*) and *Evans and Novak*, where he wasn't assured of an easy ride, yet still braved the grilling, was rapidly opening doors for him in Washington. He was gaining access in particular to a new generation of Republican politicians, thinkers, and officials who were instinctively more pro-Israel than the old establishment and more receptive to the free-market, antisocialist Likudniks. Many of them were Jewish.

While American Jews for nearly a century have overwhelmingly voted Democrat, Reagan came close in 1980 to beating Carter among Jewish voters (39–45 percent). During his presidency, a growing number of Jews, including many who formed the backbone of the nascent neoconservative movement, began to gain influence in the Republican establishment. Their parents may have thrilled at the thought of Jewish socialist pioneers building the Jewish state, but the capitalist Bibi Netanyahu was their kind of Israeli.

With the glamorous Fleur at his side, Bibi swiftly became the darling of the new wave of Reagan Republicans. Colleagues at the embassy complained that the deputy chief of mission ran his own social diary, detached from the diplomatic demands of the embassy's calendar. Arens, however, gave Bibi the backing to plow his own furrow. They were both outsiders to the diplomatic corps and enjoyed ignoring the professionals, who they knew weren't Likud voters anyway. Arens's conviction that mass media *hasbara* was the way to conduct diplomacy had been strengthened. Visual news images seemed to influence Reagan more than anything else.

During a meeting with Shamir in August 1982, Reagan spoke of being deeply moved by a photograph of a Lebanese baby girl who had lost her arms in an Israeli bombing raid. She had come to symbolize the war for him. He put the photograph, which had been taken by the UPI news agency, on his desk during the meeting, telling Shamir and Arens, "Listen, this has got to stop."[14] At Netanyahu's request, the IDF tracked down the family and discovered that it was actually a boy in the photograph. He still had both his arms; in the photo, one of them had been broken and bandaged, creating the impression of amputation. UPI subsequently corrected the caption, and the White House was notified. Netanyahu would later use embellished versions of this story to demonstrate how poorly the Israeli government dealt with propaganda.[15]

Begin initially believed that Israel was blameless for the Sabra and Shatila massacre. He thought the world holding Israel responsible for "Arabs killing Arabs" was "a blood libel." But public pressure, culminating in a mass protest of hundreds of thousands in Tel Aviv, forced him to set up a national commission of inquiry. The Kahan Commission delivered its report in February 1983, ruling that Sharon as defense minister bore "indirect responsibility," as he had ignored warnings that the Phalangists were likely to carry out mass murders in the camp. The commission recommended Sharon be removed from his post.

Bibi thought Sharon had been treated shamefully. Many years later, he said that saying Sharon "should have anticipated what others would do is a very, very surreal judgment."[16] As a civil servant, he couldn't express this view publicly. But he read in advance and approved a newspaper column his brother Iddo wrote criticizing Sharon's removal. Meanwhile, Sharon's fall created more immediate problems for Bibi. Begin asked Arens to return to Israel immediately to replace Sharon. This time, Arens relented and took the appointment as defense minister. His term as ambassador had ended after less than a year.

Arens's departure could have meant the end of Netanyahu's diplomatic career as well. The new ambassador in Washington would be unlikely to allow him the same latitude. As a political appointee, he could be removed at short notice. He began lobbying to become Arens's successor.

The idea of appointing a thirty-three-year-old with no political standing and only six months of relevant experience to Israel's most sensitive diplomatic posting may have seemed absurd, but Netanyahu believed he was the best man for the job. He was convinced he was destined for even greater things and had little time to waste. Neither was he hiding his ambition. During that period, a senior IDF officer studying at Georgetown met him on a flight from Washington to New York and had a startling conversation. "I asked Bibi on the flight, 'Where do you see yourself in ten years?' Without hesitation he answered, 'As prime minister.' 'Come on,' I said. 'You'll have to first overcome the Likud dinosaurs like Shamir, and then the Likud princes.' Bibi answered, 'The dinosaurs are dying out and the princes are too blue-blooded to fight for the crown. I'll get there.'"

Netanyahu had his supporters, particularly among his new friends in Washington. One of them, William Safire, actually wrote, in his *New York Times* column,

The Israelis should also make certain their new ambassador to the U.S., replacing Mr. Arens, is not only tough-minded and bilingual but also able to make full use of access to the U.S. public that our television offers. The current number two man in the embassy, Benjamin Netanyahu (brother of the slain hero of Entebbe), would be a superb surprise choice: a former soldier and U.S.-trained management consultant, he kept his cool and operated effectively in Washington during the worst moments of the Beirut period. He is 33 and not a professional diplomat; in this curious period, those are both assets.[17]

Arens endorsed his protégé's candidacy, but the appointment of Israel's ambassador to the United States is made jointly by the prime minister and foreign minister. Begin by then was increasingly detached from the daily business of government. Shamir, who had always been underwhelmed by Bibi, thought the idea absurd. Israel's ambassador to France, Meir Rosenne, a veteran of thirty years' service in the diplomatic corps, who, unlike most of his colleagues, also held right-wing views, got the job. Netanyahu began casting around for a new one.

14

If He Had a Sense of Humor, He'd Be a 10

For the six months between Arens's departure and Rosenne's arrival, Netanyahu was in charge of the Washington embassy. It was a relatively calm period after the previous year's Lebanon invasion. Effort went into planning another White House meeting for the prime minister. Begin's visit to the United States in November 1982 had been cut short when news arrived of the death of his wife, Aliza, before his scheduled meeting with Reagan. Begin was fading. Broken in body and spirit, he refused to set a date, and the 1983 visit was canceled.

Bibi took full advantage of groundwork laid by Arens, replacing him in the relationship with Shultz. It was no ordinary feat for the temporary ambassador of a small nation to arrange frequent meetings with a secretary of state twenty-nine years his senior. But Netanyahu had much more than an American accent to set him apart from other foreign envoys. As a graduate of MIT's Sloan School of Management, he shared lingo with Shultz, who had been a professor of economics at Sloan.

As US Marines became targets in Lebanon, views within the administration differed sharply over how to deal with the growing threat of terrorism, and Netanyahu succeeded in inserting himself in Shultz's orbit as an unofficial advisor. It was a blurring of the lines between foreign diplomat and American insider, at which Netanyahu was adept.

O N AUGUST 20, 1983, Begin addressed the cabinet, saying, simply, "I cannot go on." He never gave reasons for his resignation. For months he had barely been seen in public, closed away in his office. Broken by the death of Aliza, at home he was constantly tormented by protesters outside against the Lebanon War. The protesters held up signs with the number of Israeli soldiers killed.

As Jabotinsky's successor, he had led the Revisionists for forty years. He had led them underground and through the wilderness of opposition all the way to power.

Begin had no obvious successor. Arens was not a Knesset member and therefore could not become prime minister. He lacked the desire anyway. Two men vied for leadership. One of them was the housing minister, David Levy, a member of the generation of young Mizrahi activists who had arrived in Israel after independence from Arab lands, in his case Morocco. They had joined Likud seeking recognition and respect. The other was Foreign Minister Yitzhak Shamir, who, like Begin, had been a commander of underground Revisionist fighters during the British Mandate.

Shamir, supported by Arens, won the Likud Central Committee vote, becoming Israel's seventh prime minister and the third leader of the Revisionist movement. Levy remained a perennial and frustrated runner-up.

Originally a member of IZL, Shamir had joined the breakaway Lohamei Herut Yisrael (LHY, Fighters for the Freedom of Israel) in 1941 rather than give up fighting the British during World War II. As LHY military chief, he had commanded operations that even many Jews considered acts of terror. In September 1948 he had ordered the assassination of a Swedish count, Folke Bernadotte, a UN mediator trying to impose a ceasefire limiting the territory of the Jewish state. He later joined Mossad, where he founded the intelligence agency's special operations unit.

Shamir had joined Likud in the late 1960s to prevent Israeli pullbacks from the territories captured in the Six-Day War. There was always something of the underground commander and spy chief about him. He wasn't given to the grandiloquent rhetoric of Begin and was more ideologically rigid.

Shamir believed that Israel must brazen out any pressure to make territorial concessions. Playing on the old Arab threats to "throw the Jews into the sea," he coined a new phrase: "The sea is the same sea and the Arabs are the same Arabs." Netanyahu, whose views were closer to Shamir's than Begin's, would quote the phrase appreciatively, but

Shamir never held him in high regard. He saw Netanyahu as shallow, vain, self-destructive, and prone to pressure. Years later, he would say, "The sea is the same sea and Netanyahu is the same Netanyahu."[1]

Shamir succeeded in building a good relationship with Reagan, who appreciated the slightly gruff and straight-talking leader who, unlike Begin, didn't bore him with long speeches about the Bible.

Netanyahu wasn't in those meetings with Reagan. Ambassador Rosenne represented the embassy. Bibi was adjusting badly to being relegated once again to the number-two position. He showed Rosenne no respect and continued meeting with Shultz and making media appearances without updating him. He was skating on thin ice. Perhaps he believed that Arens's patronage still protected him, or maybe he was already considering a plunge into politics. He soon had his eye on another glittering prize.

The post of Israel's ambassador to the United Nations was about to become vacant. Bibi asked Arens to float the idea of appointing him to the post to Shamir, who remained foreign minister upon becoming prime minister. But Shamir already had his candidate for the job: Elyakim Rubinstein, a brilliant young lawyer, the Foreign Ministry's legal counsel and one of Shamir's closest advisers.

Ironically, the same ministry union that had tried to block Netanyahu's Washington posting the previous year helped him out this time by opposing Rubinstein's appointment on the grounds that he was too young (Rubinstein is two years older than Netanyahu) and lacked diplomatic experience. With an election coming up, Shamir had no time to deal with fractious diplomats, and the appointment of a new UN ambassador was postponed.

THE 1984 ELECTION delivered a stalemate. Despite the disaster in Lebanon and the economic meltdown, with annual inflation at 400 percent, Shimon Peres failed for the third time to win as Labor's leader. Neither Peres nor Shamir could form a majority coalition, and after weeks of negotiations they were forced into a national unity government, with each serving two years as prime minister. Peres took his turn first. Shamir returned full-time to the Foreign Ministry.

This was Bibi's chance. Peres still had a soft spot for Yoni's brother and failed to realize that ideologically Netanyahu was much closer to Shamir. As prime minister he had the prerogative to appoint a few ambassadors, and Shamir begrudgingly accepted his decision. So once again Peres played a key role in advancing the career of the man who would one day bring about his ultimate downfall.

Netanyahu celebrated his thirty-fifth birthday, now an ambassador in his own right, back in the city where as a child he had spent a miserable year learning English. He was returning in style. The ambassador's apartment was on the corner of Eighty-second Street and Fifth Avenue, opposite Central Park and the Metropolitan Museum of Art. Netanyahu immediately put in a request for renovations and spent the next few months living with Fleur at the Regency Hotel.

At the Permanent Mission of Israel to the United Nations, Bibi formed better relations than he had at the Washington embassy. The staff had undergone a tough period under a constant barrage of resolutions condemning Israel's war in Lebanon. Things were calmer now, and Netanyahu was not that interested anyway in the drudgery of the global organization's interminable bureaucracy. Now, with a budget of his own, he hired Israeli students to work on research. They monitored the airwaves and scoured the archives for damning quotes from Arab leaders to be used in his speeches. A large part of the mission's daily work went into planning the speeches, which typically went through five or six drafts, including Netanyahu's own extensive revisions, before he deemed them ready.

"Bibi didn't have much interest in the inner workings of the UN committees, but he saw his own speeches there as historic events," one former diplomat at the mission later said. "The fact-checking that went into them, the testing out of every idiom and nuance, were painstaking and went on for days. When he finally delivered the speech, he managed to give the impression that he was speaking almost off-the-cuff, as if the ideas had just occurred to him."

Netanyahu loved using visual aids on the podium. Once, when the Lebanese government moved to condemn Israel for its presence in their country, he screened a film of a secretary at the mission trying unsuccessfully to phone Lebanon. It ridiculed the idea that anyone controlled the country.

But Bibi saw New York as a much wider playground than just the United Nations. He still acted as if he were Israel's ambassador to the United States, communicating with senior Reagan administration officials and undertaking daily media and speaking engagements across the country.

Ambassador Netanyahu at his favorite spot—the podium at the
United Nations.

The consul general in New York is one of Israel's main diplomatic
positions, its envoy to the largest Jewish community anywhere at any
time in history. Netanyahu had little time for the consuls—Naphtali
Lavi, an old appointment of Dayan's, or his replacement, Moshe Yegar,
an old-school diplomat and historian. There could be no question who
served as Israel's senior representative in the city during Netanyahu's
three and a half years there.

Within weeks, Netanyahu was cutting a swath from UN headquarters
at Turtle Bay all the way to the *New York Times* newsroom and all the
major network studios, maintaining the friendships he had made during
his Washington posting and making new ones. He invested time in the
new cable news channels, flying to Atlanta to charm producers at CNN
headquarters. Netanyahu understood how the twenty-four-hour rolling
news cycle would reorder the news agenda and made plans to enhance his
media-monitoring operation accordingly.

From the launch of CNN's flagship interview show, *Larry King Live*,
in 1985, Netanyahu became one of its habitués. Not long before the
show's demise in 2010, King devoted an entire program to one last interview, waxing nostalgically, "We only go back, oh, almost thirty years."

King once said of Netanyahu that "on a scale of 1 to 10 as a great guest, he is an 8. If he had a sense of humor, he'd be a 10."² Netanyahu, in his methodical way, took the advice on board. His interview/speech prep must include jokes.

It didn't take long for Netanyahu's star to rise in New York society. A visiting Israeli settler leader later remembered having breakfast with Netanyahu while he lived in the Regency. "Jewish matrons kept coming up, complimenting him on his television performance and inquiring if he wasn't also an American citizen, because he should run for president one day." He also recalled Netanyahu ordering bacon and eggs and being told off by Fleur for doing so while sitting with a religious friend.

Fleur, of part-Jewish ancestry, wasn't considered Jewish by strict Orthodox law. This didn't concern the completely secular Netanyahu personally, but it would have been out of the question for a senior right-wing Israeli politician to be married to a non-Jew. Already preparing for Bibi's next career move, Fleur accepted that undergoing conversion to Judaism was part and parcel of being an Israeli political wife. For decades later, long after they divorced, there were those who claimed that she had undergone a non-Orthodox conversion and criticized Netanyahu for hypocrisy, when he nevertheless collaborated in coalitions with the anti-progressive ultra-Orthodox who would not consider her a Jew.

NEW YORK WAS Netanyahu's real introduction to the Jewish community. Having regarded American Jews, at least those he met as a teenager in Philadelphia, as weak and feckless, in New York he met the leaders of the big Jewish organizations, the mega-donors and political players.

It was shake-up time in major American Jewish organizations, especially those dealing with Israel. Getting used to Likud in power was not easy for Jews who had supported Israel during its long Labor period. For many, the heady right-wing cocktail of Likud and Reagan was difficult to stomach. Tom Dine, the savvy, liberal-leaning executive director of the American Israel Public Affairs Committee (AIPAC), courted Republican donors, who would make AIPAC both more right-wing and more influential. Netanyahu would become a star of AIPAC conferences, his presence assuring Jewish Republicans that the organization was on the right side.

The Conference of Presidents of Major American Jewish Organizations, another group shifting rightward, hired the hawkish Malcolm Hoenlein as chief executive in 1986. Hoenlein and Netanyahu became friends and collaborators. Hoenlein would introduce Netanyahu to many of the millionaires who would become his supporters.

IN EARLY 1986, allegations surfaced in Austrian media that former UN secretary general Kurt Waldheim, who was then running for Austrian president, had lied in his autobiography about his doings during the Nazi era. Israel's initial position was that it didn't believe Waldheim had been a war criminal. But as Jewish organizations and American politicians took up the case, Netanyahu joined in.

He made a great show of demanding that the United Nations reveal the file it held on Waldheim. However, the decision of Waldheim's successor, Secretary-General Javier Pérez de Cuéllar, to open the file was actually a result of a threat by Senator Alfonse D'Amato of New York to spend his reelection campaign bashing the United Nations. Ultimately, the UN file didn't hold a "smoking gun" on Waldheim, and he was elected Austrian president.

The Waldheim case was to have a profound effect on another ambassador, Ronald Lauder, scion of the Estée Lauder cosmetics empire and a Republican donor, who had been appointed by Reagan as ambassador to Austria. Lauder and Netanyahu closely cooperated on the Waldheim case. The allegations against Waldheim caused a resurgence of anti-Semitism in Austria, and Lauder, who described himself as having been a "three days a year Jew," reconnected with his roots and became involved in Jewish philanthropy and politics.

For the next two decades, until their falling-out, Ron and Bibi were close friends. Lauder introduced him to his own circle of New York millionaires, many of whom were not Jewish. That was when Bibi first met the brash real-estate entrepreneur Donald Trump, an old friend of Lauder's. Netanyahu and Trump were never close, but they remained in contact. Years later, Trump appeared on a list that Bibi compiled of millionaires upon whom he could rely for various favors.

A NOTHER IMPORTANT AMERICAN Jewish leader he met in those days was Rabbi Menachem Mendel Schneerson, the "Lubavitcher Rebbe," leader of Chabad Hasidism. Schneerson was ideologically opposed to secular Zionism but nevertheless supported Jewish statehood, and senior Israeli politicians frequently visited him in New York. His views on the Israeli-Arab conflict were ultra-hawkish; he was adamantly opposed to any territorial concessions. During the Yom Kippur War, he suggested that Israel continue its push on the Syrian front all the way to Damascus.

One of Netanyahu's former Matkal soldiers, a secular kibbutznik who had become a Chabad Hasid, took him to see Schneerson in Brooklyn in late 1984, shortly after Netanyahu's appointment to the United Nations. He arrived at 770 Eastern Parkway after midnight on the festival of Simchat Torah marking the end of the annual cycle of Torah readings. Thousands of Hasidim were waiting for the eighty-two-year-old Rebbe to start the ritual dancing with Torah scrolls. Netanyahu introduced himself, and Schneerson, to everyone's amazement, stopped to talk to him for over half an hour. According to one Hasid there, the Rebbe told Netanyahu that in each of Israel's wars, politicians had squandered the military gains, and that "when the *goyim* [non-Jews] come and demand parts of Eretz Yisrael, we must stand forcefully and deny them." Netanyahu frequently brings up another message of Schneerson's he remembers from that night: "You will go into a house of lies [referring to the United Nations]. Remember that in a hall of perfect darkness, if you light one small candle, its precious light will be seen from afar, by everyone. Your mission is to light a candle for truth and for the Jewish people."[3]

At the time, Schneerson was just another leader of American Jewry whom Netanyahu was courting. Twelve years later, the Lubavitcher's disciples would play a pivotal role in Netanyahu's ascendancy.

Meanwhile, Netanyahu was using more earthly methods to advance his career.

I N JUNE 1984, while Netanyahu was still deputy chief of mission in Washington, the Jonathan Institute was resurrected for another international conference on terror.

This time, Netanyahu was promoted from organizer to star speaker; he opened the conference before handing the mic to the keynote speaker,

Secretary of State George Shultz. It was an even higher-powered lineup than the one at the first conference. From Israel arrived Yitzhak Rabin and Arens. The American lineup included, besides Shultz, Reagan's counselor (later attorney general), Edwin Meese, and the FBI director (later CIA director) William Webster. Netanyahu's success at bringing heavy-hitters to his conference, which took place at the Four Seasons in Washington, DC, wasn't just a result of his growing influence in Washington. It was a sign of the times.

Following America's bloody episode in Lebanon, there was a growing interest in the issue of terrorism and a feeling that this was now America's problem, too. And in Reagan there was a president willing to take it on. Netanyahu has claimed that the Jonathan Institute conferences played a major role in this development. That's a gross exaggeration. Reagan hardly needed encouragement toward military action, and he saw the Soviet Union lurking behind every foreign threat long before Bibi came to Washington. But Netanyahu was certainly of the moment, and Shultz has credited him with having influenced his thinking.

On April 15, 1986, Reagan ordered an air strike on military targets in Libya, following the bombing of a nightclub in Berlin frequented by American servicemen in which 3 people (including two Americans) were killed and 229 injured. The Palestinian terrorists carrying out the bombing had been financed and directed by Colonel Muammar al-Qaddafi's regime.

It was a proud moment for Netanyahu. He had said two years previously at the conference that "if a government has harbored, trained and launched terrorists, it becomes the legitimate object of a military response." The United States had finally retaliated against a terror-supporting state. The decision to strike Libya was popular in America but roundly criticized by the "international community," including many European allies. The UN General Assembly voted 79–28 on a resolution of condemnation. Netanyahu derived great satisfaction from, for once, voting in support of an isolated United States. Usually it was the American ambassador supporting isolated Israel.

The timing could not have been better. During the week of the Libya bombing, a book containing the lectures from the Jonathan Institute conference was published in the United States. Bibi himself had written only the introduction and a couple of chapters of *Terrorism: How the West Can Win*, but for all intents and purposes, it was "Netanyahu's book."

His name appeared in bold letters on the cover ("Edited by" was much smaller). It was of the moment, reviewed in the major newspapers, and appeared on the cover of *Time* magazine, which published a seven-page excerpt. Secretary of State Shultz endorsed it and President Reagan apparently read it on Air Force One.

Netanyahu was achieving a degree of prominence that few foreign diplomats ever had. It was also the moment when Israeli media, fascinated by the amount of attention their ambassador to the United Nations was receiving, began seriously taking notice.

FROM HIS EARLIEST days in Washington, Netanyahu cultivated Israeli reporters based there as assiduously as he cultivated the American media. In return for tips on his inner dealings with the administration, he received favorable mentions as the rising star of Israeli diplomacy. After the *Time* cover, he became a superstar. The best-selling tabloid *Yedioth Ahronoth*, which would later become his strongest critic, sent a correspondent to New York to prepare a lengthy interview for its weekend magazine. The interviewer observed that "no-one now regrets the decision to appoint Netanyahu ambassador to the U.N."[4] The edgier *Hadashot* published a detailed analysis of why, ten years hence, Netanyahu and the head of the IDF's Central Command, Major General Ehud Barak, would face off as Likud's and Labor's candidates for prime minister, respectively.[5] It was a rare near-perfect political prediction. *Hadashot* got it right. The showdown with Barak took place in 1999.

Not all the coverage was positive. One left-wing daily published a list of Netanyahu's publicity stunts undermining Ambassador Rosenne and Israel's consul general, Moshe Yegar. But nearly all the reports were laudatory, describing Bibi staunchly fighting Israel's cause in the corridors of the United Nations and on America's television screens.[6]

During his trips home to Israel, Netanyahu visited newspaper offices, meeting publishers, news editors, and beat reporters. It was Bibi's honeymoon with the Israeli media, in complete contrast to what would come later. He appeared everywhere, from the political pages to entertainment talk shows, projecting a dual image as a cerebral, bookish man of the world and a down-to-earth Israeli everyman, a cigar-smoking sabra whose favorite pastime, he claimed, was hiking through the Judean

Ambassador Netanyahu
with Prime Minister
Yitzhak Shamir in Central
Park in 1987. Six years
later Bibi would replace
him as Likud leader.

Desert. In an interview with *Maariv*, he said that what bored him most
were "one-tone repetitive speeches."[7]

Netanyahu's destination on the political map was clear. Despite being
a civil servant, he allowed himself to express his own views even when
they diverged with government policy. The most striking example was in
May 1985, when the government agreed to exchange 1,150 mainly Palestinian prisoners for the release of three IDF soldiers who had been
captured by the Popular Front for the Liberation of Palestine in Lebanon. The controversial, lopsided deal was supported by nearly all the
cabinet ministers as well as by the Labor Party, Likud, and other parties,
in the hope that it would draw a line under the traumatic war.

Netanyahu defied instructions and publicly opposed the deal in interviews. In a letter to one of the ministers, he wrote: "This action has shaken
the faith of many here [in the United States] in Israel's resilience and I have

no doubt that it has deeply undermined our moral standing in Israel itself. How can we demand our soldiers endanger their lives, attacking the murderers working to destroy us, if we ourselves squander their sacrifice?"[8]

Did he think he was untouchable? Or was Netanyahu prepared to be fired in the hope that it would create the ideal circumstances for his entrance to politics? As it turned out, he got off with a light reprimand.

Under the Labor-Likud national unity government, Israeli foreign policy was run simultaneously by two leaders with very different worldviews. The result was four years of diplomatic paralysis as Shamir vetoed any effort by Peres to launch new peace initiatives. For opportunist diplomats stationed abroad, it meant a large degree of freedom.

In October 1986, "the rotation" took place. Shamir returned to the prime minister's office, and Peres became foreign minister. Two years earlier, Peres had supported Bibi's appointment. By now he had little doubt that he was dealing with a Likudnik who ignored directives to tone down his rhetoric toward the Arabs. However, replacing Netanyahu would have been difficult, as Shamir would have objected. Besides, it was clear that Bibi was about to resign in order to run in the next election. Why give him even more publicity?

15

Prime Minister? Of Course Not

Despite his initial skepticism, Shamir wanted Netanyahu to remain at the United Nations. He had enough bright young stars among the Likud "princes" and was in no hurry to see him back in Israel. Bibi had other plans.

Throughout his six years in office (1986–1992), Shamir was continuously under fire. From the left, his coalition partner, Labor leader Shimon Peres, kept trying to foist diplomatic initiatives on him. In April 1987 Shamir vetoed the "London Agreement" that Peres had signed with Jordan's King Hussein to launch an international peace conference. Shamir likened the conference to "a gallows," where Israel's neck would be in the noose. From the right, he was constantly attacked by Likud ministers David Levy and Ariel Sharon, who accused him of capitulating to Peres. At Likud Central Committee meetings, their supporters heckled the prime minister.

Likud was in a generational struggle, and Bibi needed to position himself in the party hierarchy if he didn't want the princes to get a march on him. He spent a large part of his time putting out feelers to the party. Central Committee members visiting New York received VIP treatment, including a personal briefing from the ambassador and a tour of the UN building, where they would sit with the Israeli delegation in the General Assembly.

"Everyone was charmed in the first meeting by this eloquent leader who spoke about values and ideology, not party business," recalled Gil

Samsonov, then head of the Likud Young Guard. "He got up and pointed at the map behind him. 'We have only one state,' he said. 'You have to think what's best for the nation.'"[1]

Another upcoming Likudnik visiting New York was the future president Reuven Rivlin, who was then chairman of Likud's Jerusalem branch. Netanyahu confided in him that he knew the princes would try and trip him up. Rivlin, impressed, offered to help back in Jerusalem. They would eventually become bitter rivals. "The princes thought Bibi was just a lightweight demagogue," Rivlin later recalled. "I warned them he would conquer Likud. They laughed."

These meetings were followed up with visits back in Israel, where Netanyahu began building his camp. He was recruiting his team. Embassy press officers Eyal Arad and Odelya Karmon would go on to work on his first campaign. He attended reunions of Revisionist veterans, winning them over with his extensive knowledge of Jabotinsky's writings and his insistence that their time had come.

Ministers began to pay attention. Arens was eager to have Bibi back, but others tried to dissuade him from running for national office. They sounded him out about the Jerusalem or Tel Aviv mayorships and the chairmanship of the Zionist Organization. Netanyahu brushed these offers away. He was headed for the Knesset. Besides, serving as Israel's chief protector in the American media had become less fun.

In December 1987, violent demonstrations broke out in Gaza, spreading quickly to the West Bank. Dozens of Palestinians were killed when troops responded to stone-throwing with live fire. Hundreds of foreign journalists rushed to cover the clashes. It had been five years since the First Lebanon War, and Israel was once again being portrayed as the cruel Goliath. Defense Minister Yitzhak Rabin's decision to give soldiers clubs and issue orders for them to "break hands and legs" failed to quell the Intifada (Uprising) and hardly improved optics. Twenty years after Israel had replaced Egypt and Jordan as occupiers of Gaza and the West Bank, the Palestinians were no longer prepared to remain under occupation.

In interviews, Netanyahu accused the Palestinians of wanting to destroy all of Israel and the PLO of being behind the violence. (The latter was not true, as the Intifada had begun spontaneously, though the PLO and other Palestinian organizations would later exert some control.) Bibi was outside his comfort zone. It was much more difficult to portray rock-wielding youths as agents of Syria, Libya, and the Soviet Union, as his theories of fighting terror didn't fit the new situation. Anyway, he had decided to leave before the Intifada and was already on the next stage of his career.

In his last months in New York, Netanyahu met and consulted with Republican campaign strategists, mapping his next move. He met twice with Rabbi Schneerson, who had already promised his support—though he had urged Bibi to continue his work at the United Nations. "You can continue serving her until the Messiah," the Rebbe said.[2]

He had spent six years in America's centers of power, learning the arts of television, lobbying, and fundraising. He had acquired a taste for good living, for being chauffeured and eating in fine restaurants, where someone else picked up the tab. It was another habit he took back with him to Israel, where his aides became accustomed to paying up after he left restaurants. What had he accomplished for Israel during this period?

It was Arens, Shamir, and other senior advisers who had defused the crises in the US-Israeli relationship and achieved the breakthroughs. Netanyahu had become a star of the air waves, the darling of Republican circles and the Jewish American elite, but he had had little lasting influence in the highest echelons of decision making. He was little more than a passive passenger and partisan commentator on the wide roller-coaster that took the two countries on their ups and downs. For all his high profile on television and cozy lunches with newspaper columnists, the coverage of Israel—from Lebanon to the Intifada—was hardly favorable in that period.

The United States was steadily inching toward engagement with the Palestinians. Shortly after leaving Washington, Netanyahu turned on his benefactor, the pro-Israel Secretary Shultz, who had met with two Arab Americans, Professors Edward Said and Ibrahim Abu Lughod, members of the PLO-affiliated Palestine National Council. Netanyahu claimed he had brought forward his departure to protest Shultz's paving the way for "a PLO state right in the heart of Israel, threatening our very security, our very future."[3] In December 1988, following Yasser Arafat's announcement that the PLO was renouncing the use of terror and accepting the two-state solution, the United States entered formal talks with the PLO. It was tantamount to the failure of everything that Netanyahu had worked for in the United States.

Netanyahu's real achievement was building up his new *hasbara* style of diplomacy, in which aggressive and relentless public championing of

Israel's cause became an end unto itself. When the policies of the Likud governments he served failed to gain support in the United States, he blamed a lack of motivation—in others—to argue in the policies' favor. Ultimately, Netanyahu had done a brilliant job of representing Likud's Israel, but he had mainly convinced the already convinced. Now it was time to reap that harvest.

THE RESIGNATION'S TIMING had nothing to do with Shultz. Elections were scheduled for November, and Netanyahu needed time to build up his base and run for a spot on the Likud's Knesset candidate list. Every stage of the campaign was meticulously planned. Bibi wanted to launch in a blaze of publicity. In those days, an in-depth political interview show, *Moked* (Focus), was broadcast on Thursday nights on the sole television channel. It was a prestigious venue that was usually reserved for the president, prime minister, and senior officials, not usually for aspirants. After weeks of talks with the producers, Netanyahu's team secured a March slot.

On the afternoon of the broadcast, Netanyahu was so busy briefing political reporters that he barely found the time to call the Foreign Ministry and officially resign. By then he had done more television interviews than anyone in Israeli politics. He was perfectly prepared when veteran interviewer Yoram Ronen asked him if he planned to run for prime minister. "Prime Minister? Of course not. We have an excellent prime minister, Yitzhak Shamir."[4] Shamir wasn't amused at the hasty departure of his ambassador, but many in Likud were fascinated by the shiny new creature.

The party's leader tried to befriend Netanyahu. Levy had met him in New York and was offended by his lack of respect. Sharon invited him for a meal at his farm and remarked later that he didn't trust him. As Arens's protégé, Bibi was expected to join the Shamir-Arens camp, but he tried to pass himself off as a nonaffiliated candidate.

His small and dedicated team included his former press officers, Arad and Karmon; his second cousin David Shimron, as legal adviser; and a few carefully selected party members who had volunteered their services. Netanyahu's American friends had already donated handsomely to his campaign fund, and the team set about arranging a marathon of meetings with as many of the 2,200 Central Committee members as possible. He had no job at the time but was taken care of. Bibi and Fleur lived in a central Tel Aviv apartment owned by an Australian property developer, John Gandel. The campaign used a room in the offices of a local tech firm. A Chabad Hasid who was a wealthy diamond dealer put a car and driver at Netanyahu's disposal.

Netanyahu spent his mornings meeting party members in the coffee shop of a Tel Aviv hotel. After lunch he would be driven out of town for meetings with local branches. Other candidates actually visited the cramped branch offices; Netanyahu preferred to hire event halls, where he could entertain members of a number of different branches at the same time. He crisscrossed the country, often sleeping overnight in supporters' homes. His stump speech included anecdotes from his days in the United Nations and dire warnings of the consequences of relinquishing parts of the West Bank to the PLO, which would be able to shoot down civilian airliners from the hills of Judea and Samaria.

Rival candidates and journalists ridiculed Netanyahu's fastidious habits. He traveled everywhere with a pile of crisp blue shirts, which he changed every few hours, and he used an electric razor in the car to eliminate his five o'clock shadow. It set him apart from the typical rumpled and informal Israeli politician. But instead of seeing him as a dandy, party members were impressed.

The 120 members of the Knesset are elected by a nationwide system of proportional representation. Voters vote for one party. Each party selects a numbered list of candidates, and these are allocated Knesset seats according to their share of the vote. Being high on the list makes the candidates "safe" and denotes their importance and popularity within the party. From 1977 to 1996, Likud Central Committee members selected the list by "the sevens" system. In the first free-for-all round, candidates competed for a spot on a panel of thirty-five names, with Central Committee members voting for ten candidates each.

Then came five consecutive rounds of voting in which members ranked five batches of seven. Essentially, it meant five rounds of horse-trading in which candidates were able to vie for the highest spots they aspired to without angering supporters of more powerful candidates. The top spot on the list went to Likud's leader, and other spots were reserved for members of other parties, such as the Liberals, that were affiliated with Likud. Dropping to the fifth "seven" meant relegation to the upper forties and probably no Knesset seat.

With most serving MKs already in the deals, newcomers relied on their connections with one of the main camps to boost their prospects. Candidates typically spent more time deal-making than canvassing. Netanyahu, who was affiliated with the Shamir-Arens camp, nevertheless spent months wooing members of the Sharon and Levy camps as well. He knew that he had many rivals even within the Shamir-Arens camp, especially the princes Ehud Olmert, Dan Meridor, and Ronny Milo, who were already MKs.

Netanyahu wasn't the only prominent newcomer. A year before, the "prince of princes," Benny Begin, had joined Likud. Menachem Begin's son had long kept out of politics. At forty-five, the ponderous and prematurely old geologist was running his first race. Although he had his father's name, his looks, and even his voice, he lacked the great leader's oratorical skills. Fanatically honest and frugal, he refused to make deals or spend campaign money. He traveled by bus to distant branches of the party, entering without fanfare and making short, low-key speeches. He was a Begin, and that was enough.

On June 29, the first round of voting took place in a daylong jamboree at the Herzliya Country Club. One of Bibi's donors had hired an air-conditioned RV, and there he met members of the Likud Central Committee while the rest sweated outside. As evening fell, the results were announced. Netanyahu, who had arrived from the United States only four months earlier, came in first with 1,408 votes, overtaking Begin, Arens, and Sharon. The second-biggest surprise was Levy reaching only sixth place. The housing minister was furious. He had not challenged Shamir for leadership, as he believed they had a deal that Shamir's supporters would all vote for him in return. Once again Levy felt cheated. "We'll meet in the sevens," he hissed.

Netanyahu now faced a dilemma. In "the sevens," the competition would be much closer as candidates fought for survival and each camp sought to push its people higher on the list. After his incredible showing in the first round, he was a target for rival camps. Levy was out for vengeance, and he had fixed on Netanyahu as the representative of the young, entitled upstarts of the Shamir-Arens camp. Bibi needed to decide what spot on the list to compete for. He toyed with the idea of going for number one in the first seven, but wiser heads counseled him not to push his luck. He put himself forward for the fifth spot. Any spot in the first seven would be a tremendous accomplishment for a newcomer, and he would still have to beat one of Sharon's lieutenants, David Magen, who was vying for the same spot.

This time he needed support from the Shamir camp, especially Arens, who ordered his wavering supporters to rank Netanyahu in the first seven. He scraped into fifth with 895 votes, just 8 more than Magen. Levy was first, Sharon second, and Arens made do with third. Begin closed the first seven.

Likud's national election campaign was run by the princes, who weren't interested in using Bibi's skills. He was put in charge of what was then considered a relatively minor role: overseeing polling and fundraising abroad. On a donor's recommendation, Netanyahu brought over Republican polling expert Frank Luntz. At twenty-eight, Luntz was yet to become the GOP guru of the 1990s, and few Likudniks had time for his presentations. He did, however, become a lifelong admirer of Netanyahu's style of messaging.

Likud won narrowly on November 1. The party received forty seats, one more than Labor. More importantly, the right-wing and religious parties held a small majority of sixty-three seats. But instead of forming a coalition in line with his own ideology, Shamir decided to form another national unity government with Labor. His Likud critics accused him of joining Labor to avoid having to give Levy and Sharon key ministries. Years later, Shamir claimed that his main reason for forming a national unity government was that the religious parties had demanded that Israel change its citizenship legislation to allow only those who had been born as Jews, or who had undergone a strict Orthodox conversion to Judaism, to emigrate to Israel. Leaders of American Jewry, where the non-Orthodox Reform and Conservative movements were the majority, warned that this rule would mean an irreparable rift. It was the most significant secret intervention the Jewish Diaspora had ever conducted in Israeli politics.

The deal with Labor meant fewer cabinet posts for Likud. Peres became finance minister, and Rabin remained in the Defense Ministry. Arens, Shamir's heir-apparent, became foreign minister. Levy remained housing minister, and Sharon stayed at trade and industry. Both were angry at their lack of promotion, especially as Shamir promoted the princes Meridor, Milo, and Olmert to minister positions. Netanyahu and Begin had ranked higher than the princes in the Likud list. Shamir didn't care. He refused to appoint rookie MKs as ministers. An enraged Benzion Netanyahu visited the prime minister demanding that Bibi receive a cabinet post; Shamir refused point-blank.

Arens agreed with Shamir, but he took pity on Bibi, who was calling him "three times a day." He wasn't prepared to spend time as a backbencher. Arens suggested that Netanyahu be made deputy at the Foreign Ministry. Shamir relented.

"DEPUTY MINISTER" MAY look good on a business card, but in Israeli politics it's usually a title given as compensation to a disgruntled MK. Most deputy ministers have no official responsibilities and must be content with whatever tasks their minister chooses to give them. Sworn in on December 22, Netanyahu was returning to the ministry where he'd been an employee only nine months earlier. His new role didn't give him power over the diplomats, and, mindful of how Netanyahu had treated their colleagues in Washington and New York, they avoided him, as did key advisers on Arens's staff.

Arens brought him into meetings and occasionally took him on foreign trips, but the first months were frustrating. Netanyahu spent much of his time prowling the offices and studios of foreign television networks, haranguing journalists over their coverage of the still raging Intifada. When Israelis were killed in terrorist attacks, he rushed to the scene or hospital, demanding the international media give equal coverage to Jewish victims.

Bibi continued meeting party members, lecturing small groups on the necessity of instituting harsher measures against Palestinian rioters. Most of the members of his 1988 campaign team were too busy in their new jobs to attend. A new unofficial aide volunteered to maintain the "Netanyahu camp." Avigdor Lieberman, then known to everyone as "Evet," was nine years Bibi's junior, a low-level Likud activist who had emigrated ten years earlier from Kishinev in the Soviet Union (now Chişinău, the capital of Moldova).

Lieberman, who would become Netanyahu's right-hand man over the next decade, has often been described as a thug. Nothing could be further from reality. His bulky frame, dense black beard, startling blue eyes, and gruff, heavily accented voice are intimidating, as are his extreme views. As a student he worked as a nightclub bouncer. But few Israeli politicians, with the exception of Netanyahu, are as widely read and intellectually minded as Lieberman. In those years, Lieberman, who had just moved with his young family to a West Bank settlement, bonded with Netanyahu both ideologically and personally. Evet also opened Bibi's eyes to the electoral potential of the Israeli-Russian community, a large majority of whom held hawkish views. In early 1989, he tried to get the Foreign Ministry to launch a program encouraging more Jews to arrive from the Soviet Union, but as the government was trying to reestablish diplomatic relations with Moscow, which had been cut off in 1967, there was little interest in his proposals. A few months later it happened anyway.

Meanwhile, an unofficial role had opened for Netanyahu as Israel's bulldog against the new American administration, which was proving to be increasingly critical of the Shamir government.

A month after the new Shamir government had been sworn in, the Reagan era ended with the inauguration of President George H. W. Bush on January 20, 1989. The administration's ties with Israel had taken a hit two months earlier with the recognition of the PLO, and, as James Baker replaced Shultz as secretary of state, worse beckoned. Bush and Baker had been among Israel's main critics in the Reagan White House, and now they were running the show.

Arens feared the worst and tried to get Shamir to present an Israeli peace plan in his first meeting with President Bush in April 1989. Taking the initiative, however, was against Shamir's instincts. In the key preparation meeting with Shamir, Arens took Netanyahu along "for support." Netanyahu helped to convince Shamir of the necessity of appearing to be proactive in the United States. Shamir agreed to propose autonomy talks with a Palestinian delegation whose members would be selected by Egypt and Jordan. At the White House, Bush and Baker seemed receptive to the idea, and Netanyahu was sent to sell the American media and Congress on the initiative and then go on to Ottawa, to try and get the Canadian government on board.

But Baker, along with the Egyptian regime, began pushing for a Palestinian delegation that would include PLO members. Bush and Baker shared the view that as the recipient of the largest annual sum of American foreign aid, Israel could stand to be lectured on its policies. Of all places, Baker chose an AIPAC conference in May to admonish the Shamir government, in front of hundreds of Israel's supporters.

"For Israel, now is the time to lay aside once and for all the unrealistic vision of a Greater Israel," Baker intoned. He called upon Israel to "forswear annexation," to "stop settlement activity," and to "reach out to the Palestinians as neighbors who deserve political rights." He had encouraging words for Shamir's initiatives and stern messages for the Palestinians as well, calling upon the latter to renounce violence "in all languages, not just those addressed to the West."[5] But it was the blunt admonishments to Israel that naturally were the focus of the speech. In private, Shamir described Baker as "a new hangman for the Jewish people."

The next eighteen months were to see a gradual escalation of administration pressure on Israel. Baker went behind the backs of Shamir and Arens, trying, with the help of the Egyptian government, to get the leaders of the Labor Party, Peres and Rabin, to sign off on a proposal for talks with a Palestinian delegation. Peres especially played along, quietly promising the Americans that should Shamir refuse, he could form a government of his own. Shamir was under intense pressure from Sharon and Levy, who for their own political purposes were threatening insurrection within Likud should the prime minister deliver any concession. Baker was effectively provoking a coalition crisis in Jerusalem.

Netanyahu was relegated to a supporting role. High-level diplomacy went on mainly between Arens and Baker. Arens's diplomatic adviser Sallai Meridor (the younger brother of Dan Meridor, and therefore in the princes' camp) and Shamir's favorite, Elyakim Rubinstein, who by then was a cabinet secretary, were entrusted with relaying sensitive messages and draft proposals between Jerusalem and Washington. Bibi's job was shoring up support for Israel's positions in Congress and in the media.

There were now fewer doors open to him at the State Department, however. He no longer had anywhere near the access that he had enjoyed during Shultz's tenure. He found himself meeting with a new group of advisers and Middle East experts who had been appointed to their posts during that period. Key members of this new group were different from the old generation of WASPish "Arabists" who had been instinctively hostile to Israel. Dennis Ross, Aaron David Miller, Daniel Kurtzer, and other American officials who entered the fray during those years and would remain involved in Middle Eastern diplomacy for years, were Jewish and broadly pro-Israel—just not Bibi's Israel.

For Netanyahu it was like being back at high school in Philadelphia, with all those weak American Jews who would never serve in the IDF, risking their lives for the Jewish state. They all felt that Netanyahu was condescending toward them, and he did little to change that impression. In his diplomatic memoirs *The Much Too Promised Land*, Miller recalled Bibi "yelling" at them: "I closed my eyes during his tirade and remembered my high school tennis coach yelling at me for throwing my racket." Netanyahu accused them of interfering in Israeli politics. "You can afford to give the Arabs the benefit of the doubt from the safety and security of Washington. Out here in our neighborhood, we can't and won't," he said to Miller.[6]

Netanyahu had a point. Baker was encouraging Peres and Rabin to take on Shamir, but Bibi never wanted to accept that the "unbreakable relationship" between the United States and Israel was also a vastly unequal one. Neither would he keep these thoughts private—he used every available media platform to lambast the administration's policy toward Israel. He claimed that the PLO was pulling the wool over American eyes and had not abandoned terror. Even when he was proven right, as when an attempted seaborne attack by a PLO faction on Israel's coast in June 1990 ended the US-PLO dialogue after only eighteen months, he continued to get under Baker's skin.

At one point, after Netanyahu publicly said that "U.S. policy in the Middle East is based on lies and distortions," Baker ordered him barred from entering the State Department. Robert Gates, who was deputy national security adviser, did the same. "I was offended by his glibness and his criticism of U.S. policy—not to mention his arrogance and outlandish ambition," Gates wrote in his autobiography. "I told National Security Adviser Brent Scowcroft that Bibi (Netanyahu) ought not be allowed back on White House grounds."[7]

As Netanyahu's relationship with the Bush administration crumbled, his life at home was crumbling, too. Bibi and Fleur's marriage had been difficult for a while. In their last year in New York, they had separated for months. Fleur felt neglected by Bibi's frequent absences. Netanyahu was constantly traveling back to Israel or addressing audiences across the United States. Fleur had given up her job, had converted to Judaism, and was undergoing fertility treatments, and it had all taken its toll. But she agreed to reconcile and joined Bibi in Israel.

Netanyahu tried to include Fleur in his campaign, but she had little to contribute to the intense canvassing across the country. She was by his side on the night he came first in the Likud panel vote, but as one party member who was close to the couple at the time said, "It was clear that it wasn't her scene. She was too smart just to be the woman waiting at home for Bibi to come back late at night." Fleur tried hard to fit in, lunching with other Likud wives, including Shulamit Shamir, and befriending her stepdaughter Noa. But she remained lonely and out of place.

One American friend who has remained close to Fleur and Bibi attributed the split to "a lack of maturity on both their sides. They could have worked harder. She was an extraordinary asset to him and Bibi recognized that, but he's just not that kind of a social person." Fleur left in early 1989, returning to New York, where she worked at Ron Lauder's investment company. She later married Leonard Harlan, the founder of the successful private investment firm Castle Harlan. "They both traded down," observed their friend.

Bibi never felt comfortable in Tel Aviv. On his own once again, he returned to Jerusalem. At forty, he was twice divorced and living with his parents. With a crisis engulfing the government, it looked as if he might lose his job as well.

SHAMIR CONTINUED STONEWALLING Baker regarding his demand to negotiate with a Palestinian delegation whose members included residents of East Jerusalem and deportees affiliated with the PLO. On March 3, 1990, Shamir summoned Likud ministers to discuss their position. Peres was threatening to bring the government down if they refused the Americans. Arens recommended saying yes to Baker. Netanyahu, who had just returned from Washington, disagreed, arguing that acquiescing to Baker's demand would be tantamount to agreeing to divide Jerusalem. Arens was hurt by Bibi's "uncollegiality," though, as always, he would forgive him. Shamir seemed incapable of deciding.

Ten days later, accusing Peres of undermining the government, Shamir had fired him in a cabinet meeting, and the other Labor ministers had immediately resigned. Shamir would not back down, even though Peres had already reached secret agreements with the ultra-Orthodox parties.

Two days later, the government fell in a no-confidence motion, and President Chaim Herzog gave Peres three weeks to form a new government. A mad scramble ensued between Labor and Likud for defectors from either side. On June 12, Peres had a majority on paper and was ready to present his new government to the Knesset. The five-member Agudat Yisrael, an ultra-Orthodox party, had signed a coalition agreement, but two of its MKs disappeared. Peres had already started appointing ministers, but as the hours passed, and the missing MKs failed to turn up, he was forced to notify the Knesset that he still lacked a majority. Later it transpired that a fax had arrived that night from Rabbi Schneerson in New York ordering the two MKs not to join a left-wing government.

Once again, Peres's prime ministerial designs were dashed. His colleague and rival Rabin, who had lost his position as defense minister, was scathing in his criticism, branding the farce "the stinking trick." Two months later, it was Shamir who presented a new government—the narrow right-wing coalition he had preferred not to form in 1988.

Secretary Baker, who had waited for a more favorable outcome (from his perspective), lashed out in a congressional hearing two days later, accusing Israel of lacking interest in the diplomatic process. "Everybody over there should know that the telephone number (of the White House switchboard) is 1-202-456-1414. When you're serious about peace, call us."[8]

To keep his new coalition together, Shamir had to reshuffle his cabinet. Arens moved back to the Defense Ministry, and Levy was appointed as foreign minister. It was unthinkable at first that Netanyahu would remain deputy minister under Levy, who regarded him as a dangerous upstart. Shamir agreed that Bibi move with Arens to Defense. But Netanyahu realized that at the Kirya, the military headquarters in Tel Aviv, he would have even less to do. Deputy defense ministers usually dealt with humdrum tasks, such as civil defense and logistics. Not for the last time, Bibi applied his charms to Levy, promising fealty. In a moment of weakness, the vain Levy allowed him to stay.

His cooperation lasted barely weeks. Netanyahu was too independent and he effortlessly outshone Levy, who didn't speak English. Levy's advisers convinced him that Bibi was a "plant" of the Arens-Shamir camp. Levy decided not to take him on his first visit to Washington and ordered him not to give interviews to the American media during his absence. Bibi began to wonder whether he hadn't made a mistake in not joining Arens.

But one of his big shining moments was about to come.

In May 1990, in a meeting with American Jewish leaders, Netanyahu was grilled over the latest purchase by a Jewish settler group of a building in East Jerusalem—a church building that had been converted into a yeshiva dormitory, leading to criticism from the Bush administration. He answered, sardonically, "You're right. It's a big problem for us now. But it will blow over in a week. There's a much bigger problem that won't go away. Saddam Hussein is the Middle East's, and Israel's, number one problem."[9]

Netanyahu has always maintained that the Palestinian issue is a diversion, not a central problem in the region. In the 1980s, Syria and the Soviet Union were the real issues. In the 1990s, it became Iraq, and since the beginning of the twenty-first century, he has focused on Iran. In this case, at least, he was onto something. Iraqi president Saddam Hussein would become the world's problem in three months when it invaded Kuwait. The Bush administration rushed to build an international coalition, including Arab nations, and the Israeli-Palestinian conflict was indeed a diversion it didn't need.

Saddam had threatened to "burn half of Israel," and he had an arsenal of long-range Russian Scud missiles. Intelligence analysts feared they could be equipped with chemical warheads. Israelis were given gas masks and atropine syringes to protect themselves from poison gas. Netanyahu prepared a detailed contingency plan on handling the international media in the event such an attack occurred.

In the early hours of January 17, 1991, the US coalition began its bombardment of Iraqi targets. Israelis were ordered to carry their gas masks everywhere and prepare sealed rooms in their homes. At 3:00 a.m. on January 18, the first salvo of Scud missiles hit Tel Aviv's suburbs.

Over the next forty days, thirty-nine missiles fell on Israel. Netanyahu spent the war rushing between television studios in Jerusalem, giving dozens of interviews daily to networks from around the world. He promised that Israel would retaliate, though he never specified where or when, and compared the threat of poison gas on Israel to the gas chambers used by Germany half a century earlier to exterminate Jews.

Yasser Arafat's PLO had thrown its lot in with Iraq, and as the missiles flew over the West Bank, Palestinians gathered on rooftops, cheering the

Deputy Foreign Minister Netanyahu on CNN during the Gulf War in 1991. He insisted on continuing the interview with his gas mask on.

Iraqi dictator for striking the Zionists. For Netanyahu it was a public relations bonanza. Finally, here was proof that the Palestinians were not a poor, oppressed people, but part of a much larger Arab world intent on destroying the Jewish state. In interviews, using a map that showed the missile trajectory from Iraq to Israel, he spread his hands to show the breadth of the Arab lands, and then covered tiny Israel with his thumb.

Standard-issue gas masks had the large filter in front, leaving the wearer nearly inaudible. Netanyahu obtained a mask with a side filter, through which he could be heard clearly. Finally, in the third week of the war, a missile raid caught him in CNN's Jerusalem studio. He persuaded reporter Linda Scherzer to interview him with their masks on. You could hear Netanyahu's broad smile under the mask. "I must say, this is the darnedest way to do an interview," he laughed. "What it does show, however, is the threat that Israel faces. I cannot tell you when, I cannot tell you how, but Israel will defend itself."[10]

But Israel didn't respond. Shamir and his ministers agonized over launching a counterstrike. Bush demanded that Israel not jeopardize his international coalition by attacking Iraq. On January 19, the cabinet held a rare Shabbat meeting. The pilots were already sitting on the runway, waiting to take off and bomb the launch sites. Shamir backed down. The

United States promised it was bombing the launchers and refused to open an air corridor for the Israeli attack. But Scuds continued to hit Tel Aviv. The IDF planned to land an airborne division in western Iraq, to hunt and destroy the elusive mobile launchers the Americans failed to locate. But Bush was adamant, and Shamir hoped that backing down would at least help to relieve diplomatic pressures after the war.

Netanyahu was Israel's spokesman to the world during those weeks. Levy became incensed as reports from Israel's embassies around the world, and letters from Jewish leaders, all praising Bibi, piled up on his desk. But Netanyahu was seething as well. He was furious about his lack of influence on decision making and having to deliver empty promises that Israel would retaliate.

Ultimately, Netanyahu's public relations operation had little effect, besides making him a bigger star in the international media. He even had a cameo role in Frederick Forsyth's Gulf War suspense novel, *The Fist of God*. But few Israelis at the time were exposed to foreign television networks, and fame abroad didn't boost his political prospects at home. It had been a frustrating war for Israelis—the first in which they had been attacked, taken casualties, and not fought back. And the Bush administration's policy toward Israel did not change after the war. Bush had acquired an appetite for fixing the Middle East's problems, and his pressure on the Shamir government resumed almost immediately.

But the First Gulf War was a pivotal period in Bibi's life for another reason altogether.

16

A Crime Unprecedented in the History of Democracy

After Fleur left, Netanyahu spent a couple of years as one of Israel's most eligible bachelors. The gossip pages reported him squiring various women, but they were usually wrong. Bibi was too focused on his political career. Liaisons, when they did occur, were almost always initiated by the other side and didn't last. In mid-1989, Sara Ben Artzi, a then twenty-nine-year-old El Al flight attendant, approached Netanyahu on a stopover in Schiphol Airport in Amsterdam, and after a few minutes chatting, left her phone number. Their first date was at an Indian restaurant in Tel Aviv. They continued seeing each other for a few months.

Sara was recently divorced, having ended a stormy marriage with a great deal of toxic baggage that would continue to haunt her. The marriage had lasted seven years; the divorce had been in 1987. Her friends said she had set her mind on finding a "man of consequence" and from the moment she met Bibi, wasn't going to let go. Sara had spent a frugal and austere childhood in the small town of Kiryat Tivon in northern Israel. Her father was a Bible teacher who had enforced a religious environment within their home, although it was a largely secular community. Sara's mother is remembered in Tivon as an angry woman who would shout at children in the street. It was a home that put a premium on education, and Sara's three older brothers were all brilliant and radical. One brother is today a Silicon Valley millionaire; a second is a far-left mathematics professor who refused to serve as a soldier in the West Bank; and the third is a Talmudic scholar and West Bank settler. Sara's academic career, however, failed to take off, and by the time she met Bibi, she was still struggling with her master's degree in psychology.

Many of Netanyahu's friends were taken aback by his new girlfriend, who seemed so different from his fiercely independent and career-driven ex-wives. Nine years younger than her boyfriend, Sara seemed fragile and childlike. Attending social events with Bibi, she wouldn't leave his side and rarely spoke. He was attracted to her vulnerability, but, as always, hesitant in committing, especially to someone who clung to him so closely. He continued seeing other women during 1990 and drifted away from Sara for a few months. But there was a steely tenacity to her that no one had noticed. Sara had reestablished their relationship by the end of the year, and in January 1990, as Scud missiles fell near her apartment in a Tel Aviv suburb, Bibi invited her to join him in Jerusalem. One night there, Sara informed him that she was pregnant.

For the third time, a reluctant Bibi was pressured into marriage. A few weeks after the First Gulf War ended, a small ceremony took place at his childhood home in the presence of Shamir and Arens. The next morning, a carefully staged photograph of the couple, Sara's pink dress concealing her pregnancy, appeared in the newspapers. It was the first introduction of the hitherto anonymous Sara Netanyahu to the Israeli media, which would spend much of the next decades savaging her.

At forty-one, Netanyahu bought his first apartment in Beit Hakerem, the northwest Jerusalem neighborhood where the Mileikowsky family had lived nearly seventy years before. Their first son, Yair, was born on July 28, 1991, thirteen years after the birth of his half-sister, Noa.

SHAMIR'S HOPES THE Bush administration would cut him some slack for not retaliating during the First Gulf War were unfounded. Shortly after hostilities in Iraq ended, Bush and Baker resumed their attempts to convene a peace conference with renewed vigor. They intensified pressure on Israel to stop building settlements in the West Bank.

From early 1990, a new factor came into the Israel-US equation. With the Soviet Union crumbling, hundreds of thousands of Soviet Jews were rushing to leave. Few of them were Zionists, and just like a century earlier, when Jews had fled the Pale of Settlement, most preferred emigrating to the United States. However, due to the changing political situation, America no longer regarded them as refugees, and it became much more difficult to obtain green cards. This situation served Israel, which was interested in boosting its Jewish population through emigration.

In 1990–1991, 332,000 Soviet immigrants arrived in Israel, which then numbered less than 5 million citizens. The sudden influx strained Israel's economy, which was still recovering from its near-meltdown in the mid-1980s. Israel requested $10 billion in loan guarantees from the Bush administration to ensure that it could provide housing and jobs for the new immigrants. The administration's response was positive in principle, but Baker wanted Shamir to promise that the new arrivals would not settle in the West Bank. It was a moot point, as very few of them had any interest in doing so. But to commit to the idea of Jews not being allowed to live in all of the historical land of Israel stuck in Shamir's craw. The loan guarantees were delayed.

In an attempt to pressure the Bush administration, AIPAC and other Jewish organizations deployed hundreds of activists in a concerted effort to get Congress to bypass the administration and approve the loan guarantees. On September 12, 1991, Bush retaliated in an unprecedented press conference. He reminded the press that US troops had "risked their lives to defend Israelis in the face of Iraqi Scud missiles," and that Israel was already receiving $4 billion that year. He promised that America would help Israel absorb the new immigrants, but reaffirmed that it could not allow the money to be used to build settlements. He was particularly scathing in his criticism of Israel's efforts to go around his administration. "I'm up against some powerful political forces but I owe it to the American people to tell them how strongly I feel. . . . I heard today there were something like a thousand lobbyists working the other side of the question. We've got one lonely little guy down here doing it."[1]

Shamir caved. His (almost certainly unfounded) fear that the administration would allow Soviet Jews to emigrate to the United States instead of Israel pushed him to agree to the international conference that he had likened to a gallows. He did everything in his power to empty the Madrid Conference of any real diplomatic meaning. Although he was forced to swallow a joint Jordanian-Palestinian delegation, including members clearly affiliated with the PLO, he received American assurances that the conference would just be an opening event. Actual negotiations would take place directly between Israeli and Arab delegations later on. The

Bush administration also promised that it wouldn't support an independent Palestinian state or force Israel to directly negotiate with the PLO.

The conference opening, on October 30, was officially hosted by President Bush and Soviet leader Mikhail Gorbachev. The Arab delegations were led by foreign ministers. Shamir didn't want to entrust his foreign minister with representing Israel. Until his appointment a year earlier, Levy had been Sharon's ally, pressuring Shamir from the right. As foreign minister he had shifted to the center, favoring an acceptance of the US demands. Shamir viewed him as weak and opportunistic and decided to lead the Israeli delegation himself. Levy, in a huff, announced that he would be staying home. To make things worse for him, Shamir took Netanyahu to Madrid as the delegation's official spokesperson.

Some veterans of the peace process have hailed the Madrid Conference as a key event leading to the Oslo Accords and peace between Jordan and Israel, but it is hard to escape the conclusion that it was largely theater. One senior Israeli diplomat involved in the conference said, "Shamir didn't believe there would be any real substance in the conference, which is why he brought Bibi along. He wanted *hasbara*, not diplomacy." Shamir left after the first day. He had made a speech dealing mainly with the Jewish people's historical claim to the land. During other speeches, he seemed to be dozing. He noticed, though, when the Syrian foreign minister, Farouk al-Sharaa, waved an old British "wanted" notice with his photograph and called him a "terrorist."

For Shamir, the whole event was a dangerous nuisance. For Netanyahu, it was heaven. He led a large team of press officers and spin doctors, supervised two media tents outside the conference center in the Spanish royal palace and the delegations' hotel, and gave daily briefings to the thousands of reporters gathered there, including one for Arab media that was simultaneously translated.

He reprised his role from the First Gulf War on a grander global stage. He waved the Palestinian National Covenant, highlighting the clauses calling for Israel's elimination, and demanded the Palestinians "tear up the document of hatred." He mocked the peace conference, saying he was "going around, looking for Arab representatives who will shake my hand." In response to a speech by the leader of the Palestinian delegation demanding the establishment of an independent state in the West Bank and Jerusalem, he said, "It's like someone saying I want to make peace with you but only after we amputate your hands, legs, and rip out your heart. But I certainly want to make peace with you."

Netanyahu's performance gained him admirers back home, but in making the conference a media brawl, he also helped to focus attention on his Palestinian opponent. The American-educated Hanan Ashrawi emerged as one of the most eloquent champions of the Palestinian cause on the international stage. There were many in Madrid who felt she had proven herself to be Netanyahu's equal, even surpassing him with her less bombastic manner.

After Madrid, Levy made it clear that under no circumstances would Netanyahu continue as his deputy. Bibi, who had already long ago stopped taking orders from his minister, moved to the prime minister's office, where he retained the rank of deputy minister. He was promptly sent to Washington, where separate follow-up talks between Israeli and Arab delegations were to take place. However, Netanyahu was not entrusted with actually leading one of the Israeli teams, just with their press relations. The talks immediately bogged down in arguments over formalities, as Shamir had intended.

The only tangible effect of the Madrid Conference and subsequent Washington talks was to push the three far-right parties in Shamir's government—Tzomet, Moledet, and Ha'Tehiya—out of the coalition. In January 1992, they resigned in protest over the "dangerous" negotiations, forcing Shamir to call early elections.

There was still unfinished business in the Knesset.

A FTER THE "STINKING TRICK" of 1990, there were growing calls to change the electoral system with a view to reducing the small parties' "blackmail" power over the government. The proposal that gained the most support was to add a direct vote for prime minister to the Knesset list vote. With a directly elected prime minister, the large parties would be strengthened. At least that was the thinking. Two supporters of this proposal were Netanyahu and Yitzhak Rabin, both of whom rated their prospects as candidates in a direct election to be high. Shamir and Arens, neither of whom enjoyed election campaigning, were flatly opposed to the "beauty contest" law. They enforced a whip on Likud MKs to vote against it. Netanyahu rebelled.

After strenuous arguments, Arens reached a last-minute agreement with his protégé that he would vote with Likud if it came down to the wire. On the night of the decisive vote, Bibi broke his promise, and the direct election law passed 57–56. There were dark mutterings in Likud that he had committed political suicide, but the outrage was short-lived. Shamir didn't forgive or forget, however, and years later he said that Bibi supported the law "because he sees himself a king."[2]

In an amendment, the direct election was postponed to the next elections. Meanwhile, Likud had much bigger problems. In the first party-wide primaries in Israel, Rabin had beaten Shimon Peres, regaining leadership of Labor fifteen years after being forced to resign over the foreign bank account scandal. Labor now launched its "Israel is waiting for Rabin" campaign, focusing on the image of "Mr. Security," rather than on the less popular party brand. Meanwhile, Likud was once again mired in camp warfare within its Central Committee.

In the 1992 election campaign, first Shamir went through a bruising leadership contest against Levy and Sharon, winning with an underwhelming 46 percent. In the panel vote, Netanyahu came in second this time, still impressive for a first-term MK, especially one who had just rebelled against the party line. But the big news was Levy, who still claimed to be Likud's next leader, coming in eighteenth! The Shamir-Arens camp had gone all-out to humiliate Levy. Many Likudniks felt he was splitting the party and shunned him.

A week later he salvaged a bit of self-respect, coming in third in the first "seven." Bibi was fifth again. But only a tiny handful of Levy loyalists had made the list and would be in the next Knesset. In a furious speech after the result, Levy played the "tribal card" and accused his party colleagues of anti-Mizrahi racism: "I was for some of the Likud people like a monkey that has just climbed down from the trees," he thundered, threatening to resign from the party. Arens begged Shamir to call Levy's bluff and appoint Bibi as acting foreign minister until the elections.

Shamir, however, fearing that Levy's departure would push away Mizrahi voters, gave Levy a written commitment that he would remain deputy prime minister and foreign minister in the next government. Keeping Levy in the fold did not help Likud.

On June 23, fifteen years after losing power to Likud and after four consecutive defeats under Peres, Labor finally won again. Rabin was back in office. Not only had Labor resoundingly trounced Likud as the largest party, with forty-four seats to thirty-two, but Labor, the left-wing Meretz (Vigor) party, the communists, and the Arab parties held sixty-one seats, while the Likud and its right-wing and religious allies held fifty-nine. The results, however, concealed the fact that Rabin hadn't stopped Israel's shift to the right.

More Israelis voted for the right-religious bloc than for the parties of the center-left. Due to fragmentation on the right and the higher electoral threshold of 1.5 percent, Ha'Tehiya and other small far-right parties failed to enter the Knesset, their votes lost. That, and the fact that Labor relied on Arab votes, would later feed the narrative that Rabin lacked a national mandate for the Oslo Accords.

Rabin won the elections presenting a hawkish image. He was "Mr. Security," promising not to negotiate with the PLO, never to allow the creation of a Palestinian state, and to remain on the Golan Heights. Many of the new citizens who had recently arrived from the Soviet Union held nationalist views but voted for the tough General Rabin over the tired and dispirited Shamir.

Shamir lost no time, announcing his resignation as Likud leader on election night. Although he had led the movement for nine years, he had always been a transitional figure, never fully emerging from Menachem Begin's shadow. Arens was widely seen as the frontrunner in the race to replace Shamir. On the morning after the election, Netanyahu offered to be Arens's leadership campaign manager. The next day, Arens announced that he "believed in service, not servitude," and that he was leaving politics. He didn't have the stomach for another nasty contest against Levy, or the burning ambition to lead Likud, through years of opposition, back to power.

The path was open for Netanyahu, five years after joining Likud, to announce his leadership bid.

As THE CONTEST kicked off, Netanyahu was at a disadvantage. Unlike Levy, he didn't lead a well-established camp of supporters. Many members of the now leaderless Shamir-Arens camp were planning on voting for Benny Begin. Bibi presented himself as a leader for the post-camp era, but he had competition from another candidate—

Moshe Katzav, who was popular in the Likud strongholds in the south and had served in several positions over the years, including, most recently, minister of transportation. Netanyahu relied on a new election system.

After Labor's successful first party-wide primaries, many in Likud demanded party-wide primaries as well. Most of the leadership were against holding party-wide primaries, but Netanyahu had an unlikely ally in Levy, who believed he could sign up enough new members in the mainly Mizrahi working-class towns and neighborhoods to wrap up the race.

At a post-defeat Likud Central Committee conference, Netanyahu and Levy both urged members to relinquish their power to select the party's representatives. Against them stood Begin and Sharon, who tabled an alternative plan to first revive Likud finances under a secretary-general (Sharon intended to run for this new post) and postpone primaries until the eve of the next Knesset election. Sick at the thought of spending years in opposition, 80 percent of the Central Committee voted in favor of holding primaries in eight months.

The first stage of the campaign was registering new members. Levy and Katzav relied on their existing supporters to sign up friends, relatives, and neighbors. Netanyahu's campaign set up dozens of blue booths in town centers emblazoned with Bibi's face and the slogan "Netanyahu—Choosing a Winning Leadership." In the pre-Internet era, much of Israeli political life still took place out on the street. But it was the first time anyone had actually registered new party members on the street. Registering thousands of new members weekly created Netanyahu's camp out of nothing. Campaign volunteers had an incentive to sign up hundreds of members, making them overnight leaders in their local party branches. From the start, the Netanyahu campaign had something that his rivals had not felt necessary: a computerized operation with all their supporters in a database. They also received details about existing members from party headquarters. Only Netanyahu's campaign was computer-savvy enough to make use of the new digital technologies, and all of these contacts were subjected to phone calls and campaign mail. Bibi's expensive and well-organized campaign signaled to the party that he was the one to modernize Likud and fix its finances.

By the end of 1992, Likud membership had grown over 60 percent to reach 216,000, or 4 percent of Israel's population. Likud officials estimated that over 70,000 new members had been registered by Netanyahu's campaign, while Levy succeeded in bringing in around half this number and Katzav only a few thousand. Benny Begin didn't even try to sign on new members. Once again, he was running on his name alone.

Most Likud MKs refused to openly support Netanyahu. The "princes" preferred Begin, who was one of them; they believed they would have control over him. Only three MKs joined Netanyahu's campaign—Tzachi Hanegbi and Limor Livnat, young Likudniks who had been first elected to the Knesset with Bibi in 1988, and one old-timer, Yehoshua Matza.

By the last months of the campaign, Netanyahu was the obvious frontrunner. He was running two races simultaneously: a straightforward political contest, with Levy, for control of the party, and an ideological struggle with Begin for Likud's soul. On the surface, the two Benjamins had risen from the same source. Both were sons of lifelong Revisionists, steeped in an uncompromising version of Zionism, and both opposed any retreat from the whole of the land of Israel. But both were also their fathers' sons. Begin's Revisionism, like his father's, was the parochial variety—a warmer, more Israeli ideology. Netanyahu, like his father, saw Revisionist Zionism as part of a wider Western tradition that was in tune with the conservative thinking of Ronald Reagan and Margaret Thatcher. Benny and Bibi could cooperate on many issues, but there was a difference between them that went to the core.

One morning during the campaign, they were both interviewed on the radio. Bibi was asked what he had for breakfast. A yoghurt, he answered. Begin then said, "That's exactly what the primaries are doing to the Likud. Yoghurtization. The primaries have made Likud superficial. I'm against this Americanization."[3] Netanyahu wasn't about to apologize for running an American-style campaign. He led convoys of dozens of vehicles with "Bibi" signs to towns with large numbers of Likud members. The local newspapers carried entire pages with the photographs.

Netanyahu's primary campaign brought another element of American politics to Israel: the political sex scandal.

ISRAELI POLITICIANS ARE no more straitlaced than their counterparts in other countries. In such a small country, politicians' sexual escapades rarely remain secret for long, but Israeli media traditionally does not report on these matters. It's not out of prudishness or reticence: Israeli reporters are notoriously intrusive and combative. But the unwritten understanding is that "everyone cheats" and there are far more serious matters on which politicians should be judged.

One evening in January 1993, while Netanyahu was on his way to a campaign event, Sara, at home, answered the phone. An anonymous caller informed her that Bibi was having an affair. There was a video-tape of him having sex, and if he didn't pull out of the race, it would be released.

A hysterical Sara called Bibi, who immediately returned home. When Sara finally succeeded through tears to tell him what she had heard, he didn't try to deny it. For three years he had been having an off-and-on affair with Ruth Bar, a married marketing consultant who had worked on Likud campaigns as a polling expert. Sara demanded that he leave. Netanyahu packed a few suits and left for his place of penance, his parents' home.

Over the next days, Bibi had two worries: how to keep his third marriage together and keep his campaign on the road. He ordered his campaign manager, Lieberman, to find out who the anonymous caller had been, and whether his political rivals had secretly filmed him. The conspiracy-minded Lieberman stoked Bibi's suspicions with the suggestion that perhaps party members close to Levy were involved.

Had Netanyahu been thinking clearly, he would have realized that his only problem was with his wife. As long as the relations are consensual, a sex tape is worthless in Israeli politics. There was no question of it being shown on television or reported in the newspapers. There was no Inter-net then on which it could go viral. It could, of course, be distributed to party members, but it would never have reached all of them, and besides, there was no reason for Likudniks to turn against Netanyahu just because he had sex with a woman whom few of them knew. No one had any proof that such a tape even existed. But Netanyahu wasn't thinking straight. He lodged a complaint with the police and then decided to preempt any blackmail by going public.

For once the immaculate performer wasn't composed on television. In a rumpled and angry interview he claimed that "senior people in the Likud are trying to blackmail me over a love affair I had. I had a connection with a woman that ended. We know who is behind this attempt, one of the senior people in Likud, who is surrounded by a group of criminals. Who has used methods of espionage, wiretapping and burglary, who is not worthy of being in the leadership and [whose] place is in prison."[4]

An Israeli politician speaking about his sex life was unprecedented. Menachem Begin was once asked by reporters about a secret meeting with Bashir Gemayel and answered, "You don't ask a gentleman where he spent the night." What made it worse was the explosive allegation against "one of the senior people in Likud." No one had any doubt who he was referring to. A furious Levy publicly demanded that Bibi say exactly whom he meant. The media, for the first time invited by a senior politician into his bedroom, were having a field day, dubbing the case "Bibigate" and "the hot tape." They speculated on the identity of his lover, but Bar's name came out only months later, when her husband sued for divorce.

The police investigation was eventually discontinued when no evidence of the existence of a sex tape was discovered. In going public, Netanyahu's intention had been to divert attention from his affair onto the senior Likud member who had carried out "a crime unprecedented in the history of democracy." Now he was left with egg on his face. He would forever be portrayed as not being able to handle the pressure. It was hard to see how he could remain in the same party with Levy.

Meanwhile, he worked to mend things at home. Sara was mortified by the television broadcast but allowed Bibi back the next day to see Yair and collect some clothes. They remained inside for hours as he beseeched her to reconcile. She demanded a divorce, but toward evening agreed to step outside and have their picture taken by one of the photographers who had been waiting outside since the previous night. Despite her anger, Sara was prepared to remain in the marriage, on her terms.

The lawyers met. Sara was represented by Yaakov Neeman, one of the best-connected attorneys in Israel, who would go on to serve as a senior minister in Netanyahu's governments. Netanyahu's attorneys were the feared litigator Dan Avi Yitzhak and Bibi's cousin David Shimron. Eventually Bibi and Sara reconciled. Neeman denied for years that there was a written agreement on the terms in his office safe, describing the rumors as "an urban legend."[5] The facts remain that from the last weeks of the primary campaign to this day, Sara has accompanied Bibi on nearly all his major public engagements, and especially his foreign trips, with the exception of military- and security-related events. She has had full access to his schedule and has vetted the appointments of members of his staff. What's more, the self-centered Netanyahu, who rarely acknowledges those around him, not only has borne Sara's constant presence with complete grace, indulging her every whim, but has seemed truly devoted to her, even when her demands for constant affirmation of her central role at his side have caused considerable political damage.

One place the "hot-tape" scandal didn't cause Netanyahu major damage was among Likud members.

I N ITS FINAL weeks, the campaign descended into acrimonious mud-slinging. In a televised debate, Levy called Netanyahu "Napoleon" and a "slippery eel," and diagnosed Likud as being in need of "antibibiotics." But Likud members thought otherwise.

On March 24, 1993, 52 percent of the party members voted for Netanyahu. Levy received 29 percent, and Begin only 16 percent. Whatever they thought of him personally, Likud's rank and file believed that Bibi could rebuild the party's fortunes and quickly return it to power. As dozens of young supporters chanted "Bibi King of Israel," he began his victory speech kissing Sara and thanking her for standing by him. It would be the first of many speeches in which he would name-check his wife.

The son of Benzion Netanyahu, who forty-five years earlier had been ostracized by the Revisionist leadership, was now leader of the movement.

17

A Political Failure?

etzudat Ze'ev—Ze'ev's Fortress, meaning Ze'ev Jabotinsky's—on King George Street in central Tel Aviv, the
Brutalist-style office block housing Likud headquarters, has
long been considered one of the city's ugliest buildings. When Likud's
new leader, Benjamin Netanyahu, made his way in on the day after winning the primaries in March 1993, it was one of the most depressing.
Likud, deep in debt following the previous year's lost elections, wasn't
even sure exactly how deep.

There was no money to fix the two elevators. Paying the phone and
electricity bills was a monthly struggle, and employees were instructed
to pretend they weren't there, in the hope of keeping debtors at bay.
Upon his arrival, Netanyahu installed himself in Menachem Begin's
old office, which for the past decade had stood empty. He wouldn't
spend much time there, but the symbolism was clear. This was no longer Begin's party. Then he appointed Avigdor Lieberman as the party's
new CEO.

Lieberman immediately embarked on a drastic program of cutbacks.
Veteran employees were mercilessly sacked, and allocations to local
branches, for years Likud's main hubs, were slashed to near-zero. A team
of accountants came in to work out what real-estate assets Likud owned,
and party buildings around the country were sold. Netanyahu's private
attorneys, David Shimron and Yitzhak Molcho, negotiated loan exten-
sions with the banks. Meanwhile, Bibi flew to New York, making the

191

rounds of his millionaire friends. He was now leader of the opposition, a prime-minister-in-waiting, all the more reason to open their wallets.

Likud's financial crisis was Netanyahu's opportunity to refashion the party in his image. His Likud was no longer a grassroots-orientated ideological movement. It would be transformed into an election-campaigning machine, like the national committees of the Republican and Democratic parties in the United States. It was to be Netanyahu's platform for winning the direct election for prime minister.

In the Likud Central Committee he pushed through changes to Likud's constitution, which were drafted by Shimron, giving the leader wide powers. He would appoint members to a new powerful executive that would rule on party matters. A toothless bureau, mainly a talking shop for discussing ideological issues, would also be elected. Ariel Sharon, who had been chairman of the now powerless Likud secretariat, opposed these changes in a Central Committee conference in May 1993, saying, "The leader can't be the only one deciding in the party and all its institutes emptied of content."[1] Sharon was overwhelmingly voted down. He proposed an amendment whereby a future Likud government would not be committed to diplomatic agreements signed by Labor. Netanyahu opposed this on legal grounds. There was a limit to how far Likud could go in fighting Rabin's government.

I N THE FIRST year of the new government, Likud focused mainly on its internal problems. Not that Rabin gave them much to protest in the first year of his term. With Shamir gone, the Bush administration authorized the $10 billion in loan guarantees, though settlement-building continued under Labor. By that point, the emigration from the former Soviet Union had ebbed somewhat, and the government used only two-thirds of the loan. The available cash allowed for investment in infrastructure and a boost to the private sector.

Five years in, the Intifada was on the wane. Instead of a popular uprising there were sporadic attacks against Israeli civilians and security personnel, many of them carried out by a new Islamist movement challenging the PLO—Hamas. In December 1992, following the abduction and murder of a police officer, Rabin ordered 415 Hamas activists deported to Lebanon. Despite strenuous objections from many in his government and in the Israeli legal establishment, who said that mass expulsion contravened international law, Rabin went ahead.

In July 1993, following clashes with Hezbollah on the Lebanese border, Rabin launched Operation Accountability, a weeklong bombardment of Hezbollah strongholds in southern Lebanon. Some 300,000 Lebanese villagers were forced to flee and 118 were killed, mainly civilians.

During its first year, the Rabin government was hardly left-wing. Most of its trouble came from the ultrareligious camp. Labor's two coalition partners were unlikely bedfellows—the left-wing and secular Meretz, and the Mizrahi, ultra-Orthodox Association of Sfardi Torah-Keepers, usually referred to by the acronym Shas. Without either party, Rabin would have lacked a majority (he hadn't invited the Arab and communist parties to join his coalition). The leadership of Shas was under intense pressure within the religious community to leave the coalition. In an attempt to mollify the rabbis, Rabin in June 1993 replaced the education minister, Shulamit Aloni, Meretz founder and leader, a staunch feminist, and an atheist. It brought only a short respite.

Netanyahu was eager to take advantage of the coalition strife and start taking the fight to the government, but he first had to complete a personal project.

T EN YEARS AFTER starting his career as Israel's media champion, Netanyahu summarized a decade of advocacy in his blueprint for Israel's future. Weighing in at 467 pages, *A Place Among the Nations*, published in April 1993 in the United States, is an unwieldy tome. It was relatively well received by American critics at the time, though it failed to garner the attention that his book on terrorism had. Updated in later English and Hebrew editions, it isn't easy reading, but twenty-five years later, it remains one of the most comprehensive, if extremely biased, examinations of Israel and the case for Zionism.

Netanyahu's policies today remain essentially identical to those he held as a relative newcomer to politics. Few politicians have had such a long and intensive career without their views evolving. Over the years, Netanyahu has been forced to publicly jettison some positions and present a more pragmatic image. In his actions, he has remained resolutely doctrinaire.

A Place Among the Nations is three books in one—a highly selective history of the Zionist enterprise; a polemic against the enemies of

Zionism and against weak-hearted Jews and Israelis who feel they have to apologize on its behalf; and a policy paper on the parameters for future Middle East peace (a later edition emphasizes this in the changed title—*A Durable Peace*).

Netanyahu's arc of history goes back millennia, to the days of sovereign Judea when the Jews were a fighting nation. Even after the destruction of the Temple in Jerusalem in 70 CE, they remained a majority in the land, under Roman and Byzantine occupation, until the first Muslim conquest in the seventh century. Taking a page out of his father's writings, Bibi likens the struggle of the Jews for their land to the Reconquista of Spain.[2] Benzion put the return of the Christian kings and the expulsion of Muslim Moors from the Iberian Peninsula at the center of Western history. The Christian return to Granada after 800 years prefigured the Jewish return to their ancient homeland 1,200 years after the Muslim conquest.

The modern Israeli-Arab conflict and the Palestinian issue in Netanyahu's book are inseparable from the 1,500-year struggle for hegemony over Europe and the Middle East—which is why he describes the land as an inconsequential backwater of the Ottoman Empire that remained largely uninhabited until Jewish immigration was renewed in earnest in the late nineteenth century. Netanyahu adapts Israel Zangwill's claim that it was a "nation without a land," arguing that the Arabs living there at the time were mainly nomads or relatively recent arrivals. The major landowners lived elsewhere, in Beirut or Damascus, leaving their land barren, until the Jews returned. The land was then developed thanks to the Jews, and the development of the land also encouraged more Arabs to emigrate there.

Netanyahu quotes a wide range of contemporary sources to support his historical narrative and claims that by the end of World War I, there was growing support in the West for rebuilding the Jewish homeland. The turning point was the rise of pan-Arab nationalism in the 1920s and the Europeans' sympathy toward the Arabs, alongside deep-seated anti-Semitism within the British Colonial Service.

From that point on, it would be the Arabists in the British and US diplomatic corps, Soviet communism, Nazi Germany, and the left-wing media who all in some degree collaborated with the genocidal urge of the Arab nations to destroy the Jewish presence. With the death of Egyptian president Gamal Abdel Nasser, pan-Arabism began losing its potency, but the same dynamic reappeared with individual Arab dictators and radical Islam.

"The durability of the twin fanaticisms of Pan-Arab nationalism and Islamic fundamentalism—their militarism, xenophobia, irredentism, and irreducible hatred of the existing order—is the true core of conflict in the Middle East," Netanyahu wrote.[3] Therefore the conflict is not about the Palestinians, borders, or refugees. It's not even about Israel. It rises from an implacable Arab and Muslim hatred toward the West, and Israel as the West's outpost in the Middle East. This being the case, real peace can only come when the Arabs recognize the Jewish state's right to exist. And there's little hope of that happening in our lifetimes:

> We must assume that for our generation and perhaps the next, the task of peacemaking is with the Arab world as it is, unreformed and undemocratic. The prevalence of radicalism in the Middle East— and the danger that, in the absence of any democratic traditions, a non-radical regime can turn radical overnight—means that peace in the Middle East must have security arrangements built into it. I have already noted that for the foreseeable future the only kind of peace that will endure in the region between Arab and Arab and between Arab and Jew is the peace of deterrence.[4]

Netanyahu's view of history is bleak. Writing immediately after the disintegration of the Soviet Union and the end of the Cold War, he attacked the "end of history" theory, made fashionable then by American political scientist Francis Fukuyama. The fall of communism in Eastern Europe was indeed proof that democracy could prevail, even among the Arabs, but there were no guarantees. International relations must still be based on military deterrence. There must be no question of Israel relinquishing control of the West Bank and the Golan Heights, vital buffer zones for a tiny state surrounded by enemies.

The Palestinians living there, whose existence Netanyahu begrudgingly acknowledged, should be offered, at most, limited autonomy. The millions of Palestinians were the responsibility of their Arab brothers, who had used them for too long as a cudgel against Israel and a fake cause to distract the world's attention from their own human rights violations. It was in the Arab nations' interest to make peace with Israel, to enjoy cooperation in science, medicine, and water management, Netanyahu wrote. The fact that they refused to do so had little to do with sympathy for the Palestinians' plight; it stemmed from their genocidal hatred of the Jews.

Netanyahu's other targets were Jews and Zionists who thought differently from him, especially Israelis who "believed that the Arabs loathed war as much as they themselves did and that, given a proper explication of Israel's peaceful intentions, the Arabs would embrace and welcome us." This "cloyingly sentimental approach" would only encourage further Arab demands and aggression, and while that view may gain Israel fleeting sympathy in the West, only standing firm for Israel's true interests would bring genuine respect and a "durable peace."[5]

A Place Among the Nations was the ultimate *hasbara* handbook. Many of the standard tropes of Israel's defenders were first set out there and have been echoed in thousands of Facebook posts and tweets by people who have never even read it. At its core is the belief that Israel's cause is unassailably just and that it is possible and imperative to convince all Westerners of that fact, with the exception of dyed-in-the-wool anti-Semites. Indeed, once the case for Israel has been properly presented, if you still disagree, you probably are an anti-Semite.

A quarter of a century after publication of the first edition, not only is *A Place Among the Nations* still the essence of Netanyahu's policy, but it remains an inexhaustible source for his speeches. "When we're working on a major speech, he'll still bring out his book for inspiration," said one long-serving aide. "He loves it and is convinced it still rings true." Netanyahu continues to insist that the Palestinian issue is a distraction from the real issues of the Middle East, telling foreign visitors that it's "a rabbit hole" that misinformed Westerners insist on going down.

The book's long list of acknowledgments included, besides Sara and Iddo (interestingly, not Benzion), some interesting names. Over the years Netanyahu had various groups of admirers with whom he would meet to plan political moves. One group of rotating confidants, known as "Bibi's submarine," were mainly Israeli friends and allies who, like him, were outsiders to the political system. Together they plotted how to take over Likud and win elections. He always had a second group, consisting mainly of Israelis who had either been born in the United States or had spent long periods of their lives there. Though they were all fluent in Hebrew, he preferred speaking with them in English, a habit he kept up in the prime minister's office of holding internal meetings in English.

This group is his brain trust, and three prominent members are mentioned in the acknowledgments to his book.

The eldest of them was David Bar-Ilan, an Israeli concert pianist who had lived most of his adult life in the United States. Alongside his musical career, Bar-Ilan was a prolific writer of pro-Israel columns in the American press. He was introduced to Netanyahu in 1985, when Bibi needed someone to organize the Jonathan Institute conference in Washington. They remained close friends, and Bar-Ilan became a fixture of Bibi's New York circle. Returning to Israel, in 1992 he became editor-in-chief of the *Jerusalem Post*. The venerable establishment newspaper, which had traditionally been aligned with Labor, had recently been bought by Hollinger, a media company owned by the right-wing Canadians Conrad Black and David Radler.

Under the new ownership, the paper veered rightward, leading to a walk-out of its best journalists led by managing editor David Landau. They refused to accept editorial interference. Netanyahu had a small part in this when, as deputy foreign minister, he had been angered by an interview with him and intervened through the owners to make changes. As editor, Bar-Ilan took the paper even further to the right, writing his own weekly column lambasting the left-wing Israeli media.

A second member of Bibi's brain trust who was mentioned in the acknowledgments to his book was Dore Gold, a Connecticut-born academic who had written his PhD on Saudi Arabia's support for terrorism. Gold was also Netanyahu's unofficial diplomatic adviser.

The third was Yoram Hazony, who researched the sources for the book and helped produce the manuscript (transcribing what Netanyahu dictated). A year later Hazony became a founder of the Shalem Center, a right-wing think tank and later a private college sponsored by Netanyahu's American donors, including Ronald Lauder. Shalem, they hoped, would become the vanguard of a new ideological movement in Israel.

Bar-Ilan, Gold, and Hazony were early members of the group that coalesced around Netanyahu from the early 1990s in a joint endeavor to replace the left-leaning elites of Israeli academia and media.

The first edition appeared before the Rabin government's negotiations with the PLO became known. But already then Netanyahu accused Rabin's government of dereliction of national duty, taking the Labor government to task for ordering Israel's diplomats, upon entering office, to relinquish "aggressive public relations"; for "declaring a unilateral cease-fire in the media war"; and for "not responding to the provocations of the Arab spokesmen."[6]

In a cruel irony, Netanyahu dealt at length in the book with the murderous nature of Arab regimes. He contrasted them with the Jews, who had learned their lesson from the period during the Second Temple, when "Jewish factions in besieged Jerusalem were literally knifing each other to death." This period, he said, "gave rise to the emphasis now placed on Jewish unity and the taboo on political killings among Jews, which has resulted in the virtual absence of civil war among Jews for two thousand years. With remarkably few exceptions, Jews do not kill Jews over politics."[7]

W ITH HIS BOOK published, Likud under control, and its finances improving, Netanyahu was ready to take on the government. At the end of August 1993, Likud prepared to launch an "Elections Now!" billboard campaign across Israel. Just as the first signs were going up, the news broke. On August 27, Israelis learned that for the past seven months, secret negotiations had been held between Israeli representatives and senior PLO members under the auspices of the Norwegian government in secluded locations around Oslo.

The Israeli media had had no idea. The circle of secrecy around the Oslo talks didn't even include the cabinet. Talks had been initiated in early 1993 by a deniable duo of academics, Yair Hirshfeld and Ron Pundak, meeting with Yasser Arafat's representatives. They reported to Yossi Beilin, who had replaced Netanyahu as deputy foreign minister. Rabin initially was skeptical, but for once he had allowed Foreign Minister Shimon Peres to persuade him. By August, an agreement had been reached whereby the PLO would officially recognize Israel and commit to ending the violence. Israel, in turn, would recognize the PLO as representing the Palestinian people and allow Arafat to establish, in the first stage, a Palestinian Authority in Gaza as well as in one West Bank city, Jericho. Following that, negotiations would take place regarding further Israeli pullbacks in the West Bank.

The Israelis were stunned. Could the Jewish state be on the verge of a historic compromise with Palestinian nationalism? Was Arafat, the archenemy, suddenly a partner for peace, and the PLO, which had been discredited by its support for Saddam Hussein just three years earlier, now to be rehabilitated, and allowed to arrive openly to territory under Israeli control?

Netanyahu was as surprised as anyone. None of his contacts in Jerusalem or Washington had informed him that such a breathtaking reversal of Israeli policy was in the offing. He lost little time lambasting the Oslo Agreement. "Israel faces an unprecedented threat to its security. The government is allowing the PLO to carry out its plan to destroy Israel," he declared in the Knesset. But the leader of the opposition was, for now, an irrelevant figure on the margins. The "Elections Now!" campaign (hastily canceled) and his new book, with its plans for a distant but "durable" peace, were totally overshadowed.

The world's eyes were on Rabin on September 10 as he signed the letter recognizing the PLO. Three days later, the first Oslo Agreement was signed on the White House Lawn, a beaming President Bill Clinton urging a reluctant Rabin to awkwardly shake Arafat's hand.

Netanyahu was slow out of the gate. In another Knesset speech, he likened the Rabin government to the British leadership that in 1938 had signed the Munich Agreement, ceding part of Czechoslovakia to Hitler's Germany. "You are worse than Chamberlain," he said. "He endangered another nation, but you are doing it to your own nation." But raising the ghosts of Munich was a tired and stale argument; it had been used for decades by Likud leaders warning against dangerous peace plans. The real battle against Oslo was already taking place on the streets in violent protests in Jerusalem. The protesters weren't Likudniks, but religious settlers who hadn't forgiven Likud's prime minister, Begin, for giving up Sinai to Egypt, or Shamir for going to the Madrid Conference. They didn't have much trust in Netanyahu, either, as he was still an unknown quantity.

Sticking to his Munich narrative, Netanyahu wrote an op-ed in the *New York Times* titled "Peace in Our Time?" He lambasted the agreement. "What will happen when terrorists attack Israelis in Jerusalem and return to nearby P.L.O. land? Or fire rockets from hills above Tel Aviv?" he wrote.[8] It was easier to express his views in the American media than to present himself as the leader of Israel's right wing. But that soon changed. At the start of the Oslo process, Bibi may have seemed like little more than a minor irritant, but he was soon to transform into its worst enemy. Oslo was to be the real start of Netanyahu's leadership campaign.

THE FIRST MONTHS of the Oslo process were euphoric. On the way back from Washington, Rabin stopped over in Morocco for a first public meeting with King Hassan. A few weeks later, secret talks that would soon lead to a peace agreement began with Jordan. All of a sudden peace between Israel and the Arab world seemed tangible. For a short while, a majority of Israelis were willing to believe in Shimon Peres's vision of "a new Middle East." Some polls had support for the Oslo Agreements at over 60 percent. The members of Israel's left wing felt they had finally won the historical argument. Veteran political scientist Zeev Sternhell wrote in *Haaretz* that Rabin's decision was widely popular and that "the opposition facing him is crumbling, clueless and leaderless. The air has escaped from the swollen balloon called Benjamin Netanyahu even faster than his most severe critics predicted."[9]

Oslo was the only game in town. Netanyahu went from being a frequent guest on the airwaves to someone whose press secretaries (who were constantly resigning) had to beg producers to even get his statements mentioned on the news. When he was booked, interviewers enjoyed mocking him. One television interview opened with the question, "Benjamin Netanyahu, are you a political failure?"[10]

It wasn't just widespread public support, and even wider media support, for the Oslo process. The Labor government was also presiding over a period of unprecedented economic bloom. Inflation was down to its lowest levels in over two decades. Flush with funds from the American loan guarantees and the fruits of a privatization drive, the government invested in infrastructure building and the first Israeli venture capital funds that gave the tech sector the boost it needed to begin competing with the world. The uneven distribution of the fruits of this prosperity would ultimately have dire political results for Labor; but during the early Oslo period, as foreign investment in Israel spiraled and the prospect of the Middle East opening up for business beckoned, peace and prosperity seemed unstoppable, and Netanyahu was sidelined.

In an attempt to recapture the narrative, Netanyahu formulated his own "peace plan." It was a very watered-down autonomy for the Palestinians in the West Bank and Gaza, allowing them limited self-rule in isolated cantons. It was inconceivable that any Palestinian leader would ever agree to such a plan, but Netanyahu didn't publish it. He knew the far right and the settlers would reject even the tiniest concessions and was afraid to jeopardize his ties to them. With Likud still unsettled under his new leadership, Netanyahu had few soldiers out on the streets. The overwhelming majority of those who were protesting daily against Oslo were from the religious right. Bibi couldn't afford to run afoul of them if he wanted to continue speaking at their rallies.

He did have one opportunity to prove himself to fellow Likudniks that year. In November 1993, local elections took place across Israel. Likud was still repaying its debts, but for Netanyahu this was a chance to show that his party was still electorally viable and that he could become an election winner.

The party machinery that Avigdor Lieberman had been building for the past seven months clicked into gear. Local Likud candidates were offered campaign and advertising services. Bibi once again crisscrossed the country, making speeches to support them. Labor's efforts, meanwhile, were disjointed, as government ministers had less time to spend on the stump. On November 2, Netanyahu began to reap the results, with Likud holding onto nearly all its local councils and municipalities and winning dozens of races against Labor. Most significant were the Likud victories in Israel's two largest cities.

In Jerusalem, the former health minister Ehud Olmert ended the twenty-eight-year rule of Labor's mayor, Teddy Kollek. In Tel Aviv, the former police minister, Ronny Milo, fought off Labor's candidate, a celebrated general. They had both shown how Likud, despite the unfavorable political climate, could still win elections. In Jerusalem, Olmert had struck a deal with the ultra-Orthodox rabbis, promising their representatives powerful positions in his city administration. They ordered their followers to vote for Olmert, ensuring his majority. In secular, left-leaning Tel Aviv, Milo departed from Likud national policy and indicated that he accepted the Oslo Agreements. Two and a half years later, Netanyahu would adopt both tactics when he promised diplomatic pragmatism and quietly made his own deals with the rabbis.

For Labor, losing Jerusalem, in particular, was a blow. But Rabin and his colleagues continued to see Netanyahu as a lightweight. They believed that as long as the peace process was on track, they had little to worry about.

18

Rabin Is "Not a Traitor"

On February 25, 1994, on the Jewish festival of Purim, a New York–born doctor and resident of the Kiryat Arab settlement entered the Ibrahimi mosque in the Tomb of the Patriarchs in Hebron. He wore his IDF reserve officer's uniform and carried an assault rifle. Baruch Goldstein had been a follower of the racist Rabbi Meir Kahane in the United States and a member of Kahane's ultranationalist Kach party after emigrating to Israel.

The Tomb of the Patriarchs had been a shared place of worship for Jews and Muslims since 1967, though clashes were frequent. Entering the Muslim area, Goldstein opened fire on worshipers, killing twenty-nine and wounding over a hundred before being overpowered and beaten to death. Goldstein's specific motives were unclear. He had acted on his own and left no message. Since the Oslo process had begun, he had taken to wearing a yellow Star of David, like the ones the Jews had been forced to wear in Germany during the Holocaust, in an act of protest. He probably hoped to set off a cycle of violence that would disrupt the peace process. Condemnations of the massacre came from all parts of the Israeli political spectrum, including Netanyahu and the other right-wing leaders and settlers. Goldstein's far-right supporters claimed he had acted to prevent a terrorist attack.

As rioting broke out in the West Bank, Rabin sent reinforcements to quell the violence while trying to keep the Oslo process on track. Kach, which had been barred since 1988 from contending in the elections on account of its racist platform, was outlawed, but Rabin decided not to antagonize the settlers and rejected recommendations to evict the small and fanatical Jewish settlement from Hebron. Neither did the security forces prevent Goldstein's supporters from holding his funeral on the outskirts of Hebron. One of those supporters was a twenty-three-year-old law student, Yigal Amir, who vowed to continue Goldstein's quest to end the peace process.

On April 6, after the forty days of mourning for the twenty-nine Muslims who had been murdered in Hebron, Hamas launched its first revenge suicide attack against Israeli civilians. The Palestinian Islamist movement was opposed to Oslo, but it had mainly remained on the sidelines until the Hebron massacre. A Hamas operative detonated himself next to a bus collecting schoolchildren in Afula in northern Israel, killing eight and wounding fifty-five. A week later, another Hamas bomber blew himself up inside a bus in the coastal city of Hadera, killing five. The explosive devices had been built by "The Engineer," Yahya Ayyash, a master planner of suicide bombing attacks. Arafat refused to publicly condemn the attack.

The next two years would be interspersed with suicide attacks, fueling protests against the government and putting Rabin and Peres in the impossible position of directing the security forces against Hamas while continuing to negotiate the next agreements with the PLO. As the public began turning against the Oslo process, Netanyahu rose in the polls. Peres's refrain was that pulling out of the talks would be "a prize to terror." Exasperated as they were with Arafat, in May 1994 Israel and the PLO signed the Cairo Agreement, which set out a timetable and procedures for implementing the principles of the Oslo Accords.

On July 1, Arafat arrived in Gaza City. The IDF pulled back from most of the Gaza Strip, retaining control of borders with Israel and Egypt, the Israeli settlements, and the roads leading to them. The following night, the right wing held a mass rally in Jerusalem's Zion Square. Some Likud leaders were dismayed upon arriving when they discovered giant "Death to Arafat" banners and Rehavam Ze'evi, the leader of far-right Moledet (Homeland) party, which called for "transfer"—that is, mass expulsion of Arabs—due to make a speech.

The demonstration had been organized by the settlers, who coordinated with Netanyahu loyalist Tzachi Hanegbi. Nearly all of the fifty thousand people who gathered in the square were religious settlers or their supporters. They planned to illegally march from the square toward the Palestinian neighborhoods and "paralyze" the city.[1] The Likud leadership was split. The "princes" Ehud Olmert, Dan Meridor, and Benny Begin were in favor of pulling out. Tzachi Hanegbi and Ariel Sharon demanded they stay. Netanyahu was on the fence. He supported the princes' demands, but he stayed. It would set a precedent for the next fourteen months.

Netanyahu's speeches during the period were measured. He fiercely criticized the government's policies, but he mainly avoided ad hominem attacks. Certainly his words were more moderate than what was being said by Sharon and other right-wing leaders. But he had coordinated with them and took part in some of the wildest protests against Rabin. Netanyahu tried to have it both ways, presenting himself as pragmatic and prime ministerial while riding the far-right tiger.

On October 19, the worst suicide attack up to that point took place in Tel Aviv. A Hamas bomber blew himself up in a crowded bus near Dizengoff Square, killing twenty-two. Netanyahu, who was nearby in Metzudat Ze'ev, joined the angry crowds jeering the government around the smoldering bus. The next day his political opponents and media pundits accused him of "dancing on the blood"; but most Israelis remembered the graphic footage of torn bodies, the driver lying dead at the wheel, and realized that even at the heart of cosmopolitan Israel, they were no longer safe. Polls in the aftermath of the "No. 5 bus bombing" had Netanyahu leading Rabin.

That week, Sara gave birth to their second son and Bibi's third child, Avner. The new mother didn't spend long at home with her baby. Sara was busy trying to complete her master's degree in psychology and accompanying her husband to public events and fundraising trips abroad. Her parents were drafted to take care of the two small boys, alongside a never-ending succession of nannies, none of whom met Sara's exacting standards. Avner's *brit milah* (circumcision ceremony), held at a large banqueting hall in Jerusalem, was Likud's social event of the year, as the party leadership, including rivals such as Sharon, put in an appearance. Boosted by the polls, Netanyahu already had the aura of a prime-minister-in-waiting. Only David Levy stayed away. He had rebuffed Netanyahu's half-hearted attempts to reconcile with him following the hot-tape scandal, saying, "He will be judged by his actions." An irrevocable split seemed unavoidable.

Rabin continued to dismiss Netanyahu, refusing to contemplate the inexperienced politician, twenty-seven years his junior, as a worthy rival. He rarely agreed to meet and update the leader of the opposition, and in Knesset debates he openly mocked him, much in the way Ben-Gurion had treated Begin in the 1950s. Their relationship would deteriorate as Rabin accused Netanyahu of leading the incitement against him.

One leader who was taking Netanyahu seriously was King Hussein of Jordan. Hussein, a keen follower of Israeli politics, was reading the polls. As Israel and Jordan negotiated a peace agreement, he wanted to ensure that Likud would be on board. Historically, the Revisionist movement regarded the foundation of the Hashemite kingdom, on land they claimed had originally been intended for the Jewish homeland, a travesty. "Two banks to the Jordan, this is ours and this ours as well," sang the Betar youth movement. Begin had relinquished this claim in 1965, but it had been replaced by the "Jordan is Palestine" plan, by which the Palestinians would build their state on the ruins of the Hashemite kingdom, rather than in the West Bank.

In May 1994, as talks gathered momentum, Netanyahu met secretly with Hussein's younger brother in London. Crown Prince Hassan sounded him out on Likud's positions on the agreement taking shape. Netanyahu assured him that Likud would not be an obstacle. On July 25, the agreement was formally announced in Washington and approved by the Knesset, 91–3, with Likud in favor (some members abstained). Unlike with Egypt, Israel did not relinquish territory to Jordan. For once there was consensus over an agreement with an Arab neighbor. The signing ceremony, on October 26 in the Jordan Valley, was a shining moment for Rabin and proof that the process with the Palestinians was yielding significant achievements. Although Netanyahu was not on stage, the signing provided an easy way for him to show pragmatism and statesmanship. A few days earlier, Hussein had called to personally congratulate him on Avner's birth. The next month, he was the guest of the Jordanian royal family at a memorial service at Karameh, where both he and Hassan had fought twenty-six years earlier as young soldiers.

Rabin was also pursuing a deal with Syria. He hoped an agreement with President Hafez al-Assad could also lead to a deal with Lebanon, over which the Assad regime exercised control, allowing Israel to pull its troops out of the "Security Zone" in southern Lebanon, where they were engaged in bloody skirmishes with Hezbollah. Conducted through American intermediaries, negotiations with Assad bogged down in intricate details about the final location of the border and security arrangements on the Golan. Neither side trusted the other sufficiently to disclose its true positions.

Rabin publicly accused Netanyahu of sabotage. In a television interview, he said, "The Likud chairman Netanyahu sent messages to Syria, saying they should wait until after the elections. . . . Don't close a deal now with Rabin."[2] Whatever messages Netanyahu had sent through third parties to Assad, it was disingenuous of Rabin to blame him for the failure of the talks. In the last decade of his life, Assad had negotiated with five different Israeli prime ministers and rejected every peace plan presented to him. He died in 2000, and it's highly unlikely he ever truly intended to reconcile with the Jewish state. Assad's rejection of Israel was a cornerstone of his hardline Ba'athist ideology.

Netanyahu and the Israeli right wing were also fighting Rabin's policy in Washington. Republican lawmakers worked to frustrate the Clinton administration and derail the Oslo Accords. In 1995, two Republicans from New York, Senator Al D'Amato and Representative Benjamin Gilman, chair of the House Committee on International Relations, put through legislation banning direct US assistance to the Palestinians. The funding was intended to provide support for Arafat's newly founded Palestinian Authority.

It was the first time the Israeli government had been outflanked from the right by Israel's ostensible supporters on Capitol Hill. The legislation was a breach of the unwritten rules that internal Israeli politics should not be fought in Washington. Netanyahu and the settlers had no compunction in splitting the Jewish and pro-Israel consensus. The majority of American Jews were fully in support of Rabin's policies, but the right-wing minority in control of AIPAC and the Conference of Presidents of Major American Jewish Organizations were not keen on Oslo, and in the Republicans controlling Congress they had willing allies.

The angry and violent atmosphere on Israel's streets spilled over in New York as two Israelis—Shulamit Aloni, now minister of communications, and Colette Avital, consul general, one of Bibi's early mentors during his student advocacy days in Boston—were both heckled and shoved by right-wingers at public events.

O N THE MORNING of January 22, 1995, a Palestinian Islamic Jihad (PIJ) suicide bomber detonated himself at the Beit Lid Junction, a busy intersection between Tel Aviv and Haifa, among a group of soldiers on their way to their base. Three minutes later, a second bomber blew himself up near the first responders who had rushed to the scene. Twenty-two Israelis died.

Public support for Oslo plumbed the depths. Polls in the aftermath of the Beit Lid attack had only a third of Israelis still supporting the process with the Palestinians. According to a poll conducted by the newspaper *Yedioth Ahronoth*, if elections were held in early February, Netanyahu would beat Rabin 52–38. Arafat refused to arrest the Hamas and PIJ leaders on a list presented to him by Israel. The Oslo talks were suspended for a few weeks as Israel imposed a closure on the West Bank and Gaza. But more suicide attacks took place in April, July, and August.

The ultra-Orthodox Shas had pulled out of the Labor coalition, and Rabin's government was based on a minority coalition. The Arab parties, who weren't members of the government, and Shas saved the government by not voting against it in no-confidence votes. Elections were to be held at the very latest by late 1996, and suddenly the prospect of Netanyahu becoming prime minister seemed very real. Most of his many rivals and critics within Likud piped down and got in line. They didn't want to miss out on promotion once the party got back in power. All but Levy.

Attempts to bridge the rift between them failed, and Netanyahu pushed for more constitutional changes within the party, aimed at shrinking Levy's influence. He failed to heed warnings about forcing Levy out. In June 1995, the Likud Central Committee met to decide how new members would be appointed. Levy demanded a quota system ensuring representation of his supporters. Netanyahu refused, instead proposing that the party branches, which were controlled by his people, elect most of the members of the party's institutions. Without mentioning Levy, in his speech Netanyahu compared those opposing his leadership to Arab dictators pressuring Israel. Benny Begin proposed an opposing motion, which was steamrolled—the Central Committee voted 1,074–330 for Netanyahu's motion. Levy boycotted the meeting, announcing he was leaving Likud.

On June 18, Levy formed a new party, Gesher (Bridge), and accused Likud under Netanyahu of having abandoned the party's traditional

Mizrahi voters in working-class neighborhoods and the development towns—founded in the 1950s for the immigrants arriving in the new state, mainly from Arab countries. Netanyahu wasn't perturbed. Only one other Likud MK left with Levy. Bibi was confident that he would win the next election without them.

IN DECEMBER 1994, Rabin and Peres were back in Oslo, receiving the Nobel Peace Prize together with Arafat. The world feted them as peacemakers, but many Israelis were left cold. Initial public enthusiasm had long ago evaporated. Arafat was once again seen as the terror chieftain, only now he was standing beside Israel's leaders. As suicide bombings continued, security crackdowns on the Palestinians became much more popular among the voters than peace talks or shiny diplomatic ceremonies abroad.

Surveys showed that most Israelis still respected Rabin as a strong and trustworthy leader, much more than Netanyahu. But frustrated by terrorist attacks, they were increasingly inclined to give Bibi a chance. In an attempt to broaden his appeal, Netanyahu admitted that if he was elected, despite his deep misgivings, he would not renege on agreements already signed by the government. "Reciprocity" became his watchword. He would keep to the deal, but since Arafat was a congenital liar and unreformed terrorist, he claimed the process would founder on the Palestinians' intransigence. Put on the spot by an interviewer asking whether, if elected prime minister, he would meet Arafat, Bibi answered, "I'll send my foreign minister."

He had been Likud leader for only two years but already believed that the prime minister's office was his by right. Bibi wouldn't be another Begin, waiting patiently for three decades for the pendulum to swing. He was anxious for elections. The settlers were more desperate to stop pullbacks.

ON SEPTEMBER 28, 1995, after over a year of wrangling with Arafat, Israel and the PLO signed the "Interim Agreement on the West Bank and the Gaza Strip," more commonly known as the Oslo II Accord. Israeli forces were to pull out of all the Palestinian cities, as they had from Gaza and Jericho, and from 450 villages. The territory would be split into three areas. Urban Area A would be under full Palestinian security control. Rural Area B would be under civilian Palestinian control with Israeli security. Area C, including all Jewish settlements, the roads leading to them, and borders with Israel and Jordan, would remain under full Israeli control.

Essentially, it was not that different from Netanyahu's shelved "cantons plan." Presenting Oslo II in the Knesset a week later, Rabin said it would lead to "less than a state" for the Palestinians. He promised that the settlements would not be moved, Jerusalem would remain united under Israeli sovereignty, and Israel would "not return to the 4 June 1967 lines."

Rabin's assurances were not enough. Oslo II barely scraped through in a 61–59 vote. Two hawkish Labor MKs broke with the party in protest over giving the PLO control of wide swaths of the West Bank. The government was saved by two other MKs, former members of the right-wing Tzomet (Crossroads) party, who had defected to the coalition and received ministerial posts. The right wing blasted Rabin for passing the agreement "on the votes of Arabs and for the price of a Mitsubishi [the new deputy minister's government car]." In and outside the Knesset, the Oslo II debate was the stormiest period of Rabin's premiership.

On the evening of the debate, another mass demonstration was held in Zion Square, and once again, Netanyahu spoke. He criticized the government for passing the agreement with "a non-Zionist majority," adding, "It relies on five Arab representatives who are aligned with the PLO."

The crowd was at fever pitch. When he heard people shouting "with blood and fire we will banish Rabin," Netanyahu answered them, "That's not the way. No blood and fire, just the ballot box." But his pleas fell on deaf ears, and many in the crowd chanted, "Death to Rabin." Out of his sight from the balcony overlooking the square, a few demonstrators were burning Rabin's picture. Others handed out photomontages of Rabin wearing an SS officer's cap. He couldn't see them, but television reports from the demonstration were edited to make it seem like Netanyahu had encouraged the "Death to Rabin" calls and the burning of his photograph.[3] When he was told of the goings-on in the square, he immediately denounced them, but it was too late.

Netanyahu was driven back to the Knesset for the debate. "This is the most estranged government ever from the [Jewish] heritage of Israel," Netanyahu said from the podium. "The government's alienation from the heritage is the real reason for its policies and why Hebron is to them an Arab city, Judea and Samaria the 'west bank,' the Golan, Arab land."

Rabin angrily shouted from the government seats, "You want to go back into Gaza." Netanyahu answered, "No, Mr. Rabin, I don't want to go back to Gaza, but you have brought Gaza back into Tel Aviv, and you have brought Gaza into every part of the land of Israel."[4]

Rabin retorted, "You just shut up. When Menachem Begin made the decision to withdraw from the Sinai Peninsula, you weren't even here. You have never in your life filled any kind of position involving responsibility for security."[5]

Outside the parliament, rioters spotted the prime minister's car. Rabin was not there, but members of the outlawed Kach movement surrounded it, banging on its sides. Later one of them proudly presented the Cadillac symbol he had prised off the vehicle. "Just like we got to the symbol, we can get to Rabin himself," he boasted.[6] Another member of the government, Housing Minister Benjamin Ben-Eliezer, was surrounded as he tried to reach the Knesset. When he finally made it in, shaken, the debate in the plenum was suspended for a few minutes as news of the rioting filtered in.

Netanyahu asked to make a special statement. "The first condemnation I made immediately after I heard of that calumny, during the protest," he claimed. Rabin refused to listen, leaving the plenum. Netanyahu blamed "a group of thugs, I know which illegal movement they belong to. You must not accuse an entire community because of a group of thugs." He compared the cries of "Rabin the murderer" to similar cries in the past by left-wing demonstrators against Sharon and Begin. "This was always wrong. . . . And we emphatically denounce it."[7]

But he had been there when the cries were heard and Rabin's portrait was burnt in the square. Other Likud leaders, including Meridor, Milo, and Begin, had stayed away. When Reuven Rivlin had arrived, sensing the atmosphere, he had left the balcony. Netanyahu stayed.

The next day Netanyahu told Likud's representatives to end their coordination with the far right. They ended their coordination, but it didn't change the violent tone on the streets. They weren't his people on the streets anyway.

O‌VER THE DECADES Israeli society has seen major waves of public unrest. National anger rose after the Yom Kippur and Lebanon wars, and there were protests against the peace agreement with Egypt and the disengagement from Gaza. There were rallies against corruption in politics in 1990, and there would be more in 2017. There would be "social justice" protests against the squeezing of the middle class in 2011. But there has been nothing as prolonged, as intense, and as toxic as the anti-Oslo protests of 1993 to 1995.

They were led by religious settlers who saw the process with the Palestinians as an existential threat to all they had built since 1967. They were the ideological and organizational backbone of the movement, which spanned the more moderate right and the various religious groups and at the extreme edge included the outlawed Kahanists. Together they held large rallies, blocked highways, and built dozens of illegal settlement outposts. A few of them attacked Palestinian targets in an attempt to disrupt the talks. Not all in the movement supported violence, and their shocked condemnation of Goldstein's bloodbath in Hebron was near-complete. But no one made a serious attempt to detach the violent group from the wider camp.

As the Oslo process ground on, defying terrorist attacks and political strife, the protests focused more and more on Rabin himself. Demonstrators tried to disrupt the prime minister's every public appearance, shouting him down and jostling his entourage. On Fridays, when Rabin returned for the weekend from the official residence in Jerusalem to his apartment in north Tel Aviv, they were waiting outside, shouting insults and threats. Once they called out to Leah Rabin, "You will be strung up like Mussolini and his mistress."

Rabin was at first ambivalent. When he was warned that he was personally at risk, he responded, "I was in much more dangerous situations in my army service."[8] Outwardly he remained dismissive, but as intelligence accumulated of attacks planned against both government and Palestinian targets, he privately urged the attorney general, Michael Ben-Yair, and the Supreme Court president, Aharon Barak, to agree to radical legal steps, including possibly administrative detentions against far-right activists. Neither, however, were eager to suspend the civil freedoms of the government's critics. Ben-Yair had also refused the security service's demand to be allowed to torture Palestinian terrorism suspects in the frantic attempt to prevent further suicide attacks.

Still, Rabin didn't fear for his own security. Shin Bet failed to beef up his bodyguard detail, and when they gingerly recommended Rabin wear a bullet-proof vest in public, he shot them down immediately.

The Shin Bet was aware of dark mutterings among extreme settlers and rabbis on the necessity of removing Rabin and whether it was even a holy Jewish duty. But they had no indication of an active assassination plot. In early August, Rabin finally relented to Shin Bet chief Karmi Gillon's request to be allowed to brief leaders of the anti-Oslo camp and warn them that the tone of their protests could lead to political violence, perhaps even an attempt on the prime minister's life. Gillon met with right-wing politicians, settler leaders, and rabbis. One of them was Netanyahu, who appeared to be surprised by what Gillon had to say, and skeptical that the situation could lead to serious violence. He didn't see what influence he could have on a potential attacker.

Gillon also gave a rare briefing to a small group of senior journalists. In the briefing he spoke mainly of other security matters, reaching the concern over Jewish terrorist attacks only toward the end. He said he was most worried about possible attacks against Palestinians and the mosques on the Temple Mount in Jerusalem. He added that he was worried about "UFOs," minor figures not on the Shin Bet's radar who "all day hear that Rabin is a murderer." For people like this, he said, "I have no intelligence solution. The only solution is security." He told the journalists that he had met with and warned right-wing leaders and rabbis. He didn't single out Netanyahu.[9]

The headlines the next day were of Shin Bet's warning of an attack on Rabin or Peres. Sharon attacked the government, saying that the warnings were actually incitement against the right wing, fabricated by Rabin, whom he compared to Stalin. A few weeks later in a television interview, Rabin accused his right-wing opponents—who blamed him for the terrorist attacks—of being "collaborators with Hamas."

"They are trying to dance on the blood. . . . They are not condemning the [Hamas] murderers, but attacking me for political gain. . . . I'll say it again, they are helping Hamas. . . . Hamas is relying on them."[10]

NETANYAHU'S CONDUCT IN those toxic months has remained the most indelible stain on his record. The charge that he led the incitement has become accepted truth. But at no point did Netanyahu use the vocabulary of the far right against Rabin and his ministers. He didn't join in the chorus calling for the "Oslo criminals" to be put on trial for treason. He confronted those who were chanting "Rabin the traitor," admonishing them. "He's not a traitor, [but] he's making a big mistake," he said forcefully at a rally in April. "We are dealing with political rivals, not enemies. We are one nation."[11]

But Netanyahu has been pronounced guilty of incitement by association. He did not get up and leave when the chanting began. He continued arriving at demonstrations where calls for Rabin's murder were made. Often he was not on the stage, but on the fringes of the crowd. Some Likud leaders refused to take part in these events. Others joined in. Sharon enthusiastically joined his settler allies. In a newspaper column, Sharon wrote, "What is the difference between the Jewish committees in the Ghettos and the government? There they were forced to collaborate and here the government is doing it from its free will." Sharon was never damned for likening the Rabin government to collaborators with the Nazis. Netanyahu, who didn't use that imagery against Rabin, was presented as the head inciter because he was the prime minister's rival.

What could Netanyahu have done differently? It was his duty as leader of the opposition that was fighting the government on a policy that would have historically changed Israel's foundation, disastrously in his opinion, to lead the protests. Most of the thousands who flocked to the rallies were not members of his party. The protesters burning Rabin's picture had never been Likudniks. Netanyahu had no control over them. Did he have the option of splitting the anti-Oslo camp? He could have denied them cooperation, but the right wing had lost power in 1992 as a result of its fragmentation. Likud's membership lacked the fervor and dedication of the settler movement. A more moderate Likud rally against the government would have attracted much smaller numbers.

Refusing to work with the far right would have meant Netanyahu and Likud giving up the streets. That would have limited them to speechmaking in the Knesset and being sidelined by a largely pro-Oslo media. Israeli politics was still being played out on the streets in the early 1990s, not the Internet, and the extremists made up the necessary numbers. Keeping out of the fray would have diminished Likud's voice and would have probably done nothing to minimize the incitement and violence. Netanyahu had no power to prevent what would happen on November 4.

O N OCTOBER 26, a forty-four-year-old man, using a Libyan passport with an assumed name, landed in Malta, on the ferry from Tripoli.

A few hours later, while walking through Sliema, a resort town on Malta's east coast, two men riding a motorcycle shot him in the head before speeding away. Israel had taken revenge against one of the masterminds of the suicide bombing campaign. The assassination of Palestinian Islamic Jihad's founder and secretary-general, Fathi Shaqaqi, was one of the last operations that Yitzhak Rabin signed off on.

Nine days later, Rabin took part in a rally in central Tel Aviv under the slogan "Yes to Peace. No to Violence." He had initially been skeptical about the rally. He wasn't sure whether he wanted to draw more attention to the campaign being waged against him and feared that too few supporters would come. The fears were baseless. Many members of the Israeli left wing, or, as they called themselves, "the peace camp," were fed up with the streets being dominated by the right, and turned out in strength. The square opposite city hall was packed.

"I always believed the majority of the nation wants peace, is prepared to take risks for peace," Rabin said in his last speech. "The nation really wants peace and opposes violence. Violence eats away at the foundation of Israeli democracy. It must be denounced, condemned, isolated. It is not the way of the state of Israel. There is democracy. There can be disagreements. But they are settled in democratic elections."[12]

19

Good for the Jews

As Eitan Haber, Yitzhak Rabin's chief of staff, read the government statement on the prime minister's assassination, people in the crowd outside Ichilov Hospital in Tel Aviv were already shouting "Bibi the murderer!"

The slain prime minister's body still warm, the public had yet to learn the assassin's identity, but Netanyahu was already being cast as the principal villain. Ostracized by the establishment, he was first informed that Rabin had died in the hospital by the US ambassador to Israel, Martin Indyk. The only official communication he received that night was from the Shin Bet informing him that his security was being beefed up.

After hours huddling with his advisers, Netanyahu came out to give a short statement. "The people of Israel gave up on political murder 2000 years ago," he said. "We don't replace the government by rule of gun." Netanyahu was visibly shaken. He had dismissed warnings of an actual assassination attempt. He was well aware that the media would accuse him, but was convinced that he had done nothing wrong. Privately, he blamed Rabin for not agreeing to meet in those last months and join in a call against violence. "It's the responsibility of the prime minister to bring the nation together, not split it," he complained.[1]

On the eve of the "Yes to Peace. No to Violence" rally in Tel Aviv, he had for the first time called upon the right wing not to cause a disruption. It didn't make much of a difference. Counterdemonstrators arrived. Netanyahu had no influence over the far right, certainly not over the assassin,

Yigal Amir, a law student and a supporter of the Hebron murderer Baruch Goldstein. When Amir's name came out shortly after the murder, Netanyahu dispatched Avigdor Lieberman to the Likud offices to ensure that he was not a party member.

Netanyahu wasn't surprised by the polls a few days later showing a gap of 30 percent between him and Shimon Peres. He knew the bullets that had killed Rabin had also blown away his prospects of winning the election. As far as the Israeli establishment was concerned, Bibi sat in the dock alongside Amir—and with them, the religious and settler communities.

The Likud faction gathered the next day in the Knesset. Netanyahu warned that "no one should dare blame Likud for the tragedy. It's a false accusation. The real incitement began ten minutes after Rabin's murder." He wasn't prepared to shoulder any of the blame. But some of his Likud colleagues were already convinced that the party would be better off without him. Benny Begin and Dan Meridor, who privately blamed Netanyahu for getting too close to the far right, prevailed upon him to announce Likud's support for Peres's appointment as prime minister. Agreeing, Netanyahu said to the media, "We won't let an assassin's bullet decide who is the prime minister of Israel." One of his Likud rivals muttered quietly, "The Knesset's mourning session for Rabin is the wake of Netanyahu's political career."[2]

P ERES DONNED RABIN's mantle. The rivalry between them had never gone away. Rabin had feared that Peres was planning to run against him again in 1996 for the Labor leadership. "Shimon will haunt me to my last day!" he said shortly before his death.[3] Peres was soon to discover that Rabin had kept him in the dark over negotiations with Syria. He swore to continue Rabin's legacy, but to go about it in a different fashion.

Rabin had refused to meet with Netanyahu, dismissed his religious opponents, and called the settlers protesting him "propellers"—implying that they just made wind and had no influence or effect. Peres was much more conciliatory. As he formed his new government, he sought to bring the right-wing National Religious Party, or NRP (Miflaga Datit Leumit, or Mafdal), into the fold. Until 1977, NRP had been Labor's perpetual coalition partner. Peres sent his closest aide, Yossi Beilin, to renew the "historic Mapai-NRP alliance." The NRP leaders, shocked by the murder, were willing to join, even though they continued to oppose the

Oslo process. But Labor's existing partner, the left-wing Meretz party, kiboshed any coalition with "those who had nurtured the murderer."[4] This was just the start of the political damage Meretz would cause Peres in the next months.

Despite all that had happened, Peres still retained warm feelings toward Bibi, whom he had first befriended after Yoni's death eighteen years earlier. The rancor between Netanyahu and Rabin hadn't changed that. In his speech in the Knesset recommending Peres as prime minister, Netanyahu referred to him as "Shimon my friend," adding that "Yitzhak Rabin's death commands us all to remember peace begins at home."[5]

Ten days after the murder, Peres received Netanyahu at the prime minister's office. In the interest of national reconciliation, meeting the leader of the opposition was the responsible thing to do. Peres's Labor and Meretz colleagues were angry at him for doing so—in their view, Bibi was to be shunned as the assassin's accomplice. Peres refused to shun him, however, and instead began the process of his rival's rehabilitation.

Others wouldn't forgive Netanyahu. Rabin's widow, Leah, set the tone, refusing to shake Netanyahu's hand at the mourning session in the Knesset and again at the state funeral on Mount Herzl, attended by leaders from around the world, including President Bill Clinton and former presidents Jimmy Carter and George H. W. Bush. "[Netanyahu] didn't say a word when Yitzhak was being called 'murderer' and 'traitor,' and I will not forgive him as long as I live," she said.[6] As the Rabin family sat shiva, the seven days of mourning, in their Tel Aviv home, Yasser Arafat arrived to console them. Netanyahu was advised not to come.

President Clinton agreed to meet Netanyahu after the funeral before leaving Jerusalem. Netanyahu stressed that it was Likud that had made peace with Egypt and gone to the Madrid Conference. Clinton wasn't impressed.

THE POST-ASSASSINATION WEEKS were a bitter time in Israel, verging on hysterical. The media rehashed the events of the previous months again and again, establishing the narrative of "the incitement that led to Rabin's murder." Although there was no proof he had influenced the murderer, Netanyahu was portrayed as the chief inciter.

Amir had been arrested at the scene. Two accomplices who had helped him plan his actions and prepared the murder weapon were arrested as well. But the police and Shin Bet, despite questioning extreme rabbis and far-right activists, failed to find anyone else who had been in on the plot. A national commission investigated the security failings that had allowed Amir to get close to Rabin's car and shoot him three times in the back, but it didn't have a wider mandate to probe the political atmosphere and incitement before the assassination. Peres refused entreaties from the left wing to use the murder as an opportunity for a crackdown on the settlers.

The roots of Netanyahu's deep-seated hatred of the Israeli media, his certainty that no matter what, the "left-wingers" dominating journalism would always blame him and were out to drag him down, can be found in those days. Bibi complained that blaming him for inciting Rabin's murder was "Orwellian" and that he was being silenced.

For Likud old-timers, being blamed for the assassination was a replay of the murder of the Zionist socialist leader Haim Arlozorov on a Tel Aviv beach sixty-two years earlier, when the Yishuv establishment had accused the Revisionists of the murder. The event had marked the beginning of Benzion Netanyahu's political career and the end of that of his father, Rabbi Nathan Mileikowsky, perhaps even hastening his premature death. But for Bibi, the fallout from Rabin's death was not just a collective accusation of his entire political movement, it was personal. None of his Likud colleagues, not even Ariel Sharon, who had been much more vitriolic toward Rabin, were ostracized in the same way. It was ultimate proof that he was still an outsider.

Further proof that he was being treated unfairly by the Israeli press came when his old friend Ted Koppel arrived a week after the murder to record a special edition of ABC's *Nightline*. Koppel gave Netanyahu equal airtime with Peres. In an interview with Leah Rabin, he asked what no Israeli reporter had—Why had she greeted Arafat warmly, but refused to shake Netanyahu's hand? At a town-hall debate he hosted in Jerusalem, right-wing politicians were given space to criticize the Oslo process, and their supporters were well in evidence in the audience. The left-wingers were shocked at their opponents being treated as a legitimate side to the debate so soon after the assassination. It was the first place the right had been allowed to accuse the government of using national bereavement to squelch public discourse. Facing Koppel, Netanyahu felt comfortable enough to accuse it of "McCarthyism at its purest." Leah Rabin complained afterward that "this is not the time yet for such debates and definitely not on our TV screens."[7]

There were those in Likud who felt that Netanyahu could never come back. In the days after the assassination, Galya Albin, a Likud supporter and businesswoman (who had been rumored in the past to have been in a relationship with Bibi), announced a campaign to replace him with the moderate "prince" Meridor. However, Meridor lacked a wide base of supporters, and the veteran Revisionists were rallying around their leader, who in their view was being "scapegoated by the left." Another powerful party chief who threw his support behind Netanyahu was Sharon, who detested Meridor.

Meridor never had the stomach for a fight. He would have accepted the leadership only if it was presented to him on a silver platter. He was forced to publicly foreswear any challenge.

Netanyahu's leadership was never seriously under threat, but the talk of a challenge reenergized him. Days after the murder, he was back in election mode. A date had yet to be announced, but he was already putting together his campaign team. He asked another rival, Benny Begin, to serve as campaign chairman. Begin, who would almost certainly have supported a challenge to Netanyahu, sensed that he was being used to rehabilitate Netanyahu's image and turned down the offer.

WITH HIS NEW government sworn in, Peres had to make a fateful decision. Riding high in the polls, he was told by nearly all his political advisers and ministers to take advantage of the seemingly insurmountable lead and hold elections in two months. It is almost impossible to see how Netanyahu could have closed the gap. But Peres hated the idea of winning under Rabin's shadow. He believed that in a year he would reach historic peace agreements with Syria and the Palestinians. Then, at the end of 1996, he would win the election in his own right.

For weeks, Peres dithered. Pressure within Labor to call early elections remained intense. It was Netanyahu's nightmare scenario. But one very influential voice was still calling upon Peres to wait: President Clinton convinced him that peace with Syria was within his grasp and urged him to hold off on the election. Clinton, who was well briefed on the Israeli political scene, must take part of the blame for Peres's fatal miscalculation.

One of the unheeded Labor ministers was Ehud Barak. Netanyahu's commander from his Matkal days had steadily risen to the post of IDF chief of staff. A legendary general who had been compared to Rabin, soon after his discharge he had been appointed by Rabin as interior minister. Barak, who never suffered from false humility, suggested that Peres appoint him defense minister in Rabin's place. It would have been a wise political move for Peres. The sturdy Barak would shield Peres from the inevitable criticism he would receive on security affairs while he continued to focus on diplomacy. But Peres wanted to serve as prime minister and defense minister simultaneously, just as Rabin and his mentor David Ben-Gurion had. Barak was instead promoted to foreign minister.

Peres's ambition led him to take on the burden of the Defense Ministry and push forward in two complex areas, taking on the responsibilities of serving as prime minister of a country that was undergoing deep national trauma, and maintaining leadership of a party preparing for elections. Ultimately he failed at both.

The first few weeks were promising. Israel set about implementing Oslo II, pulling out of the Palestinian cities of Tulkarm, Kalkilya, Nablus, Ramallah, and Bethlehem by the end of December. The shock of Rabin's murder held, and the settlers, for once, remained silent. A historic pullback took place with barely a murmur. Within weeks, Israel no longer directly ruled over a majority of the Palestinians. Arafat's security forces took control of the cities, and Ramallah became the new Palestinian capital. High-level talks commenced between Israel and Syria at the Wye River Plantation on the Eastern Shore of Maryland under American auspices. For a brief moment, it seemed like Peres's plans were coming together.

Netanyahu had one advantage over Peres—he could focus solely on the upcoming election. He was still lagging in the polls by more than twenty points, but more intensive polling revealed that the underlying fundamentals hadn't changed. Half the Israeli public still opposed the Oslo process, and a majority feared there were more terrorist attacks in store for Israel. It seemed that following his vilification by the media, a "shy Likudnik" tendency had taken hold, with many potential Netanyahu voters ashamed of admitting to the pollsters that they still supported him. Bibi believed that, given time, the shock would wear off, and he could beat Peres.

It would take a much more nuanced message to win back enough voters. For the first time, Netanyahu began tacking to the center. In interviews, he promised to uphold the Oslo Agreements, should he be elected.

If necessary, he said, he would even meet with Arafat. When the interviewers, off the record, asked him if he really believed he could overcome the odds and win, he answered, "I've never lost in my life."

O N JANUARY 5, 1995, "The Engineer," Yahya Ayyash, the Hamas commander who had built the explosive devices and masterminded the Palestinian suicide attacks since 1992, answered a phone call from his father. Ayyash was hiding in the basement of a friend's house in Gaza City. The friend's uncle had dealings with Israeli security, and the Shin Bet had smuggled through him a mobile phone on which they could eavesdrop on Ayyash's calls. That morning, after confirming that it was "The Engineer" on the line, a signal was transmitted that detonated a small explosive charge in the phone, blowing Ayyash's head apart.

The operation had been put in motion months earlier by Rabin, who approved adding Ayyash to the list of terror operatives marked down for elimination. Upon taking over, Peres had greenlighted the operation. As always in these cases, the Israeli government refused to explicitly take responsibility for the killing, but its leaders, including Peres, publicly expressed satisfaction at the demise of a man with the blood of so many Israelis on his hands. It was an ingenious assassination. It also turned out to be political suicide.

More encouraging news on the Palestinian front came on January 20, when Arafat was officially elected Palestinian president with an 88 percent majority. With most of Oslo II now implemented, the sides could start negotiating the next round of agreements leading to a permanent status. Peres, however, began to realize that it was highly unlikely the thorny issues of borders, Palestinian refugees, Jerusalem, and the future of the settlements could be resolved by the end of the year. Meanwhile, talks with the Syrians had once again bogged down on the myriad details of the exact location of the future border and security arrangements on the Golan Heights. Peres still held out for at least a public meeting with President Hafez al-Assad. He dreamed of sealing the election with his own Begin-Sadat moment. But Assad would never meet an Israeli leader.

Suddenly, there was a compelling case for early elections. On February 11, Peres finally announced that Israel would be going to the polls on May 29. He still led in the polls by around twenty points, but Bibi was ready. He had been planning his campaign for months.

Only two weeks after announcing elections, things began going drastically downhill for Peres.

Nearly two months had passed since Ayyash's death. During that time, there was reason to hope that Hamas's expertise in launching devastating suicide bombings had been significantly eroded, and that Arafat's men were finally taking concrete steps to prevent Hamas from reasserting itself. On March 25, the illusions were shattered. A Hamas bomber blew himself up on the no. 18 bus in central Jerusalem, killing twenty-six. It was the first of four bombings, including a second identical one against the same Jerusalem bus route in the space of eight days, in which a total of fifty-nine were murdered. Hamas carried out the attacks in retribution for Ayyash's death and to prove that his students were equally proficient in bomb-making.

In Jerusalem, the security forces posted armed soldiers at every bus stop. It wasn't just the attacks' sudden ferociousness, but their locations as well, that had security on high alert. On the main artery of Jerusalem's transportation network and then in the heart of cosmopolitan Tel Aviv, a bomber smuggled in from Gaza detonated himself outside the crowded Dizengoff Center, a shopping mall. It was the day before Purim and the scenes were etched on Israelis' minds. Parents and children at the mall to buy Purim costumes were searching for each other in the debris.

This time, Bibi didn't rush out to the scene of the bombing and issue orders to Likudniks not to join protests. Instead, it was an ashen-faced Peres on the scene. He viewed the carnage while hundreds gathered around, shouting insults against the government. It was as if Rabin's assassination had never taken place. The immunity that Peres had gained in the intervening months suddenly evaporated. Netanyahu adopted a new moderate tone. "Fight them Shimon! We will support you," he called from the Knesset podium. There was no need for him to criticize the government; it was happening on the streets without his involvement. Following the Dizengoff bombing, as the cabinet conferred in the nearby Defense Ministry, crowds closed on the compound, screaming for Peres to resign.

Had Ayyash's killing opened the gates of hell, as Hamas claimed? Some in Peres's entourage believed the assassination had been a mistake. Arafat's men had at the time been discussing a discreet ceasefire with Hamas. Peres insisted this was not the case, and that Hamas was acting on orders from its sponsors in Iran to disrupt the peace process. Few seriously questioned the wisdom of Israel's long-standing policy to take out the terror masterminds, who just kept on regenerating in younger and more destructive versions. Either way, with less than two months to election day, the campaign that had begun as Peres's inevitable procession to victory had taken a violent turn. His lead in the polls in the aftermath of the attacks halved to under 10 percent and continued shrinking.

Israel was supposed to have changed irrevocably after Rabin's death. It hadn't. It was still split between those who believed that only peace with the Arabs would guarantee long-term security and those who were convinced that security could only be achieved through eternal vigilance and deterrence. Netanyahu, no longer "dancing on the blood" at the bomb sites, was much better positioned than Peres to fight such an election. This was the campaign he had been preparing for, on his terms.

IN THE FIRST month after Rabin's murder, both candidates flew to the United States. Peres, in Washington, met with President Clinton, who received him like a long-lost brother, and presented his grand vision for Middle East peace to a joint session of Congress. Netanyahu's visit had a much lower profile. He arrived in New York with Sara on December 27 and spent only twelve hours there. He was in town to hire a campaign director.

Placing his political fate in the hands of someone who didn't speak Hebrew and had never fought an election in Israel would have been unthinkable for any other Israeli politician, but not for Netanyahu. Bibi needed someone whom he could trust to rise above party politics, and, more crucially, someone he respected enough that he would allow himself to be overruled by him. No one in Israeli politics fit that bill. But Ronald Lauder had just the man in New York.

Arthur Finkelstein had spent a quarter of a century working on Republican campaigns, including those of Presidents Nixon and Reagan, before he met Netanyahu. He had mentored two generations of Republican campaigners, but had remained in the shadows for his entire career. It was in Israel where he became a household name.

A Finkelstein campaign consisted of two key stages. First came intensive polling to identify the electorate's hidden fears and hopes as well as his client's and opponent's strengths and vulnerabilities. Based on the findings, the second stage was a relentless series of short attack ads targeting the opponent's weak spots. Finkelstein would hit upon a single word, conjuring up voters' most visceral emotions. He said his proudest achievement in decades of running campaigns for conservative candidates was turning the word "liberal" into a pejorative.

He was no magician. Finkelstein had had his fair share of defeats in the United States, and he would go on to lose in Israel as well. Lauder had first met him in 1989 when Finkelstein had run his campaign to win the Republican nomination for New York City mayor. Although Lauder had lost that race, he knew that Finkelstein's strategy had scored an impressive number of victories for no-hoper candidates taking on entrenched incumbents. Finkelstein had enjoyed one of his signature wins in 1994, when he had guided the campaign of George Pataki, a little-known state senator, to successfully unseat three-term New York governor Mario Cuomo, who had long been considered a potential heavyweight contender for the Democratic presidential nomination.

Impressed, Bibi enthusiastically accepted Lauder's recommendation. He also expected Lauder to help foot Finkelstein's $1,000-an-hour bill. The guru came not only with a hefty price tag but with a busy schedule, as it was an election year in the United States as well, and he was running dozens of campaigns back home. He would make only short visits to Israel, spending three or four days there at a time, and leave one of his assistants onsite in his absence. All polling data would have to be translated to English, and meetings with Netanyahu's campaign team would be held, in English, at Jerusalem's King David Hotel, where Finkelstein would stay under an alias.

Finkelstein was worth it. His first round of polls confirmed Netanyahu's earlier belief. Peres's lead was "soft," and the polls cited in the media failed to take into account the large proportion of "undecideds" and "shy Likudniks." With these constituencies in play, the election would be a close-run affair, Finkelstein predicted. The team began crafting Likud's messages accordingly.

Labor also had foreign advisers. Doug Schoen, Clinton's favorite pollster, had been sent to Israel in 1995 to help Rabin prepare for elections, and he continued after Rabin's death, advising Peres's team. He was not a government official, but he was a useful back channel for Clinton, who was able to remain abreast of the scene while maintaining the barely credible fiction that the administration didn't take sides in internal Israeli politics. Schoen's research pointed to conclusions similar to Finkelstein's, but his warnings remained unheeded by Labor's campaign chiefs. Peres had doled out the key campaign positions to his senior ministers, and the headquarters was riven by infighting as they competed for influence and squared off against each other in the primaries for Labor's Knesset list. They ignored Schoen's advice, regarding him as an outsider who failed to understand Israeli politics. Jacques Séguéla, the French public relations guru who had masterminded François Mitterrand's presidential campaigns, and who had also been hired, by an admirer of Peres, to work on the campaign, received similar treatment.

Likud's campaign team was more focused than Labor's. Led by former ad executive and Knesset member Limor Livnat, along with Netanyahu's old press officer from the United Nations, Eyal Arad, it included a much higher proportion of PR professionals, some of whom were left-wingers attracted by the challenge and the money. Bibi ruled that Finkelstein, not the politicians, would have the last word.

Under Finkelstein's guidance, the team zeroed in on Jerusalem as Peres's weak point. An overwhelming majority of Israelis, including those supporting Oslo, were against any concessions to the Palestinians in Israel's contested capital. The fact that Likud had zero evidence of the government negotiating with the Palestinians over Jerusalem was immaterial. "Peres will split Jerusalem" was a devastating slogan.

Finkelstein drilled the team until they understood that they had to push "Fear" and "Peace." Likud's second slogan, "Netanyahu—Making a secure peace," surprised Israelis. Even Netanyahu's most fanatical supporters hardly associated him with peace. But Finkelstein insisted they would. The negative slogan would be "No security. No peace. No reason to vote Peres." Jerusalem's mayor, Ehud Olmert, was drafted in to hold a press conference warning of Peres's designs.

Peres strenuously denied that Jerusalem had ever been on the negotiating table. But he was exposed and he knew it. The two academics, Ron Pundak and Yair Hirshfeld, who had pioneered the Oslo process, along with Peres's protégé Yossi Beilin, had discussed Jerusalem's future with Palestinian representatives. These had not been official negotiations sanctioned by Peres—they were more like academic exercises and probing—but Peres knew that if any detail of these talks should leak, it would vindicate the Likud campaign.

CRAFTING MESSAGES FOR swing voters was only a small part of Netanyahu's campaign. He began 1996 as an isolated candidate, facing not only a rampant Peres but also two other candidates running for prime minister who threatened to attract right-wing voters: former Likudnik David Levy and the leader of Tzomet, Rafael Eitan. Drafting new stars to his Likud was a key element in proving leadership.

Yitzhak Mordechai, a popular Mizrahi general, would also play a role in the campaign. Mordechai, the only officer to have commanded all three of the IDF's regional commands, was attracting suitors from left and right. He was at the end of his military career, having been passed over for promotion to deputy chief of staff. He lacked deep political convictions, however, and since the early 1990s had been discussing his future with both Labor and Likud representatives.

He preferred Labor, as they were in power, but Peres refused to guarantee him a minister's position. Peres wanted Mordechai to run in the primaries first, promising that, should he win a high place on the Knesset list, he would become a minister. This wasn't enough for the ambitious Mordechai. Within hours of being turned down by Labor, he was already hosting Netanyahu at his home. It had been less than two months since Rabin's assassination, and Bibi was anxious to achieve something. On the spot he promised Mordechai, whom he barely knew, that he would be defense minister, the country's second most powerful post, should he win the election.

Mordechai announced that he was joining Likud (Bibi's promise was an open secret). He was a valuable addition to the party, giving Likud more security credentials and filling the spot of a senior Mizrahi vacated by Levy.

Strengthened, Netanyahu set about eliminating his right-wing competitors. Rafael Eitan was the easier target. A crusty old general who had been chief of staff during the First Lebanon War, Eitan insisted that he was running for prime minister, despite knowing that Tzomet had peaked with eight seats in the 1992 election. He was easily bought off with a promise of second place on the Likud list, a ministry in the next cabinet, and seven spots for his party members in the top forty-two. It meant Likudniks would lose out on seats in the next Knesset, but it was a worthwhile sacrifice for Bibi, who was anxious to get his rivals out of his way to clear a path to the prime minister's office. It would also serve as a model for the deal with Levy.

The estranged former foreign minister was a much more difficult prospect, however. His new party, Gesher, had been launched with much fanfare six months earlier. Its members were politicians and activists from the mainly Mizrahi working-class neighborhoods and development towns. They wanted Gesher to emphasize social issues instead of taking a nationalist focus like Likud. But Levy, despite his background as an immigrant construction worker from Morocco, had been in national politics for nearly two decades, and he was unprepared to lead the type of movement they yearned for. He also lacked the fundraising skills necessary for building a new party, and Gesher was paralyzed by lack of funds.

There had been leaks in the media that senior Likud and Gesher members were in talks to engineer a reconciliation, but Levy denied it, saying, "I didn't emigrate to Israel and raise children and grandchildren here so Bibi could send them to war." He added, "The thought of him as prime minister should keep every Israeli citizen from sleeping."[8] The most damaging of these leaks was that Levy had sought a promise that should Netanyahu win, he would be reappointed as foreign minister. His idealistic followers were shocked that Levy was not demanding the Finance Ministry, where he could influence domestic social policies.

Levy was also reading the polls, and he came to the realization that he would receive only a few points as candidate for prime minister, and Gesher would win no more than a handful of seats. Fearing marginalization, he accepted a similar deal to Eitan's, who agreed to cede second place and move a spot down the list. Netanyahu guaranteed Levy the Foreign Ministry and agreed to sign an apology drafted by him.

Just like that, the sea of bad blood between Bibi and Levy had been crossed, at least temporarily. On March 12, the Likud Central Committee approved the Likud-Gesher agreement. Thousands of members cheered as Levy and Eitan joined Netanyahu on the stage. All three victoriously held their hands above their heads. Netanyahu stood between the general and Israel's most prominent Mizrahi politician, who both now supported him as the right wing's sole candidate.

Netanyahu had given up 30 percent of Likud's viable Knesset seats to Gesher and Tzomet in return for a clear run. By the end of March, as Likud held its first-ever primaries for Knesset candidates, the list was finalized. Peres's lead in the polls was down to 5 percent.

W HILE NETANYAHU WAS shoring up his right-wing base, Peres was receiving support from around the globe. Following the suicide bombings, Clinton agreed to head to the region for a March 13 summit of world and Middle East leaders in support of the peace process—and, more critically, of Peres.

Dubbed the "Summit of Peacemakers," it was an impressive event organized in just ten days. Leaders and foreign ministers of twenty-seven nations, including thirteen of the "moderate" Arab countries, met on the Red Sea at Sharm el-Sheikh, with Clinton and Egyptian president Hosni Mubarak co-hosting. Syria and Lebanon had been invited as well but boycotted the "pro-Israel" summit. There was no political substance to the summit—no concrete proposals for fighting terrorism or achieving peace, just eloquent statements. It was the international community's elite trying to boost Peres's electoral fortunes, and no one was fooled.

When Clinton left the summit, he took Peres along with him on Air Force One back to Israel. He then made an emotional pilgrimage to Rabin's grave and told a thousand students in Tel Aviv to "overcome fear, don't give into it, don't give up hope, don't let the terrorists win." A perfunctory fifteen minutes were allocated for a protocol meeting with Netanyahu.

"I hope my visit helped," whispered Clinton to Peres's entourage before leaving Ben Gurion Airport. But the polls hadn't budged, and worse was in store.

Since early 1996, the situation in south Lebanon had rapidly deteriorated. Hezbollah had intensified both rocket attacks on Israeli towns and clashes with IDF troops in the "Security Zone." More Katyushas fell on the Galilee as Air Force One was heading back. As American and French diplomats tried to broker a ceasefire, support for the government eroded. Peres and his ministers were shouted at angrily when they visited the northern town of Kiryat Shmona, whereas Netanyahu and Mordechai were greeted as heroes. Peres was convinced that the Iranian regime, Hezbollah and Hamas's paymaster, was directing the bombardments to scupper the peace process. The Israeli military intelligence chief, General Moshe Yaalon, put it bluntly: "Iran is trying to influence the elections in Israel and is behind the wave of attacks."

On April 11, Peres ordered Operation Grapes of Wrath. For sixteen days, Israeli artillery and warplanes bombarded Hezbollah targets and Lebanese infrastructure while the Israeli Navy imposed a blockade on

Lebanon's ports. But Hezbollah continued firing rockets. On April 18, a team of Israeli commandos operating inside Lebanon came under mortar fire. The commando lieutenant, Naftali Bennett, called in covering fire. Some of the shells fell near a temporary UN shelter at Qana where Lebanese civilians had gathered: 102 were killed. The Qana massacre added to the international pressure, leading to the operation's premature end and an unsatisfactory ceasefire agreement.

Operation Grapes of Wrath failed to convince Israeli voters that Peres was taking care of their security. It also damaged his standing with Israeli-Arab voters who were already angry with the closures of the West Bank and Gaza Strip after the suicide attacks.

THE NEW SYSTEM of direct elections meant that the prime ministerial candidates had to spend time before the elections wooing voters of other parties. Netanyahu had the advantage there, as he had been busy courting the ultra-Orthodox and immigrant communities for over a year, starting long before Rabin's assassination and Peres's candidacy.

Bibi felt he had to somehow atone for his "hot-tape" sin in front of the rabbis, and gave long monologues about how he had rehabilitated his marriage. He needn't have bothered. The Haredi (Orthodox) leaders considered all the secular politicians fornicators anyway. Their decision about whom to endorse was not influenced by the candidates' sex lives. But Netanyahu persevered, telling the rabbis how what happened had "caused me much harm, and my wife and children." As usual with Bibi, he was the victim.

Netanyahu's biggest fear was that the Haredi voters would cast only one ballot, making do with voting for their sectoral parties and abstaining from the vote for prime minister. In his meetings with the rabbis, he implored them to either specifically endorse him or at the very least hint that he was their preference. Peres, belatedly, also began making the rounds among the rabbis.

In his four decades in politics, Peres had built warm relations with many of the leading rabbis. On April 2, the eve of Passover, he visited Rabbi Ovadya Yosef, the spiritual leader of Shas, who blessed him, praying that "he should have the privilege of forming a brave, strong and true government." Netanyahu was also granted an audience, but his blessing was only to "succeed in all he does." But Shas followers, like most other

Haredi voters, were on the right politically, and they especially hated Peres's coalition partners, the members of the ultra-secular Meretz party. The political leader of Shas, Arye Deri, was at pains to emphasize that Rabbi Yosef would not be endorsing a candidate.

In his meetings with Haredi groups, Netanyahu spoke emotionally of how his son Yair was learning his prayers at a religious kindergarten. Both candidates promised the Haredim government funds and political power if they should win the election. The rabbis respected Peres, and in many cases shared his dovish politics. But there was a limit to how far they could go against their hawkish followers, and Peres received very few rabbinical endorsements. Netanyahu, who in his personal life was just as secular as Peres, if not more so, had the advantage of Likud's image as a more traditionally Jewish party. Labor was historically associated with its godless socialist founders, and, of course, partnered with Meretz. Ultimately, most of the rabbis let it be known that they favored Netanyahu.

Another significant group of voters ostensibly up for grabs was the recent immigrants from the Soviet Union. Peres had appointed liaisons to the Russian community and made sure they had a representative on Labor's list, but he relied mainly on what he believed was a shared background. Born in Vishnyeva in today's Belarus, Peres thought the immigrants from Russia and other former Soviet republics were similar to his generation of pioneers arriving in Palestine seven decades earlier from Eastern Europe, and therefore natural Labor voters. It was a dangerous assumption.

Netanyahu had in his Moldovan-born right-hand man, Avigdor Lieberman, a much more influential ambassador to the Russian community. Netanyahu was also close, since his days at the United Nations, with Natan Sharansky, the Jewish Russian human rights activist and famed Gulag prisoner. Netanyahu had campaigned for Sharansky's release, and the two shared a belief that the only way to make peace in the Middle East was for the Arabs to first embrace democracy.

In March 1996, Sharansky founded Yisrael B'Aliyah (Israel on the Rise), an immigrants' party. Both Peres and Netanyahu appeared at its conference, appealing for support. The prime minister listed all that his government had done for the immigrants, but he seemed condescending. Netanyahu received a much warmer reception. His tough-talking commitments not to make further concessions to the Palestinians were much more in tune with their thinking. Four years earlier, many of them had voted Labor, out of appreciation for "Mr. Security," Rabin. Peres failed to inspire them.

THE LAST MONTH of the campaign was the television stage. Israeli law forbids the purchase of airtime for political purposes. Instead, parties are allocated fixed broadcasting slots according to their electoral size. Until Finkelstein came along, political ads sought to educate viewers on the opposing worldviews of the parties. The ads were so ponderous that some parties interspersed their messages with political stand-up comedy routines.

The anti-Peres ads that Finkelstein crafted for Netanyahu's campaign were short, simple, and monochrome—for example, dark glass shattering, giving way to a blurry photograph of Peres and Arafat together. Peres was portrayed as an aging and deluded dreamer, easily tricked by the devilish Arafat. Netanyahu, by contrast, was shown in soft colors, with a mock-up prime minister's office in the background to lend him gravitas and a dove of peace flying above. Bibi's soundbites were moderate and upbeat, extolling "our wonderful country," a phrase that has stuck to him to this day.

Labor's ads were more low-key, presenting Peres as Israel's elder statesman. Arafat did not appear in the footage, and both Rabin and Netanyahu were relegated to only occasional cameos. Labor's campaigners were afraid to make unwelcome comparisons between the slain leader and Peres and didn't want to present Bibi as his worthy challenger.

As a result of the ad campaigns, Netanyahu was winning the battle of the airwaves even before the debate. Labor's campaign chiefs were under no illusions their man could beat Likud's accomplished performer onscreen. As the two parties' representatives met to discuss terms, Likud had one objective—making sure a debate, any debate, took place. They knew Bibi would win and accepted Labor's demands. They would hold just one thirty-minute debate, to be recorded at Labor's studios and moderated by the Peres-supporting broadcaster and *Haaretz* columnist Dan Margalit.

The debate was set for Sunday, May 26, three days before the election. Netanyahu spent the weekend, a total of twenty hours, rehearsing in a mock studio. Meridor played Peres, and he attacked mercilessly.

At one point he asked Bibi, "Why should the public believe you? Even your colleagues Benny Begin and Dan Meridor don't believe you."⁹ But Netanyahu took it all in stride, preparing answers for every potential attack line. Peres, who hated the whole idea of a debate, would agree to spend only a couple of hours preparing, and he never did a full rehearsal. His strategy was to not treat Netanyahu as an equal, and he stuck to it throughout, looking at the moderator rather than the camera or his opponent.

The result was horrendous. Peres looked tired, frozen, and robotic. Complaining about Likud's accusations over Jerusalem, he sounded petulant. Netanyahu, who had arrived at the studio a bag of nerves, came alive as soon as the cameras started rolling, and he was animated and eloquent. Deflecting Margalit's questions, he took the battle to Peres. "Many watching us now get up in the morning and ask themselves when the next terror attack will happen," he said accusingly. The soundbites were well crafted and well aimed. "My ambition isn't to tour the palaces of Europe, like Mr. Peres," he said, mocking his opponent.

Margalit asked him about the "hot tape." Netanyahu calmly replied, "It was a mistake that hurt my wife," and immediately parried. "The bigger mistake is what Mr. Peres has done over the last four years and that has hurt all of Israel."

The final stage of the debate was a single direct question from each opponent. "What happened to the New Middle East you promised us?" asked Netanyahu. Peres, in turn, refused to ask Netanyahu a question, instead demanding he apologize for Likud's accusations. Even the most partisan viewer had to admit that Bibi had won by a knockout.

Throughout the campaign, Peres's staunchest supporters were foreigners without a vote. In April he flew to the Gulf states of Oman and Qatar, in the hope of demonstrating to Israelis that the fruits of peace and regional cooperation were just around the corner. Later that month he was in Washington again. Clinton showered him with compliments, arms deals, and joint statements scheduled for prime-time news in Israel. A US president had never made such overt efforts to influence a foreign election. When, on the eve of the election, Clinton promised Israelis continued American support if they chose peace, there was no doubt whom he was endorsing.

But Clinton was up against another American with more influence in Israel—even though he was dead. The Lubavitcher Rebbe, Chabad leader Rabbi Menachem Mendel Schneerson, had passed away on June 12, 1994, disappointing his followers by not appearing as the messiah. But they were still resolved to fulfill his wishes and support Netanyahu, who they believed would keep the Land of Israel whole. Ten days before the election, Sharon organized a secret meeting with the main Chabad rabbis. He told them that Netanyahu still needed a last push to overcome Peres. Netanyahu, arriving toward the end of the meeting, explained that he could not abrogate the Oslo Agreements, but as Arafat himself was not in full compliance, he would make sure they went nowhere.

The Chabad rabbis were on board. The movement officially would not take part in politics, but its thousands of members were drafted into an unofficial last-minute campaign. An Australian Chabad donor, the diamond millionaire Joseph Gutnick, promised to foot the bill, which would come to millions. Entire printing presses were hired to prepare banners, leaflets, and stickers of all sizes with the slogan "Netanyahu is good for the Jews," which some criticized for being racist, since it ignored the fact that only about 75 percent of Israeli citizens are Jewish. Seventy-two hours before the polls opened, the Chabadniks spread out across Israel, plastering them on every available space and at intervals of a few hundred meters on highways. It was a stunning blanket surprise campaign. When Netanyahu was asked about it, he feigned innocence: "I'll be good for everyone. Arabs and Jews as well," he responded.

The rabbis were falling into line. Two days before the election, a ninety-four-year-old Kabbalist sage, Rabbi Yitzhak Kaduri, received Netanyahu, saying in his blessing over him that he would become prime minister. Netanyahu kept a serious face, masking his disdain for the sage's mystical form of Judaism. Shas campaigners had been handing out amulets signed by Kaduri to their voters, and it was a roundabout way of getting that party's endorsement as well. In Haredi neighborhoods, banners went up with the slogan, "With God's Help, Netanyahu."

And yet, despite having run a dismal campaign, on the morning of May 29, as Israelis went to vote, the polls were predicting a narrow 51–49 victory for Peres. Just more than half the country seemed to still believe in Peres's vision for peace and wanted him to continue where Rabin had tragically been cut off. Labor's strategists were convinced that they held the lead. Labor had run a non-campaign designed not to anger wavering

voters. The party had decided not to bring up the accusations that Netanyahu had incited against Rabin, assuming that the trauma of his assassination was still fresh in voters' minds.

Instead, the campaign had focused on how good the economy was
doing—on the fact that Israelis were buying new cars and computers and
taking vacations abroad. But the majority, who had yet to share in the
fruits of the new prosperity, only felt left behind. Labor organized gath-
erings of cultural figures and show-business people, and set up events
with luminaries such as the renowned writer Amos Oz, under a banner
reading, "The Nation for Peres." But this approach only highlighted the
narrative of the elites versus the outsiders.

Peres's campaign believed that when the moment of truth came, most
voters would realize there was no comparison between their candidate,
who over forty years had built Israel's military, established its nuclear program, and brought the economy back from the brink in the mid-1980s,
and a man whose only accomplishment was being a star TV pugilist.
Peres had served in every key ministerial post as well as prime minister.
Netanyahu had never even been in the cabinet or taken responsibility for
life-and-death decisions. Israelis had always placed their fate in the hands
of wise old men (and one wise woman). Surely they weren't about to
change tack and elect a charlatan, no matter how many tactical mistakes
Labor made in its campaign.

B OTH CANDIDATES BEGAN election day upbeat, voting early and touring
regional headquarters, meeting enthusiastic supporters. As the day
drew on, Peres received updates from Labor's main office, which suggested that voting in the Arab towns, where he was expecting to win by
a landslide, was sluggish. He rushed to central headquarters in Tel Aviv
and spent the last hours frantically calling local party bosses to get out
the vote.

Likud's field operation, run jointly by Lieberman and Mordechai, was
much more efficient. By evening, Netanyahu grew withdrawn. The campaign had succeeded beyond expectations, and Finkelstein, who had left
Israel on Sunday morning, had predicted a wafer-thin victory on the basis
of his polling. But on the brink, he was suddenly gripped by doubt. Benzion had said that no matter what, the left-wing establishment wouldn't
let Bibi win. A group of Netanyahu's American supporters had arrived in

Israel for election night, taking suites in a Tel Aviv hotel. Bibi joined them for a few minutes, but then sat alone with Sara in another room to await the exit polls at 10:00 p.m.

Both television channels had the same result—Peres in the lead with 50.7 percent to Netanyahu's 49.3 percent. Statistically it was too close to call. That didn't stop hundreds of Labor members gathered in the Tel Aviv Cinerama from bursting into cheers. Across town in the Convention Center, Likudniks were desolate. They had felt throughout the day that victory was within their grasp. The cameras zeroed in on the tearful face of a young blonde activist, the then anonymous Tzipi Livni.

Lieberman knocked on Bibi's door. "The exit polls are wrong. My reports from the field put us in the lead."[10] But Netanyahu believed the numbers on television. After midnight, he left the hotel for the Convention Center to face his supporters, this time without Sara by his side. "A very large part of the nation supports our way. I love you. I'm proud of you. I salute you," he said to them.[11] It wasn't quite a concession speech, but Netanyahu was already launching his battle for survival against the Likud rivals who were preparing to challenge his leadership.

The Convention Center began to empty as Likudniks drifted home and television crews started to pack up. The Cinerama was still packed with Labor members singing peace songs. Peres, at home in his Tel Aviv apartment, was already receiving congratulatory phone calls from around the world. The White House called asking if it could issue a formal congratulation. Peres counseled waiting for actual results and went to bed, after scheduling a meeting in the morning with his advisers to discuss the next stage of negotiations with the Palestinians.

Peres was asleep when at 2:45 a.m. the television announced that the trend had reversed. The results coming in had made them update their prediction, putting Netanyahu in the lead. Hundreds of Likudniks streamed back, chanting, "There is a God!" and "Peres go home!" The trend held, and four hours later the analysts called it for Bibi. He had won with 50.5 percent of the vote, beating Peres by 29,457 votes.

Peres realized belatedly that he had taken the country he had served all his life for granted. He had won handily in places like secular middle-class Tel Aviv, but had lost overall by 11 percent among Jewish voters, and had succumbed to a majority comprising a coalition of outsiders. He said after the election that "the Jews had beaten the Israelis."

Bill Clinton took two lessons from the election that he had tried so hard to help Peres win. One, according to Dick Morris, Clinton's political consultant, was that "the candidate who used American-style polling and media won." The other, Morris wrote, quoting Clinton, was that "you can't push people faster than they are ready to go. If they're not ready for peace, there's not much you can do about it."[12]

Clinton was being uncharitable. Israelis wanted peace, but they were afraid of making concessions to their enemies, just like any other nation. It had been Peres's election to lose. He had failed to convince enough Israelis that his vision for peace could be achieved. And it was the victory of one man who had read the undercurrents of the electorate. Benjamin Netanyahu had stoked Israelis' deepest fears, and believing in his inevitability, had transformed himself, in less than seven months, from pariah to prime minister.

PART FOUR

"Israel's Serial Bungler"

1996–2009

20

The Bedrock of Our Existence

At forty-six, Benjamin Netanyahu was the youngest prime minister in Israel's history, the first who had been born after independence. He was also the first to be elected by direct vote. As such, Bibi believed he had the right to go about things very differently from his predecessors.

Netanyahu planned a presidential-style administration with far-reaching powers for his prime minister's office (PMO). He wanted national security and economy councils and a special *hasbara* unit under his aegis. Powerful government departments, such as the Civil Service Commission and the Treasury Ministry's budget department, would also be moved to the PMO. He had served as a special forces officer, had a master's degree in business management from MIT, and had been a BCG management consultant. He was convinced he could hold the reins of Israel's military and economy.

He was determined as well not to repeat what he saw as the mistakes of the previous Likud prime ministers, Begin and Shamir. "Leftist" holdovers from Labor governments would not be allowed to influence policy.

Many of Netanyahu's ideas made sense. Israeli prime ministers have historically lacked staff powerful enough to effect significant change and stand up to entrenched civil servants, IDF generals, and Treasury Ministry economists. The problem was that the ideas flew in the face of political reality.

Direct election of the prime minister hadn't changed Israel's parliamentary system. Worse, many Likud voters had made do in 1996 with casting one ballot for Netanyahu and another for a different sectoral party. As a result, Likud had only thirty-two seats. To build a Knesset majority, Netanyahu had to make deals with five other parties and grant them ministries. This left Likud with only four key ministries and a clutch of junior ones. David Levy had been promised the Foreign Ministry. Netanyahu believed he would run Israel's foreign policy himself anyway. Yitzhak Mordechai got the Defense Ministry. That left Finance and Justice.

Ariel Sharon and Dan Meridor had both put aside their rivalries with Bibi during the elections. Sharon had been key in bringing Levy back into the fold and was Netanyahu's plenipotentiary to the ultra-Orthodox rabbis. Meridor had been the "moderate" face of Likud's campaign. They both expected to be rewarded. Avigdor Lieberman, who was to remain Netanyahu's right-hand man as director-general of the PMO, urged him to keep Sharon and Meridor out of the cabinet. Bibi needed little urging. He appointed Yaakov Neeman, the secretive lawyer who had helped him reconcile with Sara after the "hot-tape" scandal, as justice minister. He planned to appoint the governor of the Bank of Israel, Yaakov Frenkel, who was also a former economist for the International Monetary Fund (IMF), to Finance. But he was blindsided by a cabinet revolt even before the cabinet was sworn in. Levy, who saw in Sharon a potential ally, refused to serve if Sharon was kept out. Benny Begin, who had initially accepted the Science Ministry, made Meridor joining a condition.

Netanyahu's first crisis broke out on June 18, 1996, the day he was to present his government to the Knesset. He was forced to back down. Meridor became finance minister, and the furious Sharon was mollified by a "National Infrastructure Ministry," which was hastily cobbled together from parts of other ministries. The press, which had briefly been stupefied by Bibi's shock victory, had a field day as prospective ministers criticized their soon-to-be boss off the record. Finally, as evening fell, Netanyahu was sworn in as Israel's ninth prime minister. Benzion, Tzila, and Sara watched proudly from the gallery. But it was a sour ending to what Bibi hoped would be a perfect day. As the ministers were sworn in and took their seats beside him, there was an acrimonious atmosphere. Following the election, because of his incredible win, Netanyahu's old rivals had been prepared to forgive previous trespasses. Now they were getting the feeling that he saw them as superfluous courtiers. They had to be prepared to protect their new fiefdoms.

Netanyahu would suffer from a fractious cabinet from Day One, a situation that was only exacerbated by the ineptitude of his personal team. Bibi's staff at the PMO was the opposite of his professional election campaign staff. He selected his aides, who then had to be approved by Sara, according to their loyalty rather than for their expertise. This was the case for Lieberman, the domineering director-general, whose sole managerial experience was purging Likud of Bibi's enemies. Netanyahu appointed a classical pianist and right-wing polemicist, David Bar-Ilan, as director of policy planning and communications. His diplomatic adviser was Dore Gold, an academic with no actual diplomatic experience. The cabinet secretary would be the ineffectual but loyal Danny Naveh, a former aide to Arens. Efforts to hire a professional chief of staff foundered. In the space of eighteen months, four men would try—and fail—to impose some sort of order on the prime minister's office. But Bibi, preparing for his first trip to Washington as prime minister, was still oblivious to the chaos around him.

B ILL CLINTON IS only three years older than Netanyahu. Perhaps that is why he never seemed to have the same kind respect for him that he had for the elder statesmen Rabin and Peres. As politicians, however, Clinton and Netanyahu had much in common. Both reached the highest office in their country at a young age with relatively meager records. Both had risen largely because they presented a fresh image and were able to connect with their constituents. But whereas Clinton was naturally trusting and optimistic, Netanyahu believed the worst of people and was eternally suspicious. He refused to meet US diplomats to prepare for the meeting in advance. It would be him and POTUS meeting as equals.

As they sat down in the Oval Office on July 9, Clinton was anxious for assurances that Netanyahu would continue the Oslo process. Instead, Netanyahu delivered a lengthy lecture on the Arabs and why his government, while honoring previous agreements, would first need to review outstanding issues with the Palestinians. After Bibi left, an exasperated Clinton remarked, "Who the fuck does he think he is? Who's the fucking superpower here?"[1] But outwardly, the president remained all smiles and compliments to his guest.

Clinton was hardly comforted the next day by Netanyahu's rapturous reception at the Republican-dominated Congress. In a rare honor for a freshman foreign leader, he was invited to address a joint session. Netanyahu used the word "peace" sixty-two times but did not once mention his interlocutor, Palestinian president Yasser Arafat. He promised that Israel was "ready to resume negotiations with the Palestinian Authority," as well as with Syria and Lebanon, but insisted on strict security conditions for any peace agreement.[2]

By far the biggest standing ovation came when he announced that "in the next four years, we will begin the long-term process of gradually reducing the level of your generous economic assistance to Israel."[3] Two decades since that speech, the process has yet to begin. The United States gives even more annually to Netanyahu's Israel now than it did then, though now it's called "defense assistance" instead of "economic assistance."[4]

Though Clinton pressured him to get the peace process back on track, Netanyahu regarded his Washington visit as a resounding success. To his indignation, much of the Israeli media focused on the fact that the taxpayers had paid not only for Sara to join him, but also his small children, Yair and Avner. Photographs of nannies carrying them onto the plane filled the papers. By then Sara and the nannies were a national issue.

A week before the trip to Washington, reporters in Jerusalem had been alerted to a young woman on the sidewalk outside the Netanyahu residence. Weeks earlier, Sara had hired Tanya Shaw, a young South African, as a nanny, and then summarily fired her for "burning a pot of soup." Shaw's belongings had been dumped outside the door, by security, after another employee had been ordered by Sara to open her bags and shake out the clothes to ensure that she had not stolen anything. Shortly after Shaw spoke to the press, two other nannies came forward to relate their own stories of short and traumatic employment under Sara. They were the first in a long list of domestic employees and secretaries who left in tears, in many cases suing for abusive employment.

What had been a closely guarded secret in Likud circles was now public. Ever since Sara had allowed Bibi to return home after the "hot-tape" scandal, she had demanded, and received, full control of his schedule and vetted his aides. Upon Netanyahu's election, she received her own taxpayer-funded staff. She wasn't the first prime minister's wife to attract negative attention. Part of the problem was the lack of an established practice regarding the prime minister's wife or a budget for her staff. It had never been much of an issue until Sara arrived. She received two secretaries from the PMO staff and a personal public relations adviser who was hired under the guise of being the "prime minister's adviser on religious issues."

The extensive coverage of Sara's affairs in the Israeli media could have been regarded as unfair if not for the endless string of employees complaining of abuse, the stories of her demands for gift-bags at every event she attended, her detailed demands regarding hotel rooms before foreign trips, which she relayed through Israeli embassies, and other abuses of the system. Sara had made herself "fair game" by involving herself in every detail of her husband's job, insisting on attending nearly every public event he attended to stand at his side. She had made sure that their children received attention in the media during the election as well. She had even demanded her own election ad, insisting that she was an electoral asset. The campaign team humored her and filmed an ad, which was then sent for editing, but it was not completed in time for election day.

Netanyahu, despite paying a heavy price in the media, never tried to curb Sara. Instead he has severely chastised journalists. He paid another heavy price in his relationship with his eldest child, Noa, with whom he has been close, despite never having lived together. Their meetings became much less frequent after he married Sara. When Bibi entered the prime minister's office, he placed a photograph of Noa on the bookshelf, alongside one of Sara and their two sons. A few weeks later, it disappeared. A friend who inquired about it was told that it had been sent for reframing. Twenty years later, Bibi has grandchildren from Noa, but his office décor has never included their pictures. Nor has Noa's picture reappeared.

T OGETHER WITH SARA stories, the main issue early in Netanyahu's term was when he would meet Arafat.

In his victory speech, four days after the election, Netanyahu said, "We intend to further the process of dialogue with all our neighbors to reach a stable peace, a real peace, a peace with security." But he was in no hurry: "First and foremost, peace must be reached at home," he insisted.[5]

For weeks, he allowed others to maintain contact with the Palestinian leadership. Dore Gold called the Palestinian president's office to intro-

Netanyahu and Arafat during their awkward first meeting in 1996 on the border with Gaza.

duce himself the day after the election. Foreign Minister Levy was sent first to meet Arafat, though he was not given any mandate to negotiate. Meanwhile, Netanyahu received Arafat's deputy, Mahmoud Abbas, for a cordial but meaningless meeting. After nearly three months in office, Netanyahu finally relented to American pressure and to threats from Israel's president, Ezer Weizman, who said that if Netanyahu didn't meet with Arafat, Weizman himself would open negotiations with the Palestinians, though he had no political powers.

The first meeting between the Palestinian president and the leader of the Zionist Revisionist movement, which until recently had refused to even recognize the existence of a Palestinian people, took place in a cramped meeting room at the Erez border crossing to the Gaza Strip. Anxious to escape one of Arafat's famous embraces, Netanyahu awkwardly shook hands across the table. Little of substance was said as he exchanged banalities with the man whom he had been sent to capture as a young soldier in 1968 on his first operation.

In a statement after the meeting, Netanyahu stressed three concepts: reciprocity, security, and prosperity. These would remain the elements of his policy toward the Palestinians. His demands for reciprocity and security arrangements would stymie the development of any meaningful agreement moving forward, and the promise of economic prosperity for the Palestinians became a substitute for actual statehood.

There was no follow-up meeting. Instead, anxious to appease his base in the aftermath of meeting with Arafat, Netanyahu authorized the building of 1,500 new homes in the settlements and threatened to close down Orient House, the PLO's "foreign ministry" in East Jerusalem. As far as he was concerned, not canceling the Oslo Agreements and sitting down with Arafat was as much as anyone should expect for the time being. But the Oslo II agreement included further commitments.

The Israeli pullback from the Palestinian cities was completed by the end of 1995, except from Hebron. In a forlorn attempt to gain their endorsement, Peres had acquiesced to the rabbis' demands to delay the Hebron pullback because of its special place in Jewish history (both as the site of the Tomb of the Patriarchs and the location of the 1929 massacre) and the difficulty of organizing security for the settlers living within the city. To help Peres, Arafat had agreed to reschedule the pullback to June 15, two weeks after the election. Netanyahu was committed to standing by former agreements, but he had also promised the settlers and the Chabad rabbis that he would stand by them, saying, "You can trust me on Hebron." The date passed, and Netanyahu stonewalled, telling the Americans that he was still reviewing the Palestinians' compliance with the security requirements of the Oslo Accords. If the Palestinians were out of compliance, it would give him an excuse to stop following the pullback schedule.

The deadlock was broken from an unexpected direction. For nearly three decades, Israeli archaeologists had been excavating under East Jerusalem, revealing the base of the massive Western Wall, the edge of the Jerusalem Temple rebuilt by King Herod, and the street level of ancient Jerusalem. It was a scientific, religious, and political project underlining the Jewish connection to the city. The Jerusalem Islamic Waqf objected to the dig, claiming falsely that the tunnel was damaging the foundations of the Haram al-Sharif mosques on the Temple Mount. For years there was only one entrance to the tunnel. An exit existed behind a wall in the Old City's Muslim Quarter, but it had remained sealed for fear of provoking an outbreak of violence.

On September 23, the night after Yom Kippur, Netanyahu came under pressure from Jerusalem mayor Ehud Olmert and Jewish American religious-nationalist donors to assert Israeli sovereignty by opening the exit to the tunnel. The security chiefs, in a rushed consultation, gave their guarded assessments, saying they thought violence could be averted. Netanyahu gave the order, and the exit was unsealed.

The Waqf protested, saying that the Al Aqsa Mosque was "in danger," and there were angry denunciations from Arafat, who quoted Koran passages calling upon believers to "kill and be killed" in protection of their possessions. The message was clear. The following morning, violent clashes broke out throughout East Jerusalem, the West Bank, and the Gaza Strip. Palestinian security personnel, who for two years had been patrolling the area with the IDF as part of the Oslo security arrangements, now turned their guns against the IDF.

For three days, battles raged, as all the Oslo procedures collapsed. For the first time since 1967, the IDF began to deploy tanks around Palestinian cities. Netanyahu, on a visit to Germany, frantically tried to manage the situation over the phone with Defense Minister Mordechai, while at the same time fielding calls from the US secretary of state, Warren Christopher. Arafat now wasn't answering his calls. Netanyahu was forced to cut his trip short and return to Jerusalem. Finally, after Washington cajoled him and Netanyahu threatened to send the IDF into Palestinian cities, Arafat ordered his men to stand down. Seventeen Israeli soldiers and nearly a hundred Palestinians had been killed.

Netanyahu justified opening the tunnel because it "touches the bedrock of our existence." It was the most grievous blow to the Oslo process since Rabin's assassination. Trust between Israeli and Palestinian security forces had been shattered. Netanyahu was accused at home and abroad of provoking the Palestinians, and Arafat now had the diplomatic upper hand. Clinton summoned them, along with Jordan's King Hussein, for an emergency summit, to be held on September 30.

Bibi was rattled. He had spent barely three months in office, and he was experiencing his first security crisis. He was being criticized at home for not having held proper consultations with the military and intelligence chiefs before opening the tunnel. At the White House, Hussein spoke to him sternly, accusing him of arrogance and disrespect. A chastened Netanyahu sat by Arafat on a couch and began to work his charms. Bizarrely, it seemed to work, as the two men spoke for hours.

"I found a friend in the White House," Netanyahu announced. But his sudden embrace of Arafat, and the relief among the Americans and

Jordanians that he and Arafat were getting along, obscured the fact that little had been accomplished, except for Netanyahu's agreement to launch intensive negotiations on the Hebron pullback. It would take three and a half months of frustrating shuttle diplomacy between Jerusalem and Gaza by US negotiator Dennis Ross before the Hebron Agreement could be reached. Arafat was a much more difficult customer now, and Netanyahu, who rapidly grew less affectionate toward the Palestinian leader after their White House meeting, sent his personal attorney, Yitzhak Molcho, to "babysit" the Israeli negotiators. The tunnel crisis had forced the Clinton administration—which since the start of the Oslo process had largely been cheerleading from the sidelines, while Israelis and Palestinians did their own negotiating—to take to the field. Clinton was invested and he would remain in the game, no matter how much both sides disappointed him.

It was a miserable compromise. The 450 Jewish settlers in the heart of the Palestinian city were not relocated. Hebron was split into two parts, with 80 percent of the city under Palestinian control and 20 percent under Israeli control, though the settlers constituted only 0.3 percent of its population. The deal meant that thousands of Palestinians, as well as the city's old commercial center, would remain under Israeli military occupation.

Even this compromise—not moving one settler and keeping full Israeli control of the Tomb of the Patriarchs—was met with an outcry from the ideological right, however. Former prime minister Shamir said that "anyone who voted Netanyahu should be tearing his hair out."[6] More damaging was the resignation of Science Minister Begin, who, in protest, established an opposition faction within Likud. On January 16, 1997, the Knesset passed the Hebron Agreement 87–17. Most of those voting against it were members of Netanyahu's coalition.

The Hebron Agreement included a redeployment of Israeli military forces that had already been agreed to in Oslo II, and it affected only a tiny portion of the West Bank. It was historic nonetheless. For the first time, a Likud prime minister had ordered Israeli troops to pull out from part of the historical Land of Israel and allowed the Palestinians to take control of a piece of the historical Jewish homeland.

O F ALL THE Israeli elites Netanyahu tried to break, the ones who would prove most obdurate were the members of the legal establishment. The followers of Jabotinsky had been taught to revere the law. Menachem Begin famously heralded a Supreme Court ruling by exclaiming, "There are judges in Jerusalem!" The Likud "princes" had been part of Jerusalem's Rehavia neighborhood milieu, where most of the Supreme Court justices lived. Socially, Netanyahu also belonged to this group—his uncle, Benzion's brother Elisha, was married to Supreme Court justice Shoshana Netanyahu. Politically, however, he was much closer to a new generation of Likud activists who saw the Supreme Court, under the presidency of "legal activist" Professor Aharon Barak, as a group of left-wingers sabotaging the decisions of an elected government.

Netanyahu's political allies, the far right and religious politicians, accused the Supreme Court of standing up for the rights of Palestinians at Israelis' expense (though the Supreme Court rarely challenges Israel's security policies) and upholding "secular" values over the commandments of the Torah. When his political allies attacked the Supreme Court, Netanyahu failed to speak up for the justices, and in the coalition agreement he gave the National Religious Party chairmanship of the Knesset Justice Committee. His appointment of Yaakov Neeman, a religious and socially conservative lawyer, as justice minister was an attempt to get the justices to toe the line.

Seven weeks after his appointment, Neeman was indicted for attempting to suborn a witness and lying in court and forced to resign. Neeman and Netanyahu were convinced that the charges, of which Neeman was ultimately cleared, had been trumped up by the legal establishment. Netanyahu appointed another loyalist, Tzachi Hanegbi, as justice minister, vowing to get back at the judicial elite by naming an attorney general who would sort out the legal system.

The identity of the new attorney general announced by Hanegbi on January 10, six days before the Knesset vote on the Hebron Agreement, astonished even many of Netanyahu's supporters. Ronny Bar-On was a successful commercial lawyer and veteran Likud activist, but he was largely unknown outside of Jerusalem, had never been considered a leading legal mind, and had scant experience of public service. Previous attorneys general, who in Israel are both the government's senior legal adviser and head of the state prosecutor services, had all been prominent legal scholars, former judges, or senior prosecutors. Bar-On simply didn't fit the bill, and his appointment was met with intense criticism, which only intensified when some ill-timed sightings of Bar-On gambling in

London were reported. (While there was nothing illegal in his activities, the Israeli public had a puritanical streak when it came to non-sports betting.) Two days later, Bar-On decided he didn't want the job after all. The Jerusalem district judge Elyakim Rubinstein, the man who fourteen years earlier had been the leading candidate for ambassador to the United Nations, before Netanyahu elbowed him aside, became attorney general instead. It was just another botched appointment in a series of many.

Israel's Channel 1 reported that Bar-On's appointment had been part of a deal to secure the votes of members of Shas, the Mizrahi ultra-Orthodox party, in favor of the Hebron Agreement. According to the report, Bar-On, as attorney general, was to have approved a plea bargain for Shas leader Arye Deri, who was on trial for accepting bribes from a Torah seminary in return for government funding. Netanyahu, Lieberman, Hanegbi, and Deri were all alleged to have been in on the plot.

For the first time, an Israeli prime minister was accused of being involved in bribery. Netanyahu denied any knowledge of an illegal deal, but the police who were called in to investigate believed he had been part of it. In another first, Netanyahu was questioned twice as a suspect, and within weeks the police recommendation that Netanyahu be indicted was leaked to the media. Those were the worst days of his first term. By Israeli law, the prime minister does not have to resign if indicted, but such a situation was unprecedented. Senior Likud ministers made it clear they would not remain in the cabinet if Netanyahu was to stand trial. Their departure would almost certainly have led to a stampede and the fall of the coalition. Under siege, Netanyahu kept his silence, while his aides darkly spoke to the media of a plot to bring down the prime minister.

Less than a year in power, Netanyahu faced the prospect of an ignominious end. His fate was now in the hands of his old rival Elyakim Rubinstein, who, as attorney general, had final say on the indictments of senior figures.

On April 20, Rubinstein announced his decision. Sufficient evidence for an indictment had been found only against Deri. He accepted the police findings that there had been a criminal plot to appoint a lenient attorney general in exchange for votes for the Hebron Agreement among Shas members, but did not believe there was enough evidence to put Netanyahu, Hanegbi, and Lieberman on trial. Rubinstein issued a "public report," however, in which he admitted that the prime minister's actions had been "questionable."

A relieved Bibi rushed to appear on television, insisting that he had been exonerated, but accepting that he had made mistakes; he said he had learned from the affair. Treasury Minister Dan Meridor and Communications Minister Limor Livnat both kept him waiting for another twenty-four hours while they "studied" Rubinstein's report before deciding not to resign. For Meridor, who was being lampooned by TV satirists for being a weak and ineffectual kitten, it was a political mistake. He was already on a collision course with Netanyahu.

O NE OF NETANYAHU's greatest frustrations during his first term was that, despite considering himself an expert, he failed to fundamentally change Israel's economy. He had sweeping plans to push ahead privatization, cut personal and corporate taxes, shrink the government, and liberalize the money markets. In three years, these policies were to remain largely on paper.

The Labor government's major investment in infrastructure had widened the deficit, making it impossible to cut taxes—especially as Netanyahu's coalition partners had extracted commitments for increased spending on benefits and subsidies for special-interest groups such as religious communities, ultra-Orthodox families, Haredi schools, and settlements. His attempts to achieve structural changes were opposed by the veteran Finance Ministry bureaucracy, supported by their minister, Meridor. Netanyahu clashed frequently with the minister he had never wanted to appoint.

"My opponents don't understand the main thing, because they've never worked in the economy. Never been in the market," he once remarked. He preferred to talk economics with his original candidate for the Finance Ministry, Yaakov Frenkel. From early 1997, Frenkel and Meridor were locked in a conflict on the best method for keeping inflation down. Since the near-meltdown of Israel's economy in the mid-1980s, the Bank of Israel had maintained strict controls on the shekel's rate of exchange. Frenkel believed the Israeli economy was strong enough to ease these controls and instead use other methods, particularly the interest rate, to control inflation when necessary. Meridor, on the advice of the ministry economists, strenuously objected. Netanyahu supported Frenkel's reasoning, but Meridor demanded that as minister, it was his call. Netanyahu overruled him, and on June 20, Meridor resigned.

Meridor and Netanyahu had been rivals for the past decade, practically from the moment Bibi had entered politics. But Meridor never had it in him to put up a hard fight, and Netanyahu outfoxed him every step of the way. When Meridor finally struck back, he chose an obscure economic issue—which most of the public barely understood—as his issue to stand on. Had he chosen to resign over the Bar-On Hebron scandal, he may have started a chain reaction that would have brought Netanyahu down. Instead, his departure was just another resignation, one more in a series of blows that were slowly eroding the prime minister's authority.

"THE PREVIOUS GOVERNMENT ignored the terrible terror wave. I set myself a goal to stop this terrible thing we had here and it's hard, but we've done it," Netanyahu bragged in a television interview on July 28.[7] But as his predecessors Rabin and Peres had learned, terrorist attacks came at the worst and most unexpected moments. Two days later, two Hamas bombers disguised as Haredi Jews detonated themselves simultaneously in Jerusalem's crowded Mahane Yehuda Market. Sixteen Israelis were killed and 178 wounded in what for decades had been the most iconic of Likud strongholds, the first stop on any budding Likudnik candidate's campaign tour.

The security cabinet authorized striking at Hamas leaders, and Netanyahu called in Mossad chief Danny Yatom, who proposed, as a target, the Hamas political bureau chief, Khaled Mashal. Assassinating Mashal would mean overturning Rabin's order from three years ago to cease clandestine operations in Jordan. The team chosen for the hit would not have much time to study Mashal's movements between his home and his office in Amman. Another Hamas suicide bombing took place on September 4 on Jerusalem's Ben Yehuda Street, a pedestrian mall, killing five, which added further urgency.

To avoid angering Jordan, the plan against Mashal was to use an aerosolized toxin that wouldn't be detectable in a postmortem. But as the Mossad team approached Mashal as he was leaving his car on an Amman street, he turned to his daughter, whom the team had not noticed sitting in the back. The spray hit Mashal's ear, and realizing that he was under attack, he dove back into the car, shouting to the driver to take him to the hospital. Mashal's bodyguard gave chase, grappling with the two Mossad agents. A crowd gathered, leading to a Jordanian police officer detaining the two, who were carrying fake Canadian passports. Four other agents in the getaway team escaped to the Israeli embassy.

The agents' covers didn't stand up for long, and a furious King Hussein soon discovered that Israel had been carrying out assassinations in his capital. Mossad chief Yatom flew immediately to Amman in an attempt to extricate the agents. Upon arrival, he was informed that should Mashal die, they would be accused of murder. On Netanyahu's orders, the antidote, which was being held by the team in case of accidental discharge, was rushed to the hospital, saving Mashal's life. Hussein still refused to release the two agents under arrest or allow the other four to leave the embassy. He threatened to tear up the peace agreement.

Israel's ambassador to the European Union, Efrayim Halevy, who in his previous position, as deputy Mossad chief, had led the secret diplomacy with Jordan, and had become close to Hussein, was sent to Amman to negotiate a solution. The outcome proved a further humiliation for Israel. Netanyahu was forced to agree to the release of Hamas's founder, Sheikh Ahmed Yassin, and seventy other Palestinian prisoners, a step that helped boost Hussein's standing among his Palestinian subjects.

Netanyahu was barely keeping the Oslo process alive, and he had been on the brink of losing the other peace agreement he had inherited, one he actually supported. He had been publicly shamed by Mossad's botched assassination. Yatom resigned a few months later, after a string of operational mishaps, and was replaced by Halevy. However, much of the blame stuck to Bibi, who had failed to inform the defense minister, Mordechai, and the IDF chief of staff, Amnon Shahak, in advance of the operation. A year into his premiership, he was looking increasingly impetuous and accident-prone.

The Economist, one of the few newspapers Netanyahu truly respected, ran a cover story calling for his resignation, branding him "Israel's Serial Bungler."[8]

21

Dragged to Wye

The Israeli elites, having lost the election in 1996, set about delegitimizing Netanyahu. Yitzhak Rabin's former chief of staff, Shimon Sheves, said on the day after the election, "The state is finished." Leah Rabin remarked, "I'd like to pack a suitcase and very quickly disappear from here." A *Haaretz* columnist, Ari Shavit, wrote, "For us, for the enlightened elite, since the morning of May 30, we have been forced to contend with a situation we could not control. . . . The mechanism we have developed to work our way out of this tangle is to work up a psychosis of hatred for the elected prime minister."[1] Netanyahu had many things in common with the Israeli left—he was well-educated, cosmopolitan, and secular. Perhaps part of their hostility to him was that they were so similar, yet he shared the ideology of the "other Israel."

The antipathy was mutual. For Netanyahu, the vanguard of unjustified hatred toward him was the media. In his victory speech, he told Likudniks they had beaten "a hostile and mud-slinging press." Winning would not cure him of the obsession. At a literary event in November 1997, he complained that "most of the media organizations are not objective and their reports are unreliable." If it wasn't for the media, he was certain the entire public would realize what a success his government was. It was the media enticing his recalcitrant ministers to incessantly speak against him instead of toeing the line.

Typically, Netanyahu's first daily staff meeting, after reading the intelligence briefing, was with his press officers, analyzing the newspapers.

Throughout his first term he was continuously giving interviews and calling up journalists at all hours. He would usually complain, but he would also call with praise. "The press is always attacking me. When a balanced article is so rare, I feel the need to speak with the person and say thank you."

He conveniently forgot the first decade of his public career, before Oslo, when he had been the media's star. Bibi never grasped the irony that thanks to the abominable media, he had risen so quickly to the top. And as unfair as the coverage could be, it couldn't be blamed for all the endless blunders and falling-outs during his tenure.

T HE MEMBERS OF the IDF General Staff were Netanyahu's age. As a young Matkal officer, he had served with some of them. Many had served with Yoni. But the moment he became prime minister, there was a barrier. It wasn't just Bibi's insecurity and his need to assert himself as their political master. He had spent five years in a small elite unit and had never shaken his disdain for "the big and stupid army." Netanyahu had little trust in unwieldy armored divisions and was inclined to favor secret, special operations.

The generals of 1996 had been promoted by Netanyahu's political rivals. Rabin, the IDF's commander in 1967, was their father figure. They had been on the negotiation teams that had crafted the Oslo Accords. In Netanyahu's eyes, they were all politically suspect. One of his first decisions was to stop including serving officers in talks with the Palestinians. It was time for them to "change disk," he said, making an analogy to changing the programming for a computer. Senior generals routinely attended cabinet meetings. Now Netanyahu ordered them to leave once they had finished their briefings.

He suspected that they had been tainted by politics, and therefore he doubted their loyalty. His suspicion was confirmed when *Maariv* exposed a major general who had continued briefing Shimon Peres months after the election.

Relations were particularly rocky with the chief of general staff, Lieutenant General Amnon Shahak. The charismatic officer, a protégé of Rabin's, was doubly suspect in Netanyahu's eyes for having established a warm working relationship with Arafat. In one cabinet briefing,

Netanyahu reprimanded Shahak, saying, "It isn't the [chief of general staff's] role to provide political analyses."[2]

Shahak clashed with members of the cabinet who demanded decisive action against Hezbollah in south Lebanon. He told them it was unrealistic to expect the Shi'a militia to stop attacking Israel. But as talks with the Palestinians foundered, Netanyahu found that he had no choice but to bring the generals back in. There was no one else to provide security assessments.

As serving officers, they obeyed the government's orders, but the division between the prime minister and the General Staff quickly found its way to the media. When Netanyahu claimed to have received intelligence that Arafat had "given a green light to terror," generals told reporters it wasn't that clear-cut. When Shahak's term as chief of general staff ended in June 1998, it was widely assumed that he would soon join politics in opposition to Netanyahu.

The low morale of the generals spread, infecting an influential community, the senior reserve officers, many of whom signed petitions against Netanyahu's policies and in 1999 volunteered for the Barak campaign. The IDF has always been the most respected institute in Israeli society. Of all the elites, it would ultimately be the nonpolitical officer corps that caused him the most political damage.

Netanyahu's relationship with other parts of the security establishment were better. These entities were directly responsible to the prime minister and never leaked information to the press. The Mossad chiefs Danny Yatom and Efrayim Halevy praised Netanyahu in their memoirs for backing them up, even after operational mistakes.

Netanyahu was particularly enthusiastic in his position as chairman of the Israel Atomic Energy Commission, paying visits to the Israeli nuclear reactor in Dimona and increasing funding for the nuclear project. He challenged the Israeli defense orthodoxy of "nuclear opacity," advocating more acknowledgment of the country's arsenal. In February 1998, as Saddam Hussein refused to allow UN inspectors to visit his military facilities, a "senior source in the prime minister's office" was quoted threatening Saddam, saying that if a missile with a chemical warhead was fired at Israel, the response would be a neutron bomb.

This report caused consternation within the security establishment, and Netanyahu put major changes to nuclear policy on hold. A few months later, he demanded, and received, written assurances from President Clinton that the Fissile Material Cut-off Treaty his administration was proposing would not force Israel to abandon its opacity. But Netanyahu would revisit the issue later, arguing that Israel's deterrence strategies would be enhanced by acknowledging its full capabilities.

MEANWHILE, NETANYAHU WAS busy fighting the Oslo philosophy that peace would bring security. He would always insist that only security could eventually, one day, bring peace.

In August 1996, Netanyahu had to decide how to respond to intelligence reports that Hafez al-Assad of Syria was planning a surprise attack to snatch back part of the Golan Heights, which Syria had lost in 1967. The reports came from a legendary Mossad agent-runner who claimed to have received details from a retired Syrian general. A Syrian division had just returned from Lebanon, and forces were exercising near the border. The IDF's intelligence branch disputed the Mossad report. Shahak and Mordechai counseled caution, and Netanyahu accepted their views. The IDF quietly put its units on alert without calling up reserves or launching a preemptive attack. It was a difficult decision for a new prime minister. He remembered rushing back in 1973 to an Israel under surprise attack by Syria and Egypt.

One of the first questions the Americans had for Netanyahu was whether he would honor the commitment that Rabin had secretly given them, that he would withdraw from the Golan for peace with Syria. Netanyahu argued that it was not a signed agreement and he had no obligation to follow it. Reluctantly, Secretary of State Warren Christopher agreed and gave Netanyahu written assurances confirming that. Netanyahu told the Americans that he would be willing to pull back on the Golan, to the edge of the ridgeline, but he would not permit a retreat down the cliffs, to the original border. For Assad, this was a nonstarter.

In mid-1998, Netanyahu's position suddenly changed. He sent his friend Ronald Lauder to Damascus to meet Assad. This was classic Netanyahu diplomacy, using unaccountable personal emissaries instead of diplomats. Lauder met Assad nine times, and they reached a number of points of agreement, including one specifying that the border would be on "the line of June 4, 1967," as the Syrians demanded. To continue negotiating, Assad wanted a map on which the border would be drawn.

Netanyahu has categorically denied ever promising Assad the Golan. Senior Israeli and US officials have claimed that he was prepared to send a map, but members of his inner cabinet, Mordechai and Sharon, vetoed him. No map was sent, and the Lauder mission ended in September 1998. Lauder has backed up Netanyahu, saying the proposals were his own ideas.

Lauder may have been exceeding his mandate. A complete withdrawal from the Golan certainly would fly in the face of everything Netanyahu has ever written and said publicly. However, it's clear that Netanyahu was deeply involved in Lauder's secret diplomacy. His old friend and benefactor was acting with the prime minister's blessing. While Lauder was secretly negotiating with Assad, Netanyahu commissioned at least six polls to gauge the Israeli public's positions on a withdrawal from the Golan Heights. The lack of enthusiasm among Israelis for such a move played a part in the demise of the talks.[3] Netanyahu, throughout his political career, has been obsessed with polls. His pollster in his first term, Shai Reuveni, was one of his closest advisers, often eating Shabbat meals with the Netanyahu family, and had instructions to call him at all hours with the latest poll results.[4]

Netanyahu was hoping the Syrian negotiations could relieve the pressure from the Clinton administration to make progress with the Palestinians. He also hoped that by opening a channel to Assad he could obtain his support in disarming, or at least curbing, Hezbollah. Since 1985, on average, twenty IDF soldiers had been killed annually in the "Security Zone" in south Lebanon. The year 1997 had been the bloodiest for over a decade, with seventy-three servicemen dying in September in a collision between two packed helicopters flying to Lebanon. In September, twelve more soldiers died in a commando raid on the Lebanese coast.

The IDF's presence in Lebanon was becoming a deeply unpopular and dangerous liability. Israel needed an exit strategy that would allow it to pull out while guaranteeing the safety of its civilians living near the border. Netanyahu tried to engage with the Lebanese government, in the hope that it would rein Hezbollah in, but Prime Minister Rafik Hariri made it clear that Assad was calling the shots.

Netanyahu failed, just like Rabin, Peres, and Barak, to overcome Assad's deep suspicion of Israel. Unlike them, he denies even trying.

W HILE LAUDER WAS meeting Assad in Damascus, another set of
secret talks was taking place in Jerusalem.

By the summer of 1998, Ehud Barak, Netanyahu's old Matkal commander, had been Labor leader for a year. Like Bibi in 1992, he had
begun his leadership campaign immediately after the election defeat.
Unlike Bibi, who had a clear run after Shamir's resignation, Barak had
had to contend with Peres, who insisted on remaining leader for another year, until the primaries of June 1997, which Barak won by a
landslide.

Now Barak was finding it difficult to acclimatize to a civilian environment where his orders weren't obeyed unquestioningly. It showed in
his public appearances and on television. No one doubted his brilliance.
One-on-one, Barak could be both charming and devastatingly persua-
sive. In larger settings he still appeared aloof and standoffish. Many
considered him to be arrogant, and many in Labor resented him—
behind his back, he was called "Napoleon."

After the first year of chaos, Netanyahu's administration had attained
a level of precarious calm. The blunder rate was down, and he was relatively secure in the polls. Meanwhile, in Labor, the frequent complaint
was "Ehud isn't taking off."

Throughout that summer, Barak held a series of secret meetings with
Netanyahu's consigliere Yaakov Neeman on forming a Likud-Labor
national unity government. Neeman, who had recently been cleared in
court, had been appointed finance minister in Meridor's place. He and
Netanyahu had two major reasons to desire a more centrist coalition.
Clinton was pressuring Netanyahu for further redeployments in the
West Bank, which would enrage the right-wing and ultra-Orthodox parties, whose demands for more sectoral funding was making it difficult to
deal with the deficit.

Barak, languishing in the polls while facing two more years in opposition, followed by the prospect of another defeat to Netanyahu,
wanted to prove himself in government. Under the deal he negotiated
with Neeman, Labor would be an equal partner, and Barak would be
defense minister. It wasn't the first attempt to form a national unity
government. Immediately after the elections, Labor had been eager to
do so, but Netanyahu, after stringing them along, preferred a right-wing
religious coalition. Another attempt in early 1997, this time initiated by

Bibi, was kiboshed by Barak, who believed the government was about to fall as a result of the Bar-On Hebron scandal.

The deal was almost done. But it was leaked to the press, probably by Mordechai, who was anxious not to lose the Defense Ministry. There were reports as well of a separate deal being negotiated by Peres behind Barak's back. He cut contact.

With national unity off the table, Barak swung into full campaign mode. Elections weren't even on the horizon, but he was determined to take Bibi down. He attacked Netanyahu's alliance with the ultra-Orthodox, knowing he was unlikely ever to get votes in that constituency. Just as right-wing politicians could always fall back on their voters' hatred of Arabs, the center-left could rely on resentment of Haredi "parasites" who studied Torah, lived on government handouts, and refused to serve in the IDF.

Netanyahu's alliance with the religious Jews was an easy target. He had done everything he could to curry favor with the rabbis, even though not all of them respected him. In July 1997, Rabbi Ovadya Yosef had publicly mocked his bungling, calling him "a blind goat." Bibi continued courting them. In a meeting with Rabbi Yitzhak Kaduri, a radio-journalist's microphone caught Netanyahu whispering in the sage's ear that "people on the left forgot what it is to be Jewish. They think we will get our security from the Arabs. We'll give them part of our land and the Arabs will take care of us. Unheard of."[5]

The Haredim made unprecedented inroads during Netanyahu's first term. He showered them with subsidies and ministries. Under Haredi pressure, the Transport Ministry closed Jerusalem's Bar-Ilan Road to vehicles on Shabbat, although the high court ordered the main transportation artery reopened.

Shas leader Arye Deri became Bibi's political confidant, speaking with him on the phone every few hours. The secular Netanyahu always had a deeper trust in religious allies than in his own Likudniks. He hired Uri Elitzur, a settler leader and prominent National Religious Party member, as his fourth chief of staff in 1998.

In April 1998, Israel celebrated fifty years of independence. The star-studded main event, attended by Netanyahu and guest of honor Vice President Al Gore, was scheduled to include a number by the Batsheva Dance Company. Before the event, religious politicians objected to the piece, which had been performed earlier in another venue, because the dancers would be scantily dressed. Refusing to adapt their costumes, the dancers withdrew at the last moment, and the company's director read a letter complaining of censorship from the stage.

Netanyahu's subservience to the rabbis angered many moderate Likudniks as well as some of his American supporters. It was also one of the factors leading to his irrevocable split with Foreign Minister Levy.

Netanyahu was falling out with his Likud ministers one after another. In November 1997, a stormy Likud conference had voted on canceling the primaries for the Knesset list and returning power to the Central Committee. Only five years earlier, Netanyahu had championed primaries. Now his ministers were convinced that he was behind the move to abolish them, as part of a plan to use the Central Committee, which was dominated by Bibi loyalists, to cut them down to size. One by one they faced the rowdy Likudniks. "Did we come to power just to dole out jobs [to party cronies]?" asked Communications Minister Limor Livnat. She was shouted down by cries of "Yes! Yes!" Sharon pledged Netanyahu his support, but added, acerbically, "I don't know whether to help your right hand or your left hand."[6]

Netanyahu denied being behind the proposal, but his right-hand man, Lieberman, certainly was. Lieberman's people were caught surreptitiously filming party members planning to vote against the proposal. A few weeks later, exasperated at what he saw as Bibi's failure to assert himself over his ministers, Lieberman resigned. Netanyahu would later blame him for many of the mistakes in his first eighteen months in power. The Likud chaos receded somewhat, but the loss of his chief political enforcer confirmed the impression that even Bibi's oldest allies no longer wanted to work with him.

David Levy had never been an ally, but Netanyahu had recognized that he needed him in Likud, in order to keep the party's Mizrahi working-class constituency together, and had honored his commitment to appoint him as foreign minister. But foreign minister was an empty title. Netanyahu only saw the ministry as a *hasbara* platform. Foreign policy was to be run through his office, by his personal messengers, not through leftist professional diplomats. Netanyahu's team begrudgingly allowed the security experts to take part in the negotiations with the Palestinians, but the Foreign Ministry remained in the dark. Levy was constantly finding out about the latest developments in his meetings with American diplomats. He remonstrated with Netanyahu, who promised to include him. Nothing changed.

Levy led his Gesher faction of five MKs. As the 1998 budget was prepared for its Knesset vote, Gesher presented a list of demands for social projects. Most were turned down by Neeman, who claimed lack of funding. As the final version was brought to the Knesset, an enraged Levy discovered that similar demands made by Shas, as well as increased funding for the ultra-Orthodox community, had been met, and were now being presented as Deri's achievements on behalf of the Mizrahi working-class sector. On January 4, 1998, he announced his resignation, telling reporters, in an emotional press conference, "I've finished with this partnership."

Gesher officially remained part of the coalition, but Netanyahu could no longer rely on its votes. His coalition was down to the bare minimum of sixty-one MKs. He didn't rush, however, to appoint a replacement for Levy as foreign minister, leaving the post vacant for another nine months.

Two weeks after Levy's resignation, Netanyahu was back in Washington. Since the Hebron agreement in January 1997, the diplomatic process with the Palestinians had barely budged. Israel was committed to further redeployments, but Netanyahu constantly found reasons to delay, and the deadlines lapsed. The indefatigable Dennis Ross managed to engineer a Netanyahu-Arafat summit in October, after the two leaders hadn't met for eight months. But while Bibi and Yasser were now comfortable in each other's company, even friendly, there was no breakthrough.

The Clinton administration fully recognized that Netanyahu had his work cut out for him getting his right-wing coalition to go along with any pullback, and Clinton and those who represented him in discussions with Bibi had infinite patience for him. But even infinity was wearing thin. They began to suspect that coalition troubles were just another item on Netanyahu's never-ending list of excuses that allowed him to delay. Along with requests for revisions in the security arrangements, and the (partly justified) accusations that Arafat was turning a blind eye to terrorist attacks and allowing murderous incitement against Israelis, there were demands to limit the number of Palestinian security personnel, and to finally amend the Palestinian Charter. Meanwhile, Arafat had his own growing list of demands and infringements. Israel had yet to allow the Palestinians to operate an airport in Gaza, would not release prisoners, would not arrest violent settlers, and would not stop building in the settlements, on top of not carrying out the further redeployments in the West Bank.

As the new US secretary of state, Madeleine Albright, prepared for her first visit to the region, she planned to deliver Netanyahu a stern lecture. But once again terrorism changed the agenda, with the two Hamas suicide bombings on Ben Yehuda Street in Jerusalem in September 1997. Albright found herself lecturing Arafat instead on the "revolving door," whereby suspects were arrested and then released, a practice that allowed Hamas militants to walk free. Arafat grumbled that he could not be expected to fight Hamas while Netanyahu authorized more settler homes. Albright took the Israeli line, responding, "There is no moral equivalency between suicide bombings and bulldozers, between killing innocent people and building houses."[7]

Once again, President Clinton was prepared to put his own credibility on the line. He invited Netanyahu and Arafat to separate meetings in Washington. The timing could hardly have been worse. Netanyahu arrived in the White House on January 20, 1998. Clinton tried to concentrate on the issues at hand, but he was continuously called out of the room for mysterious consultations. Arafat was due on the 22nd. On the 21st, news broke that Clinton was accused of having enjoyed sexual relations in the Oval Office with a White House intern.

Bibi called Clinton to commiserate. As someone who had survived a sex scandal, he promised him "it will all blow over."[8] He was not entirely convincing. A weakened administration would obviously work in his favor. Neither could Clinton miss the fact that while Netanyahu had been in Washington, he had met with GOP leaders who were now calling for impeachment, and had addressed rallies alongside his fieriest critics, such as the evangelical leaders Jerry Falwell and Pat Robertson. Small wonder that Arab media was full of conspiracy theories casting the Jewish Monica Lewinsky as a Mossad agent.

It wasn't just the Lewinsky affair causing delays. The Clinton administration was dealing with the threat of war in Iraq, with Saddam Hussein defying the United Nations Special Commission (UNSCOM) inspectors. Despite all these personal and international troubles, and despite facing crucial midterm elections, which could define the last two years of his presidency, Clinton was determined to continue with

Clinton did everything he could to prevent Netanyahu's election.

the peace process. He needed to complete his joint legacy with Rabin, and he wanted to prove to the American public that he would not let the scandal deny him his place on the international stage.

But Netanyahu, who was hearing from his Republican friends that Clinton's chances of impeachment were increasing, was in no hurry to make deals. In March, he sent David Bar-Ilan, one of his most right-wing aides, to Washington to brief congressional leaders on Arafat's support for Hamas terrorists. Netanyahu believed that he could continue to get away with dragging feet on the diplomatic process, just as he had a year earlier, when he had authorized a new neighborhood in East Jerusalem.

Mayor Ehud Olmert and the settler leadership held more sway over Netanyahu during that period than the US president. The Har Homa settlement in East Jerusalem had originally been planned by the Rabin government, but had not yet been built. In early 1997, after the Hebron pullback, Netanyahu approved construction and allowed bulldozers to go to work on the rocky hilltop. American diplomats were sympathetic when Arafat complained that Israeli construction on the site was driving a wedge between Bethlehem and East Jerusalem, but they also understood Netanyahu's political constraints. When the United Nations voted to condemn the work, the United States vetoed the resolution.

Netanyahu promised to delay the next phase of construction permits. More construction was approved in 2014. To most Israelis, it is now just another neighborhood in Jerusalem, but by international law, it is an illegal settlement.

A year later, the US administration was growing fed up with Netanyahu's political problems. Albright favored calling him out publicly; National Security Adviser Sandy Berger agreed and accused Bibi of "playing rope-a-dope with us."[9] The media carried headlines about a crisis between Jerusalem and Washington, but Clinton preferred to try and work with Netanyahu rather than against him. Clinton had no reason to fear a backlash from his own considerable Jewish base—polls consistently showed that 80 percent of American Jews supported Clinton's approach on pressuring Israel to freeze settlement building and make concessions to the Palestinians for peace. Bibi's Republican choir was in a clear minority. But Clinton either felt weakened by the ongoing Lewinsky scandal or truly believed that playing hardball with Netanyahu wouldn't work.

The main obstacle remained the overdue redeployment. The Palestinians already had military or civilian control of 27 percent of the West Bank. Jerusalem, the settlements, and "security areas" were to be discussed in the "permanent status" talks. The redeployment was expected to include the remaining territory, and Arafat insisted this would give him control of 91 percent of the West Bank. Netanyahu had a very different security map, according to which Israel could cede less than 40 percent. In months of grueling back-and-forth diplomacy, the American negotiators settled on redeployment from 13 percent as the maximum they could hold Netanyahu to and get Arafat to accept. But Bibi wanted to go lower.

Ross had told Netanyahu that the minimal redeployment would have to be in the "lower teens," but when he came up with thirteen, Netanyahu, the master of the English language, complained that he had "understood eleven." After further haggling, he agreed to transfer 10 percent to Palestinian control and define a further 3 percent as "nature reserves," to be administered by the Palestinian Authority. Any building there would have to receive Israeli authorization.

It had taken a year and a half to reach this formula. Clinton was once again prepared to invest political capital, inviting the sides to a joint summit where they would cross the finishing line. He was taking a major risk in committing himself for as long as it would take when it was just weeks from the midterms. Arafat agreed to arrive. Netanyahu said yes, then twice tried to find reasons to postpone. But ultimately, he had no choice.

The day before leaving for the summit at the Wye Plantation, Netanyahu made a deft political move. He appointed Ariel Sharon as foreign minister. Fifteen years after being forced out of the Defense Ministry in the wake of the Sabra and Shatila massacres, the man who had been shunned as an international pariah since 1983 was back in a top cabinet job. Sharon had been positioning himself for months, toning down his criticism of Netanyahu. He had even invited Arafat's deputy, Mahmoud Abbas, to his farm.

A few months earlier, the US administration had ended its long ostracism of Sharon when Ross met him to discuss the peace process. They were willing to accept Sharon back into the fold to secure a breakthrough. As foreign minister and a senior member of the Israeli negotiating team, the settlers' champion was expected to help Netanyahu sell the Wye agreement to the right wing. Upon his arrival at the summit, Clinton invited Sharon for a private conversation, sitting with him past midnight. The Americans were so eager to have Sharon on board that they were prepared to overlook his rudeness when, upon meeting the Palestinian delegation, he refused to shake Arafat's hand.

THE WYE RIVER Summit of October 1998 lasted for nine days. It seems incredible that an embattled US president spent so much time and effort trying to solve a conflict over a tiny, by American standards, parcel of land so far away. It attests to Clinton's dedication and the obduracy of Netanyahu and Arafat. The outcome, determined in advance by nearly two years of diplomacy, was, as far as the Americans and Palestinians were concerned, just an interim stage before the permanent status talks. But nothing less would have brought Netanyahu to finally sign a further withdrawal agreement in the West Bank.

Secluded in Wye River's pastoral surroundings on Maryland's rural Eastern Shore, the Americans had hoped that an agreement could be reached in four or five days. But the sides reopened and fought over nearly every detail. Toward the end, King Hussein, who was dying of Non-Hodgkin's lymphoma, was flown in from the Mayo Clinic to urge them to completion.

As the summit ground on to its ultimate end, Netanyahu precipitated three crises. On the seventh day, feigning an objection to the security memorandum in the draft, Netanyahu had the Israeli delegation pack their suitcases and inform the Americans that they were about to fly home. He later agreed to stay for another day, and talks on the interim peace accord continued. The first crisis had been averted.

The next evening, Clinton lost his temper. Israel had demanded that the Palestinians arrest a number of men who appeared on a list of terrorist suspects. Netanyahu seemed to hint that one of them, a high-ranking Palestinian officer, ought to simply be assassinated on Arafat's orders. Clinton burst out at him, "This is chickenshit, I'm not going to put up with this kind of bullshit." The self-pitying Bibi sat on a couch, complaining to Ross, asking, "Why is Israel treated this way? Why am I treated this way? What have I done to deserve this?" Eventually, Bibi backed down. The second crisis was over.[10]

Shortly after he agreed to sign the Wye River Memorandum, Netanyahu added a couple of caveats. He told the Clinton administration that to appease Israel's right wing, he would have to authorize building permits in Har Homa. In addition, of the 750 Palestinian prisoners he had agreed to release, most of them would be common criminals, not the "political prisoners" whom Israel considered terrorists.

At 6:30 a.m. on October 23, as they were finally wrapping up and about to put out press statements announcing that an agreement had been reached, Clinton dropped a bombshell on Netanyahu. A few days earlier, Netanyahu had privately asked Clinton to release Jonathan Pollard, an American Jewish US Navy analyst who was serving a life sentence for spying for Israel. Netanyahu had been the first Israeli prime minister to publicly acknowledge that Pollard had been in Israel's service. Pollard's release, he told Clinton, would help him sell the Wye agreement to his supporters in Israel. Clinton was favorable to the request, but his team was against it, some adamantly. CIA Director George Tenet said he would resign if Pollard was released.

The news from Clinton, which came just before the signing, brought about the third crisis, with Netanyahu withdrawing to his room and refusing to speak to the Americans. The Israelis still believe that Clinton reneged on a promise to release Pollard, though Clinton claimed he never actually said yes. In the end, it was Sharon who urged Netanyahu to come out and proceed with the deal. Bibi once again folded under pressure.

Netanyahu had agreed to a three-stage redeployment from 13 percent of the West Bank over a period of twelve weeks. As part of the implementation process, Clinton promised to fly in December to Israel and Gaza, where he would attend a meeting of the Palestinian National Council, finally amending the Palestinian Charter. With breathtaking optimism, the Wye River Memorandum included a commitment from both sides to try and reach a "permanent status" within six months, by May 4, 1999.

On Friday afternoon, the teams scrambled for helicopters to make it to the signing ceremony at the White House before sundown and the beginning of Shabbat. For the American hosts and the Palestinians, there was relief, but also bitterness. So much effort had to be expended to obtain such a meager result. There was none of the jubilation of the previous Oslo signing ceremonies with Rabin and Peres. For Netanyahu, there remained the grim job back home of trying to get his crumbling coalition to sign off on the agreement as well. He knew his government might not survive Wye.

22

They. Are. Afraid.

When he returned from Wye Plantation, Netanyahu could have used the moment to reboot his premiership. He had achieved an agreement that had the support of more than three-quarters of Israelis, a much higher approval rating than the Oslo Agreements. By continuing the peace process with the Palestinians, while driving a hard bargain and keeping an eagle-eye on security, he had done what the majority of the nation wanted. The right wing was threatening to bring down his government, but Netanyahu was leading Ehud Barak in the polls. He could have called on Barak at that point to form a national unity government that would implement the Wye River Memorandum, and work together on the permanent status negotiations. If he had done so, Barak would have had a hard time saying no. It was Bibi's opportunity to secure two more years in power, followed by a likely second term.

Netanyahu, however, instinctively turned rightward, toward the 20 percent of the population that was against Wye—the hardcore Revisionists and settlers. They were his political tribe, and like them, Netanyahu hated the agreement he had just signed in the White House. He lost no time in trying to sabotage it.

Begging coalition trouble, he told the Americans he needed time to implement the agreement. It took three weeks just for him to present it to the cabinet and the Knesset. In the cabinet, it passed 8–4, with five abstentions. It passed the Knesset thanks to Labor's votes. Netanyahu promised his ministers that each stage of the redeployment would be authorized in a separate vote. Any statement by the Palestinians, any lack of compliance, real or imagined, would be reason for more delay.

The slow pace of implementation failed to assuage the hard right. Former prime minister Yitzhak Shamir slammed Netanyahu, calling him "an angel of destruction." "Who gave him permission to promise more parts of Judea and Samaria to the Arabs? How is he better than Rabin or Peres?" Shamir fumed. "He has a desire for power for its own sake."[1] Neither were they mollified by the construction permits issued for Har Homa. Ariel Sharon backed Netanyahu in public, but privately he urged the settlers to take advantage of the weak prime minister quickly, by illegally occupying hilltops throughout the West Bank.

The first stage was implemented in November 1998. The IDF dismantled a few disused outposts, pulling back from 2 percent of the West Bank, mainly wasteland. When Clinton arrived a few weeks later, Netanyahu explained that he needed time to get his coalition in order before the next redeployment. The members of the president's team were enraged, but Clinton merely shrugged. By that point he knew he had gotten as much as he could expect out of Bibi and was clinging to the hope that he would soon be gone. Instead Clinton focused his visit on the Palestinian side, singing carols in Bethlehem and making an emotional speech to the Palestinian National Council in Gaza, saying, "I am honored to be the first American president to address the Palestinian people, in a city governed by Palestinians, for Palestinians."[2] At the Erez Crossing, he brought Arafat and Netanyahu together for their last meeting. It was an unhappy couple of hours yielding no results.

Clinton was still fighting impeachment and would soon have to order air strikes on Iraq and the Serbs in Kosovo. He had not given up on peace between Israelis and Palestinians. He had invested too much of his presidency into it. But he had given up on Bibi.

Many have criticized Clinton for being so patient with Netanyahu for two and a half years. He never blamed him in public or went behind his back to the Palestinians. But Clinton had succeeded in squeezing out of Netanyahu two signed agreements. Hebron and Wye may have been only tiny, incremental steps, but he had gotten an ideological Likud leader to withdraw from parts of the West Bank. The Oslo process had slowed down to a crawl, but it had not been derailed. The Knesset was preparing to vote for early elections. Clinton had reason to hope that Oslo would outlast Bibi.

Y THE TIME Clinton returned to his impeachment battles in Congress, there was close to a majority in the Knesset for bringing elections forward. Frantically, Netanyahu tried to hang on, but he had fallen
out with the right wing in his coalition for signing Wye, with the moderates for not implementing it, and with pretty much everyone else over his
own conduct. Even the loyal Yaakov Neeman resigned as finance minister on December 18, when Netanyahu failed to back him in acrimonious
budget talks with the ultra-Orthodox parties. His government was going
to fall either by an early election motion, by not passing the 1999 budget,
or in a no-confidence vote. Netanyahu clutched at straws.

He reached out once again to David Levy, offering to give him Neeman's position as finance minister in return for the five Gesher MKs
supporting the government. But the deal fell through. Finally, he made a
last-minute appeal to Labor to enter a national unity government. Had
he done so two months before, when returning from Wye, Barak would
have been put on the spot. By then, however, everyone—the Knesset, the
media, the whole nation, it seemed—was simply fed up.

"The right thing is to go for elections. This government has exhausted itself," answered Barak. Netanyahu himself was exhausted from
the struggle to stay in power. He had visibly aged since entering office,
putting on weight, the makeup he perpetually wore on his face failing to
hide the sagging pouches of tiredness.

On December 16 at a Hanukkah lighting in Metzudat Ze'ev, he announced early elections. Five days later, the Knesset voted to dissolve
itself. Elections were set for May 17, 1999. Netanyahu's first government
had held together for only thirty months. And there were more splits to
come before Israel went to the polls.

Defense Minister Mordechai, the star of the last election, again
weighed his options. Relations with Netanyahu had been tense throughout the term. Mordechai treated the Defense Ministry as his birthright,
not a post he was filling at the prime minister's pleasure. He shot down
Netanyahu's plans to establish a national security council to oversee
the IDF and intelligence community. As Bibi rowed with the generals,
Mordechai invariably took their side, though he usually did so quietly,
allowing others to take the flak.

Mordechai had expected to be the government's point man on all
security-related matters, but constantly found himself in the dark. Netanyahu used his own confidants, or sent Sharon on sensitive missions.

Like the other senior ministers, he had given up on establishing a stable working relationship with Netanyahu. For months he had been holding talks with the two "princes" who had left Likud—former finance minister Dan Meridor and Tel Aviv mayor Ronny Milo. They had linked up with the recently discharged IDF chief of staff, Amnon Shahak, in a new centrist party with one purpose—to bring down Netanyahu. Mordechai was tempted to join, but loath to give up the Defense Ministry.

As in the previous elections, Mordechai was dealing with both sides. He simultaneously negotiated with the centrist trio, demanding leadership of the new party, should he join, while seeking assurances from Netanyahu that he would remain defense minister if he stayed in Likud. With the media closely following the Bibi-Mordechai struggle, Netanyahu preempted his defense minister.

On January 23, a government driver knocked on Mordechai's door. He was inside with Meridor, Milo, and Shahak as the dismissal was delivered. Minutes later, Netanyahu was on television, surrounded by the remaining Likud ministers, reading out a long, harsh letter telling Mordechai that his "personal ambition is stronger than any other consideration." It was an unprecedented humiliation. The second most powerful man in Israel was being fired live on television.

Netanyahu had intended it as a demonstration of strong, decisive leadership, destroying Mordechai's credibility. It failed. Mordechai joined the new Center Party (Mifleget Ha'Merkaz) as leader and candidate for prime minister. The party's electoral prospects were unclear, and the four men at its helm all felt they should be captain, but to Netanyahu they were kryptonite. Three top Likudniks, two of them senior ministers in his government, had joined his IDF chief of staff, all now devoted to eliminating Bibi. And they were far from alone. Every other week, another former member of Netanyahu's government announced that he was founding a new party.

On the far right, former science minister Benny Begin founded Herut, using the same name as the historical forerunner of Likud, which had been led by his father. Ex-foreign minister David Levy relaunched Gesher, breaking away again from Likud. As did Netanyahu's other partner from 1996, Agriculture Minister Rafael Eitan, who ran with his Tzomet party. Avigdor Lieberman, who had spent five years at Netanyahu's side as Likud CEO and director-general of the prime minister's office, launched his own political platform, Yisrael Beiteinu (Israel Our

Home), aimed mainly at bringing together immigrants from the former Soviet Union.

It was a mad stampede out of Netanyahu's Likud, with the "princes" in the lead. One thing all the new parties had in common was that they claimed to represent Likud's values, unlike that unprincipled charlatan Netanyahu. Many who still remained in the party disputed his leadership.

Likud held its leadership primary on January 25. Netanyahu had hoped to be reelected unopposed, but Uzi Landau, the man who twenty-five years earlier had first introduced him to political activism on the MIT campus in Boston, announced that he would be running against him, to represent the true Likud. Landau dropped out of the race within weeks, however, to make way for the man who had launched Netanyahu's career.

Six years after leaving politics, now at the age of seventy-three, Moshe Arens announced that he would be running against Netanyahu in the primary. Arens had never sought to lead Likud or become prime minister, but he felt responsible for his protégé's actions and had opposed the Hebron and Wye agreements. He also quietly resented the fact that Netanyahu had not heeded his advice since becoming Likud leader. One of the very rare gentlemen of Israeli politics, Arens had barely ever criticized Bibi in public, and even then, he had kept it low-key. His surprise leadership bid had no realistic chance of success, but it was a damaging statement on Netanyahu's leadership nevertheless.

Anxious to minimize the damage, Netanyahu offered Arens the Defense Ministry just vacated by Mordechai. The cynicism of Bibi's offer was not lost on Arens. With only months to the election, he would only be a caretaker defense minister anyway. But his sense of national responsibility prevailed. He agreed to Netanyahu's offer, but added that he would take the job only after the primary. On February 25, Netanyahu beat Arens 80–20. Two days later, Arens became defense minister under the man who had twice been his deputy.

Three years earlier, Netanyahu had run against the seventy-two-year-old Peres as a fresh young leader. In Likud's 1999 campaign, a visibly aged Bibi was running with two septuagenarians, Arens and Sharon, flanking him as chaperones.

NETANYAHU'S CAMPAIGN TEAM in 1999 was like the negative image of the team that had worked so well three years earlier. Arthur

Finkelstein was still on retainer and flying in for visits every few weeks, but the turbulent years had taken their toll on Netanyahu's circle. They were no longer disciplined or receptive to Finkelstein's direction. As it was, his style of campaigning was much more suited to an insurgent candidate, not a tired and discredited incumbent.

One of the two leaders of the original team, Eyal Arad, Netanyahu's old UN press officer, had long ago fallen out with him. He had been frozen out of the newly elected prime minister's team three years before, marked down by Sara Netanyahu since the "hot-tape" scandal as someone who may have known about Bibi's affair. Now owning his own public relations company, Arad was working for the Center Party, his services at the disposal of Netanyahu's nemeses.

Communications Minister Limor Livnat, who had led the team in 1996 with Arad, like many talented and attractive women around Bibi, had also fallen afoul of Sara. Still, because of her popularity in the party, Netanyahu had no choice but to appoint her to the cabinet. Like the other Likud ministers, Livnat was disillusioned by his leadership and entertaining an offer from her friends Milo and Meridor to defect to the Center Party. Her loyalty to Likud prevailed, but it took considerable urging from Netanyahu to get her to lead the campaign team again.

It was an unhappy band that gathered at party headquarters. As prime minister and a proven winner, Bibi was no longer content to allow the professionals to call the shots. Sara had to have her say as well. They interfered in the messaging and editing of broadcasts. Bibi, on Finkelstein's advice, urged the campaign to go on the attack against Barak. Livnat believed Barak was still a Teflon general, and preferred to target their fire on other Labor politicians who would lead Barak astray leftward. Sara constantly demanded that they present the achievements of "the best prime minister" Israel had ever had—and of course showcase his wonderful family.

Despite the discord, Netanyahu was initially optimistic. Likud's polling showed that 28 percent of those who voted for him in 1996 were not planning to do so again. But this time there would be more than two candidates for prime minister—in addition to him and Barak, Begin, Mordechai, and the Palestinian Israeli politician Azmi Bishara were all planning to run. With so many candidates from left and right, no one would cross the 50 percent threshold, and there would be a second round between the two frontrunners, most likely Netanyahu and Barak. Bibi believed that he could rely on his coalition of right-wing, Russian, and religious outsiders to put aside their misgivings and turn out in the second round to beat the left.

But the early optimism soon gave way to creeping hysteria. In one of his first campaign rallies, Netanyahu entered the venue wearing a heavy bullet-proof coat, on the Shin Bet's instructions. Bibi began whipping up the crowd against the left. "You know who we're dealing with," he told the baying Likudniks. Turning to a camera crew: "Channel 2? I thought you were Labor's TV." Back at the crowd: "You say there's no difference?" He paused. "Is there anyone here who isn't a Likud member?" As they crowed "No!" he theatrically shrugged off the bullet-proof coat. His die-hard supporters lapped it up, but many Israelis, including Likud voters, were disgusted by the divisive tone.[3]

Meanwhile, Barak learned the mistakes of Labor's previous campaign and what Netanyahu had done right. He kept most of Labor's politicians out of the campaign itself, instead building his team from driven young activists and special forces officers from his time in the army. Clinton also learned from his mistake in 1996 and now kept out of the elections. But key Democratic operatives from the United States were advising the Barak campaign, including Clinton's 1992 campaign manager James Carville (who had been introduced to Barak by Hillary Clinton's mentor, the American Jewish peace activist Sara Ehrman) and pollster Stan Greenberg. Another foreign leader quietly rooting for Barak was British prime minister Tony Blair. Blair's pollster, Philip Gould, also assisted the campaign. Barak closely studied Blair's "New Labour" 1997 campaign, which had won a landslide in Britain, and modeled his own "war room" on Labour's Millbank headquarters.

One key lesson Barak learned from Blair was the need to rebrand Labor, opening the party to communities who were not prepared to vote for "the left." Barak's version was unveiled in March—"One Israel." To diversify his lineup, he had added two small parties whose leaders were promised cabinet positions and slots for their members on the joint list—the moderate, pro-peace religious party Meimad (an acronym for Medina Yehudit, Medina Demokratit, or Jewish State, Democratic State), and the biggest surprise, Gesher. David Levy, Likud's longest-serving MK, the man who symbolized the party's connection with the Mizrahi working class, had developed such a resentment toward Netanyahu that he was prepared to join Likud's historical rival.

Levy had not converted, and many Labor members grumbled that he wasn't that popular among his own constituency. But Barak hadn't brought Levy in for his voters. He needed the veteran Likudnik to dilute Labor's left-wing image. Besides, he cared less for Labor votes in the party ballot than Barak votes in the direct election for prime minister.

Barak's campaign presented him as Rabin's successor, in the "Mr. Security" role, not necessarily as a peacemaker. He remained vague on how he planned to continue the peace process, sticking instead to two popular policies.

On February 28, Brigadier General Erez Gerstein, commander of IDF forces in south Lebanon, was killed by a Hezbollah bomb, along with two of his men and an Israeli radio journalist. The next day, Barak promised that, should he be elected, within a year the IDF would pull back from the "Security Zone," as part of a wider agreement with Syria and Lebanon.

Barak's second campaign promise was "One Israel, One draft." He would end the Haredi yeshiva students' exemption from military service. He didn't explain how he would change the policy, which had been approved by David Ben-Gurion; he just wanted to link the unpopular Haredim to Netanyahu in the voters' minds.

Not that he had to try very hard. The 1999 election was the consummation of Netanyahu's affair with the Haredim. Bibi had not changed his secular, hedonistic ways, but they had never expected it of him. Netanyahu had no interest in affairs of synagogue and state and was perfectly happy for the ultra-Orthodox hegemony to remain. Neither was the increase in benefits for Haredi education and large families a major price to pay in return for automatic support from the Haredi MKs and ministers in security and diplomatic matters. It was the perfect political alliance.

Netanyahu was prepared to anger his American supporters with his alliance with the ultra-Orthodox. Legislation they proposed would have marginalized the Reform and Conservative movements, to which most American Jews belong. It led to the unprecedented, until then, move by some Jewish federations to cut their donations to the United Israel Appeal, giving millions instead to Israeli movements promoting religious tolerance and pluralism—essentially funding critics of the Netanyahu government.

After a string of Supreme Court rulings challenging the legality of various regulations in favor of the ultra-Orthodox, including their exemption from military service, Netanyahu promised the rabbis that after the elections he would form a commission to examine the Court's powers.

On the eve of the elections, the rabbis told their followers to vote "for the candidate whose party is closer to acting in the spirit of religion." No one had any doubt who that was. The political leader of Shas, Arye Deri, was even more explicit, calling at campaign rallies to "Vote Shas and Netanyahu!"

On March 13, Deri was convicted of bribe-taking, fraud, and breach of trust and sentenced to four years in prison. With the verdict on appeal, he continued to lead Shas. Barak announced that should he be elected, he would not conduct coalition talks with Shas as long as Deri remained leader. Netanyahu failed to see how Deri tainted him and did not distance himself.

The close connection with Shas damaged Netanyahu with another key constituency. The secular "Russian" voters saw the Haredim, especially the Shas Mizrahim, as backward, oriental clerics. In one of his sermons, the Shas spiritual leader, Rabbi Ovadya Yosef, called the pork-eating Russians "completely evil," warning that they weren't even Jewish. Shas controlled the Interior Ministry, with its baffling bureaucracy for newcomers. The immigrant party Yisrael B'Aliyah ran a campaign in Russian calling for the Interior Ministry to be "under its own control." Its leader, Natan Sharansky, who had once been Netanyahu's close ally, had also become estranged. Sharansky suspected that Lieberman's Yisrael Beiteinu party was actually a Likud satellite, coordinated with Netanyahu, to entice away his voters.

Barak calculated that he had nothing to lose by running an "anti-Haredi" campaign. The ultra-Orthodox were voting for Netanyahu anyway. But he could attract many of the 68 percent of former Soviet Union immigrants who had voted for Netanyahu in 1996. Barak's campaign printed campaign literature in Russian. A sanitized Russian edition of a glowing new biography of him was printed in tens of thousands of copies, delivered for free to immigrant voters' homes. Any connection to the old socialism of Labor was airbrushed out. The candidate was presented to the Russians as the tough "General Barak" who would have no patience for those religious parasites.

The campaign, emphasizing Barak's military record, included a photograph of him from 1972, as a Sayeret Matkal commander, on the wing of the Sabena airliner that had just been captured from hijackers. Labor didn't mention that the young Lieutenant Netanyahu had been wounded during the operation.

B Y FEBRUARY, THE polls had begun to turn decisively against Netanyahu. On February 7, King Hussein died. The next day, as Netanyahu mingled with Clinton, Blair, and dozens of other world leaders at the funeral in Amman, they found it hard to conceal their relief at the thought of not having to meet him again. In early March, he made a rare appearance at the memorial service for Menachem Begin on the Mount of Olives. Herut leader Benny Begin edged away from Netanyahu and cut the service short. People were beginning to shun Bibi as they had after Rabin's assassination. One of the more popular stickers of the campaign called on Israelis to vote for anyone, even a goat, "Just not Bibi!"

Netanyahu's slogan didn't try to appeal to moderates. It was "Just Netanyahu! A strong leader for a strong nation." A negative slogan, "Ehud Barak—too much ambition, too few principles," rang particularly hollow, as most voters saw it as an apt description of the incumbent.

As his numbers in the polls continued to shrink, Netanyahu's rhetoric turned even more tribal. "The rich, the artists . . . these elites. They hate everyone," he told Likudniks in April. "They hate the people. They hate the Mizrahis, they hate the Russians, hate anyone who is not them. Everyone who isn't with them, Ethiopians, Mizrahis, Russians, everyone." At a rally a few weeks later, he accused the media of working with the left to bring him down and led the crowd in chanting, over and over, "They. Are. Afraid. They. Are. Afraid. They. Are. Afraid."

It didn't work, but Netanyahu had been written off before, only to win. Some began to worry that Bibi was a "magician" who could read the Israeli public better than the pollsters. The "tom-tom drums" of the Likud tribe were calling the voters home. Netanyahu was still relying on a second-round showdown with Barak where he could work his magic. Labor was worried about this outcome as well, and the other candidates, Mordechai, Begin, and Bishara, were all under intense pressure to withdraw in favor of the frontrunner, Barak.

At the debate, Netanyahu scored a point when he got Mordechai to commit not to drop out of the race under any circumstance. Bibi had eagerly agreed to the debate, expecting to land another knockout like he had with Peres. Barak declined to participate, preferring to lose points for his absence than to give Netanyahu the opportunity to outshine him onscreen. Mordechai was hesitant to debate Netanyahu, but his partners in the Center Party, which had been losing votes to Labor for weeks, prevailed upon him to accept. Meridor and Arad, who had prepped Bibi for his debate against Peres in 1996, now rehearsed his opponent.

It was a lopsided and strangely compelling spectacle. On Finkelstein's advice, Netanyahu largely ignored Mordechai, as well as the moderator, Nissim Mishal, choosing to focus instead on the empty chair representing Barak. This opened him up to constant attacks from a sneering Mordechai, who chuckled as Netanyahu spoke and belittled his achievements as prime minister. Mordechai claimed that Israel was more secure not thanks to Netanyahu, but because he and the security chiefs had reined in the prime minister.

"Keep your calm Bibi, keep your calm, I know these outbursts of yours," he berated him. "I know in what military situations we could have been, and you know." When Mishal asked them a question about negotiations with Syria, Netanyahu denied that he would ever retreat from the Golan. Mordechai interjected, "Look me in the eye, Bibi."[4] The prime minister was humiliated on live television. Mordechai hadn't gained any points, either. He came over as too nasty. Barak, who stayed home, won the debate.

Even Netanyahu's sole achievement, Mordechai's promise to stay the course, turned out to be worthless. In the last days of the campaign, Begin, Bishara, and finally Mordechai on the eve of the election, all dropped out. So great was the desire, across the political spectrum, to be rid of Netanyahu, that the far right, the far left, and the center all gave Barak a clear run against him. Mordechai, especially, had served Barak well by running nearly to the end. Many right-wing voters who were disappointed with Netanyahu, but found it impossible to contemplate voting for the left wing's candidate, first made up their minds to vote Mordechai. When he dropped out, some went back reluctantly to Netanyahu. Others, having already chosen in their minds the gateway candidate, found it easier now to shift to Barak.

I N 1996, NETANYAHU had built a coalition of underdogs and outcasts to achieve his breathtaking victory over Peres. He had then spent the next three years smashing that coalition to smithereens. His camp of outsiders had turned in on itself in a feeding frenzy. Bibi had satisfied no one. Not the settlers, the moderates, the old Revisionists, or the newcomer Russians. Only one section of the electorate remained true to Netanyahu—the ultra-Orthodox. In some Haredi neighborhoods, he received over 99 percent of the vote.

Israel's first right-wing prime minister, Menachem Begin, so despised by the Netanyahu family, had spent decades building Likud as a warm home for both Revisionist veterans and Mizrahi immigrants. As prime minister, he had tried, unsuccessfully, to unify Israelis from all walks of life. Netanyahu instead played up the tribal divides. It had worked in 1996, when anyone who did not belong to the left camp was denied a place in the national mourning after Rabin's assassination. But by 1999, Bibi had driven too many out of Likud, broken too many promises to his partners, and divided Israel too deeply.

It wasn't a totally ineffective strategy. On May 17, Ehud Barak was elected prime minister with 56 percent of the vote. It was a handy majority, yet not quite a landslide. After all that had happened, Netanyahu still received 44 percent. And Barak had to run as a hawkish and centrist general, which is what he was, to win. At least half of all Israelis were still reluctant to risk their votes for peace.

Netanyahu's concession speech, twenty minutes after the exit polls were out, even before the first real results began trickling in, was his best of the campaign. It was short and elegant. For once, he blamed no one. He of course thanked Sara, but he also thanked one more person—Ariel Sharon, the only senior Likud minister standing by him that night in the Tel Aviv Hilton ballroom.

He went back upstairs to his room. He wasn't morose or disappointed. As a great believer in polling, Netanyahu had been aware for weeks that he was facing certain defeat. Mordechai dropping out a day earlier had merely confirmed it. Later that night, he stood on the hotel balcony with a few of his closest supporters, those who remained loyal to him, and analyzed what had gone wrong. He was taking a time-out from politics, resigning from the Likud leadership before anyone challenged him, and from the Knesset as well. He would make some money in the private sector, and before long, he would return. That's why he had made sure to thank Sharon. Netanyahu planned to recommend him as temporary leader in his absence. At seventy, Sharon wasn't about to be an obstacle to Netanyahu's return. He would just be the old caretaker.

As Bibi summed up his lessons from the disastrous campaign, he assumed some responsibility. It wasn't his policies or capabilities, but he was willing to take part of the blame for not having paid enough attention to the ministers around him. Politics, he admitted, was also about getting along with other people. But more than anything else, it had been the media who had brought him down. He vowed to change that next time around.

23

A Concerned Citizen

Two days after losing the election, Benjamin Netanyahu was searching for a new house in Jerusalem. The apartment he had recently bought in Rehavia was not large enough to host guests in style. Besides, Bibi and Sara felt their standing warranted a private home, a status symbol in the cramped city. But the economic boom of the past decade had put the kind of house they had in mind in a central neighborhood out of the price range of a man who had lived for the past fifteen years on a government salary and the munificence of his wealthy friends.

As he traipsed after the estate agent, viewing desirable residences in the upscale German Colony of Jerusalem, and meeting polite, quizzical smiles when he asked the sellers for a discount, Netanyahu realized he would have to go through with his plan to make a clean break from politics for a while. By Israeli law, MKs are prohibited from having outside employment to parliamentary duties. Unlike previous prime ministers, who had retained their seats after losing an election, Netanyahu announced his resignation from the Knesset. He consoled himself that it was only a short break from politics to obtain financial security for his family, and he would soon be back in power.

On one count at least, Netanyahu was right. His successor, Ehud Barak, would have the shortest term of any prime minister in Israel's history. Barak had been marketed as the antithesis to Bibi. If anything, he was the upgrade. Barak would lose his staff, fall out with his coalition, bomb out in negotiations with the Palestinians and Syria, and be dumped by the electorate in half the time it had taken Netanyahu.

Barak's energetic and brash approach to the two diplomatic processes was the opposite of Netanyahu's hesitant and cagey one. Within six months of taking office he was at Shepherdstown, West Virginia, for talks with Syria's foreign minister. Six months later there was another full-blown summit with the Palestinians, this time at Camp David.

Barak believed he could cross the finish line and deliver a peace deal with Syria and permanent status agreements with the Palestinians. He had Bill Clinton's full backing. Nevertheless, he totally failed. Neither Hafez al-Assad nor Yasser Arafat had ever been prepared to go the final mile and resolve the conflict, or, just like Egypt's Anwar al-Sadat, they were simply incapable of compromising on anything less than every inch of territory captured by Israel in 1967. Both negotiations failed spectacularly.

The Oslo veterans had advised Barak not to rush headlong into an all-or-nothing summit with Arafat. But he wasn't one to heed advice. Clinton had some misgivings, but nearing the end of his presidency and on his fourth Israeli prime minister, he was anxious to seal his Middle East peace legacy.

By the time Barak took off for Camp David, he had lost all but one of his coalition partners, leaving him with a minority government. A year after his confident victory, his administration was falling apart.

What was it about this new generation of Israeli leaders, Bibi and Barak? They were self-confident and suspicious and impervious to counsel, efficient as campaigners, yet incapable of building anything resembling a harmonious team or maintaining a stable coalition once in power. There seemed to be something in the Sayeret Matkal DNA that transformed its officers into secretive solo operators who were focused on their targets but oblivious to their surroundings.

NETANYAHU HAD NO time to gloat over his successor's misfortune. Three months after leaving office, the police began an investigation against him over charges that the prime minister's office had paid a Jerusalem contractor, Avner Amedi, nearly half a million shekels to settle Netanyahu's outstanding bill. According to allegations published in *Yedioth Ahronoth*, most of the bill was for private services such as renovations performed at the Netanyahus' residences. It was alleged that Amedi had also carried out similar services for Sara's parents.

Amedi's demands for payment had been ignored for years—until Netanyahu was elected prime minister, when the contractor suddenly became the recipient of lavish government contracts from his office. As the investigators dug dipper, they discovered that one of Amedi's last contracts had been to box up and remove, on Sara's instructions, the contents of a room containing hundreds of gifts Netanyahu had received during his term as prime minister. By law, the gifts were state property. Police, accompanied by media camera crews, raided the Netanyahus' private residence, taking a case of documents. Seven hundred gifts were repossessed by the state; another 150 had disappeared.

For a year Bibi and Sara remained under the shadow of a criminal investigation, with the results threatening to land them in court and prevent his political comeback. "They are afraid I will return," he complained to sympathetic journalists. Once again he blamed an unholy alliance of leftist law-enforcement and media. Passing a photograph of Yitzhak Rabin in the corridor of the police headquarters, he said to the officers, "I know you're all leftists." The couple claimed to have been unaware of the government contracts awarded to Amedi and insisted that they believed the gifts were legally theirs.

The media, which previously had gleefully reported on Sara's passion for goody bags, and the monthly budget at the prime minister's office of 11,700 shekels for Bibi's favorite Cuban cigars, continued to show a keen interest in the couple's greediness. Bibi had been known for years in Jerusalem restaurants as someone who left others to pay the bill. Sara was his perfect partner in entitlement. But while the majority of the media may have been hoping for the investigations to seal Netanyahu's political demise, the scandals were having little effect on the right-wingers, who were beginning to pine for him.

As in the Bar-On Hebron case, the police recommended an indictment. The state prosecutor concurred. But the attorney general, Elyakim Rubinstein, once again overruled the prosecutor, saving Netanyahu with his ruling on September 27, 2000. There was insufficient evidence to secure a conviction, he said. Rubinstein, however, did condemn Netanyahu's conduct as "ugly," and remarked on the "insufferable ease" with which he had ignored the norms expected of a public servant.[1]

Tzila Netanyahu didn't live to see her son and daughter-in-law cleared. The young woman who had written poems and studied law and then devoted her life to her husband's and sons' careers passed away on January 31, 2000. Shortly beforehand, she told one of her friends that "87 years [was] enough." Even in death she became part of Yoni's pantheon. On her tombstone was written, "In upstanding glory, she bore the grief of the falling of her son Jonathan, of the noblest of heroes of the state of Israel in all its wars."

Tzila's death, taking place at a low point in Bibi's career, was a rebuke to him, a reminder of how his parents were never fully satisfied, even by his greatest success. Benzion, with his habitual bluntness, had criticized his son's term in office, saying in a rare interview in 1998, "He doesn't know how to develop manners to captivate people by praise or grace," and "He doesn't always succeed in choosing the most suitable people." Praising his son's statesmanship, Benzion said, "He may well have been more suited as foreign minister than head of state. But at this moment I don't see anyone better." These words led Netanyahu's critics to say, unfairly, that even Bibi's father didn't think he should be prime minister.[2]

Netanyahu was determined to return to office and prove his father and everyone else wrong. Meanwhile, he needed to make money. For three and a half years as a private citizen, Netanyahu was on the lucrative circuit of ex-presidents and prime ministers making the rounds as "consultants" for international companies, giving private "talks" to billionaire businessmen, and lecturing for high fees, which in his case went as high as $60,000 for a single appearance. He has never released his financial records and is not required to do so by Israeli law, but the Israeli business press assessed his earnings during that period at around 15 million shekels (about $3.7 million). The family remained in their Rehavia apartment, but in 2002 they bought a 5 million shekel weekend villa by the sea in exclusive Caesarea.[3]

The Israeli media compared Netanyahu's hedonism unfavorably with the frugality of David Ben-Gurion and Menachem Begin, as well as with Peres and Rabin, who lived off their government salaries. Netanyahu's assets, consisting primarily of the family's two homes and those inherited by Bibi and Sara from their parents, was estimated by *Forbes Israel* in 2015 at around 42 million shekels (about $11 million),[4] similar in scale to estimates for contemporary Israeli leaders' assets. Ehud Barak in his periods outside politics was on the same circuit. Ariel Sharon built up one of the largest cattle farms in Israel. Until the law forbade MKs to have extra-parliamentarian business interests, Ehud Olmert enjoyed income from his successful law firm. And all four of Israel's most recent prime ministers have been investigated for corruption.

A YEAR AFTER LEAVING office, Netanyahu made his first political intervention. In a television interview, he slammed Ehud Barak, who was then at the Camp David summit with Arafat and Clinton, for his proposals to pull back from 90 percent of the West Bank and share parts of East Jerusalem with the Palestinians. When asked whether he was speaking as a politician, Netanyahu answered, "I'm speaking as a concerned citizen." The Israeli media has lampooned him ever since as "the concerned citizen," but it was a clear signal both to his supporters and his rivals. As the months passed, he began making more media appearances, usually with "soft" interviewers, such as the credulous talk-show host Yair Lapid, to whom he said, in February 2002, that he was traveling the world to present Israel's case: "I'm not interested in the money, as you well know."

In between business trips, Netanyahu was working on rehabilitation. His diary was full of meetings with Likudniks, journalists, and even senior members of other parties. The monologue he delivered included assurances that since his downfall he had learned "to listen," and that "I am not working on my own." In meetings with settlers and far-right activists who had attacked him for signing the Hebron and Wye agreements, he explained that he had implemented "an interpretation of the [Oslo] Agreement that would allow me to stop the gallop to the '67 lines."[5] Most on the right, especially the old Revisionists, were forgiving, and still saw in him their best hope of blocking Barak's plans. Not that Barak was getting anywhere with them.

After fourteen days, the Camp David summit ended with the Israelis and the Palestinians incapable of bridging their differences. "I'm a colossal failure, and you've made me one," Clinton told Arafat bitterly.[6]

In one year's frenetic activity, Barak had been on the brink of deals with the Palestinians and Syria. Keeping his election promise, he had pulled the IDF out of the "Security Zone" in southern Lebanon in early June. But without an agreement with either Syria or Lebanon, the pullback was disorderly, and Israeli posts were soon taken over by Hezbollah, crowing over how they had "banished" the mighty Israeli army.

The shine had gone off Barak's premiership, but the very thought of Likud leader Ariel Sharon replacing him still seemed outlandish. Even within Likud, few regarded him as more than a caretaker. He had won the leadership primary in 1999, beating Ehud Olmert with 53 percent of the vote, but this was largely due to Netanyahu's supporters backing him, in the belief that the seventy-one-year-old pariah would never be an obstacle to Bibi's return. But Sharon was playing a long game. He was lulling Netanyahu into a false sense of security while transforming his old image as a warmonger into that of a benevolent grandfather.

Sharon's team of advisers now included Eyal Arad, Netanyahu's old press officer, who had sworn to keep his old boss out of office, and Arthur Finkelstein, who had been hired once again by Likud to advise the impending election campaign. It was Finkelstein, who was still convinced that Jerusalem was a winning issue, who urged Sharon to make a visit to the Temple Mount on September 28, the day before Rosh Hashanah. Sharon's tour of the contested Haram al-Sharif compound was intended as a challenge to the Barak government, but it sparked off a wave of Palestinian riots. The rioting quickly spread throughout the West Bank and Gaza as well as to some Palestinian-Israeli communities within the Green Line (the pre-1967 border).

As the spontaneous rioting gave way to gunfights between the IDF and Palestinian militias, Israel's intelligence services argued over whether Arafat was orchestrating the violence or merely taking advantage of it. It made little difference. The Second Intifada was to rage for another four and a half years, until after Arafat's death. In the last months of his administration, Clinton, as a lame-duck president, made a last-gasp attempt to forge an agreement, bringing Barak and Arafat together for meetings in Paris and the United States. Both sides "accepted" the "Clinton parameters," though with significant reservations. But it was too late. Barak was going down. The Second Intifada was the death knell of his government and of the Oslo process.

ON NOVEMBER 28, Barak was forced to admit that he had no mandate to remain in power. "You want elections? I'm ready for elections," he said in the Knesset, adding that he had won every election he had run in.[7] Which was exactly what Netanyahu had said two years earlier. Likud now had to decide between its leader and its leader-in-exile.

Under the direct-election law, the very law that Netanyahu had defied Likud over in 1992, providing the crucial vote that passed it, a special election for prime minister could be held without dissolving the sitting Knesset. Now Barak would use that same law to prevent Netanyahu's return.

Having resigned from the Knesset, Netanyahu could not run for prime minister. After coming under fire from the opposition for blocking his opponent, Barak agreed to pass an amendment that would allow candidates who were not MKs also to run for prime minister. But he still refused to dissolve the Knesset. On December 13, the Knesset overwhelmingly passed the "Netanyahu Law." Netanyahu's path back to power was clear. The polls gave him a clear edge over a plummeting Barak.

At that point, Netanyahu made the biggest miscalculation of his political career. He had left Likud after the 1999 elections with only nineteen seats. That would be insufficient, he reasoned, to build a stable coalition and remain in power for more than a few months. "I can be prime minister in sixty days . . . but with this anarchy and internal paralysis nothing can be achieved," he insisted.[8] He would only run if elections for a new Knesset were held as well. Sharon was loath to give up his leadership, but Likud and most of the other opposition parties supported Netanyahu's demand. Shas didn't.

The ultra-Orthodox party on which Netanyahu had lavished so many resources and so much energy during his first term had come close to overtaking Likud in 1999, winning seventeen seats, having attracted many of Likud's traditional voters. Well aware that they would struggle to repeat that performance, the leaders of Shas refused Netanyahu's entreaties to vote in favor of dissolving the Knesset. Everyone expected Netanyahu to go back on his word and run for prime minister anyway. The opportunity seemed too good to resist. But Netanyahu was convinced that no matter who won the direct election, with the current Knesset, another election would happen in a matter of months. Had he decided to run, he would almost certainly have been back in office less than two years after leaving. The miscalculation meant it would take him eight more years.

As Barak and Sharon squared off, the polls indicated that a majority of Israelis still found it hard to contemplate Sharon, the man who had been blamed with pushing the country into a disastrous war in Lebanon, as prime minister. But the intensifying Second Intifada, coupled with what many saw as pointless talks continuing with Arafat, ate away at Barak's support. With the slogan "Only Sharon Will Bring Peace," and footage of him on the farm hugging grandchildren and feeding lambs, Likud's campaign repackaged the angry old warlord as elder statesman.

Labor, in vain, tried to remind voters of all the times Sharon had dragged Israel into some very bad corners. They even distributed hundreds of thousands of mock emergency call-up papers, for the "next war" Sharon would bring. Barak's defeat was crushing. On February 6, 2001, Sharon won with 62 percent of the vote.

Israelis hadn't given up on peace. They had given up on the young generation of leadership represented by Barak and Netanyahu, in favor of a member of Rabin and Peres's generation. Barak's abbreviated term wasn't just the end of the Oslo process, it was the end of Labor's image as Israel's responsible party of government. For Labor, Barak's defeat opened a prolonged period of constant infighting, low election results, and Likud dominance.

"YOU DIDN'T WANT him as defense minister, you'll get him as prime minister," said Ariel Sharon's hagiographer, Uri Dan, after Sharon had been forced to resign as defense minister in 1983.[9] It had taken Sharon eighteen years to fulfill that prophecy, and he had no plans to serve only as interim PM. Defying Netanyahu's predictions, he succeeded in forming a stable coalition with Labor. The rivalry between him and Netanyahu, who was making no secret of his intention to run in the next leadership primary, was out in the open.

As the Second Intifada grew more bloody and suicide bombers returned to Israel's streets, Netanyahu asked in an interview, "How have we reached the situation that every day there is an industry of murder here?" Sharon's people said that "Bibi is inciting against Sharon, just like he incited against Rabin."[10] Sharon refused to negotiate with the Palestinians as long as the violence continued. Netanyahu went one step further and called for Arafat to be deported.

After Al Qaida terrorists flew planes into the World Trade Center and the Pentagon on September 11, 2001, Netanyahu was eager to reprise his role as the American media's terrorism expert. His first reaction, recorded by the *New York Times*, wasn't particularly well-phrased. When asked "what the attack meant for relations between the United States and Israel," he said, "It's very good." He then backtracked: "Well, not very good, but it will generate immediate sympathy." He said it would "strengthen the bond between our two peoples."[11]

Netanyahu would claim that he had predicted the 9/11 attack in one of his books on terrorism. What he had actually written was that if the West didn't wake up to threats, "in the worst of such scenarios, the consequences could be not a car bomb but a nuclear bomb in the basement of the World Trade Center."[12]

A year after the attacks, he appeared before a congressional committee to support President George W. Bush's plans to launch a war against Iraq. In a rare, for Netanyahu, reference to Menachem Begin, he recalled how Israel in 1981 had attacked the Iraqi nuclear reactor: "Two decades ago it was possible to thwart Saddam's nuclear ambitions by bombing a single installation. Today nothing less than dismantling his regime will do."[13]

On the eve of Netanyahu's first visit as prime minister to Washington back in 1996, a group of neoconservatives, including Richard Perle and Netanyahu's old friend Doug Feith, calling themselves the "Study Group on a New Israeli Strategy Toward 2000," had published a paper titled "A Clean Break: A New Strategy for Securing the Realm." The paper was presented as a policy report for Netanyahu and included recommendations for attacking Syria and Iraq. It wasn't a paper Netanyahu ever seriously considered, and the "Study Group" was mainly using his name for their own publicity. Nevertheless, it has been used ever since as grist for the mills of conspiracy theorists eager to portray Bush's "War on Terror" as a Zionist plot.[14]

Back home, Netanyahu continued to clash with Sharon, who was making intriguing hints in his speeches regarding a Palestinian state. Netanyahu, sensing the opportunity to score points, challenged Sharon to a vote in the Central Committee. "Self-rule for the Palestinians—yes. A state—no," he thundered in his speech. "A Palestinian state means no Jewish state and a Jewish state means no Palestinian state." Sharon in return mocked Netanyahu over his own conduct as prime minister, without mentioning his name. "The Oslo agreements were accepted by someone else," he said, and it had been other prime ministers who "warmly, perhaps naively, shook Arafat's hand. One of ours as well. I never shook Arafat's hand."[5] Sharon lost the vote, with only 41 percent of the Central Committee members supporting him.

Sharon was careful not to open too wide a breach with Netanyahu. He even sent him that month on an official *hasbara* tour on behalf of the government to Israel's supporters in Washington. But the showdown was inevitable. Netanyahu's people were openly calling Sharon "Bibi's predecessor." When Sharon went to the United States in October 2002 to discuss with the Bush administration, among other matters, the impending Iraq war, and "the day after Saddam," Netanyahu sneered, saying, "He won't be prime minister after Saddam."

As the primary neared, Netanyahu was confident he would be the first to ever depose a serving Likud leader. The party members' dilemma was between Netanyahu, who appealed to their right-wing ideology, and Sharon, a more popular figure with the wider electorate. Three weeks before the primary, Sharon sprung a trap. On November 2, Labor had left the coalition, to put some distance between Labor and Sharon's government before the election (which would be for the Knesset only, the experiment in direct elections abandoned). Sharon offered Netanyahu the Foreign Ministry, which had just been vacated by Peres. Netanyahu didn't want to be seen endorsing Sharon's policies, but turning Sharon down would look like refusing to serve the nation. Netanyahu accepted the post, while emphasizing that he was still running in the primary.

It was a master move by Sharon. Now Likudniks could vote for him as leader, confident that they would be getting Netanyahu as well, as part of the package. Sharon, on the other hand, had made it clear that if he lost, he would retire.

In the last days of the campaign, the veteran Revisionists rallied to Netanyahu. To them, Sharon, whose agrarian roots were in the hated Mapai, had always been a dangerous opportunist, without allegiance to Jabotinskean ideology. Among them was Moshe Arens, who reconciled with his wayward protégé. It wasn't enough. Most Likudniks believed that Sharon was a better candidate for the general election.

On November 25, Sharon won the primary with 55 percent of the vote. For Netanyahu it was a second defeat, as crushing as losing to Barak in 1999. He had lost on his home turf, receiving only 40 percent of the vote.

O N JANUARY 28, 2003, Sharon's Likud easily trounced Labor, which was under the short-lived leadership of the earnest left-wing former general Amram Mitzna. Likud had won thirty-eight seats, its best result in four elections (and one that under Netanyahu it has not surpassed).

Netanyahu expected to remain in the post that he had occupied for only two months, and was looking forward to transforming the Foreign Ministry into a *hasbara*-style propaganda organization. Sharon had another surprise in store. He appointed the bland Silvan Shalom as foreign minister and suggested that Netanyahu become finance minister. When Netanyahu objected, he was shocked to discover that he was being given no choice. Sharon's motives were mixed. He had been itching to take Netanyahu down a notch, and now was his chance. But Sharon also believed that Netanyahu was the right person to take on the Israeli economy, which was reeling from a recession that had been caused by the burst of the dotcom bubble and the Second Intifada.

Netanyahu spent twenty-four hours mulling it over with his advisers in snowbound Jerusalem. He issued Sharon a long list of conditions and was surprised when they were all accepted, even his demand that a second minister be appointed beneath him in the Finance Ministry. Sharon promised Netanyahu full autonomy on all financial issues. In effect, he would be Israel's "financial prime minister." Just before he said yes, Netanyahu added another request—to be "designated acting prime minister."

Israeli law doesn't require prime ministers to designate a minister who will replace them, if for some reason they are unable to continue serving. Most have been averse to doing so. Sharon certainly didn't plan to designate Netanyahu as his potential successor, and he turned down this condition. By then, Netanyahu had already agreed to take the job. Few noticed the next week, on the eve of the new cabinet's swearing-in, when Sharon compensated the new industry, trade and employment minister, Ehud Olmert, who had believed that he would get Finance, with the "designated acting prime minister" title. It meant little at the time. Sharon was going nowhere.

Moving down the street to the Ministry of Finance, Netanyahu set about his new job with unexpected relish. It was the only time in his career when he was responsible for a specific field of policy, and it was a role he had always claimed to be uniquely capable of performing, as few Israeli politicians had a grasp on economics.

A firm believer in open markets and small government, Netanyahu accelerated the economic trends that were already in place, slashing corporate and individual taxes, cutting social benefits, and firing four thousand government employees (he likened the public sector to "a fat man being carried by a lean man," the private sector). He privatized the national airline, El Al; the state shipping company, Zim; and the telecommunications giant Bezeq. He forced the banks to divest their pension divisions and phased out fixed-interest government bonds, releasing large sums of money for investment in, among other things, tech companies.

His policies showed swift results. Within two years, unemployment and inflation were down, the deficit was almost zero, and growth was up. Israel's GDP grew between 2004 and 2008 by 5 percent or more annually. Deregulation of financial services opened up a new investment sector that had barely existed before.

However, the impact of Netanyahu's thirty months in charge of Israel's economy has been exaggerated. The country was put on the path to budgetary restraint and neoliberalism already in the mid-1980s, by the unity government headed by Peres, which had been forced to restructure the economy to rein in massive inflation. The Rabin government in 1992 had made the key investments that transformed the high-tech industry, making it Israel's leading export sector. Long detached from its socialist roots, Labor's economic policy going into the twenty-first century was not that different from Likud's. After taking power in 1999, Ehud Barak implemented the budget that had been prepared by the Netanyahu government largely untouched. The Sharon government passed Labor's budget in 2001 without change.

Netanyahu deserves credit for helping to create the conditions for Israel's speedy recovery from recession, continuing the liberalization of its financial markets, and boosting the prosperity that was a factor in cushioning the Israeli economy during the global downturn from late 2008. However, had Netanyahu continued running the economy, some of the deregulatory plans he had yet to implement could have left Israel more exposed to the global storms. And a larger part of the credit for Israel's economic success during Netanyahu's period goes to the improvement in the security situation as the Second Intifada petered out and trade boomed.

Israel's "left" is only left on matters of war and peace. On the economy, the "leftists," who belong to the wealthier and more highly educated parts of Israeli society, tend to lean rightward. The Israeli media largely reflects the affluent upper middle class, which hated Netanyahu as prime minister, but loved him as finance minister. He spoke the language of the business press, and his image of success from that period is as much due to public relations as to results.

At the same time, Bibi had a tin ear for the concerns of those on the lower rungs who weren't enjoying the prosperity. Poverty and inequality rates grew rapidly in that period, and those suffering the most were Likud's traditional voters. "No one is helping the poor more than me," he insisted, and he may have been right in the long term. But in the short term, his voters were hurting, and Netanyahu failed to even pretend that he felt their pain.

In July 2003, Vicky Knafo, a Likud-voting single mother, began a solitary march from Mitzpe Ramon, deep in the Negev, to Jerusalem, to protest the cuts in benefits to unemployed single parents. She drew a great deal of attention and sympathy, but Netanyahu complained that the media were "making a hero out of a woman who is walking all the way to Jerusalem. She probably does jogging every evening."

Netanyahu was impervious to criticism. He had Sharon's backing, and with the coalition's support, he could push nearly all his reforms through the Knesset, drowning out the objections of his old allies from the ultra-Orthodox parties, whose voters were among the casualties. He would only realize much later that his policies had driven a wedge between him and his electorate.

As NETANYAHU WAS busy being "financial prime minister," the real prime minister was working on his own explosive policy. By mid-2004, the rate of suicide bombings within Israel was starting to decline. The Palestinian Authority was beginning to slowly reestablish security coordination, though Arafat remained isolated in his Ramallah headquarters. Israel was in advanced stages of the construction of a "separation fence," in some places a concrete wall, within the West Bank, which was designed to keep the attackers out. Israelis had learned to live with the Intifada, but Sharon feared renewed diplomatic pressure on Israel to make concessions to the Palestinians. He was also anxious to deflect the media's attention away from police investigations into his murky financial affairs.

In December 2003, Sharon unveiled his plan to unilaterally "disengage" from the Gaza Strip. To most Likudniks, the idea of ceding the southernmost part of the Mediterranean coast to total Palestinian control, and worse, uprooting the eight thousand Israeli settlers living there, was absolute anathema. But once Sharon came out with the plan, he wouldn't be budged. What's more, it was popular among the wider public and with the media.

In private, Netanyahu called disengagement "Sharon's surrender plan." Unilateral retreat was the opposite of all he believed in. But he was wary of jeopardizing his position as finance minister by openly opposing Sharon. For a year and a half, Netanyahu refused the entreaties of the settlers and right-wingers who begged him to lead the anti-disengagement camp. Instead he gave the plan his qualified and grudging public support, proposing conditions that Sharon usually ignored. On May 2, 2004, Likud held a party-wide referendum on disengagement, which Sharon lost 60–40. He continued anyway, making only cosmetic changes to the plan.

With a sinking heart, Netanyahu continued voting in both the cabinet and the Knesset in favor of disengagement, knowing that if it went through, his constituency would never forgive him. At the crucial Knesset vote in November, along with two other Likud ministers, he announced that he would refuse to vote if a nationwide referendum wasn't called on the issue. Sharon, who had made clear that ministers not voting in favor of disengagement would be fired immediately, refused to speak to him, remaining seated in the plenum for hours as Netanyahu held anxious talks with his coconspirators in the corridors. It was a name vote, and when Netanyahu's name was called out, he was still outside. The Knesset clerk read out the names of the absent MKs again, and at the last second, Bibi rushed in to vote yes amid jeering from all sides of the house.

In a collection of essays published before disengagement, he made his views clear. He believed that "putting a fence on an agreed border between us and the Palestinians won't end the conflict and release us from its threat, until the Palestinians release themselves from their intention to destroy the Jewish state. . . . In unilateral retreat without anything in return there is existential danger."[16] But he was still not prepared to resign. Ten days before disengagement, he responded angrily to a journalist, saying, "You want me to resign? I'm the real Likud."

Two days later, on August 7, he resigned.

Later Netanyahu would claim to have "always opposed disengagement," but said he had stayed on until the last moment to make sure his financial reforms were securely in place and that he was leaving the economy in good shape. Sharon was scathing in his rebuke, saying, "After supporting disengagement four times, Bibi ran away."[17]

Once again Netanyahu was cast out of the government, with his biggest rival firmly in power.

24

My Own Media

Despite fears of violent clashes between Israeli settlers and the Israeli security forces evicting them, disengagement from Gaza was over with few casualties in eight days in August 2005. Most Israelis were relieved. For Likudniks, however, it was the deepest crisis in the history of the Revisionist movement. A Likud government had voluntarily, without international pressure and without receiving anything in return, relinquished part of the Land of Israel and uprooted Jewish communities. For twenty-eight years, since Menachem Begin first came to power in 1977, the movement had struggled to bridge the growing chasm between ideology and pragmatism. Ariel Sharon's disengagement from Gaza was a bridge too far.

Likud was irrevocably split between Sharon's supporters, who justified disengagement, and those determined to punish Sharon and ensure Likud never again repeated such a travesty. Netanyahu sought to lead the latter camp, though many of its members found it hard to forgive him for voting in favor of disengagement and resigning only a week before the eviction.

At a stormy Likud Central Committee meeting in September, the microphones were mysteriously disconnected just before the prime minister's speech, and Sharon barely managed to fight off a challenge from Netanyahu to hold an early leadership primary. Senior party members tried to broker a compromise whereby Netanyahu would be ensured the number-two and senior ministerial position in return for not running against Sharon. It was pointless. The two men were never going to cooperate again.

On November 22, Sharon left Likud and announced that he was dissolving the Knesset. It was a seismic shift in Israeli politics—the "big bang" that would blow away the Likud-Labor dichotomy in favor of a new centrist entity, or so at least many believed. Fifteen Likud ministers and MKs joined Sharon's new party, Kadima (Forward). They included the likes of Ehud Olmert and Tzipi Livni, who had literally been born into the Revisionist movement and made ideological journeys to the center-left, and old Netanyahu allies, such as Tzachi Hanegbi, who believed in Sharon. Senior Labor members joined as well, including, most astonishingly, the eighty-two-year-old Shimon Peres.

Kadima was to be the new pragmatic establishment—a Mapai for the twenty-first century. Likud, reduced to its ideological rump, was once again the redoubt for extreme and detached holdouts.

Netanyahu expected those remaining to acclaim him as leader. But the remaining Likudniks were split between those who accused Bibi of pushing Sharon out and those blaming him for not moving against Sharon earlier. Many believed he wasn't the man to rebuild the party. Five candidates challenged him in the leadership primary. Defense Minister Shaul Mofaz dropped out of the race to join Kadima, and Uzi Landau, once again running to Bibi's right, agreed to stand aside. Even then, Netanyahu failed to achieve a convincing win. On December 19, he was elected Likud leader, six and a half years after resigning the post, with just 44 percent of the vote.

The demoralized Likudniks knew they were facing a wipeout. Sharon was reaching epic heights of popularity, having extricated Israel from the accursed Gaza and looking tough while doing so. At seventy-eight, he was the man who had isolated Arafat in Ramallah until Arafat's mysterious death in November 2004, and then forced the Palestinians to end the Intifada. And he wasn't afraid of taking on the settlers either.

It wasn't just the Sharon surge. Other waves were crashing over Likud. Its traditional working-class voters, suffering from the results of Netanyahu's cuts to social benefits, were deserting. Desperate to fill Likud's war chest, Netanyahu tried to set up meetings with potential donors in the local business community. A few months earlier, they had been eager to meet their darling finance minister; now they weren't even returning his calls. The stink of impending defeat stuck to Likud. Not since Rabin's assassination had Netanyahu felt so isolated.

HAD SHARON RUN in 2006, Likud and Netanyahu's career may indeed have been wiped out. But on the evening of January 4, it was Sharon's bloated and much-abused body that gave out first. As the doctors confirmed that Sharon might never rise from the coma caused by his second stroke and massive brain hemorrhage, the prime minister's military secretary took the designated acting prime minister, Ehud Olmert, to a secure room and handed him the files containing the secret protocols regarding Israel's strategic assets.

Olmert was an accidental prime minister. Sharon had never seen him as a potential successor, awarding him the "designated acting" title only as compensation for giving the Finance Ministry to Netanyahu. A veteran politician, in the Knesset since his twenties, Olmert had nursed a deep personal rivalry with Netanyahu from the moment the former ambassador returned home. As Jerusalem's mayor, Olmert had actively sabotaged the Likud's 1999 campaign by hosting Barak in city hall and saying, on camera, that the Labor leader could be trusted on Jerusalem.

Olmert, born into a staunchly Jabotinskean family, had made a rapid transition from the far-right mayor who pressured Netanyahu to open up the Western Wall tunnel and build in East Jerusalem to Sharon's outlier on disengagement. A brilliant, ruthless, and famously corrupt operator, he was deeply unpopular in Likud, where in the 2003 primaries he had only reached the thirty-second spot on the Knesset list.

Had there been time to hold a leadership primary, Kadima would probably not have fielded Olmert as its candidate. But the new party's strategists had little choice but to go with the acting prime minister, relying on the sleeping Sharon's aura to guide them to victory.

Nothing by then could save Likud. Not the last-minute change of Kadima's leader or the surprise victory of Hamas in the second elections for the Palestinian Legislative Council, seemingly confirming Netanyahu's prediction that Gaza would become a Hamas stronghold and terrorist base.

On March 28, Kadima won twenty-nine seats. It was nowhere near the unprecedented numbers that polls had been promising the party under Sharon, but enough to form a government. For the first time, a party that was not Likud or Labor had won the election. Olmert was now prime minister in his own right and already talking of a second pullback from settlements deep in the West Bank. This pullback was dubbed the "Convergence Plan," and later sometimes the "realignment plan."

But the real story of the election was Likud's collapse. At twelve seats, it was the party's worst result since 1951. It had dropped to fourth place, after Kadima, Labor, and Shas, only narrowly leading Avigdor Lieberman's Yisrael Beiteinu by 116 votes. It was inconceivable that Netanyahu would remain leader after such a downfall. It was his third defeat in a row. He had lost to Barak in 1999 and to Sharon in the 2002 primaries, and now Olmert, with a lot of help from the comatose Sharon, had beat him. The knives were being sharpened the moment the exit polls were out at 10:00 p.m. Half the members of the drastically shrunken Knesset faction were already planning leadership challenges.

Netanyahu needed to take immediate action. Having watched the exit polls at a friend's apartment in Tel Aviv, he rushed to the small hall where Likud was holding its election night event. The plotters were not there, just a few young MKs and a crowd of perhaps fifty disconsolate supporters and bored journalists. The journalists were exasperated at not having been sent to cover the wild scenes of drunken jubilation at Kadima headquarters.

As Netanyahu entered the hall, he steeled himself for booing. But there was silence. Many there expected another resignation speech. He took to the stage and launched into the speech he had been preparing on the way over. "I received the party in its most difficult days. . . . We will rebuild the movement and continue on our path, sticking to it. We've seen better days and we will see better days again. . . . Our way is the right and only way to bring security to the state."[1] The few dozen supporters began cheering his fighting words, and the young MKs, who minutes ago had been busy calculating whom to support in the leadership challenge, joined him on the stage. Alongside them was one member of the older generation—the jovial Jerusalem lawyer Ruvi Rivlin, once a stalwart of the David Levy camp and never a close ally of Bibi's. That night, in the interests of the party, he lent his gravitas to the embattled leader.

On television, it looked like a valiant display of Likud unity. The would-be challengers sheathed their knives for the time being. It was a concession speech that secured Netanyahu's political future.

LIKUD IN 2006 was a very different creature from the party Netanyahu had arrived to rebuild in 1993. Israeli party politics were no longer about maintaining a large grassroots organization with branches across the country. Campaigns were moving from the streets to the Internet. Messaging was much more important than organizing. Netanyahu was no longer a young star, but even in his late fifties, he was peculiarly adept at this new age of politics.

At MIT, Netanyahu had written papers on the effects of computer systems on business organizations. In his private life he is a technophobe. Bibi has very rarely ever operated his own computer or mobile phone. He always relied on aides to do that for him. As finance minister, he was surrounded by a team drawn from the finest in Israel's civil service. With his resignation they dispersed. Back in opposition and embarking on yet another stage in his long slog back to power, Netanyahu went about rebuilding the support groups that had served him well back in the days he fought Rabin and Oslo. They were a combination of old loyalists, who stuck by him despite everything, and newcomers.

He fell back on "Bibi's submarine," the mix of right-wing academics and journalists who were still determined, like him, to replace the old elites. One notable addition to his unofficial team was Ron Dermer, the son of a former Democratic mayor of Miami Beach, who had emigrated to Israel in 1996. Dermer had worked for Netanyahu's ally Natan Sharansky, helping him write the best-selling *The Case for Democracy*, a book that George W. Bush said had deeply influenced his thinking. Netanyahu had appointed Dermer as the economic envoy in the Israeli embassy in Washington, and the two had remained very close, often talking daily when in different countries. Dermer was to become one of the closest of Netanyahu's advisers outside of his family and is regarded by other aides as "Bibi's brain."

Dermer also conformed to Netanyahu's preferred profile for his aides—he was loyal, right-wing, religious, and American-born. So many of Netanyahu's advisers are native English speakers that he often holds staff meetings in his office in Jerusalem in English, which makes him feel like he's back at the Boston Consulting Group, a much more professional environment, to his taste. Another young aide in this mold was Ari Harow, who had emigrated to Israel from California, lived on a West Bank settlement, and returned to study in New York after his military service was complete. While there, Harow ran the American Friends of Likud, a fundraising operation, and when he returned to Israel in 2007, became Netanyahu's adviser. One of the main roles of Netanyahu's American-born advisers was to maintain his long list of foreign donors and when necessary connect them speedily to the boss.

Naftali Bennett was another of this crop of new aides. Born in Haifa to American parents, like Netanyahu he had spent parts of his childhood in North America and at the age of eighteen joined Sayeret Matkal. After serving as a special forces officer and studying business management at Hebrew University, Bennett had moved to New York, where he founded a start-up software company with Israeli partners. He became a millionaire when the company was sold in 2005 to RSA Security. As a teenager, Bennett hero-worshiped the mythologized Yoni Netanyahu and saw himself as following in his footsteps. In late 2006, he began to work for Netanyahu following the crisis that fatally weakened the Olmert government.

O LMERT, A VETERAN politician who had rarely dealt with high-level security affairs, appointed Labor's leader, Amir Peretz, a trade unionist with even less relevant experience, as defense minister. They inherited as IDF chief of staff Lieutenant General Dan Halutz, a combat pilot. With its focus on war on the borders, the IDF had always been led by army generals who had commanded armored divisions and territorial headquarters, never by a man whose experience of the battlefield was from thousands of feet above. But Halutz had been one of Sharon's favorites, a potential successor, and when appointing him, Sharon reckoned that as long as he was in power, there would be no lack of military experience.

The government and the IDF were woefully unprepared when a Hezbollah attack on an IDF patrol at the Lebanon border, on July 12, 2006, led to rapid escalation. The Iranian-backed militia had intended to capture Israeli soldiers, but ended up killing five and snatching two of the bodies back over the border. They hadn't intended to start a war. In retaliation, Israel launched a massive air campaign against Hezbollah's strongholds, wiping out many of the organization's missile sites—but not all, by any account. Hezbollah responded with its own mortar and rocket barrages on Israeli towns and villages in the Galilee. A week into what had become Israel's Second Lebanon War, ground troops were sent in.

Six IDF divisions, the entire air force, and most of the navy were involved in the fighting, which lasted thirty-four days. In the end, 121 Israeli soldiers and 44 civilians were killed, and while Hezbollah and Lebanese casualties were much higher, the war ended in what most Israelis felt was a humiliating stalemate. Despite being the overwhelmingly superior side, Israel had not stopped Hezbollah from firing on its towns throughout the war and had failed to take out Hezbollah's top commanders.

A more experienced political leadership may have known when to hold back and not commit Israel's military to an unnecessary all-out war. A chief of staff fully aware of the condition of his ground forces would have known that the IDF—tired after years of Intifada skirmishes in Gaza and the West Bank, its units, particularly the reserves, depleted and lacking in training from years of cutbacks under Finance Minister Netanyahu—was ill-prepared in the summer of 2006 to enter a war against a small but resourceful enemy. Six months after taking power, Olmert's credibility was drastically eroded.

During the war, Netanyahu supported the government to the hilt. "Fight them, hit them, smash them. We're with you," he said, addressing Olmert in the Knesset.[2] Once again, he toured the television studios, giving forceful interviews to the international networks, justifying the invasion of Lebanon. Israel's two major supporters were President Bush and British prime minister Tony Blair. But Blair was taking a large amount of flak at home, from members of his own Labour Party and the British media, over his support for Israel's "disproportionate response." Olmert asked Netanyahu to fly to London, on another *hasbara* mission, to back Blair up. Netanyahu immediately agreed.

The government was prepared to pay for business-class tickets and five-star accommodation for Bibi and Sara. However, Sara demanded a higher-level first-class flight and a superior luxury hotel, as well as a personal assistant to fly with them. The solution was to get a Jewish British businessman, Joshua Rowe, who was prepared to pay thousands of pounds for the honor of sponsoring Netanyahu's mission, to foot the bill for the upgrades. The Netanyahus stayed in a suite at The Connaught. Their penchant for luxury travel, sponsored by members of their millionaires club, was to come back and haunt them years later.

Netanyahu's benefactors also helped fund the wages of a much larger staff than the Knesset and Likud were willing to fund. Another, more discreet contribution went to the organizers of the reservists' protests after the war. As civilians who had been called up to fight in Lebanon returned, demanding that the politicians take responsibility for the failure of the war, Netanyahu kept a low profile. But he was coordinated with the organizers of the protests against Olmert. One of them, Naftali Bennett, who had rushed back from the United States to fight with his commando unit deep in Hezbollah territory, was recommended to him as a useful addition to the team. Bennett joined as Netanyahu's new chief of staff, but would last less than two years before falling out with Sara.

T HE DONORS WERE listed in four categories. The top tier combined both high net worth and high willingness to help out. Since Netanyahu had entered politics and holding primaries had become more popular with Israeli parties, the laws regulating political finance had been toughened up. Private donations were capped, corporations were forbidden to donate, and the candidates and parties had to give a full accounting of every shekel to the state comptroller. But there were other ways to use money.

Netanyahu's main conclusion from his disastrous first term was something he constantly repeated in meetings with his benefactors: "I need my own media." He had given up on Israeli journalists being honest enough to present him as the country's only true leader. He was convinced that friendlier newspapers and TV channels would make all the difference. It wasn't enough for those journalists to lean rightward. Bibi demanded loyalty from what he saw as his own "court reporters." Even though it was under the ownership of friendly investors, he routinely tried to bully the editors of the *Jerusalem Post*. In 2004, he called the young editor, the American conservative columnist Bret Stephens, to complain of a passing reference in the paper to the "hot-tape" incident. "My children can now read English," he thundered. Stephens, while supporting many of Netanyahu's policies, refused to rein in his writers. Undeterred, Netanyahu continued to urge his rich friends to invest in the Israeli media.

Ron Lauder agreed to buy a majority share in Israel's Channel 10, but changing the culture of an existing news organization was difficult, and there was a limit to how far Lauder was prepared to go in imposing his will on the channel's editorial policy. A British Israeli businessman, Shlomo Ben-Tzvi, hoping to get close to Netanyahu, bought three small right-wing newspapers, but a lack of funds and chronic mismanagement stymied his plans to combine them into a new nationwide daily. But help was on the way from the top name on the list.

Sheldon Adelson had made his millions in computer trade shows, and his billions in mega-casino and hotel complexes. Based in Las Vegas,

Adelson had not been on Netanyahu's radar during his time in New York. After meeting his second wife, Miri, an Israeli doctor, Adelson began developing an interest in his Jewish roots and Israel. He was introduced to Netanyahu in 1990, and Netanyahu had helped the couple receive the unprecedented permission to have their wedding reception in the Knesset.

Over the years Adelson had donated hundreds of millions of dollars to Republican candidates, mainly through super PACs. Israeli law forbids such loopholes, but Adelson was able to support Netanyahu in other important ways.

Adelson founded *Yisrael Hayom* (Israel Today) in July 2007. The free daily paper was not a throwaway, like those distributed around the world with minimal original editorial content but plenty of advertising. Instead, it had a large team of journalists, some of them among the best-paid in Israel, and carried few ads. With Adelson paying for a circulation of over a quarter of a million copies across Israel, industry insiders estimated that he was losing over a hundred million shekels annually on the project (an amount equivalent to about $25 million). Adelson didn't mind—he created a media outlet that could, and would, slavishly support Netanyahu.

Two loyal crewmembers of "Bibi's submarine" were drafted in. Amos Regev, a veteran journalist, was appointed editor-in-chief, and Nathan Eshel, an old National Religious Party activist, and a particular favorite of Sara's, became CEO. *Yisrael Hayom*'s editorial line was resolutely on the right, glowing in its coverage of Netanyahu and his family and intensely critical of Olmert. Not that a hostile tabloid was the worst of Olmert's troubles.

ALLEGATIONS OF CORRUPTION had dogged Olmert for much of his career. After becoming prime minister, they went into overdrive. In little more than eighteen months, five separate police investigations were launched into his financial affairs. Olmert insisted he had done nothing wrong, but evidence of bribery and fraud accumulated. On May 27, 2008, the Jewish American businessman Morris Talansky testified in a pretrial hearing at the Jerusalem District Court, describing in detail how he had regularly passed envelopes stuffed with cash on to Olmert.[3]

By Israeli law, a minister can remain in office until indicted, and a prime minister only has to resign following a conviction. Olmert insisted that Talansky was lying and that he had no plans to resign. However, following Talansky's graphic testimony (which ultimately would not lead to a conviction), Ehud Barak, who had recently returned to politics, replacing Peretz as Labor leader, threatened to leave the coalition if Olmert stayed on. On July 30, Olmert announced that he would resign as soon as Kadima appointed his successor.

On September 17, Foreign Minister Tzipi Livni won the Kadima primary. The young anonymous woman who had been seen crying at Likud headquarters on the night of the 1996 election, when they thought Netanyahu had lost, was old Likud aristocracy. Her father, Eitan, had been the IZL's operations commander and a Knesset member. After a brief career as a commercial lawyer, and an even shorter period as a Mossad operative, she had launched her own political career. Netanyahu in 1996 had counted Livni a loyalist and appointed her to the coveted position of director-general of the Government Companies Authority, which regulates state-owned companies. After Netanyahu's departure, she had fallen under Sharon's spell, and as her political views began shifting leftward, she relinquished her parents' Greater Land of Israel dreams.

Livni should have had no problem keeping Olmert's coalition together and becoming Israel's second female prime minister. But Livni, who had spent the past two years fruitlessly negotiating with the Palestinians, was terrible at coalition horse-trading. To makes things more difficult, Netanyahu was quietly dealing with his old ultra-Orthodox allies in Shas and United Torah Judaism (Yahadut Ha'Torah). Livni failed to meet their demands for extra funding and religious legislation, and on October 26 she was forced to announce that she could not form a coalition. Early elections were set for February 24, 2009.

The plan to replace Likud with a new centrist party was in jeopardy, but the ex-Likudniks who had joined Sharon in Kadima were still convinced they had been right. At his last cabinet meeting before the election, Olmert said, "The dream of the Greater Land of Israel is over and doesn't exist anymore and anyone who talks about it is deluding himself."[4] Netanyahu was determined to prove them wrong.

25

Threats Are What Work

For the 2009 campaign Likud hired a Republican strategist from the United States, John McLaughlin. (Finkelstein had been hired by Netanyahu's rival on the right, Lieberman.) McLaughlin advised Netanyahu to run a "winner's campaign" and not act the underdog, as he had in past elections. This time Bibi needed no urging: he simply couldn't conceive of an outcome in which the people wouldn't want him back in office. But he couldn't always trust the people. The strategy was for Netanyahu not to mention his rivals at all. He was to be presented to the Israeli public as the only competent and experienced candidate on offer.

The strategy worked for Netanyahu as long as Likud was leading Kadima—which was still associated in the public's mind with Olmert's corruption—by a wide margin in the polls. But the gap narrowed as Kadima's campaign, presenting Livni as "Ms. Clean" and Netanyahu as just another failed corrupt ex-prime minister, began to hit home. Netanyahu authorized attack ads against Livni, accusing her of being a leftist endangering Israel's security. These ads mainly served to draw more center-left voters into the Kadima tent and highlight Livni as a viable alternative.

Netanyahu worked hard, traveling to places across the country hit by his economic policies. He explained and apologized and promised that his next government would be more sensitive to the concerns of Likud's traditional voters. In what was a huge personal sacrifice, he canceled the publication of a book he had spent two years writing. *The Israeli Tiger* was to have been his economic manifesto and the story of how he had wrought wonders as finance minister. But he realized it would be political suicide to trumpet those achievements—especially because, with the global economy in crisis, owing largely to lax controls on Western banks, deregulation of the financial system suddenly didn't sound like such a great idea. *The Israeli Tiger* never saw the light of day.

O N FEBRUARY 10, 2009, the day of the elections, Netanyahu toured the Likud strongholds south of Tel Aviv, which in the last election had voted for Kadima.

"Everyone thinks I have already been elected prime minister," he complained to a reporter. "And now they're allowing themselves to be enticed by niche parties."[1] As far as he was concerned, all voters wanted him back as prime minister. But he was concerned that right-leaning voters were voting for other potential coalition partners, and that Likud would not be large enough.

In the last hours of voting, the data from exit polling was troubling. The reports were of right-wing voters wavering between Likud and Lieberman's Yisrael Beiteinu and a strong showing for Kadima, especially in the Tel Aviv area. "We have to call our branches and start threatening them the left is rising," said Gilad Erdan, a young MK who had been an aide in the prime minister's office during Netanyahu's first term, anxious to reestablish his loyalty. "Threats are what work. We're paying the price now for not running a negative campaign against Kadima and Livni."

Netanyahu spent most of the day visiting regional Likud headquarters, delivering pep talks to volunteers. As night fell, to the consternation of his security detail, he shifted to direct interaction with voters. In Ashdod he ordered the convoy to stop at a shopping mall and went inside, mingling among shoppers and popping into restaurants. "Did you vote already?" he asked each person he came up to, waving a Likud ballot paper. "Finish your soup and then go to the polling station," he jocularly admonished one table.

As shoppers gathered to see the candidate, his entourage was squashed between the public and the extra police who had been called in to ensure security for the former—and perhaps future—prime minister. "From tomorrow we won't have to suffer this," sighed Ari Harow, who had replaced Bennett as chief of staff. "Either we'll be in the prime minister's 'sterile zone' or we won't need security at all."

A few hours later, as the results started to come in, it turned out that Netanyahu was right to have been worried.

L IKUD HAD MADE an incredible comeback from the catastrophic result three years earlier, when only one in ten voters had favored Netanyahu's party. He had more than doubled their 2006 tally to twenty-seven seats. The right-wing-religious bloc of parties held a Knesset majority of sixty-five seats, virtually ensuring him a coalition.

But Livni could and would also claim victory. Kadima under her leadership had received more votes than Netanyahu's Likud. It was the tiniest of margins—less than thirty thousand votes, which translated into just one more Knesset seat. Her success had come at the expense of the rest of the center-left camp. Kadima voters who had returned home to Likud had been replaced by Labor and Meretz voters, particularly women. Livni had emerged from the election still the leader of the Knesset's largest party.

Both Netanyahu and Livni proclaimed victory. Netanyahu could claim, with some degree of justification, that a clear majority had voted for parties likely to support him as prime minister. But Livni had received more votes than him.

It was a classic electoral stalemate. Most of the Israeli media, except Sheldon Adelson's *Yisrael Hayom*, were treating the results as a tie— further proof to Netanyahu that the old elites would do anything to prevent his return to office. "They are trying to steal the elections from the people," he fumed to his aides.

President Shimon Peres once again was to play a pivotal role in Netanyahu's rise to power. Israel's president is required by law, after consulting with the Knesset parties, to call upon the party leader with the best chances of commanding the support of a majority to form the new government. This was likely to be Netanyahu, but in the past it had always been the leader of the largest party.

Netanyahu was frustrated with Lieberman and the Shas leader, Eli Yishai, for remaining noncommittal about whether they would recommend that Peres call upon Netanyahu. That was normal following an election for the smaller parties, because they sought to maximize their opportunities for extracting promises from prospective prime ministers. For Lieberman and Yishai to have acted in any other way would have been out of character—and bad tactics. But Netanyahu was impatient with anyone seeking to delay his new government's swearing-in and convinced that behind his back, secret talks were in progress to form an alternative Livni coalition.

Lieberman played on Netanyahu's fears. Yisrael Beiteinu had exceeded expectations by gaining fifteen seats, even more than Labor, making it the third-largest party in the new Knesset. "Everyone knows we now hold the key to the next government," Lieberman said in his victory speech, without indicating whose door he would open with that key. Hours after the election ended, Lieberman flew off for a week's vacation in Minsk. Netanyahu's office tried for days, in vain, to locate him in the Belarusian capital, and when they finally succeeded in getting him on the line, Lieberman refused to make any promises.

When they finally met, Lieberman made it clear he expected one of the top three posts in the new government—Defense, Finance, or Foreign Affairs. Netanyahu acquiesced. Following Lieberman's lead, the other right-wing and religious parties also announced they would be recommending Netanyahu to the president. He now had a potential majority of sixty-five Knesset members.

Meanwhile, Livni's potential coalition was unraveling. Labor and Meretz, smarting at the way in which Kadima's leader had enticed away their voters, refused to recommend her, telling Peres he should make his own choice. She may have been the leader of the largest party, but with only twenty-eight Knesset members, she couldn't form a coalition.

TEN DAYS AFTER the elections, Netanyahu was summoned to the president's residence. In private, before officially instructing him to form the new government, Peres implored Netanyahu, "for the good of the state," to engage with Livni and form a national unity coalition with a wide base.

There were few Israeli politicians who irritated Netanyahu as much as Livni. He couldn't forgive the disloyalty of the woman he had promoted from obscurity. He was deeply offended by anyone who could conceive of Livni as a credible alternative to his leadership. Netanyahu was especially affronted by Livni's expectation that he would agree to splitting the premiership term with her. Any partnership with her was out of the question. But Netanyahu did want a wide and stable coalition, with at least one center-left partner. He didn't want to be at the mercy of his far-right partners, as he had been in his first term.

Netanyahu was aware of his hardliner reputation outside Israel and was anxious to project a more moderate image—especially as he was soon to meet the new president, Barack Obama, in Washington. For two weeks, he went through the motions of holding coalition talks with Livni, who drove a tough bargain, insisting the new government commit to the two-state peace solution with the Palestinians. The prospective prime minister seemed unfazed, promising to form a national unity government: "With goodwill we can bridge over the differences," he told her.[2] But as the talks dragged on, and Netanyahu signed coalition agreements with the right-wing and religious parties, Livni got the message. She ended the sham negotiations. But she never was the moderate partner Netanyahu had been after.

After leading the Labor Party to the worst election result in its history, Ehud Barak told his party that "the voters' verdict has sent us to opposition. I have informed Netanyahu that we will be a constructive and responsible opposition."[3] But he was already holding secret talks with his old soldier Bibi. The personal ties between the two men had survived the animosity of the 1999 elections. The history they shared transcended party divides, and they both despised Livni. They were natural allies. Netanyahu was happy for Barak to continue as defense minister in his new cabinet. He had promised the ex-IDF chief of staff Moshe Yaalon, who had joined Likud at one of its lowest points, that he would be defense minister once they returned to power. But Netanyahu had no problem shafting Yaalon, who had little time to build up his own support base within Likud.

Barak unleashed his political earthquake—he would be proposing a coalition agreement with Likud at the Labor convention. His party members were livid at what they justly saw as an abrupt change in party policy without any form of consultation. But Barak managed to push the coalition deal through the conference by a small majority of party delegates voting in favor.

Ehud Barak, the man who had ended Netanyahu's first term, would prove to be the closest thing he ever had to a political soulmate. For the next four years, the two men would work together in harmony to a degree they had never enjoyed with their own party colleagues. These two deeply suspicious, ego-driven individuals found joint purpose, seeing in themselves Israel's only "responsible grown-ups," surrounded by despised, incompetent political hacks. Netanyahu now had his wide coalition and moderate partner.

Fifty days after the elections and 3,556 days, nearly ten years, after leaving the prime minister's office, Netanyahu gave his second inaugural Speech. Toward the Palestinians he was surprisingly emollient, promising their leaders that "if you really want peace, we can reach it. The government I head will work to achieve peace. We don't want to rule over the Palestinians and we'll aspire to reach a permanent arrangement. The Palestinians will have all the authority to rule themselves except those that will threaten our state." The tough talk was reserved instead for Iran's president, Mahmoud Ahmadinejad, whose "calls to destroy us are accepted by the world without firm condemnation, almost as routine. The Jewish people have learned their lesson not to dismiss megalomaniac dictators threatening to exterminate us. Unlike the Holocaust, when we had no salvation, today we are not without a shield. We have a state and we know how to defend it."[4]

These would be the twin themes of Netanyahu's second term. Promises to the Palestinians, if only they would prove serious about making peace, and warnings of a genocide planned by an Iranian leadership against which the Jews had no choice but to fight for their lives. Just before midnight on March 31, following the first vote of confidence in his new government, he was sworn in, with ninety-nine-year-old Benzion Netanyahu gazing sternly from the gallery.

The next morning, the members of the new government gathered at President Peres's residence for the traditional group portrait. Only a hundred people were allowed to attend, and there was intense jockeying for invitations. Minutes before the ministers took their places, a black van stopped by the gates and a white mobility scooter was lifted out. A ruddy-faced elderly gentleman, his hair dyed bright red, trundled up the path, followed by his energetic wife. He maneuvered the scooter into the hall, parking in a front-row space that had been reserved in advance. With unabashed pride, he looked on as Netanyahu uneasily took his seat, his knees pointing outward. Sitting beside him, Peres seemed to shrink in resignation. This was the moment Sheldon Adelson had worked for and paid for. Bibi was back in power.

PART FIVE

Stuck on Top

2009–2018

26

A New Pragmatic Bibi?

oth men were elected leaders of their countries in their mid-
forties, with little political experience but enough eloquence and
charisma to defy the entrenched political establishments. But
despite similarity between their political trajectories, there was never
much hope of Benjamin Netanyahu and Barack Obama getting along.
Nevertheless, of all Israeli PM–POTUS duos, Bibi and Barack spent the
longest period working together—Netanyahu returned to office two
months after Obama's inauguration and was still there in January 2017
when Obama's presidency ended.

Their first meeting, in Washington, where they both addressed
AIPAC's annual conference, was in March 2007. Obama, a freshman
senator at the time, had launched his presidential campaign three weeks
earlier, and when he appeared before the pro-Israel lobby he hit all the
right notes. He described Israel as "our strongest ally in the region and
its only established democracy," called Iran "one of the greatest threats to
the United States, to Israel, and world peace," and waxed lyrically on his
first visit to Israel the previous year.[1]

At that first meeting, which took place at Obama's request, he mainly
listened as Netanyahu delivered his standard speech on the region. At the
time, Bibi hoped the unlikely candidate would surprise everyone and beat
Hillary Clinton to the Democratic nomination. He assumed he would
be back in power soon, and the last thing he wanted was to face another
Clinton in the Oval Office.

They next met seventeen months later in Jerusalem. Obama was by then the Democratic candidate. Netanyahu was still leader of the opposition, but anticipating Ehud Olmert's downfall. It was the last stop on Obama's whirlwind seven-nation tour to burnish his paltry foreign policy credentials. He joked with Netanyahu that he "could fall asleep standing up"—not that it stopped Netanyahu from delivering another lecture on the Iranian nuclear threat, or Obama from studiously taking it all in.[2]

At their next meeting, predicted Netanyahu, smiling, we will both be in office. Obama wasn't naïve enough to believe that Bibi favored him. There was no question that he was rooting for his Republican opponent, John McCain, who just that day had criticized Obama for being too soft on Iran.

Netanyahu's American allies had vetted Obama's record. They knew that in Chicago the young state senator had been close to the local Palestinian community, and that he had demanded a more "even-handed" US policy in the Middle East. He also had close ties to many prominent Jewish figures in Chicago, some of whom played pivotal roles in his ascendancy. But they all were from the liberal wing of the community and not enamored of Netanyahu. Once in national politics, Obama presented himself as staunchly pro-Israel, but he had also made clear in a meeting with Jewish leaders that "there is a strain within the pro-Israel community that says unless you adopt an unwavering pro-Likud approach to Israel that you're anti-Israel, and that can't be the measure of our friendship with Israel."[3]

Sheldon Adelson and Netanyahu's other benefactors were all donating heavily to McCain's campaign. Bibi's old friend Malcolm Hoenlein, leader of the Conference of Presidents of Major American Jewish Organizations, said in Jerusalem that "of course Obama has plenty of Jewish supporters, and there are many Jews around him. But there is a legitimate concern over the zeitgeist around the campaign."[4]

Obama's first appointments after the election did little to allay Netanyahu's fears. Hillary Clinton was the new secretary of state, and the new White House chief of staff, Rahm Emanuel, had been one of the senior aides urging Bill Clinton to confront Netanyahu.

Prior to his first White House meeting with Clinton in 1996, Netanyahu had insisted on no advance meetings. Before his first meeting as prime minister with Obama in May 2009, a team of Netanyahu's closest aides flew to Washington to work the agenda. Netanyahu wanted Iran at the top of the list, but Obama had other ideas, and nothing could have prepared Bibi for that meeting.

The statements and pleasantries in the open part of the meeting were friendly. Obama kept the bombshell for when he sat alone with Netanyahu. To get the diplomatic process with the Palestinians back on track, he demanded that Israel completely "freeze" building on the settlements.

Obama's foreign policy team had analyzed the past eight years of the stagnant process and reached the conclusion that once the level of violence had been significantly reduced, the main obstacle was construction on the settlements. In a dramatic departure from the Bush administration's approach, Obama had decided to remove the obstacle.

As a tactic for jump-starting talks, it was a mistake. Obama was telling a freshly elected right-wing prime minister to take a step no previous Israeli prime minister, not even the "leftist" Rabin and Peres, had agreed to. More crucially, Obama was setting a threshold for Palestinian leader Mahmoud Abbas, who in the past had grudgingly negotiated with Israel while it continued building. How could Abbas countenance doing so in the future once the demand had been made by the Americans?

The US administration had briefed Israeli journalists that for enhanced support on the Iranian issue, Netanyahu would have to show flexibility toward the Palestinians. Ultimately, it would work the other way around. Public clashes with Netanyahu during Obama's first term would revolve mainly around the Palestinian issue, while differences over Iran remained largely below the surface. In his second term, Obama would openly break with Bibi on Iran, but give up on peace with the Palestinians.

O BAMA AND NETANYAHU were on a collision course from that point on, all the way through the next seven and a half years. Netanyahu's GOP supporters established the narrative early on that Obama had "thrown Israel under the bus," an accusation that three years later would become a constant refrain of Republican candidates on the campaign trail. Obama insisted that he had Israel's best interests at heart, but made no attempt to deny there were deep disagreements. In a meeting with Jewish leaders in July 2009, he said that "when there is no daylight [between Israel and the United States], Israel just sits on the sidelines and that erodes our credibility with the Arab states."[5] This sentiment shocked

Israelis, as did the administration's refusal to adhere to the letter from President George W. Bush to Ariel Sharon in 2004 as US policy. That letter had stated that in the permanent status, Israeli settlement blocs in the West Bank would remain part of Israel.

Three groups were stoking the impression of a no-holds-barred conflict between Obama and Netanyahu. One consisted of members of Obama's team who felt that the more the president was seen as being at odds with Netanyahu, the more the administration's credibility in the rest of the Middle East was enhanced. The second group consisted of those in the media, both Israeli and international, who were eager to cast the two men as belligerents, with Netanyahu clearly the "bad guy."

While the antipathy between Netanyahu and Obama was unmissable, often the perceived slights and insults were manufactured retroactively, and not even noticed by either of them when allegedly taking place. Every nuance of body language, or whether or not they posed for a photograph during a meeting, or if Netanyahu was invited on any particular visit to stay at Blair House, the presidential guest quarters, became proof of "tension" or "snubs." When the White House released a photograph of Obama speaking to Netanyahu on the phone, his feet on the desk, the prime minister's people interpreted what had originally been intended as a display of casual intimacy as deliberate "dissing" of Bibi. When, in front of the cameras during a White House meeting in May 2011, Netanyahu explained at length, to a bemused Obama, why Israel could not retreat to the 1967 lines, Obama's aides described it as an "intolerable lecture," though the president had not been overly perturbed. In September 2012, after Netanyahu publicly criticized Obama's Iranian policy, his ambassador to the United Nations, and later National Security Adviser Susan Rice, complained to an American Jewish leader that Netanyahu had done everything but "use the N-word" against the president.

The third group stoking the negative atmosphere was Netanyahu's own team. This seems counterintuitive—Israeli prime ministers usually have an interest in being perceived as getting along with the US president. Netanyahu had paid a political price in 1999 for Clinton's obvious displeasure. But Netanyahu's aides were speaking openly about how much "Obama hates us," saying, "If our friends in Washington don't stand by us, we're lost." It wasn't only an appeal to Netanyahu's American supporters: Bibi was intentionally defining Obama in the consciousness of the Israeli public as the nation's enemy.

OBAMA'S PRESSURE EVENTUALLY yielded results. On November 25, 2009, Netanyahu became the first Israeli prime minister to officially announce a freeze on settlement building. It would only be for ten months, and it was not a total freeze—Netanyahu insisted that building would continue in East Jerusalem, and in the West Bank only new construction would be frozen, while existing projects would be completed. Palestinian president Mahmoud Abbas used these qualifications to delay entering talks for another nine months. When Abbas finally relented, in mid-2010, Netanyahu, citing coalition pressure, refused to extend the freeze by more than another month. Other events in the region would soon intervene anyway and reduce the pressure on him. But meanwhile, some were tempted to believe that Netanyahu had been forced by Obama to make a significant shift on the Palestinian issue.

On June 14, 2009, at Bar-Ilan University near Tel Aviv, Netanyahu gave his first major policy speech since returning to power. He worked on the speech for weeks after returning from Washington. For once, there were few leaks from his office, and the Obama administration was not sent its text in advance.

By Netanyahu's standards, it was a radical departure. In a rare nod to Menachem Begin, he said he shared the vision of peace Begin had pursued with Anwar al-Sadat, and that he "fully" supported Obama's "idea of a regional peace" and "desire to bring about a new era of reconciliation in our region." To this purpose, Netanyahu for the first time acknowledged "[Israel's] need to recognize [the Palestinians'] rights" and said that Israel "will be ready in a future peace agreement to reach a solution where a demilitarized Palestinian state exists alongside the Jewish state."[6]

This was the same Netanyahu who seven years earlier had demanded that the Likud Central Committee censure Ariel Sharon for even mentioning a Palestinian state, insisting, "Self-rule for the Palestinians—yes. A state—no! A Palestinian state means no Jewish state and a Jewish state means no Palestinian state." But a closer look at the Bar-Ilan Speech showed that beyond his rhetorical concession, Netanyahu's core policy remained unchanged. He had not given any details of the shape and nature of the "demilitarized Palestinian state."

At Bar-Ilan University, Netanyahu promised that while negotiating, Israel had "no intention of building new settlements or of expropriating additional land for existing settlements," but stressed that the settlers must be allowed "to raise their children like families elsewhere." In addition to complete demilitarization, Netanyahu placed an absolute condition—the "Palestinians must clearly and unambiguously recognize Israel as the state of the Jewish people."[7]

"In my vision of peace," he said, "in this small land of ours, two peoples live freely, side-by-side, in amity and mutual respect. Each will have its own flag, its own national anthem, its own government. Neither will threaten the security or survival of the other." But there was nothing to suggest that beyond the words "Palestinian state," and self-rule in a cluster of enclaves, hemmed in by settlements and military bases, Netanyahu was prepared to give the Palestinians anything. It was the same plan as the one he had proposed on the eve of Oslo fifteen years ago, just with a different name.[8]

To Netanyahu, for whom words are everything, the Bar-Ilan Speech was monumental. The rest of the world remained underwhelmed. Even the settlers didn't bother taking him too seriously. Netanyahu had to match his speech with actions first. But he didn't even try to get his own party to accept the speech as its policy. The Likud platform continued to oppose a Palestinian state.

Obama and his team continued to hope that Netanyahu would show a more pragmatic side, and not just in words. In March 2010, Vice President Joe Biden, one of the more pro-Israel voices in the US administration, traveled to Jerusalem. Biden's visit, intended both as an overture to the Israeli public and reassurance to Netanyahu that Obama was serious about dealing with the Iranian threat, quickly developed into a full-blown crisis when the Jerusalem District Planning Council issued building permits for hundreds of new apartments in an ultra-Orthodox neighborhood in East Jerusalem. The United States considered that neighborhood to be a settlement.

The Obama administration was certain it was a deliberate provocation. In a stormy phone call, Secretary of State Clinton yelled at Netanyahu as she relayed the president's demands. The White House followed the call up with a heavy round of negative briefings to the press. Netanyahu insisted that the issuance of the permits was a bureaucratic procedure of which he had had no prior knowledge, and he may have been telling the truth. He promised that the new apartments would not be built for at least two years; still, trust between him and Obama had been further eroded.

Negotiations with the Palestinians continued in fits and starts. During 2010, the Obama administration cajoled Netanyahu and Abbas into meeting three times, but little progress was made. Israel cut off talks when Abbas's Fatah faction signed a reconciliation agreement with Hamas. The administration wouldn't accept the Fatah-Hamas agreement, which was never implemented, as sufficient reason for suspending negotiations.

In May 2011, it was time for another speech. The Speaker of the new Republican Congress, John Boehner, invited Netanyahu for his second joint session address. The White House noted what was a clearly partisan gesture of support by the GOP to the embattled prime minister, but Vice President Biden was in his chair, beside Boehner, when Netanyahu took to the podium. His rhetoric went even further than it had in the Bar-Ilan Speech. "I am willing to make painful compromises to achieve this historical peace," Netanyahu promised. "I recognize that in a genuine peace we will be required to give up parts of the ancestral Jewish homeland." But once again he demanded that the Palestinians recognize Israel as the sovereign state of the Jewish people, and once again he refused to go into any specifics over the size of the Palestinian state, emphasizing that Israel "will not return to the indefensible borders of 1967."[9]

Netanyahu milked his audience, getting twenty-nine standing ovations. The speech was a challenge to Obama, who two days earlier had made his own speech calling for negotiations on a two-state solution based on the 1967 lines. Netanyahu politely thanked Obama for his support for Israel while using the Republican Congress (and a large number of applauding Democratic representatives as well) to demonstrate his power in Washington.

But both Netanyahu and Obama were to discover that there was a limit to what can be achieved by speeches.

NETANYAHU'S BAR-ILAN SPEECH had partly been in response to an earlier one by Obama. Two weeks after their meeting in the White House, the president had landed in the Middle East, fulfilling his campaign promise to visit a major Arab capital and repair the relationship between the United States and the Muslim world. Obama's June 4 speech at Cairo's Al-Azhar University, titled "A New Beginning," addressed a wide range of subjects, including the Israel-Palestine conflict. He reaffirmed America's "bond" with Israel, describing it as "unbreakable," and called out anti-Semitism and Holocaust denial in Muslim countries. He spoke more eloquently than any previous American president on the Palestinians' plight under Israeli occupation. The "daily humiliations—large and small—that come with occupation," he said, were "intolerable."[10]

However, what angered Israelis more was the suggestion in Obama's speech that their state had been founded because of the Holocaust—an old Palestinian claim against the West—rather than because of the Jewish people's ancient claim to the land. Obama hadn't actually said that, but he had juxtaposed the statement "The aspiration for a Jewish homeland is rooted in a tragic history that cannot be denied" with words on the Holocaust, which implied a strong connection. The Israelis were also offended that Obama had visited Cairo and the Saudi capital, Riyadh, but had not found time to land in Israel before continuing, ironically, to a tour of the Buchenwald concentration camp in Germany. A stopover in Israel had been considered by the White House, but discarded in the interest of demonstrating that Obama was indeed "different" in his attitude toward Israel.

Later in Obama's term, some of his advisers would admit that it had been a mistake not to grasp the opportunity to engage earlier with the Israeli public and counter the image being created by Netanyahu's people of the president as an "Israel-hater."

But the more significant mixed message from Obama's Cairo Speech was to the Arab public, not just in Cairo, but across the Arab world. While making it clear that the United States was no longer interested in imposing its order on other countries, he also extolled the virtues of democracy and human rights. Obama had set out to show the Arab world that the United States was not their enemy. As he warmly greeted the dictators of Egypt and Saudi Arabia, President Hosni Mubarak and King Abdullah, respectively, assuring them that America was out of the regime-change business, many Arabs, especially young people, were asking themselves if Obama really was their friend.

A year and a half later, as millions of Arab citizens took to the streets, first in Tunisia, then in Egypt and other Arab countries, clamoring to "remove the dictator," Obama became determined to change his dictator-friendly image and put himself on the right side of history. America's allies in the Middle East looked on horrified as, in January 2011, Obama cold-shouldered Mubarak's appeal for support as chaos reigned in the streets of Cairo, and publicly declared that the transition of power in Egypt "must begin now."[11]

Netanyahu appealed to Western leaders to stand behind Mubarak. For two decades, the tough old tyrant had maintained Egypt's cold but stable peace with Israel, kept Islamic extremism under his iron thumb, and anchored a regional alliance against Iran. Bibi ominously warned that the "Arab Spring" would be followed by an "Islamic winter." America's Arab allies were sending Washington identical warnings, fearing that the Muslim Brotherhood would take over Egypt and other countries. But in the heady months of early 2011, Obama was willing to give the Brotherhood's brand of political Islam a chance.

ISRAEL WAS TO have its own, much more benign—but for Netanyahu politically threatening—version of the Arab Spring.

In July 2011, thousands of young Israelis camped out on the grassy thoroughfare in the middle of Tel Aviv's Rothschild Boulevard. It had started with graphic designer Daphni Leef, who built a tent and set up a Facebook page protesting the rising cost of rent. It quickly spread to a much wider protest movement over the straitened circumstances of Israel's middle class. There was very little violence. Many of those marching chanted a slogan adapted from the Tahrir Square protests: "The people demand social justice!" Most of them were ordinary young people, including couples and families, not people who had been particularly interested in politics in the past.

The "tent protests" evolved into the "social protest movement," involving hundreds of thousands of people across the country, and exposed one of the weakest links in Netanyahu's economic policies. Hidden behind the healthy financial statistics and the headlines heralding yet more multimillion-dollar high-tech startup "exits," the majority of Israelis were struggling on their salaries to afford housing and keep up a Western-standard lifestyle without incurring crushing debt. A similar protest movement would take place in the United States shortly thereafter, in September 2011, when Occupy Wall Street began, and Europe saw protests over economic inequality as well. But for Israel, in the Middle East, the Arab Spring resonated more than in other places where "occupy" movements took place. The awkward truth was that Netanyahu's Israel had two economies: a healthy technology-driven economy, trading with the world and bringing in handsome rewards for its successful entrepreneurs and software engineers, on the one hand, and, on the other, a second economy in which most of the middle and working classes floundered.

For once, the Israeli media focused almost entirely on social issues—and naturally blamed Netanyahu for the situation. The recommendations of a hastily assembled government committee on ways to rein in the housing market and alleviate the suffering of the middle class failed to assuage the protesters. Even an Islamist terrorist attack on the Egyptian border, killing eight Israelis, and Netanyahu's subsequent decision to allocate billions to building a new border fence, didn't dislodge them from the headlines for more than a few days. Netanyahu was convinced that left-wing nongovernmental organizations (NGOs) with European funding were orchestrating the protests, but his attempts to cast aspersions failed miserably. The protests were causing real political damage, and Bibi plummeted in the polls.

What finally pushed the protests off the public agenda was one of the most uncharacteristic decisions of Netanyahu's career.

I N A SMALL country where nearly everyone serves in the military, MIAs and POWs have always been a highly sensitive issue. High-profile campaigns have been ongoing for decades to discover the whereabouts of missing soldiers, even after the intelligence community presumed them dead. In cases where Palestinian and Lebanese organizations held live captives, or even just bodies, Israel was often prepared to release hundreds of jailed terrorists in return for them. In 1985, Israel exchanged 1,150 prisoners for 3 Israeli soldiers who had been captured in Lebanon.

Netanyahu, whose brother Yoni had been killed in the Entebbe operation, when Israel refused to exchange prisoners for the hijacked hostages, adamantly opposed such lopsided exchanges. He had risked his job as ambassador to publicly criticize the deal in 1985, describing it as a "critical blow to all Israel's efforts to form an international front against terror."[12] On the other hand, in 1997, under pressure to save six Mossad agents and the peace treaty with Jordan, he had released Hamas founder Ahmed Yassin. At the Wye River Summit, the most difficult detail for Netanyahu to swallow had been releasing Palestinian prisoners who had killed Israelis. It took intense pressure from President Clinton to get him to sign off.

Back in power, he had inherited another, similar dilemma from his predecessor. On June 25, 2006, Palestinian fighters had emerged from a tunnel under the Gaza border and attacked an Israeli tank, killing two of the tank crewmembers and wounding another. Grabbing the fourth crewmember, they rushed back into Gaza. For over five years, Gilad Shalit was held in an underground cell in Gaza while Israel's intelligence efforts to locate him failed.

Hamas had demanded that Israel release a thousand Palestinian prisoners, including hundreds who had been convicted for killing Israelis, in exchange for Shalit's return. The negotiations, conducted through Egypt and Germany, drew on for years.

In March 2009, Ehud Olmert had spent most of his last days as prime minister trying to finalize the deal. Netanyahu dearly wanted him to succeed, because it would save him from having to make difficult decisions. But Hamas wouldn't budge, and Olmert balked at the price. Taking office two weeks later, Netanyahu reviewed the details and made it clear that he would not deal with Hamas on those terms. The German negotiator continued for a few months, going back and forth, but by the end of 2009 had abandoned hope. The Shalit family launched a well-funded and star-studded campaign under the slogan "Gilad Shalit—The child of all of us," pressuring Olmert, and then Netanyahu, to pay whatever price was necessary. Every Israeli knew Gilad's face, and most of them supported his parents' demands.

In the late summer of 2011, there were signals that Hamas might be prepared to moderate its demands. A new German negotiator went to work, shuttling between Jerusalem, Gaza, and Cairo. The Syrian Civil War had begun, and the Syrian regime's forces, under Bashar al-Assad, with Iranian backing, were gunning down Sunni demonstrators on the streets. Many of those killed were members of the Syrian Muslim Brotherhood, Hamas's ideological Sunni allies. The movement's leaders, whose political headquarters were in Damascus, were being pressured to cut ties with their Syrian and Iranian sponsors. Anxious for a public relations coup to distract their critics, Hamas's political leaders needed to show that they had forced Israel to release prisoners. But the Hamas military commander, Ahmed Jabari, still insisted on a thousand-for-one ratio in the exchange.

Ultimately, Hamas's concessions were minimal. They accepted Israel's veto on three senior prisoners on their original list and agreed to some of the prisoners being released to Gaza, instead of the West Bank, where it was feared they would organize a new terrorist campaign, both against Israel and against their Fatah rivals in the Palestinian Authority. But Jabari got his thousand. In fact, Israel released 1,027 Palestinians, including 280 who had been sentenced to life behind bars for murder.

Netanyahu, who authorized the deal and pushed it through a dramatic all-night cabinet meeting, gave a number of reasons for his change of heart: Hamas had reduced its demands, the security chiefs had agreed to the deal, and there was a threat that if Israel did not respond this time around, "Shalit would disappear for many years." In Israel's security establishment, even those who supported the deal were critical of this reasoning. Hamas had barely reduced its demands, and the threat of Shalit's disappearance was almost certainly a bluff—a live Israeli soldier was the most powerful lever of pressure Hamas had over Israel, not something they would make disappear. And besides, Yoram Cohen, the Shin Bet chief, who gave his professional cover for the deal, had recently been a surprise appointment of Netanyahu's, who had chosen him over the likelier candidate. He owed Bibi his job.

At the end of the day, Netanyahu had gone against his principles and paid the heaviest price any Israeli prime minister ever had for a single soldier. There is no evidence Netanyahu made the call for political or popularity reasons, though many senior Israeli figures have said so in private.

On October 18, Jabari handed Shalit over to Egyptian officials at the Rafah border crossing, and from there he was transferred to Israeli territory. As the helicopter carrying him landed at Tel Nof Airbase, Netanyahu was on the tarmac to greet him.

For weeks, Israeli media reported on nothing but the deliberations leading to the Shalit deal, the preparations, the implementation, and Gilad's first days back home with his family. The social protest movement, already unsure about how to proceed after a successful summer of protests, was starved of publicity. Protesting against a prime minister who was working to bring "everyone's child" home would have gone down very badly with the public. By the time the Shalit festival finally died down, the widespread passions behind the protests had petered out.

At the height of the protests in August, Netanyahu's approval ratings stood at 29 percent, their lowest point since his return to power. Two months later, with Shalit safely home, 51 percent of Israelis, more than at any other time during that term, were pleased with their prime minister.

In Jerusalem and Washington, there were some who allowed themselves the illusion that there was a new pragmatic Bibi in Israel, a Bibi who was prepared to release prisoners, freeze settlements, and allow a Palestinian state.

27

Your Father Wrote History.
You Are Making History.

Israel has two nuclear doctrines. The first—nuclear opacity—was formulated by David Ben-Gurion and Shimon Peres in the early 1960s in response to the Kennedy administration. Israel and the United States agreed to a formula whereby "Israel will not be the first nation to introduce nuclear weapons to the Middle East" and will not publicly acknowledge whatever military nuclear capabilities it has.

The second is the Begin Doctrine, whereby Israel will never allow one of its enemies to acquire nuclear weapons. In 1981, Begin ordered an air strike on Saddam Hussein's Osirak nuclear reactor to block Iraq's nuclear ambitions.

In his first term, Netanyahu struggled with the opacity doctrine, proposing that Israel deter its enemies by unveiling its capabilities. One of his advisers was quoted threatening Iraq with a "neutron bomb." In his second term, Netanyahu struggled to fulfill the Begin Doctrine as he sought to prevent Iran from developing nuclear weapons.

In September 2007, Ehud Olmert ordered an air strike on a nuclear reactor that the Assad regime had secretly built in northern Syria with North Korean assistance. To prevent further escalation, Olmert decided that Israel would not acknowledge the attack on Syria, allowing President Bashar al-Assad to save face.

As conflicting reports swirled through the international media, Israeli journalists were prohibited from reporting what they knew. Of all people, it was the leader of the opposition, Netanyahu, who first broke the official silence, two weeks after the strike. "I was a partner to the strike from the first moment," he boasted. "I congratulated Olmert personally."[1] Olmert, who had indeed conferred with Netanyahu before ordering the operation, was enraged at Bibi for jeopardizing his non-attribution policy, which had prevented a Syrian retaliation.

Netanyahu considered himself an expert on the nuclear threats facing Israel, especially from Iran. He vividly remembered sitting in the United Nations in 1985, hearing the Iranian ambassador call for Israel to be "excised like a cancerous tumor" and "thrown into the dustbin of history."[2] For years, much of the talk in international forums was of Saddam Hussein's "weapons of mass destruction." Netanyahu would routinely make sure to mention Iran, along with Iraq, as another rogue nation trying to acquire nuclear weapons.

In his book *A Place Among the Nations*, Netanyahu had stipulated that in the peace agreement he envisaged Israel signing one day, there would have to be provisions for sanctions to prevent countries like Iran from developing nuclear weapons.[3] In his first term as prime minister, he would often bring Iran up during meetings with foreign leaders. Visiting China in 1999, he implored President Jiang Zemin not to allow the People's Republic to sell the Islamic Republic equipment that could help the Iranians with their nuclear research.[4]

For Netanyahu, the threat of Iran's nuclear bomb was on par with the extermination of six million Jews in the Holocaust. As early as 1996, on a visit to the Bergen-Belsen concentration camp in Germany, he had spoken of Iran as a new incarnation of Nazi Germany.

In his three years as leader of the opposition after losing the 2006 election, with little else to occupy him, Iran became his primary obsession. Without explicitly saying so, he implied that the Kadima government was not doing enough to counter Iran's nuclear ambitions. Ariel Sharon's policy was "Iran is the world's problem." Sharon believed that Israel should not be seen leading the anti-Iran campaign. He preferred working closely behind the scenes with other governments on the issue, particularly on intelligence-sharing and secret sabotage operations. Olmert continued Sharon's policy.

Netanyahu was convinced that Israel must sound the alarm bells. He saw himself as Ze'ev Jabotinsky, who had spent the 1930s warning an uncaring world of the impending Holocaust. In every meeting with a foreign delegation or speech to a Jewish American organization, he issued a constant warning: "It's 1938 and Iran is Germany. And Iran is racing to arm itself with atomic bombs."[5]

I N HIS FIRST White House meeting with Obama in May 2009, Netanyahu was dismayed to discover that Obama wasn't interested in talking about Iran at any length. For Bibi, the Palestinian issue was a distraction from the real threat, not just to Israel, but to the entire world. How could Obama expect Israel to waste time and resources on a local side-show and make dangerous concessions to the Palestinians while its very existence was being threatened by Iran?

Obama's approach was the exact opposite. He argued that the best way for Israel and the international community to confront Iran was through a joint diplomatic front to pressure it, through sanctions, to negotiate, and that solving the Israeli-Palestinian conflict was the key to building that front. Netanyahu was all in favor of sanctions, but he countered that Iran, through its financial and military support for Hamas and the Palestinian Islamic Jihad, was sabotaging any chance of peace. Iran had to be dealt with first. But Obama at that point was still convinced Iran was Netanyahu's excuse to avoid dealing with the Palestinians. He was only half-right. Netanyahu was desperate to avoid the Palestinian issue. But the Iranian threat was no excuse. It was the core reason Netanyahu believed he was destined to lead Israel.

On Obama's orders, the US military was preparing withdrawal plans from Iraq at the time. He hoped to end the war in Afghanistan as well in the not-too-distant future. Nothing was further away from his thinking than a third war. Obama instead believed he could engage with the Shi'a Iranian regime, even partner with it in "balancing" Sunni extremism. On the campaign trail, Obama had said he would reach out to the Iranian people and their leaders. With the rabidly anti-Western president Mahmoud Ahmadinejad in office in Iran, that seemed impossible, but, undeterred, Obama sent Iran's supreme leader, the Ayatollah Ali Khamenei, a personal letter in May 2009 in the hope of opening a dialogue.

A month later, Khamenei referred to the letter in a speech in Tehran, citing it as proof that the United States and other foreign powers had interfered in Iran's presidential election. It was a baseless accusation as far as Obama was concerned. Not only had the United States done nothing to interfere in the June 12 election, but after thousands of Iranians took to the streets to protest widespread fraud during the vote-counting in favor of Ahmadinejad, defying the Basij paramilitary forces who fired on the crowds, killing dozens, and the mass detentions and torture of thousands, it took Obama ten days to condemn the Iranian government's actions. He finally said, "The United States and the international community have been appalled and outraged by the threats, beatings, and imprisonment."[6] But there was no questioning of the legitimacy of the elections, or the regime itself. Nothing came even close to Obama's demand for the transition in Egypt to "begin now," eighteen months later, when demonstrations broke out against America's old ally Hosni Mubarak.

Obama was anxious to avoid any impression of trying to effect regime change in Iran. In his defense, it has to be said that the Iranian protesters and the leaders of the "Reformist" camp were anxious not to be tainted by foreign support. Regretfully, Obama conceded that for the time being, direct negotiations with Iran were unlikely. Meanwhile, he was resolved to prevent Netanyahu from making matters worse with a military attack on Iran's nuclear installations.

EVEN WHEN NETANYAHU was not prime minister, Israel was preparing for a possible strike on Iran. During his decade out of office, Israel had purchased squadrons of long-range F-15I and F-16I fighter-bombers from the United States, developed and launched spy satellites, and spent billions enhancing Israel's strategic intelligence and strike capabilities. "Ninety percent of our equipment and training is for a much larger war. The fighter jets weren't built for attacking Gaza or even Lebanon," said one squadron commander.

Both Olmert and Sharon had considered preemptive strikes against Iran's nuclear plants. They had decided that Israel had time to first try and slow down Iran's nuclear development by other means. Neither wanted to act without the blessing of the United States, and George W. Bush had enough on his hands in Iraq and Afghanistan. American intelligence assessments also differed with Israel's over how close Iran was to a nuclear military capability, or if it even was working on one.

The United States was aware of Israel's plans under Olmert, and it knew about the long-range sorties the Israeli Air Force was conducting over the Mediterranean to simulate the 2,000-mile flight path to Iran and back. But US officials were fairly confident that Olmert would not surprise them. They had no such confidence in Netanyahu.

It was Ehud Barak who convinced the Obama administration that Netanyahu wasn't just using Iran as an excuse to avoid negotiations with the Palestinians. When he had returned to Labor leadership and to government, as defense minister, in July 2007, Barak had agreed with Olmert's low-profile policy on Iran. Two years later, he still didn't agree with Netanyahu on the issue, saying, in an interview, "I am not among those who believe Iran is an existential issue for Israel."[7] Soon after that, however, he adjusted his views to those of his new boss. For the next three years, Bibi and Barak would hold the Obama administration in suspense regarding their plans to attack Iran.

Barak still had credibility in Washington, where he was seen as the "moderate" pole of Netanyahu's government. For three years, he was Israel's real ambassador to the United States, flying there twice a month and meeting with senior administration officials. Israel's official ambassador, the American Israeli historian Michael Oren, a fellow at a Jerusalem think tank funded by Sheldon Adelson, had the full confidence of neither Netanyahu nor the US administration.

When Barak told US administration officials how serious his government was about using military force to destroy Iran's nuclear program, they were dismayed. Unlike Netanyahu, Barak didn't indulge in historical doomsaying when describing the threat to Israel. Instead he employed crisp and detailed strategic analysis. He failed to convince the US administration of the urgent need to act, but he scared the hell out of them over Israel's intentions.

Back in Israel, he was Bibi's soulmate, their political rivalry forgotten. Thirty-five years earlier, in Matkal, Lieutenant Netanyahu had worshiped his unit commander as a hero. Behind his back he called Barak "the wise man." Now he outranked him, but they were in effect equals, sharing the same intimate language and codes, cocooned from the rest of the cabinet. It was the closest political relationship either of them ever had.

The United States has never fully trusted its Israeli ally, devoting considerable intelligence resources to finding out what Israel is up to before the Israelis deign to tell them. But there was no precedent for the effort that the Obama administration put into ensuring that Israel was not about to launch a strike on Iran. For three years, beginning in late 2009, there was all manner of surveillance and intelligence-gathering.

The procession of high-ranking administration officials, from the vice president on down, landing at Ben Gurion Airport and making the rounds between Jerusalem and Tel Aviv was never ending. There were periods in which it seemed like a week couldn't go by without the CIA director, the chairman of the joint chiefs of staff, or the national security adviser, or at the very least a deputy secretary of state, arriving to visit with Israeli officials.

They all asked the same questions, made the same arguments, and issued the same warnings. Before leaving, they gave the standard assurance that Obama had Israel's back and personally guaranteed that he would never allow Iran to acquire nuclear weapons. They all returned to Washington without crucial answers to whether and when Israel planned to attack.

Israel gave them plenty to guess about. The long-range exercises of air force squadrons intensified. New military technologies, many shared and even financed by the United States, were quickly made operational. Meanwhile, the secret war against Iran continued. Mysterious explosions at arms plants destroyed missile assembly lines and killed Iranian generals. Nuclear scientists were assassinated in daylight on the streets of Tehran. Shipments of military and nuclear materials disappeared at sea. The prime suspect, Israel, never took responsibility.

The United States was a partner in the secret campaign against Iran. Bush had authorized the cooperation, which continued, and even intensified, under Obama. Their most famous success was Stuxnet, a malicious computer worm that found its way into the operating system of Iran's uranium enrichment centrifuges. According to the *New York Times*, Stuxnet had been developed by a joint American-Israeli team in "Operation Olympic Games" to sabotage Iran's nuclear program.[8]

Contrary to the "throwing Israel under the bus" narrative pushed by Netanyahu's people in Jerusalem and Washington, Obama authorized taking the intelligence-sharing and operational coordination between the two countries to unprecedented levels. Israel's intelligence and security chiefs were also Obama's unlikely allies in his effort to hold the war plans of Netanyahu and Barak at bay.

WHEN NETANYAHU RETURNED to office in March 2009, he inherited Meir Dagan as Mossad chief and Yuval Diskin as head of the Shin Bet. Both had originally been appointed by Sharon, and their old boss's deep disdain for Bibi, whom he called "the male model," had rubbed off on them. Dagan, in particular, enjoyed rubbing Netanyahu the wrong way. He had been close to Sharon since the early 1970s, when as a young officer under Sharon's command he had led an IDF death squad, eliminating PLO fighters in the close alleyways of Gaza. Dagan detested the sight of Netanyahu sitting in Sharon's chair. He regaled his friends, and even journalists, with stories of the prime minister's lack of decisiveness.

Dagan was the only person in government who allowed himself to clash openly with Netanyahu. In their weekly meetings to approve sensitive operations outside Israel, he insisted that the prevaricating Netanyahu take responsibility and give precise instructions. Once, he created a scene at the prime minister's residence. While he was briefing Netanyahu, Sara walked in. Bibi asked him to continue, as Sara was privy to all his secrets. That wasn't enough for Dagan, who inquired whether she had official Shin Bet clearance. Sara left. Dagan was never asked back to the residence.

In some ways, Dagan resembled Netanyahu. He believed Iran was a mortal threat to Israel. In his office at Mossad headquarters hung a photograph of a religious Jew kneeling down before Nazi soldiers. For Dagan it symbolized "my grandfather just before he was murdered. I look at this picture every day and promise that the Holocaust will never happen again." But Dagan believed the clandestine war he waged as Mossad chief in 2002 was the only way to fight Iran. A military strike would be a blunt and ineffective instrument, to be used only as a last resort. He didn't believe in Netanyahu as Israel's leader.

There was no consensus in the security establishment over military action against Iran. But Dagan and Diskin had a crucial ally in the IDF chief of staff, Lieutenant General Gabi Ashkenazi, a gruff and aggressive Golani Brigade veteran who disliked Matkal sophisticates, including his direct boss, Barak, and the prime minister, Netanyahu. Ashkenazi was a soldier's soldier, and he never shied away from a fight, whether in the field or in the corridors of the Defense Ministry. But he believed that a long-range operation in Iran would unnecessarily expose Israeli pilots and jeopardize cooperation with the United States.

Most of the details of how the three service chiefs worked to block a strike on Iran have yet to emerge. Opposing their elected political masters was no easy matter, however, and supporters of Netanyahu have described their actions as tantamount to "a military coup." But they did have the blessing of the president of Israel.

S HIMON PERES, STILL the eternal optimist at eighty-five, in his last role of seven decades of public service, wanted to believe that the Netanyahu who returned to power in 2009 was a more grown-up and pragmatic Bibi than the one of 1996–1999. For months, Peres assured world leaders that "Bibi has changed" and advised they give him a chance. Netanyahu reciprocated, allowing Peres to open up his own back channel to Palestinian president Abbas, on the condition that Peres report back on everything. Peres held five secret meetings with Abbas in 2010, making progress on permanent status issues. However, Netanyahu's suspicions eventually got the better of him and he pulled the plug on the talks, ordering Peres to cancel a sixth meeting shortly before it was to take place. Peres fumed, but he was forced to accept the limits of his largely ceremonial position.

But Peres refused to accept the limits when it came to a strike on Iran. He was the only president to have previously served as prime minister, and had been privy to all of Israel's secrets. Olmert, who had lobbied for Peres's election (presidents in Israel are elected by the Knesset in a secret ballot), valued Peres's advice and authorized his continued access to confidential materials. The communications infrastructure in the president's office was connected to the "black" network, and his new military adjutant was a veteran intelligence officer. Netanyahu, discovering this upon replacing Olmert, was perturbed, but was loath to insult Peres by downgrading his access.

With Sharon in a coma, Peres was the last of the founding generation in government. During that period, one senior officer who opposed the Iran operation described him as "our Western Wall"—a combination of father-confessor and ringleader. One of Peres's closest aides put it more bluntly—"Shimon is doing everything to help Ashkenazi and the service chiefs to stop this Iranian madness."

Ashkenazi was both responsible for preparing a military strike against Iran and at the forefront of trying to stop it from taking place. In 2010, he twice played a key role in preventing what could have been an actual strike. Earlier in the year, Barak had ordered the army to be ready for an operation, and Ashkenazi had responded that in his professional opinion, intelligence was lacking and other logistical preparations had to be made before the IDF could guarantee it was capable of carrying out the operation. Barak disagreed with Ashkenazi's assessment, but had no choice but to defer. He ordered the necessary preparations to be made as soon as possible.

A few months later, there was a showdown between both Barak and Netanyahu, on the one hand, and, on the other hand, the security chiefs at Mossad headquarters north of Tel Aviv. It was the most dramatic political-military clash since the eve of the Six-Day War, when the generals had demanded that Prime Minister Eshkol give an attack order. This time, the roles were reversed, with the generals holding back the politicians.

Netanyahu and Barak ordered Ashkenazi to place the IDF at its highest alert status, essentially on a war footing. The status alert, using a term that in Israeli military slang means "cocking the gun," meant discreetly calling up essential reserve personnel, canceling all leave, placing aircraft and missiles on twenty-four-hour readiness, and opening emergency storage facilities. It would cost the army millions of shekels a day and keep it just hours from actually launching the strike. Sensing that the two leaders were trying to sneak something behind the government's back, Ashkenazi said that "cocking the gun" was equivalent to an act of war and by law had to be authorized by the full cabinet. Barak insisted it was a legal order, and that an alert status was not the same as going to war. A heated exchange ensued, with Dagan joining Ashkenazi.

"If you play with this accordion, music will come out," warned Ashkenazi. "You could be making an illegal decision to go to war," added Dagan. Netanyahu remained silent during the argument, and eventually Barak backed down.[9]

In an attempt to influence public opinion, Ashkenazi and the officers close to him briefed journalists, informing them that an attack on Iran would cause Iran's proxy, Hezbollah, to counterattack immediately by firing thousands of rockets at civilian targets in Israel. "We are facing a war with thousands of civilian casualties," warned one of the officers in an off-the-record briefing. "It's going to be like nothing we've experienced before." And those opposing the Iran attack weren't just briefing Israeli journalists.

"We assumed the Americans knew everything about the operation and also about the opposition to it," said Barak in April 2017. "There was someone among us talking to them on a daily basis."[10] Barak confirmed what had been an open secret for years in the Israeli establishment—that senior Israeli officials were leaking details of the ongoing argument within the Israeli leadership to the Obama administration. Peres and Dagan were the main suspects.

A year earlier, in an interview with Dagan that appeared on Israeli TV after his 2016 death, he described how he had been in contact with CIA director Leon Panetta when he felt that Barak was not truthfully presenting the Obama administration's objections to an attack on Iran to the cabinet. In a subsequent interview, Panetta said that Dagan had "indicated the frustrations with them [Netanyahu and Barak] moving forward."[11]

"I think he was worried that decisions were made for political reasons and I think that troubled him," Panetta recalled. Dagan, Panetta said, was "very concerned that somebody [would] push the wrong button."[12]

Whether there was actual collusion between Israeli officials and a foreign government to thwart Israel's elected leaders is still not clear. With both Dagan and Peres dead, the truth may never be fully known. Naturally, views in Israel on the presumed actions of the officials involved are split between those on the right, who would accuse those who spoke to the Obama administration of treason, and those on the left who praise the same men for doing whatever was necessary to prevent a potentially illegal order and avert a disastrous war.

WITHIN THE FIRST five months of 2011, Dagan, Ashkenazi, and Diskin all ended their terms. They were replaced by security chiefs selected by Netanyahu and Barak who were less likely to strenuously object to an Iranian strike.

Finally a civilian, Dagan lost no time in openly continuing his crusade against a military strike, telling journalists that Iran was still at least four years away from developing a nuclear weapon, and that within the Iranian leadership there was "deep division on continuing to develop the nuclear program."[13] The message was clear—there was no need to rush and strike. The secret sabotage campaign, together with diplomatic pressure and sanctions, were working.

With the three combative security chiefs out, the battle within the Israeli leadership over attacking Iran moved to the "Octet"—the inner cabinet of eight senior ministers. But despite all of Netanyahu and Barak's arguments, a majority of the forum opposed the attack. On January 17, Barak announced that he was leaving the Labor Party, along with four other hawkish MKs. He blamed the rest of the party for acting against its elected leader and trying to pull Labor in a "combative, leftist-socialist" direction. Barak continued as defense minister, while the remaining Labor MKs left the coalition. But his hopes that a coalition positioned further to the right would help to shift opinion in the cabinet proved groundless. At least half the Octet continued to oppose a strike. An earlier attempt by Netanyahu to boost the pro-strike faction by appointing one of his protégés, Finance Minister Yuval Steinitz, to the inner cabinet, which had only seven members at that point, had failed as well.

With the battle now becoming more political, the Obama administration focused its campaign against a strike on the cabinet. Individual cabinet members were invited to Washington for meetings with senior administration officials. Octet meetings were devoted to long discussions on the Iranian issue, with Netanyahu and Barak delivering interminable lectures, but a firm group of four ministers held out.

From 2010 to 2012, the tension and debate over a possible strike reached a crescendo every spring and summer. A complex long-range operation stretching the Israeli Air Force to its limits could almost certainly be carried out only in perfect weather conditions. In early 2012, as the indicators in favor of a possible Israeli strike came around again, the debate spilled out into the open. The Obama administration embarked on a new tactic to influence both decision-makers and public opinion in Israel—it started to cast doubt on whether Israel could destroy Iran's nuclear program by itself.

Pentagon analysts briefed journalists on how difficult such an operation would be. There would be multiple targets, many of them hidden underground within reinforced steel and concrete bunkers. Former senior officials were trotted out to deliver their verdicts, including former CIA director Michael Hayden, who said, in January 2011, that an attack against Iran was "beyond the capacity" of Israel.[14] It was a high-risk tactic, potentially pushing Israel to prove that it could indeed pull it off, and had the effect of undermining Israel's deterrence capability in Iranian eyes. It also wasn't entirely truthful.

Israel's armed forces may be only a fraction of the size of America's, but Israel had been preparing and building up for such an attack for two decades, ever since the Iraqi Scud missiles had hit Tel Aviv in the 1991 Gulf War. Israel's military planners fully appreciated the difficulties and had prepared various options for a series of attacks against multiple fortified targets. They had at their disposal sufficient warplanes and aerial tankers to carry out a sustained bombing campaign in waves, as well as back-up from land- and submarine-launched missiles. There was also the option of inserting special forces on the ground to destroy some of the more difficult targets. All of these options were high-risk. There would be casualties, and aircraft and pilots would be lost. There were fierce arguments within the Israeli defense establishment over whether the operation would be worthwhile.

But the real argument was not over the viability of the operation, but just how much damage it would cause to the Iranian nuclear program and how long it would take Iran to get back on track. One particularly gung-ho air force general said that if the government ordered a strike, "my pilots will be breaking down my office door to be on it, no matter the risks. And we don't have any illusions that the Iranians will rebuild and we will have to bomb them again three years later."

Netanyahu dithered. For all the tough talk coming out of Jerusalem, the Octet was not convened again to discuss a strike on Iran throughout 2012. In their discussions with Obama and other senior US officials, Netanyahu and Barak refused to say whether or not Israel would attack. Obama had ordered upgraded intelligence-sharing, but as Israel refused even to guarantee sufficient warning time before launching an attack, the US intelligence community began withholding information from Israel that could help Israel's generals in a strike.

The anti-Iran rhetoric and threats to act yielded at least one significant result: the United States and European leaders, in particular Prime Minister David Cameron in Britain, had ramped up sanctions against Iran, effectively cutting its financial system off from the international banking networks and ending its oil sales to the West.

The sanctions would eventually bring Iran to the negotiating table, but this wasn't enough for Netanyahu, who wanted a more credible military threat against Iran from the United States. Obama refused to publicly go beyond his standard formulation—"All options are on the table," and the United States would "do what is necessary." The United States was indeed working on operational plans to strike Iran if necessary. For

Bibi with Benzion at age 101.

one, it was developing massive bunker-buster bombs capable of taking out the underground uranium enrichment plants. But what Israelis and Iranians heard was a president who had no intention of going to war and who would do whatever it took to prevent Israel from doing so.

O N APRIL 30, 2012, Benzion Netanyahu passed away at the age of 102. Well into his late nineties, he had soldiered on with his research, spending long periods in the United States, where he often read and wrote in the New York Public Library. He never moderated his views. In his last interview, shortly after his son's Bar-Ilan Speech, he denied that Bibi had made an ideological concession by offering the Palestinians a state. "He doesn't support [a Palestinian state]. He supports conditions that they [the Palestinians] will never accept. That's what I heard from him. . . . This land is Jewish land, not for Arabs. There is no place here for Arabs and won't be. They will never agree to the conditions."[15] In another interview a few months earlier, he had said, "We are under threat of extermination. People think the Holocaust, the threat, is over. It isn't over. It continues all the time."[16]

At his funeral, Netanyahu eulogized him at length. Trying to show a softer side of the stern father, he recalled how in a New York snowstorm, when the young Bibi was clamoring for food, Benzion went out, returning drenched with a hot tray. He recounted how he had played soccer with his sons in Central Park. His best memories of his father were from America.

Bibi said he had learned from his father that "a vital characteristic of every living organism, and a nation is a living organism, is the ability to identify danger in time. An ability our nation lost during the period of exile."[17]

President Peres also spoke, ending his eulogy with a message to the prime minister: "Bibi, your father wrote history. You are making history. With the same feeling, the same destiny, the same heritage."[18] The last historical showdown between Netanyahu and Peres was reaching its peak. This time, Peres would win.

DURING BENZION's shiva, secret talks were in progress with Kadima. In March, Tzipi Livni had lost the centrist party's leadership primary to Shaul Mofaz, the former defense minister, a political ally turned fierce critic of Netanyahu. On May 8, Netanyahu and Mofaz appeared together, announcing a new coalition deal. Netanyahu, who had been in danger of losing his majority, owing to disagreements over a new state budget, now enjoyed the largest majority of any government in Israel's history.

Two weeks later, Netanyahu was back on the cover of *Time*, the magazine that had boosted his popularity twenty-six years earlier with a cover story on his prescriptions against terror. This time he was crowned "KING BIBI." *Time* managing editor Richard Stengel profiled him, noting that he was "poised to become the longest-serving Israeli Prime Minister since David Ben-Gurion, the founding father of Israel. He has no national rival. His approval rating, roughly 50%, is at an all-time high. At a moment when incumbents around the world are being shunted aside, he is triumphant." Faced with the challenge of a nuclear Iran and resolving the Palestinian issue, wrote Stengel, "the question is whether he is a prisoner of that history or he can write a new narrative."[19] The answer was to be negative.

Mofaz joined the cabinet and became the ninth member of the Octet. But Netanyahu's hopes that he could win Mofaz's support for a strike on Iran were soon dashed. The new minister flew in June to Washington for talks with the Obama administration and returned firmly opposed to a unilateral Israeli operation. The new coalition lasted only two months. Netanyahu had promised Kadima that he would pass a new law on drafting Haredi yeshiva students into the IDF, but once again his alliance with the ultra-Orthodox parties took precedence. Early elections loomed.

T HE LATE SUMMER of 2012 was the peak period of Iran war talk in Israel. On August 10, an interview with a source called only "the decision-maker," a very thinly veiled Barak, appeared in *Haaretz*. "The decision-maker" strongly argued in favor of a strike. "A nuclear Iran is one of the most serious things that can happen to Israel," he said. "If Iran goes nuclear, everything here will be different. Everything. We will move to a different mode of existence. If Iran goes nuclear, down the road, Israel will face a threat of existential proportions."[20]

Horrified by the tone, a group of five former senior intelligence officers, including ex-commanders of Sayeret Matkal, sent Netanyahu and Barak a private letter. All of them knew Barak well and were convinced that he was dragging Netanyahu and the rest of the country to war. They warned them of "terrible chaos that will come in various ways after the euphoria of victory." Striking Iran would cause "a war in which the damage will not be measured only in casualties, but in long-term damage for Israel's economic and social functioning." It would be "a dramatic and colossal historical mistake to try and force the US into a war against its will."

With an election months away, many in government and in the opposition began to talk of "political motives" behind a possible strike. In the polls, nearly 60 percent of Israelis opposed the strike, but Netanyahu's right-wing voters were overwhelmingly in favor, and a successful operation would change the minds of many more. Peres, who in 1981 had lost an election to Likud right after the attack on Iraq's Osirak nuclear reactor, decided to free himself of the restraints of the Israeli presidency and speak out in public.

On August 16, he gave a series of interviews to the main Israeli news organizations. "It's clear to us we can't do this on our own," he said. "We can postpone [Iran's nuclear development], but it's clear to us we need to go together with America." He urged Israelis to trust Obama, who a month earlier had decorated Peres in the White House with the Presidential Medal of Freedom. Denying Iran nuclear weapons, said Peres, "is an American interest and Obama sees that. He doesn't just say it to make us feel good."[21]

Peres didn't mention Netanyahu or Barak by name, but the address was clear. Bibi was livid. "Peres forgot his role as president," Netanyahu's people told the media. "Peres forgot as well that he promised a new Middle East after Oslo and instead a thousand Israelis were murdered." Peres, they said, had also opposed the Osirak bombing, which had saved Israel and the world from Saddam Hussein's nuclear bomb.[22]

Netanyahu, in public, refrained from attacking Peres or the opponents of an operation. He had called the public debate "irresponsible and damaging to national security. . . . The political leadership decides. The professional level executes. I have not yet decided."[23]

On September 27, Netanyahu addressed the United Nations General Assembly. Most of his speech focused on the Iranian nuclear issue, "because the hour is getting late, very late." At the global forum he put forward his strongest case for military action against Iran. "Iran uses diplomatic negotiations as a means to buy time to advance its nuclear program," Netanyahu said. And "sanctions have not stopped Iran's nuclear program either."[24]

He had even brought a diagram, in the shape of a cartoon bomb, on which he drew with a marker a thick red line, highlighting the 90 percent uranium enrichment threshold. From the red line, "it's only a few months, possibly a few weeks, before they get enough enriched uranium for the first bomb. . . . The relevant question is not when Iran will get the bomb. The relevant question is at what stage can we no longer stop Iran from getting the bomb. The red line must be drawn on Iran's nuclear enrichment program because these enrichment facilities are the only nuclear installations that we can definitely see and credibly target."[25]

Netanyahu was imploring Obama and the world to stop Iran from crossing the red line. The implication was that if they wouldn't, he would.

THE SUMMER OF 2012 passed without an Israeli attack on Iran. Netanyahu, meanwhile, had other problems. Despite a growing deficit, his coalition partners refused to pass a new state budget including sweeping cutbacks in social programs. On October 15, Likud tabled a motion to dissolve the Knesset and bring the election forward to January 22, 2013. In his speeches Netanyahu continued to constantly warn of the Iranian threat, but reports and leaks on strike plans disappeared.

On November 26, Barak announced that he would not be running in the election; he was leaving politics to spend more time with his family. At seventy, he had hoped to lead Israel in one last war. Now he realized it wasn't going to happen, and he had better things to do with his time. Three days later, he flew to Washington for his last working visit at the Pentagon. Defense Secretary Leon Panetta, who together with so many other senior administration officials had spent so much time over the past three years trying to stop Barak and Netanyahu from striking Iran, awarded Barak the Defense Department's Medal for Distinguished Public Service.

Unlike Peres and Barak, Netanyahu was not about to receive any medals from the Obama administration. Barack Obama had been re-elected president on November 6. Throughout the campaign, as Republican candidates accused him of having "thrown Israel under the bus," and Netanyahu's benefactor, Sheldon Adelson, plowed $93 million into the GOP campaign, Netanyahu did little to fix the impression that he couldn't wait to see Obama kicked out of the White House.

In July, Netanyahu's old colleague from the Boston Consulting Group, the recently nominated Republican candidate, Mitt Romney, arrived in Jerusalem. Netanyahu could of course argue that Obama had also flown four years earlier as a candidate to meet Israel's leaders. But there was no mistaking the rapture in Netanyahu's greeting of Romney at his office. Later that day, they met a second time, for an intimate dinner at the prime minister's residence. Romney held a fundraising event in Jerusalem, where there was no mistaking the correlation between Romney's donors and staunch Bibi supporters.

Netanyahu, with his insider knowledge of American politics, might have been expected to be a bit more circumspect, but he had been convinced by his Republican contacts that the polls predicting an Obama victory were not to be trusted.

Disappointed with the re-election, Netanyahu should have taken some time to reflect on how to engage with Obama in his second term. But he had an election of his own to fight.

Five years after his resignation, Barak, no longer an ally, hinted that in 2012 Netanyahu had become less eager to attack Iran, and had instead been pinning his hopes on somehow getting the United States to strike. This sounds likely only under a Romney administration.[26] Obama had given Netanyahu little reason to believe this was a serious option.

Many in Jerusalem and Washington alike are convinced that Netanyahu and Barak never seriously planned to strike Iran—that all the preparations, the "cocking of the gun," the tough talk that scared Obama, were all an elaborate bluff. Netanyahu, of course, denies this, claiming he was prepared then, and still is prepared, to bomb Iran's nuclear installations.

Only Netanyahu and Barak know the true answer. Nearly all of those who retroactively accused Bibi of bluffing were certainly taken in during those three years. If he was bluffing, he succeeded in making the Western governments dramatically ramp up their sanctions on Iran. And the focus on Iran significantly reduced the pressure on Netanyahu to make concessions to the Palestinians. By the start of his second term, Barack Obama no longer had much faith in his ability to solve the Israeli-Palestinian conflict. He still had high hopes, though, for his engagement with Iran.

On November 14, 2012, an Israeli drone flying over Gaza City fired a missile, killing Ahmed Jabari, the Hamas military chief who had held Gilad Shalit and forced Israel to release 1,027 prisoners in exchange for the soldier. It was the starting shot for Operation Pillar of Defense. Israel attacked hundreds of Hamas targets in Gaza, and Hamas fired rockets at Israeli cities. Eight days later, the Muslim Brotherhood government in Egypt brokered a ceasefire. Six Israelis and 223 Gazans, three-quarters of them members of Hamas and the Islamic Jihad, had been killed. Tens of thousands of ground troops were on stand-by, but Netanyahu opposed sending in ground troops.

Obama supported Israel throughout, branding Hamas the aggressor for firing on civilian targets. Israeli casualties were low, though Hamas rockets reached as far as Tel Aviv. Nearly all the missiles threatening urban areas were intercepted by the Israeli-built Iron Dome system. The Obama administration had allocated Israel, in addition to the annual $3 billion in military assistance, hundreds of millions of dollars to build more

Iron Dome interceptors. Some on the Israeli left accused Netanyahu of an "elections war." The operation was widely popular in Israel.

The election on January 22, 2013, gave Netanyahu the easiest win he had ever experienced. Kadima, which only seven years earlier had replaced Likud as the party of power, was wiped out. Labor, under yet another new leader, Shelly Yachimovich, a former journalist who valiantly tried to run a campaign focused on social and economic issues, was a shadow of its former self. As the center-left votes split between five different parties, there was no real alternative to Bibi.

Likud, which on Arthur Finkelstein's advice had linked up in a joint list with Lieberman's far-right party Yisrael Beiteinu, hardly covered itself in glory. Likud Beiteinu received a quarter of the votes—translating into thirty-one seats—eleven less than the two parties had together in the outgoing Knesset. But all the other parties in the new Knesset were much smaller.

Netanyahu, having spoken about little else besides Iran during the campaign, won his third term in office virtually unopposed.

28

The Arab Voters
Are Moving in Droves

Netanyahu began his third term as "King Bibi," master of all he surveyed. But his kingdom was divided.

No other party leader emerged from the 2013 election with a chance of forming a coalition, but the Knesset arithmetic put Netanyahu at the mercy of his potential partners. The joint Likud Beiteinu list had received only thirty-one seats. Together with Bibi's old allies, the ultra-Orthodox parties, they were still ten seats short of a majority. Surprising everyone, Netanyahu signed a coalition agreement with Tzipi Livni, who was now leader of a new centrist party, Ha'Tnuah (The Movement). Livni would hold the dual role of justice minister and chief negotiator with the Palestinians, giving Netanyahu's government a moderate gloss. That still left the coalition four seats short.

The natural partner would have been another traditional Likud ally—the National Religious Party, now rebranded as HaBayit HaYehudi (Jewish Home). But along with its new name, Jewish Home had a new leader—Naftali Bennett, Netanyahu's chief of staff before their falling-out in 2008. Bennett had committed the cardinal sin of saying to Sara, who demanded a full report on Bibi's whereabouts, "I work for your husband, not for you."

With Bennett vetoed, Netanyahu turned to Labor, but its socialist leader, Shelly Yachimovich, turned him down. There was a third option—the new ultra-centrist party Yesh Atid (There Is a Future), led

by talk-show host Yair Lapid, which seemed incapable of taking a position even minutely deviating from the mainstream. Yesh Atid had attracted
middle-class voters, leapfrogging over Labor to become the second-
largest party in the Knesset. But Lapid was a strident secularist, and the
ultra-Orthodox vetoed him. The Haredi veto overrode Sara's. Netanyahu
was forced to open talks with Bennett, who had a surprise in store.

Bennett and Lapid had secretly established a "bond of brothers." Bennett refused to enter government without Yesh Atid. Netanyahu fumed
that he had "a mandate from the nation" and that Bennett couldn't dic-
tate to him which other partners to choose. Bennett, enjoying seeing
his old boss squirm, wouldn't budge. Netanyahu was forced to ditch his
Haredi friends and form a coalition with three party leaders he deeply
distrusted—Bennett, Lapid, and Livni. It was to be an unhappy and
short-lived Netanyahu government.

O N MARCH 20, 2013, Obama landed in Israel. Many of his aides,
including some who felt it had been a mistake not to fly to Israel
after the Cairo Speech in 2009, didn't see the point by then in a presidential visit. Bibi and Barack were never going to trust each other, and
the president no longer rated his chances of making progress in the
Israeli-Palestinian diplomatic process to be very high. Obama was to
meet with Palestinian president Abbas as well. He had not brought any
new diplomatic plans with him, but he was willing to humor his new
secretary of state, John Kerry, who never gave up faith.

Both consummate actors, Obama and Netanyahu managed to make
the three-day visit seem friendly enough. None of the meetings with Israelis or Palestinians contained substantive policies. The visit was mem-
orable only because of two moments at the very start and finish, on the
Ben Gurion Airport tarmac. Upon landing in Air Force One, Obama was
taken for a quick tour of an Iron Dome battery, which had been brought
to the airport. The missile defense system, developed indigenously by
Israel, would have been useless in intercepting incoming Hamas rockets without sufficient interceptor missiles, which Obama had agreed
to fund. The tour over, the two leaders walked back to the motorcade,
Obama nonchalantly shrugging off his jacket. Netanyahu quickly copied
him, affording the photographers the enduring not-quite-mirror-image
of the svelte Barack and the slightly pudgy Bibi, identically attired in

Obama and Netanyahu putting
on a show of friendship for the
sake of the Israeli-US relationship
in March 2013.

dark trousers, white shirts, and light blue ties, with their jackets slung
over their shoulders, walking side-by-side in the sun—two men who
hated each other's guts, putting on an amiable show for the sake of the
enduring American-Israeli relationship.

Just before his departure on March 22, Obama held a final meeting
with Netanyahu in a portable cabin on the runway. Obama had Turkey's
Recep Tayyip Erdoğan on the phone and pressured Netanyahu into reading out an apology that had been prepared in advance. It was an exercise
fraught with tension, as the hyper-suspicious Israeli and Turkish leaders
had no channel of communication, and the US ambassador in Israel, Dan
Shapiro, was redrafting the wording of the apology all the way to the
airport. What had once been a strategic alliance between Israel and Turkey had been going downhill for years, even before Netanyahu's return to
office. Diplomatic relations were finally cut following an Israeli raid on a
flotilla that had been trying to break the blockade that Israel had imposed
on Gaza. In the May 2010 raid, nine Turkish activists had been killed.
The apology to Erdoğan allowed Obama to leave Israel feeling he had

achieved something; if nothing else, he had brought two of America's wayward allies together. But it would take another three years for Israel and Turkey to resume diplomatic ties, and even then, there was little hope of them rebuilding an alliance.

No one was under illusions that the outwardly successful visit had repaired the relationship between Netanyahu and Obama. Four months later, Netanyahu appointed his closest adviser, Ron Dermer, as Israel's new ambassador to Washington, replacing Oren. Dermer was known as a virulent critic of Obama, so much so that at one point there was concern the administration would not accept his appointment. This "nuclear option" was not exercised, but it was clear that the new envoy was Israel's ambassador to the GOP. Dermer's appointment was a snub to Obama, and he would receive little access to the administration.

With Netanyahu's representative in Washington, virtually a persona non grata with the administration, Ambassador Shapiro in Israel often remained the only effective personal link between the two leaders. Appointed in 2011, Shapiro was a consummate professional. He was personally committed to Obama, on whose 2008 campaign he had worked as senior policy adviser and Jewish outreach coordinator. He often found himself torn as an American Jew with a deep connection to Israel, as well, when having to maintain a working relationship with an Israeli prime minister whose policies he firmly opposed and who openly dismissed the views of the president he served.

The White House did not keep up any pretenses either. Over the next few years, there would be a steady stream of invective from unnamed senior officials criticizing Netanyahu, including calling him "a coward" and "chickenshit."[1] Meanwhile, Netanyahu may have given up on a military strike against Iran, but he focused all his rhetoric and lobbying on trying to prevent an agreement between Iran and the United States.

D URING THE VISIT, Obama was asked by journalists about his reaction to reports of sporadic use of chemical weapons by the Assad regime in Syria. Evidence at that point was sketchy, but Obama said, "We have been very clear to the Assad regime—but also to other players on the ground—that a red line for us is we start seeing a whole bunch of chemical weapons moving around or being utilized. That would change my calculus."[2]

The United States had "led from behind," reluctantly joining other Western and Arab nations to intervene on the side of the rebels in Libya. Dictator Muammar al-Qaddafi had been deposed and then brutally murdered in October 2011. In the midst of the chaos of the Arab Spring and the Libyan Civil War of that year, the American diplomatic compound in Benghazi was attacked, claiming the life of US Ambassador J. Christopher Stevens and three other Americans on September 11, 2012. The Libyan quagmire convinced Obama not to get involved in the even bloodier civil war in Syria, where the Assad regime, backed by Iran and Hezbollah, was killing hundreds of thousands of civilians. However, incontrovertible proof of chemical weapons use would be a different matter. Or so, at least, Obama had promised.

For Israel, Syria, just across the border, was a much closer concern. In the early months of the Syrian Civil War, many Israeli intelligence analysts gleefully predicted Bashar al-Assad's imminent downfall. Netanyahu was more ambivalent. He had no love for the Assad family, whose soldiers he had fought together with his brothers Yoni and Iddo in 1973. Assad was an ally of both Iran and Hezbollah. But he had also been a stable presence, preventing escalation on the Golan. In Assad's absence, Netanyahu feared, Syria could become the playground of Hezbollah and other Islamic jihadists. In the first years of the civil war, he counseled other Western leaders not to supply weapons, especially shoulder-launched antiaircraft missiles, to the rebels. There was no way of telling in whose hands they might end up, he warned.

In early 2013, Israel launched the first in a series of air strikes on Hezbollah convoys and storage facilities in Syria. Israel officially refused to take responsibility for the attacks, but no one in the region had any doubt as to their origin. The objective was to prevent Iran's Lebanese proxy from transferring advanced weapons to its strongholds in Lebanon's Bekaa Valley. Netanyahu established a series of his own red lines in Syria—Israel would not allow Hezbollah to acquire advanced weaponry, would respond forcefully to any firing on its territory, and would prevent Iran or Hezbollah from establishing a presence on the Golan.

On August 21, 2013, Obama's red line in Syria was blatantly crossed. The Assad regime attacked rebel-held Ghouta, east of Damascus, with sarin gas, a highly toxic nerve agent, killing 1,429 civilians. Obama had no choice but to order preparations for a missile strike on the regime. And then he dithered, seeking congressional approval as a delaying tactic. Stating his reasons for holding back, he explained that one strike wouldn't topple the regime, and there was no one prepared to take over in Damascus if the regime did topple. Many suspected him of being loath to jeopardize negotiations with Iran by attacking its Syrian ally. Russia snatched Obama's chestnuts from the fire, brokering a deal whereby Assad committed to dismantling his chemical weapons arsenal under international supervision as an alternative to being on the receiving end of an American strike.

Israel and America's other allies in the region were shocked by Obama's backing down. It served as proof that their skepticism about his truthfulness when he said, in regard to Iran, that "all options are on the table" had not been unfounded. For Israel, the elimination of most of Syria's chemical arsenal, which originally had been manufactured to attack Israel, was a strategic windfall. It eliminated an arsenal of weapons of mass destruction across the border and allowed the Netanyahu government to save hundreds of millions in civil defense preparations. But that hardly made up for the strategic vacuum created by Obama's indecision—a vacuum that would soon be filled by ISIS, Russia, and Iran.

Obama, impervious to criticism from Washington's foreign policy establishment for having "tarnished America's credibility" in the Middle East, would be sucked back into Syria a year later, when the Islamic State, a group he had dismissed as "a jayvee team," began beheading Western hostages. All that, however, was in the future as Obama tuned out the foreign policy "experts" and Netanyahu, focusing his efforts instead on reaching a deal with Iran.

In June 2013, a new Iranian president, Hassan Rouhani, had been elected. Rouhani was a member of the clerical class that had been behind Ayatollah Khomeini's Islamic Revolution in 1979, but, unlike his predecessor as president, Mahmoud Ahmadinejad, who had led an outwardly hardline attitude toward the world, the Western-educated Rouhani projected a more flexible image. Netanyahu, in both public appearances and in conversations with other Western leaders, tried in vain to convince his interlocutors that Rouhani and his new government were simply a more user-friendly face of the same extreme regime, and that the real power in Tehran still resided with Supreme Leader Ali Khamenei and the Islamic Revolutionary Guard Corps (IRGC). But the leaders of the West, especially Obama, were eager to find a way to engage diplomatically with Iran openly, and the soft-spoken Rouhani, along with his sophisticated foreign minister, Mohammad Javad Zarif, offered them the opening they had been looking for. Essentially, Netanyahu was right. Rouhani governed at the supreme leader's pleasure, and on the ground in the Middle East, especially in Syria and Lebanon, the IRGC commanders did not take orders from him. But after nearly a quarter of a century of treating Iran as a pariah, the Western political classes warmed to the silver-tongued Zarif, who, just like Netanyahu, had spent some of his formative years in the United States, and served as a diplomat at the United Nations. As one Israeli diplomat put it, "The Iranians have pulled a Bibi," appointing an English-speaking charmer as their chief diplomat.

THE SHARON GOVERNMENT had unilaterally withdrawn from Gaza in September 2005 after dismantling the settlements there. No arrangements were put in place to help alleviate the plight of the Palestinians in Gaza, over one and a half million people living in a narrow coastal strip stuck between the Mediterranean, Israel, and Egypt (an area measuring 365 square kilometers, or 141 square miles). In June 2007, Hamas launched a coup in Gaza, ousting the Fatah-dominated Palestinian Authority. In response, Israel imposed a blockade, allowing only basic foodstuffs and medications to get through. The blockade failed to stop Hamas from smuggling in and building an impressive array of rockets. In response to the Hamas attacks, Israel launched a series of operations in Gaza—Summer Rains, Hot Winter, Cast Lead, and Pillar of Defense—causing hundreds of Palestinian deaths and widespread damage to the already crumbling infrastructure.

In the lulls between fighting, Olmert, and then Netanyahu, had more pressing matters to attend to than searching for a solution for Gaza's population. The National Security Council (founded in 1999 on Netanyahu's instructions, but awarded no real powers) had drawn up comprehensive plans for Gaza's future, but the cabinet routinely ignored them.

On June 12, 2014, three Israeli teenagers were kidnapped and then murdered by Hamas members in the West Bank. Their fate unclear, the government ordered the IDF on a widespread search operation with the additional objective of degrading Hamas networks. Four hundred Hamas operatives were arrested, including fifty who had been released three years earlier in the Shalit prisoner exchange deal.

Hamas, in response, launched daily salvos of rockets from Gaza against Israel. Most of the rockets threatening built-up areas were intercepted by Iron Dome and there were no casualties. But despite the intensifying Israeli air strikes on Hamas targets in Gaza, the salvos continued, with Hamas firing at targets deeper within Israel. On July 8, Israel announced Operation Protective Edge.

At every stage of the operation, Netanyahu, with backing from Defense Minister Moshe Yaalon, held out against demands from the IDF General Staff and the more combative members of his cabinet to expand the operation to a wider ground campaign. At one point, he even fired Deputy Defense Minister Danny Danon for criticizing him in public for holding back. Netanyahu was concerned the IDF would get bogged down in a high-casualty conflict in Gaza's narrow alleyways. Even after finally authorizing a ground campaign on July 17, he stipulated the incursions would be limited to a few kilometers.

What forced Netanyahu's hand was Hamas's use of tunnels reaching under the border into Israeli territory. The IDF demanded time to destroy the tunnels before any ceasefire. Israeli intelligence had been aware of Hamas burrowing under the border for years, but Netanyahu's cabinet had only cursorily debated this threat to Israeli civilians. The IDF had devoted scant resources to the tunnels, and its units going into Gaza were untrained and lacked suitable equipment for underground warfare.

Netanyahu was anxious for a ceasefire, but unlike in previous rounds in Gaza, this time Egypt was less enthusiastic about mediating. The new military regime of General Abdel Fattah al-Sisi regarded Hamas as the proxy of its enemy, the Muslim Brotherhood, and was happy to see Israel bleed them. Secretary of State Kerry arrived in the region, but he enraged the Israelis by seeking to include Turkey and Qatar—both supporters of Hamas—in the ceasefire talks. It took fifty days of fighting until the Egyptians finally roused themselves to broker a lasting ceasefire on August 26.

Operation Protective Edge was the closest thing to full-out war in Netanyahu's entire time as prime minister thus far. It ended in bitter stalemate. The number of Palestinians who had been killed reached 2,100, half of them civilians. Tens of thousands of buildings in Gaza were destroyed, but Hamas received only empty promises for ending the blockade and rebuilding the Strip. On the Israeli side, 73 soldiers and civilians were killed. The IDF, with its overwhelming firepower, had significantly degraded Hamas's arsenal, but rockets were still launched daily, throughout the operation, against Israel's cities, including Tel Aviv and the vicinity of Ben Gurion Airport, leading to most foreign airlines suspending services to Israel for forty-eight hours.

As the ceasefire held, there was desultory talk of long-term solutions for Gaza, but Netanyahu's attention quickly became focused elsewhere. His conduct during the Gaza conflict highlighted two contradictory traits in his leadership: a deep reluctance to address burning issues on the Palestinian front, alongside his extreme aversion to risk and large-scale military adventures.

O N MAY 30, 2014, a French citizen of Algerian origin who had spent a year fighting for ISIS in Syria opened fire inside Brussels's Jewish Museum of Belgium, killing four people, including two Israelis. It was the first terrorist attack that had been carried out by a follower of the Islamic State outside the Middle East and the start of a global spree of attacks against Western civilians. Jewish communities were often chosen as targets. On January 9, 2015, two days after the attack on the *Charlie Hebdo* offices, killing twelve and wounding twelve others, four Jews were killed in an attack on a kosher supermarket in Paris.

Israeli officials pressured the families of the four victims to have them buried in Israel. Netanyahu, anxious to be seen as protector of all Jews, attended the state funeral. He insisted on traveling to Paris, despite President François Hollande's office trying to dissuade him, and attended a march organized by the French to demonstrate unity following the Paris terrorist attacks, pushing himself to the front row. Many other world leaders had arrived to show their support for France—Netanyahu was the only one who had been asked to stay away. He also demanded an invitation to join Hollande on his solidarity visit to Paris's Grand Synagogue, where he was met by cheers from the largely Zionist congregation. But as Netanyahu ended his twenty-seven-minute speech with a call "to join your Jewish brothers in our historical homeland, in the land of Israel," they responded by singing the French national anthem, "La Marseillaise."[3] It was a typically French response to Netanyahu advising they abandon the country they considered their homeland.

Most Jews are not Israeli citizens, and many more Jews voted for Barack Obama than for Netanyahu's Likud. Yet Netanyahu regarded himself as the "representative of the entire Jewish people."[4] His attitude polarized Jews around the world like no previous Israeli leader. Many were enraged by the way Netanyahu monopolized the memory of the Holocaust to brand Israel's enemies as reincarnations of the Nazis and his own critics as collaborators. At the AIPAC conference in 2012, Netanyahu brought up the historical controversy over President Franklin Roosevelt's decision not to bomb Auschwitz. "My friends, 2012 is not 1944. Never again!" he cried, to stormy applause from the pro-Bibi crowd.[5] Many other American Jews were scandalized by what sounded like an admonishment of Obama for ignoring a second Holocaust.

Three years later, Netanyahu invented his own history, telling the Zionist Congress in Jerusalem that Mufti Haj Amin al-Husseini, the godfather of Palestinian nationalism, had suggested that Hitler exterminate the Jews in their meeting in November 1941. "Hitler didn't want to exterminate the Jews at the time, he wanted to expel them," claimed Netanyahu.[6] Husseini had indeed been a virulent anti-Semite and admirer of Hitler, but no serious historian agrees that he had been the author of the Final Solution.

Netanyahu had no patience for his Jewish Diaspora critics. Since his teens in Philadelphia, he had developed a deep disdain for liberal American Jews who had the chutzpah to not support Israel, and its leader, unquestionably.

Throughout most of his public career, most of the American Jews surrounding Netanyahu have been part of the admiring minority supporting his views. The few Jewish critics he has met have tended to be administration officials, diplomats, and journalists—habitual sell-outs of Jewish values, as far as Netanyahu is concerned. Earlier during his career, Netanyahu made more of an effort to hide these feelings and worked on his relationships with liberals. But as he stayed in power, it became more obvious that he did not respect them. In private, he has agreed with assessments that they will eventually assimilate and disappear. "He has a true disdain for progressive Jews," said a senior official in the Obama administration who was intensely proud of his Jewish heritage. "He talks about stuff they like—high tech and gay rights—but it's clear he disrespects people who put their liberalism on par with their Jewishness."

Sheldon Adelson, the casino mogul who was prepared to spend $100 million trying to oust Obama in 2012, and at least twice that on the Netanyahu-worshiping *Yisrael Hayom* newspaper, came to embody the best of American Jewry for Bibi. Netanyahu even ended his decades-long friendship with Ronald Lauder, who since 2007 has been the president of the World Jewish Congress. Lauder had refused to force Israel's Channel 10, in which he was a majority shareholder, to stop conducting its "Bibitours" investigation into the lavish travel arrangements the Netanyahu couple demanded, and received, from wealthy benefactors. Once Adelson delivered Netanyahu his "own media," Lauder was cast out of Netanyahu's circle.

On November 12, 2014, the Knesset held a preliminary vote on the "Law for the Advancement and Protection of Print Journalism in Israel." It was an anti-dumping bill, preventing free newspapers from being distributed nationally. Its target was *Yisrael Hayom*, which would be forced to charge readers a minimum fee, eliminating its Adelson-sponsored advantage over competing newspapers that were critical of Netanyahu. The vote passed 43–23, with most of those voting in favor members of the coalition. Netanyahu turned on his ministers and cried "shame."

Three weeks later, he suddenly escalated his routine legislative disagreements within the coalition and gave Finance Minister Lapid an ultimatum to follow his orders or resign. Without waiting for an answer, Netanyahu announced the firing of Lapid and Livni the next day, citing their "attacking the government and its head from within the government."[7] Livni had voted in favor of the "Yisrael Hayom Law," as had members of Lapid's Yesh Atid party.

Netanyahu's third government had served for only twenty months. Bibi was calling early elections, squandering the time remaining in his term, two and a half years, to save Adelson's free newspaper.

NETANYAHU EXPECTED THE 2015 election to be a rerun of 2013. With the Israeli political scene as splintered as ever, none of the other party leaders seemed to jeopardize his primacy. The campaign strategy was to be the tried and true candidate who could be trusted. He would run as the only politician with the experience and will to stand up to Obama over the Iranian issue and deny the Palestinians a share of Jerusalem. To demonstrate the clear gulf of competence between the prime minister and his would-be rivals, Likud produced humorous online campaign ads in which Netanyahu played himself as the "Bibisitter," the only person trusted to take care of the nation's children, and as a kindergarten teacher, dealing with an unruly mob of urchins who played the other parties' leaders. His next move was less amusing.

On January 21, 2015, House Speaker John Boehner announced that Netanyahu would be addressing a joint session of Congress. It was an unprecedented breach of protocol. Although the Speaker does officially invite foreign leaders to address Congress, it had never before happened without prior consultation with the White House. Ron Dermer and the Republican leadership had hatched their plan in secret, blindsiding the Obama administration, which was informed about the visit just an hour before the invitation became public.

It wasn't just the absence of any consultation that was the problem, or even that Netanyahu would be addressing Congress only two weeks before the Israeli election. The leader of an ally of the United States was coming to Washington to tell Congress to oppose the president's key foreign policy initiative—the nuclear deal with Iran.

In November 2013, Iran and the United Nations Security Council's P5+1 group of world powers, led by the United States, had reached an interim agreement in Geneva whereby Iran accepted some temporary limits on its nuclear program in return for sanctions relief. As part of the deal, some of its frozen assets would be released. It was a time-limited partial agreement, and the parties struggled to reach a final deal throughout 2014.

Netanyahu surprised no one in lambasting the interim agreement, calling it "not a historic agreement, but a historic mistake." It had made the world, he said, "a much more dangerous place because the most dangerous regime in the world has taken a significant step toward attaining the most dangerous weapon in the world."[8]

But the real battle with Obama would commence over the final deal. Netanyahu's speech to Congress was a preemptive strike. He was relying on the Republican-dominated Senate to block the president. Shrugging off criticism, he insisted this was no election stunt. He would be speaking in Congress "not just as the prime minister of Israel but as a representative of the entire Jewish people."[9] Nothing deterred him, not the Jewish American leaders discreetly begging him to reconsider, or the dozens of Democratic representatives threatening to boycott his address, or the White House itself, which made clear that Netanyahu would not be meeting the president or any other member of the administration while in Washington.

On March 3, with his guests Adelson and the Holocaust survivor and author Elie Wiesel, looking on from the gallery, Netanyahu became only the second foreign leader in history to address Congress three times—equaling the record set by his hero and role model Winston Churchill. He opened with a nod to bipartisanship, singling out old Democratic friends and singing Obama's praises for all he had done for Israel. But there was no mistaking the message that came next.

Netanyahu pronounced the Iran deal that Secretary Kerry was working on "a bad deal that will at best curtail Iran's nuclear ambitions for a while." It would allow Iran to keep its nuclear infrastructure intact, imposing only a decade-long moratorium on further development and uranium enrichment. And it wouldn't curtail Iran's support for the Assad regime or terrorist organizations. "It's a very bad deal," Netanyahu intoned. "We're better off without it."[10]

He had thrown down the gauntlet to Obama, months before the Iran deal was even signed. The Republicans, and some Democrats, applauded him rapturously, interrupting the forty-five-minute speech with twenty-six standing ovations. That night on *The Daily Show*, comedian Jon Stewart said it was "by far the longest blowjob a Jewish man has ever received."[11]

It was also an abject failure. The speech failed to boost Netanyahu in the polls back home. And when, four months later, the nuclear agreement was finally signed, it was clear that it had failed to deliver a veto-proof majority.

EVEN BEFORE NETANYAHU took off for Washington, it was clear that his campaign strategy had backfired. Six years of Iran-talk had wearied Israelis. Not that the voters blamed Netanyahu for damaging Israeli-US relations. Obama-hatred remained an electoral asset, and a large majority still believed the president was anti-Israel. But the scare tactics that had worked in 2009 and 2013 had lost their potency. Too many Israelis were just too tired of hearing Bibi go on about Iran while they couldn't afford to buy a decent-sized apartment.

In mid-February, the state comptroller published a report on the prime minister's residence budget, revealing a rise of hundreds of thousands of shekels in public money spent on the upkeep of the Netanyahu family. Israelis had long known that Netanyahu lived a lavish lifestyle at their expense, but enough of them were still willing to vote for him as long as they believed he was taking care of their interests. Fewer now seemed convinced of that. A week later, a second comptroller's report came out severely criticizing the Netanyahu government for not acting to rein in the spiraling cost of housing.

In a speech responding to the report, Netanyahu reprimanded those who fretted over such minor things. "When we talk about housing prices and the cost of living, I don't forget for a moment life itself. And the biggest threat facing us in our life as Israeli citizens and as a state is the threat of Iran acquiring nuclear energy weapons with a stated intention of exterminating us."[12] Netanyahu had badly misjudged the public mood. "Life itself" instantly became a byword for his disconnect from the daily concerns of ordinary Israelis.

With only a month until the elections, Likud was tied in the polls with the Zionist Union (HaMahaneh HaTziyoni), a joint list of Labor and Tzipi Livni's Ha'Tnuah. The latest Labor leader, Isaac "Buzhi" Herzog, a slight and mild-mannered lawyer with a high-pitched voice, was an unlikely challenger. Herzog's strategists even tried artificially adding some stubble on his campaign photographs, to give him a more rugged image. And yet, by the end of February, Herzog had opened up a small but steady gap.

The polls and atmosphere on the streets were beginning to feel like a rerun of the 1999 election, when Netanyahu lost to Barak. Whether it was a rekindling of the social protests of 2011, or simply Netanyahu-fatigue, there was an "Anyone but Bibi" dynamic. Parties from left and right barely spoke about the issues; it was all about replacing Netanyahu. Likud was hemorrhaging votes in all directions, in particular to Bennett's Jewish Home and to Kulanu (All of Us), a new center-right party led by Moshe Kahlon, a popular Likud minister who, like so many others, had fallen out with Bibi. Kahlon presented himself as the "real Likud" of the working classes. By the time Netanyahu left for Washington, Likud was down to nineteen seats in the polls. Returning to Israel on March 4, thirteen days before the election, Bibi was dismayed to discover that his speech to the US Congress had failed to deliver a bounce in the polls.

On March 7, Meir Dagan, the Mossad chief who had clashed with Netanyahu over the Iran strike, addressed an "Israel Wants Change" rally in Tel Aviv's Rabin Square. Dying from liver failure, he told a reporter on the eve of the rally, "I have to keep my last shreds of strength to push him out." In tears, Dagan delivered the only political speech of his life, telling fifty thousand Israelis, "For the first time in my life I'm afraid of our leadership. This the biggest leadership crisis in the state's history. We deserve a leadership that will serve the public and not itself."[13]

But the pollsters and pundits predicting Netanyahu's political demise were reckoning without Bibi's base. Netanyahu, who hadn't given an interview to the Israeli media for nearly two years, stormed the airwaves, predicting a divided Jerusalem and an Islamic State on Israel's borders if the weak and ineffectual "Buzhi and Tzipi" were to win. Settler leaders were called in for meetings with Netanyahu, who sternly warned them that anything but a vote for Likud would lead to the rise of the left and a resumption of the Oslo process. Few of them were great admirers of Netanyahu—they had known him for too long—but many of them were convinced. Meanwhile, millions of text messages were being sent to a million targeted recipients, warning that the right wing was in danger of losing power.[14]

Three months earlier, Netanyahu's campaign team had determined that many traditional Likud voters were tired of Bibi and planned to vote for another party or stay home. Their contingency plan was to broadcast panic. As the settler activists fanned out throughout their communities, the text-message bombardment intensified. Likud sent eighteen million text messages in the last week of the campaign, five million on election day.

The last media polls, broadcast two days before the election, had Likud lagging behind the Zionist Union by four seats. But they were out of date. By then, Netanyahu's private pollsters had already picked up a resurgence of support, putting him back in the lead. Nevertheless, in all his public appearances, Netanyahu stuck to the panic message, saying, "The right wing is in danger."

All pretenses were dropped as Bibi played shamelessly to his base. In an interview with the settlers weekly *Makor Rishon* (First Source), which Adelson had recently acquired, Netanyahu promised, "If I'm elected, there won't be a Palestinian state." In a second interview, he elaborated, saying, "Anyone today who wants to establish a Palestinian state and retreat from territory is giving radical Islam a launching-pad to attack Israel."[15]

On previous election days, Netanyahu had crisscrossed the country, bringing out the vote. On March 13, 2015, he made do with one short visit to a run-down pedestrian mall in the southern coastal town of Ashkelon. He spoke for three minutes, warning, "There is still a gap between the Zionist Union and Likud."[16] On previous election days, he had been surrounded by ambitious MKs who were angling for cabinet positions. Sensing Likud's defeat, they had now disappeared. This time, only an old rival, Energy Minister Silvan Shalom, turned up. He was preparing to challenge Netanyahu on the day after the election. But Netanyahu was relying on text messages, Facebook, and racism.

Wavering right-wing voters received a steady stream of messages. "Turnout is three times higher in the Arab sector." "Herzog promised to appoint an Arab minister to his cabinet." "Hamas called on Israeli-Arabs to go and vote."

At noon, a twenty-eight-second clip was posted on Netanyahu's Facebook page: "The right is in danger of losing power, the Arab voters are moving in droves to the polling stations," he warned. "We only have you. Go to vote. Bring your friends and relatives. Vote Likud to close the gap between us and Labor. And with your help, and God's help, we will form a national government that will protect the state of Israel."[17]

Hours before the voting ended, a relatively low turnout was predicted. At 10:00 p.m., the exit polls forecast a tie between Likud and the Zionist Union. Loud cheers went up in Likud headquarters. They had closed the gap, and the predicted results of the other parties suggested that Netanyahu would be able to build another right-wing religious coalition. But the exit polls had closed two hours earlier than the actual voting stations to give the pollsters time to tabulate their results. They missed a massive surge of over half a million voters in the last two hours. Turnout was the highest since 1999.

As the official results started coming in, Likud's lead grew. In the last days and hours of the campaign, disappointed Likudniks planning to vote for Jewish Home or Kulanu had been panicked home to Likud. The night ended with Likud on thirty seats, six more than Zionist Union. Israelis may have been tired of Bibi, but he had won a fourth term.

29

A Bad Mistake of Historic Proportions

Barack Obama was not surprised by Netanyahu's fourth election victory. As his aides gleefully pored over the latest polls predicting Bibi's downfall, he advised they keep their hopes down. "[Obama] didn't think Herzog could win and said the Israeli people have been consistent in supporting Bibi and weren't about to change their minds," a senior administration official later recalled. "He said Abbas hadn't helped either." By the last quarter of his presidency, Obama had long realized that the foreign policy holy grail of American presidents, Israeli-Palestinian peace, was beyond his grasp. Disappointed by Netanyahu and his Palestinian counterpart, Obama was pinning all his hopes on the Iranians. Just like Netanyahu, he was already preparing for a battle on the Hill over the Iran deal.

For years, the two allies had been playing a double-game with each other. US diplomats routinely briefed their Israeli counterparts on the state of play in the P5+1 negotiations, and the Israelis made their comments, which were usually critical. Beneath the surface, the administration engaged with the Iranian leadership through a secret Omani back channel. Obama sent secret letters to the Iranian supreme leader Ali Khamenei urging him to renew the nuclear talks and proposing an alliance against ISIS. Mossad discovered the backchannel's existence and Israel informed the administration that it was aware. The US National Security Agency maintained surveillance on Netanyahu, even after he'd given up on an Iran strike in late 2012, to keep tabs on his conversations with Jewish American leaders and his Republican allies, in which they suspected Netanyahu of leaking details of the P5+1 talks that he had received from the administration. It wasn't the first time the United States and Israel had cooperated while spying on each other.

After countless rounds of talks, on July 14, 2015, John Kerry and the Iranian foreign minister, Mohammad Javad Zarif, signed the deal, along with the other P5+1 representatives. The details of the Joint Comprehensive Plan of Action were much as Netanyahu had described in his speech to Congress. Iran would freeze its nuclear development for a decade. Its nuclear infrastructure was to remain largely intact, and Iran was allowed to continue its low-grade uranium enrichment, subject to international supervision. In return, all nuclear-related sanctions would be removed.

In a tense phone call, Netanyahu told Obama that it was "a bad mistake of historic proportions."[1] Obama tried taking a conciliatory tone, promising America's continuing support and proposing that the two countries take advantage of Defense Secretary Ash Carter's upcoming visit to Israel to begin negotiating a new ten-year military assistance treaty. But Netanyahu wasn't interested in negotiating. He needed one more showdown with Obama in Congress. For history's sake.

There followed two and a half months of intense lobbying, quarterbacked in Washington by Ron Dermer, to get Congress to oppose the deal. The Jewish community and the pro-Israel organizations would be split between the president and the prime minister. For Netanyahu, it was a lost cause. He had all the Republican senators, but Obama needed only thirty-four Democrats to support him to deny his opponents a veto-proof majority. The deal was not technically a treaty, so it didn't have to be ratified by the US Senate. Instead, to oppose it, Congress would have to pass a resolution of disapproval, and to do so it would have to break a Democratic filibuster. No amount of lobbying would make more than a handful of Democratic senators abandon their president on a "legacy" vote.

Obama had another ace up his sleeve—the Israeli security chiefs. He already knew that, although in their professional opinion, the deal could have been much better, they still realized it would effectively give them a ten-year break from Iran's nuclear program. That break would allow Israel's security establishment to focus on more immediate threats. Once again, the IDF generals were conspiring against Bibi.

By September 2, it was all over. Thirty-four senators had publicly confirmed their support. Obama had his Iran deal. A month later, Netanyahu delivered his concession speech at the United Nations General Assembly. He was still very critical of the deal. "After three days of listening to world leaders praise the nuclear deal with Iran," he said, "I begin my speech today by saying: Ladies and gentlemen, check your enthusiasm at the door." But for the first time he admitted there were good points to the deal, which "does place several constraints on Iran's nuclear program." Finally beaten by Obama, he was reduced to imploring the international community to "make sure that the inspectors actually inspect."[2]

OBAMA AND NETANYAHU's relationship would never recover. It had already taken a turn for the worse following the election in March. Obama had pointedly waited two days before calling to congratulate Netanyahu on his victory, demonstrating his displeasure at the "Arabs in droves" remark and the promise not to establish a Palestinian state during his term.

Netanyahu tried to walk back his pledge to the settlers, saying he was still committed to a "sustainable, peaceful two-state solution." In an interview two days later, Obama said, "We take him at his word when he said that it wouldn't happen during his prime ministership, and so that's why we've got to evaluate what other options are available." On the "Arabs in droves," Obama noted, it "starts to erode the name of democracy in the country."[3]

Netanyahu, aside from a weak apology to Israel's Arab citizens a week after the election, made no attempt to prevent his Likud MKs from making a stream of racist anti-Arab statements. The 2013 and 2015 elections had brought a new crop of populist Likudniks to the Knesset. Likud still officially called itself a "national-liberal party," but not a shred of liberalism remained. The only active senior Likudniks still espousing the Jabotinskean tradition of "decorum," combining Jewish nationalism with a commitment to human rights and the rule of law, were Benny Begin, a lone voice on the backbenches, and President Reuven Rivlin.

Netanyahu had fought tooth and nail against Rivlin's election in 2014. Not only was he an old rival, but Rivlin was too independent for Netanyahu's taste. As Knesset Speaker, Rivlin had once insulted Sara by seating her next to Tzipi Livni at an official event. Bibi did everything he could to find an alternative candidate, even calling the non-Israeli Elie Wiesel in New York, hours before the ballot, begging him to put himself forward as candidate for president. But the popular Rivlin was ultimately elected president. From his new position, Rivlin lambasted the wave of anti-Arab racism. But even the prime minister continued to indulge himself occasionally. After a terrorist attack carried out by Israeli Arabs in January 2016, Netanyahu arrived on the scene, promising, "We won't allow two states here, one law-abiding state for Jews and another one without the rule of law."[4]

The racism was stoked by a new wave of Palestinian violence that began in October 2015. Unlike previous waves, when attacks were usually carried out by members of Palestinian organizations, this time the perpetrators were young nonaffiliated individuals, often just teenagers motivated online to take a kitchen knife, a makeshift gun, or a vehicle to ram into Israelis. The violence was bred of desperation among Palestinians at the lack of any progress toward independence. Religious incitement online accused the Jews of "defiling" the Haram al-Sharif mosques.

It wasn't a full-fledged intifada. The violence failed to spread to wider swaths of Palestinian society and petered out after a few months. But the period of nearly daily stabbings and shootings were a stark reminder that the conflict wasn't going away. It also exposed a deep divide within Israeli society, as populist politicians called for making sure attackers "didn't leave the scene alive." Once again, it was the generals calling for moderation. The IDF chief of staff, Lieutenant General Gadi Eisenkott, angered the politicians when he said in a lecture that soldiers didn't always need to shoot to kill. "I don't want to see a soldier emptying a magazine on a 13-year-old girl holding scissors," he said.[5]

On March 24, 2016, Sergeant Elor Azaria was captured on camera shooting a wounded Palestinian assailant to death. By the time the shooting took place, however, the assailant had been lying on the ground for ten minutes, after he was injured in a stabbing attempt. Azaria was arrested and later put on trial for manslaughter, and the IDF High Command, as well as Netanyahu's defense minister, Moshe Yaalon, condemned his action. But a large proportion of the public, and nearly all the right-wing parliamentarians, were scandalized that an IDF soldier was under arrest for shooting a terrorist. Netanyahu had initially condemned, but quickly changed his tune, calling Azaria's parents to express his support.

Yaalon's views on the Palestinian issue were virtually indistinguishable from Netanyahu's. He had no problem saying publicly that there was no chance of a Palestinian state being established this century. But he was no racist, and as a stickler for military discipline, he abhorred Azaria's act of vigilantism. The pro-Azaria chorus and growing criticism of the IDF commanders isolated him within Likud. In May, he discovered that Netanyahu was holding secret talks with Avigdor Lieberman on Yisrael Beiteinu's return to the coalition. Lieberman demanded the Defense Ministry. Yaalon resigned from the government, the Knesset, and Likud before Netanyahu could fire him. He and Netanyahu had also clashed recently over the prime minister's insistence on buying more submarines for the navy, a demand that only later on would begin to make sense to him.

With Lieberman back in his cabinet and Likud purged of yet another moderate voice, Netanyahu now headed his most right-wing coalition ever. Dan Meridor, the moderate Likud "prince" who had returned to the party in 2009 in the hope of finding a more pragmatic Netanyahu, said that "Bibi isn't a racist himself, but he is adept at using racism for political purposes. He gave up on centrist voters ever supporting him again and now only appeals to his base."

ALONG WITH RACISM, during his fourth term Netanyahu began to show an increasing tendency toward authoritarianism. He left the post of foreign minister vacant. Ostensibly, this was to allow for a coalition deal with Labor in which Herzog would become foreign minister. But Netanyahu preferred to run the Foreign Ministry himself, having always seen the role of Israel's diplomats merely to project his own policies and beliefs and serve as *hasbara* envoys. On delicate diplomatic missions he preferred to send one of his old confidantes—Ron Dermer; his lawyer Yitzhak Molcho; Dore Gold, whom he appointed as the Foreign Ministry's director-general; or a new addition to this group, the former deputy Mossad chief Yossi Cohen, who had won Netanyahu's trust as national security adviser.

Traumatized by Meir Dagan's rebelliousness, Netanyahu had taken to appointing Mossad chiefs he could trust. Dagan was replaced by Tamir Pardo, who had served under Yoni Netanyahu in Sayeret Matkal and had been beside him at his death in Entebbe. But Pardo had been a disappointment, not fully backing Netanyahu on Iran. In a private meeting in July 2014, he said the Palestinian conflict was a more existential issue for Israel than the Iranian threat. His remarks were reported by Barak Ravid of *Haaretz*, enraging Netanyahu.[6] When Pardo's term ended in December 2015, his deputy (called only "N" because his name was classified) was frontrunner to replace him. Hours before the announcement, N received a phone call from Netanyahu with a strange question. "Will you be loyal to me?" N answered that he would do everything necessary to protect the state. "I'll get back to you," said Netanyahu. But that evening, the appointment went not to N, but to the loyal Yossi Cohen.[7]

Another obsession Netanyahu could never let go of was the media. In 2012, he said in a private meeting, "We have two enemies, the *New York Times* and *Haaretz*. They set the agenda for an anti-Israel campaign all over the world."[8] *Haaretz*, Israel's oldest newspaper, is staunchly liberal-Zionist. But for Netanyahu, its criticisms of his policies made it anti-Israel. Holding an early election to block the legislation against Adelson's *Yisrael Hayom* hadn't been enough. In his fourth term, he appointed himself communications minister, and the coalition partners had to sign an agreement promising to support him on any media legislation.

Netanyahu appointed another loyalist, his former chief of staff and 2015 campaign manager, Shlomo Filber, as director-general of the Communications Ministry. Together they set about "breaking the media monopolies." The license-holders of Channel 2, Israel's most popular station, were forced to divide it into two weaker stations. But their efforts to force Channel 10, the combative station that had broadcast hard-hitting investigations on Netanyahu's financial affairs, to close down over unpaid licensing fees was stymied by Finance Minister Moshe Kahlon. A campaign to prevent the new public broadcasting corporation, a result of legislation in Netanyahu's previous term, from going on air was blocked by the Supreme Court.

Meanwhile, Netanyahu as communications minister was in charge of authorizing mergers for the owner of the telecommunications giant Bezeq, Shaul Alovich. Alovich, a personal friend of his, also owned one of Israel's largest websites, Walla. Walla's coverage of Bibi and Sara had become increasingly positive since Alovich had acquired it. In February 2017, the Israeli Supreme Court put an end to the farce, ruling that due to conflict of interest, Netanyahu could not continue as communications minister.

For two and a half years after the election, Netanyahu's only interviews with the Israeli media were to the obscure "Heritage Channel," which is owned by an Israeli-Georgian oligarch friendly to Netanyahu. Its sycophantic interviewers could be relied upon to deliver softball questions and nod along with the answers. Occasionally, Netanyahu would meet with groups of journalists for off-the-record sessions. In one of them, he turned to Ilana Dayan, the anchor of Channel 2's investigative journalism show, asking, in all seriousness, "Why don't you do an investigation on how much I'm admired abroad?"

Dayan had recently broadcast an investigation into the goings-on in Netanyahu's office. Netanyahu had responded by accusing Dayan of having "not even a drop of personal integrity" and being "one of the leaders of a concerted frenzy against Prime Minister Benjamin Netanyahu, aimed at toppling the right-wing government."[9] It took Dayan six minutes to read the entire response onscreen. Having failed to tame or shut down Israel's adversarial press, Netanyahu was going for the jugular, accusing the media of trying to bring down an elected government.

Most of the professional staff in his press office had been replaced by young online gunslingers, who helped Bibi overcome his technophobia and communicate with the public by Facebook and Twitter, bypassing the heads of the mainstream media. When Donald Trump came along, Netanyahu eagerly adopted his "fake news" terminology, branding with it most of Israel's news organizations.

As 2016 BEGAN, Netanyahu was counting down the months until Obama's departure. It had been seven long years, in which they had achieved little together. Obama had prevented Netanyahu from launching a war in Iran, which could well have drawn in the United States. Netanyahu had failed to prevent the Iran deal. No progress whatsoever had been made on the Palestinian front, although Obama blamed Abbas for this as well. That the West Bank had remained relatively calm for most of the period could be chalked down as an achievement.

Back in 2011, Obama and French president Nicolas Sarkozy had been overheard by journalists discussing Netanyahu at a G20 summit. "I cannot bear him, he's a liar," complained Sarkozy. "You're fed up with him?" answered Obama. "I have to deal with him every day."[10] Sarkozy was long gone from the Élysée Palace, and Obama was fed up as well. Soon he would be leaving the White House and wouldn't have to deal with Netanyahu at all.

Long after Obama had given up hope, Netanyahu continued to string along would-be peacemakers who believed they could somehow force the pragmatic Bibi out of him and get him to sign a historic agreement with the Palestinians. Shimon Peres tried and failed in 2011. In 2013, Tzipi Livni tried for twenty months after being appointed chief negotiator—until she got fired. All that time, in the background, Tony Blair, the "Quartet" envoy to the Middle East, had been traveling back and forth to Jerusalem and Ramallah, while maintaining in London a secret backchannel between Netanyahu and the representatives of Abbas.[11] After the 2015 election, Netanyahu had promised Labor leader Herzog that should he join his government, he would be the one leading the negotiations. In a secret summit in Jordan in February 2016, King Abdullah and Egypt's President Abdel Fattah al-Sisi proposed to jointly host negotiations. There was talk of the Saudis getting involved.

Some of these tracks continued for years, but they never reached their destination. Netanyahu or Abbas, often both, would always find a reason to derail talks at the crucial moment. There was political pressure back home, and there were unilateral steps taken by the other side, or demands for further security arrangements, settlements, or prisoners, or Hamas lurking on the sidelines.

While even the most seasoned diplomats were eventually replaced by new hopefuls, Netanyahu and Abbas had been doing this for over twenty years, and they knew every pothole to get stuck in down the road. Ultimately, they both had an interest in maintaining the status quo, and were incapable of making the difficult decisions necessary for a breakthrough. However, they did maintain security cooperation between their officers, for the sake of keeping Hamas out of the West Bank. While nearly all the other Israeli prime ministers over the past three decades—Rabin, Peres, Barak, Sharon, and Olmert—had looked for ways to achieve a breakthrough with the Palestinians, Netanyahu, like Shamir, is intent on preserving the status quo. Unlike Shamir, who was forced to contend with the Intifada, Netanyahu inherited the Oslo framework, and he has learned over the years how to utilize it to his own benefit. He realized that while being dysfunctional, and nothing even close to the Palestinians' aspirations, the semiautonomous Palestinian Authority in the West Bank had created a political and financial base that Abbas and the Fatah leaders around him were loath to give up on. As leader of the opposition in the early 1990s, Netanyahu had lambasted the Oslo Agreements. Twenty years later, he emerged as Oslo's most valiant defender. The framework put in place by Rabin and Peres had left Netanyahu with the means to preserve a fragile calm in the West Bank. While his critics continue to insist that Israel's occupation of the Palestinians is "unsustainable," Oslo allows Netanyahu to continue sustaining it and to prove to Israelis that Israel does not have to make peace with the Palestinians to enjoy financial prosperity and improving international relations. "Abbas is even more useless than Bibi," said one senior Western diplomat at the end of yet another fruitless trip. "But Bibi has all the power."

No one traveled down that road with more hope than John Kerry. In his four years as secretary of state, no matter how many times Netanyahu let him down, Kerry never lost faith in him. He continued trying to bring the Israelis and Palestinians together from wherever he was in the world, often holding video-conferences with them from exotic locations. He was continuously calling Netanyahu, speaking with him for hours on the phone. One American diplomat estimated that Kerry had called Netanyahu four hundred times during his tenure. Sometimes Kerry would phone from his home, out of the blue, without notifying his aides and without a note-taker listening in on the call. Such was his forlorn faith in Bibi.

Obama let Kerry founder, as Netanyahu refused to commit to fixed borders, or even to present the Americans with a map marking out proposed territory and borders for a two-state solution.

In July 2013, Kerry achieved his one breakthrough. After three years with no official negotiations, Israel and the Palestinians agreed to hold permanent status talks for nine months. During this period Israel committed to release 104 prisoners in four tranches, and the Palestinians suspended their requests to be accepted as an independent state by international organizations. Tzipi Livni was to represent Israel at the talks, but Yitzhak Molcho, who was there to report every detail back to Netanyahu—making sure maps never came up—gave Livni a limited mandate.

By April 2014, the talks were bogged down. The Palestinians presented Livni with a list of demands, starting with a written commitment from Netanyahu on a Palestinian state based on the 1967 borders, with Jerusalem as its capital. When no answer was forthcoming, they renewed their application for full membership in the United Nations. In response, Israel announced that it would not release the last tranche of twenty-six prisoners and issued building permits for hundreds of new homes in East Jerusalem.

"Both sides wound out in a position of unhelpful moves," a woeful Kerry told the Senate Foreign Relations Committee three days later. "The prisoners were not released by Israel on the day they were supposed to be released and then another day passed and another day, and then 700 units were approved in Jerusalem and then poof—that was sort of the moment."[12] Kerry sounded as if he was placing most of the blame on Israel, but no serious pressure came from the Obama administration to renew talks. Obama needed Kerry for the Iran negotiations, and with the administration hoping soon to sign the nuclear agreement, which Netanyahu would hate, it wasn't the best of times to try and force anything on him. Ultimately, it was the Iran deal that saved Netanyahu from making progress with the Palestinians.

Kerry would go on trying to renew negotiations to the very last days of the Obama administration. In the administration's twilight, there was an expectation that Obama would deliver his "parameters" for the permanent status. Netanyahu was anxious to prevent that from happening. Parameters would set clear guidelines for negotiations with the Palestinians under future administrations. Netanyahu thrived on blurred lines. Obama was unsure whether the parameters were at all realistic and deferred his decision until after the election, not wanting to hamper Hillary Clinton's campaign with an unnecessary Bibi case. After the election it was too late.

Kerry was to have the last laugh. On December 24, the United States decided to abstain rather than veto a UN resolution defining Israel's settlements as illegal. Netanyahu was furious, saying that "the Obama administration not only failed to protect Israel against this gang-up at the UN, it colluded with it behind the scenes."[13] But he really had no reason to complain. Every previous administration had decided at some point not to veto resolutions condemning Israel. It had taken the Obama administration nearly eight years to reach that point. Besides, a new president was about to be inaugurated and things would never be the same. Donald Trump hadn't even entered the White

House, yet his transition team were already falling over themselves to try to prevent the UN vote. Their overtures to the Russian ambassador would feature, a year later, in the Mueller investigation into Trump's ties with the Kremlin.

O BAMA WOULD NOT take revenge for all the times Netanyahu had confronted him. It seemed that he had meant what he said when he had promised to continue supporting Israel, despite Netanyahu. Or else Obama was simply trying not to create trouble for his hoped-for successor. He never did throw Israel under the bus. Bibi's critics, who had accused him of causing irreparable damage to the US-Israeli relationship by going to speak in Congress, were astonished at Obama's equanimity. Not only was Netanyahu not forced to pay a price, but as soon as the Iran deal passed Congress, talks began on the new ten-year military assistance agreement.

The Obama administration was prepared to give Israel an unprecedented package, but Netanyahu prevaricated for months. Some of his Republican friends were urging him not to sign with Obama, in the hope of getting a better deal from the next administration. But as the Republican primaries drew to their astonishing result, Netanyahu decided he would be better off signing with Obama than having to renegotiate with Hillary Clinton. On October 15, the United States and Israel signed the memorandum of understanding for a ten-year $38 billion military aid package.

A week later, Netanyahu and Obama met at the United Nations General Assembly for what was supposed to be their last meeting with Obama in office. Bibi joked that now that Obama would have lots of time to golf, he must come and visit their weekend home in Caesarea, near Israel's only golf course. Obama looked mainly relieved that it was their last meeting. Netanyahu couldn't hide his satisfaction. His old foe was leaving and he was still in power.

But they were to meet again just eight days later.

On September 28, Shimon Peres passed away at the age of ninety-three. Obama, the Clintons, and Kerry all flew to the funeral. In the VIP tent, Obama was disgusted to spot Sheldon Adelson, a man who literally stood for the opposite of Peres's values in every possible way.

In his eulogy, Obama ruefully reflected on Peres's "unfinished business" and recalled Peres saying to him that "Jews were not born to rule over another people." Peres, said Obama, "showed us that justice and hope are at the heart of the Zionist idea" and "believed the Zionist idea would be best protected when Palestinians too had a state of their own."[14]

It was a speech that many Israelis had hoped they would one day hear from their own prime minister. But Netanyahu preferred in his eulogy of Peres to dwell on their frequent arguments. Bibi was soon to be released from the shadow of three rivals—Peres, Clinton, and Obama—and with their departure, he hoped to be finally released of the irksome legacy of the Oslo process.

Mahmoud Abbas had arrived as well to pay his respects. But as Netanyahu laboriously name-checked each and every foreign dignitary, even the Grand Duke of Luxembourg, he pointedly left out the Palestinian president.

30

Nothing Will Happen,
Because Nothing Happened

Hillary Clinton was the last politician Netanyahu wanted to see in the Oval Office after the US election. As First Lady and then secretary of state, she had played key roles in both of the administrations he had clashed with over matters he considered vital to Israel's security. In an interview with CNN, Hillary Clinton had said, "I've known Bibi a long time. And I have a very good relationship with him, in part because we can yell at each other and we do. And I was often the designated yeller."[1] That wasn't exactly what Bibi was looking for in a president.

Had Netanyahu not given up his US citizenship upon becoming an Israeli diplomat in 1982, he would have instinctively voted Republican. But this year's candidate was no kind of Republican he had ever dealt with before. He wasn't even a politician.

"Bibi is a risk-averse politician. He dislikes instability and Donald Trump is the opposite of the kind of leader he wants to deal with," said a former aide who spent time with Netanyahu in the United States. Another former member of his team put it more bluntly: "Bibi is scared of both candidates."

Netanyahu had learned from his mistake in 2012 and was keeping well away from the campaign. He had sent strict instructions to Israel's diplomats in the United States to show no favor to either candidate under any circumstances.

What made it even more difficult was that his benefactor Sheldon Adelson, who had first supported Lindsey Graham and then Marco Rubio, was now firmly on the Trump bandwagon, plowing millions into the campaign. Things with Adelson had not been going smoothly of late. In September 2016, Sheldon and his wife, Miri, had been absent for the first time from Netanyahu's annual speech at the United Nations General Assembly. Sara had been complaining about her photographs not appearing frequently enough in *Yisrael Hayom*, and Bibi was beginning to wonder whether the paper was that helpful to him anyway. "Market share isn't necessarily power," he had said recently, remarking that the paper had "little influence." On his relationship with Adelson, he said, "Do you think I can tell that redhead what to do?"[2]

Like everyone else, he had gone to sleep on November 8 expecting four years of Hillary Clinton. Waking up to Trump, Netanyahu reflected that while this wasn't exactly the GOP president he had dreamed of working with, after so many years of arguing with Democratic administrations, he did see some unique benefits in having a President Trump.

While other world leaders were still working out how to contact the president-elect, putting calls through to the Trump Tower switchboard, Netanyahu was the only one who was already personally acquainted with him. Bibi and Donald had met back in the 1980s, during Netanyahu's UN days—they had been introduced by Ronald Lauder, Bibi's friend who was also an old friend of Trump's.

Trump's name had even appeared on one of Netanyahu's handwritten millionaires' lists, though he was in the lowest category, indicating that he was good for an occasional favor, but not much more. In 2013, Trump had appeared in a YouTube clip, calling upon Israelis to "vote for Benjamin. Terrific guy, terrific leader. Great for Israel" (though it wasn't part of the Likud campaign and had been made by one of Netanyahu's American admirers on his own initiative).

Netanyahu knew other key figures in Trump's circle. The family of Trump's son-in-law and soon-to-be senior adviser Jared Kushner were old supporters—Jared had once had to move out of his room when Netanyahu came to stay with them in New York City. And he was familiar with the Breitbart News Network crowd.

Breitbart's CEO, Larry Solov, had written that the website had been "born in the USA" but "conceived in Jerusalem," and that the idea to set it up had come to him and cofounder Andrew Breitbart when they were on a junket for conservative bloggers to Israel in 2007. One of the highlights of their trip had been a meeting with Netanyahu, who was then leader of the opposition. The website that Solov and Breitbart envisioned, Solov said, "would be unapologetically pro-freedom and pro-Israel. We were sick of the anti-Israel bias of the mainstream media and J-Street."[3]

Most American Jews were horrified by Trump's victory and by the reports of the alleged anti-Semitic views of Steve Bannon, who had been Breitbart's editor-in-chief and was now Trump's chief strategist. But Ron Dermer, who knew Bannon, reported that he was "very pro-Israel." To Netanyahu, that was all that mattered. Netanyahu and Bannon shared a unique historical belief. Both had been brought up—Bibi by his historian father and Bannon by his Catholic parents and teachers—to view the "Reconquista," the fifteenth-century Christian victory over the Muslim Moors in Spain, as a key moment in history when "Western civilization was saved" from the Muslims.[4] Benzion taught Bibi that this was the precedent for the return of the Jews to their land.

On the face of it, there seems to be little in common between the self-made diplomat and politician and Trump, the bumptious salesman. Netanyahu is an intellectual and an ideologue, while Trump finds it difficult to remember any books he's read, and his only dogma has ever been promoting his brand. But there are similarities as well. Both men are fundamentally insecure, lacking in introspection, and have an uncanny ability to sense their rivals' weak spots and sniff out their voters' inner fears. Netanyahu's perpetual campaign mode also resembles the Trump presidential campaign, with its reliance on constantly stirring up resentment and divisions between parts of the electorate. Shortly after the election, Netanyahu began daily urging his aides to "be like Trump." One Trump trait that the Netanyahu team was quick to adopt was branding unfavorable reports in the media as "fake news."[5]

Trump, promising to build a wall on the US border with Mexico, had repeatedly mentioned Israel's border fence as his model, saying, "Walls work. Just ask Israel." Netanyahu, trying to curry favor, Tweeted, "President Trump is right. I built a wall along Israel's southern border. It stopped all illegal immigration. Great success. Great idea," causing a diplomatic spat with Mexico and angry protests from the Mexican Jewish community.

Netanyahu was even more delighted when Trump appointed his team for the Israeli-Palestinian issue. Kushner was to be in charge overall, while two of Trump's lawyers also received key appointments: Jason Greenblatt was to be special representative for international negotiations and David Friedman the new ambassador to Israel. All three men belonged to the right kind of American Jewry, as far as Netanyahu was concerned—conservative, right wing, and Orthodox. They were prime specimens of the minority of American Jews who supported the settlement policy. Greenblatt had studied at a yeshiva in the West Bank, and Friedman had helped with fundraising for one of the settlements. Vice President-elect Mike Pence, a stalwart of the ultra-pro-Israel Christian evangelist movement, was also a reassuring figure. The Trump team proved itself during the transition by trying to convince Russia's ambassador to avert the UN resolution condemning the settlements.

After his election, Trump had called a peace agreement between the Israelis and Palestinians "the ultimate deal" and said that "as a deal maker," he wanted to seal "the deal that can't be made. And do it for humanity's sake."[6] But it quickly became clear that he had no idea how to go about doing it. On February 15, 2017, Netanyahu arrived in Washington for his first White House meeting with a Republican president. At their joint press conference, Trump was asked for his opinion on the two-state solution. Abandoning nearly two decades of American foreign policy, Trump answered, "I'm looking at two-state and at one-state and I like the one that both parties like."

There was a more jarring note for Netanyahu when Trump, answering another question, turned to him and said, "Hold back on settlements for a little bit."[7] But Netanyahu didn't mind holding back on settlements for Trump. It wasn't the total freeze that Obama had demanded in their first meeting, and besides, Netanyahu was happy to have an excuse to rein in his rival, the education minister Naftali Bennett, and the rest of his coalition's far right wing, who were demanding a massive settlement-building drive, including even extending Israeli sovereignty to parts of the West Bank. Netanyahu didn't want to jeopardize his security coordination with the Palestinian Authority.

For all his rhetoric and opposition to formal settlement "freezes," Netanyahu has never been particularly interested in building more settlements. During his tenure, fewer new settler homes were built in an average year in the West Bank than under any of his predecessors in the past three decades.[8] He has continued to receive the grudging support of the settlers because, unlike his predecessors, he is also not

planning to attempt any diplomatic initiative that could lead to some of them being evicted.

Only two months after Trump's inauguration, Dermer, speaking at the annual AIPAC conference in Washington, said that "for the first time in many years, perhaps in decades, there is no daylight between our governments."[9] In early May, there was a flurry of reports from Washington that Trump was planning "something big," that Netanyahu's old friend Ronald Lauder was urging him to put pressure on Netanyahu—and that, of all people, the Trump team was being advised by Tzipi Livni. Netanyahu had been able to portray Obama as a "hostile" president, and therefore defying him was interpreted by many Israelis as a sign of his strength. Saying no to a "friendly" president like Trump would have been more difficult to explain to the Israeli public. But on May 22, as Trump arrived in Israel, Netanyahu's fears evaporated.

Unlike Obama, who had waited five years to make his presidential visit, Israel was on the itinerary of President Trump's very first international tour. Arriving directly from the Saudi capital, Riyadh, Trump stepped off of Air Force One in Ben Gurion Airport and told his hosts, "We just came from the Middle East." Not to be outdone, Sara Netanyahu told the president and First Lady, "We're just like you. The media hate us but the people love us."[10]

Trump spent twenty-four hours in Israel, making speeches that could have easily been written by Netanyahu. At one point Bibi even said, "I think we quote each other." On the peace process, Trump said he was "personally committed," but that he had no plans. In the many speeches he made during his whirlwind visit, he barely mentioned the Palestinians, and never once a Palestinian state or the settlements. Beyond mentioning that both sides would have to make "tough decisions" to reach peace, he offered no specifics. But he was hopeful, after his meetings with Arab leaders in Riyadh, where he said he had discovered that "there's a lot of love out there" in the Middle East.[11] On the other hand, he had plenty to say about Iran's malignant influence in the region.

In the short closed meetings he had with Netanyahu, Trump had some vague ideas about working with the Saudis and other Sunni states, but nothing much beyond that. In his brief meeting with President Mahmoud Abbas in Bethlehem, Trump mainly demanded that the Palestinians crack down on incitement against Israel in their schools and media and stressed the need to fight terrorism. As Trump made his final farewell speech at the Israel Museum in Jerusalem, Sheldon Adelson, in the first row, watched proudly. He had spent millions to bring the two men to power. It had been the perfect visit.

Greenblatt and Kushner made a few more trips to the region, usually telling either side what they wanted to hear, but not proposing any new plans. Meanwhile, in Washington, there were reports that Trump, beginning to realize how complicated the Israeli-Palestinian conflict was, had lost his initial enthusiasm for achieving the "ultimate deal."

In August, Abbas met with a group of left-wing Israeli MKs in Ramallah. "I have met with Trump's envoys about 20 times since the beginning of his term as president of the United States," he reported wearily. "Every time they repeatedly stressed how much they believe in and are committed to a two-state solution and a halt to construction in the settlements. I have pleaded with them to say the same thing to Netanyahu, but they refrained. They said they would consider it but then didn't get back to me."[12]

Ten days later, Netanyahu was guest of honor at a settlement not far from Ramallah to celebrate fifty years since the beginning of the settlements. "We are here to stay, forever," he said. "We will deepen our roots, build, strengthen and settle."[13] This time there was no American president on the phone demanding explanations.

Worse was in store for the Palestinians when Trump broke with nearly seven decades of US foreign policy by announcing that the US would recognize Jerusalem as Israel's capital. Like all other governments, the US had refrained from officially recognizing Jerusalem until a final Israeli-Palestinian agreement could be reached. President Abbas responded that the Palestinians would no longer recognize the US as an "honest broker," nor accept a Trump peace proposal, if any would ever be put forth. Trump fired back by threatening to cut US funding for UNRWA, the UN agency helping Palestinian refugees.

THERE WERE DRAWBACKS to having an administration so detached from the region. In July 2017, when a short round of violence broke out following the killing of two Israeli police officers on the Temple Mount in Jerusalem, and Netanyahu's hasty decision to set up metal detectors at the entrance to Haram al-Sharif, no US secretary of state was willing to make marathon phone calls to Abbas, ensuring security cooperation with

Israel. Netanyahu was forced to swallow the humiliation of dismantling the metal detectors. At least calm was restored.

Where Trump's lack of any real interest in foreign policy irked Netanyahu most was Syria. For six years, Israel had watched anxiously from its northern border as the Assad regime lost control of most of the country, which was being torn up among rival rebel factions and the jihadists of the Islamic State. Into the vacuum had come Iran and its Lebanese proxy Hezbollah, who propped up the failing Assad. Israeli intelligence kept its eagle eye focused on Hezbollah and Iran's Quds Force officers, and every few weeks came news of mysterious explosions and air strikes on depots and convoys of advanced weapons that Hezbollah was hoping to spirit away to its arsenal in Lebanon's Bekaa Valley.

Netanyahu's Israel had been careful not to get sucked into the terrible war across its border, but over six years it had carried out nearly a hundred operations in Syria, trying to prevent Hezbollah from building up its military capabilities. On January 18, 2015, a group of senior Hezbollah commanders and Iranian officers including a general had been killed in an air strike on the Golan Heights. This wasn't just another night attack on an arms convoy, but the elimination of an Iranian and Hezbollah command group in Syria that had been planning to expand its operations to Israel's border.[14]

At no point in Netanyahu's premiership was Israel so close to being "on the brink of war with Hezbollah and Iran," as one senior IDF officer described it months later. Israel braced for a response, which came in the shape of a missile attack a few days later on the Lebanese border that killed two Israeli soldiers. And then all was quiet. Iran and Hezbollah were too invested in the survival of the Assad regime for a further escalation with Israel. The gamble had paid off—Hezbollah kept away from the Golan.

Even Netanyahu's most bitter critics in the security establishment had been forced to praise him for safeguarding Israel's northern interests as Syria descended into chaos. But by early 2017, that achievement seemed to be eroding. In September 2015, Russia, taking advantage of Obama's inaction in Syria, had deployed its air force to Syria, and had begun ruthlessly bombing the rebel areas. Within eighteen months, Vladimir Putin had saved his client Bashar al-Assad from losing power, and the regime was back in control of most of the country. Iran, which had backed Assad from the start, with military assistance and billions of dollars, now demanded, in return, to be allowed to establish permanent bases on Syrian soil. Netanyahu's entreaties to the Trump administration to intervene on Israel's behalf with Putin to block Iran's entrenchment failed to result in action. Netanyahu was forced to rely on Putin, who relished the opportunity to keep both Iran and Israel off-balance.

It would be a gross exaggeration to say that Netanyahu was beginning to miss Obama, but he realized he wouldn't be able to rely on Trump either.

NETANYAHU REVELED IN finally having the Palestinian monkey off his back. Halfway through the Obama presidency, he had already identified rapidly diminishing international interest in the issue. Aside from John Kerry, France's President Hollande, and a handful of European foreign ministers, fewer world leaders were bothering him about the Palestinians. The optimistic decade after the end of the Cold War, when democracy was on the march and even the most intractable conflicts seemed solvable, had been forgotten. New autocratic leaders were coming to the fore, and "illiberal democracy" was spreading. With the Arab world in turmoil, the European Union in crisis, and Asian powers rising, the world just stopped caring about the Palestinians. And Israel had technology to offer.

Netanyahu had failed to convince the world that Israel was justified in keeping the settlements, but he had succeeded in taking the settlements off the global agenda. He had changed the old diplomatic paradigm whereby the Israeli-Palestinian conflict was the source of all the problems in the region.

Netanyahu expanded Israel's diplomacy in the Far East, where leaders were especially eager to acquire Israeli technology and had little interest in the Palestinians. He established a special rapport with nationalist leaders, such as India's Narendra Modi and Japan's Shinzo Abe.

"Bibi loves meeting Asian leaders," said one senior Israeli diplomat in 2015. "They just want to talk business. Recently he sat down for an hour with the leader of one of the major Asian powers, and the entire meeting was about technology deals, until the last minute when one of the diplomats cleared his throat and put a note in front of the leader. It was a thirty-second statement on the importance of the peace process. The leader read it and asked Netanyahu if he wanted to respond. Bibi said no, and they went off to lunch."

Netanyahu loved playing the statesman, and there were plenty of prime ministers and presidents constantly visiting Jerusalem to give him the impression that it was him they were seeking. Not a month passed without a foreign trip, with Sara at his side. In some months he made two or even three excursions abroad. He had become one of the most recognized world leaders—at the British prime minister's office on Downing Street, "a call from Netanyahu" would be the code used by aides to bring meetings to an end.[15] He expanded his Asian outreach to Africa and Eastern Europe and started holding multinational regional summits, where he could dispense wisdom to half a dozen leaders at a time. The fascination was real. Netanyahu was the leader of a small country who had brazenly defied two presidents of the United States and emerged unscathed.

Another group of leaders who were gradually willing to engage with Netanyahu were the Arab Sunni dictators, who saw him as a partner both in their joint rivalry with Shi'a Iran and as a useful ally to have when dealing with Trump's Washington. After the years of turmoil following the 2011 revolution in Egypt, a new strongman had emerged in President Abdel Fattah al-Sisi, who came to power in 2014 and immediately reinforced the Egyptian military's iron grip on power. Under Sisi, the security relationship with Israel, cooperating against Hamas in Gaza and ISIS in Sinai, intensified. Sisi smilingly told interviewers that he had useful conversations with Netanyahu and that they spoke over the phone "a lot."[16]

Beneath the surface, cooperation with other Arab states that, unlike Egypt, had no diplomatic relations with Israel were improving as well. While no details were being acknowledged in public, Netanyahu's emissaries and senior figures in the Saudi leadership were coordinating their moves against Iran.

In many ways, Netanyahu felt more at ease with leaders like Sisi, Trump, Putin, and Modi—"strongmen" with a disregard for liberal democracy who saw in Netanyahu a kindred spirit and a veteran challenger of international consensus.

FROM EARLY 2017, the trips were Netanyahu's only respite from a relentless barrage of police investigations into his and Sara's financial affairs. Those of his closest associates came under scrutiny as well.

Upon returning to power in 2009, Netanyahu was determined not to allow the legal system to badger him or his wife again. His loyal justice minister, Yaakov Neeman, appointed Yehuda Weinstein, a defense lawyer specializing in white-collar cases, as the new attorney general. At one time or another Weinstein had worked for most of the senior Israeli politicians who were facing allegations of corruption, including Netanyahu. In 2016, Weinstein was replaced by Avichai Mandelblit, who for the previous three years had been Netanyahu's trusted cabinet secretary.

Mandelblit, a painstakingly meticulous former IDF military advocate general, was reluctant to investigate his old boss. The first case brought before him regarding Netanyahu was the "Bibitours" investigation in January 2017. Despite evidence of half a million shekels being paid by private individuals and organizations to upgrade tickets and hotels for Bibi and Sara during the period that Netanyahu had been finance minister, Mandelblit ruled there was no criminal case for them to answer.[17]

In December 2015, Netanyahu had appointed Roni Alsheikh, former deputy head of Shin Bet, as police commissioner. He believed Alsheikh wouldn't investigate him, but the spy-chief directed his officers to probe the prime minister's affairs. Mandelblit couldn't ignore the mounting evidence of the Netanyahus' sense of entitlement and indifference to any code of public standards. In October 2016, he authorized widening the investigation into multiple allegations that Sara had misappropriated funds destined for the upkeep of the prime minister's official residence. In December 2016, he ordered a second investigation into crates of champagne, boxes of Cuban cigars, and jewelry that Bibi and Sara had received. The couple didn't deny receiving them, but insisted they were just "gifts" from "close friends."[18] As the gift list lengthened, to the tune of 1 million shekels, and with it the names of well-known tycoons from Israel and abroad who had sent them, police officials favored indicting Netanyahu for taking bribes. While Mandelblit mulled the case, ordering additional inquiries and authorizing police to question Bibi and Sara, more came up. Police investigating fraud allegations against Netanyahu's former bureau chief, Ari Harow, discovered, on Harow's smartphone, recordings of Netanyahu and his media enemy, Arnon Mozes, publisher of *Yedioth Ahronoth*. In meetings before the 2015 election, Netanyahu and Mozes discussed a deal whereby Mozes would have his newspaper improve its attitude toward Bibi. In return, Netanyahu would prevail on Adelson to limit circulation of *Yisrael Hayom*, which was eating into *Yedioth*'s profits.[19]

The two archenemies failed to reach a deal, but police were convinced they had the basis of a bribery indictment. This time, the police questioned not only Bibi, but also Sheldon Adelson and his wife, Miri. In August, the Supreme Court upheld a Freedom of Information petition requiring Netanyahu to divulge the frequency of calls he had with Adelson and the editor of *Yisrael Hayom*. He was forced to reveal that in 2012–2015 he had spoken over the phone 160 times with Adelson and over 300 times with editor Amos Regev.[20] The Adelsons' relationship with Bibi, which had grown a bit distant in the past year, became even more remote. In September 2017, for the second year running, they didn't attend Netanyahu's UN General Assembly speech, and suddenly began to be seen more in the company of Netanyahu's rival on the right, Naftali Bennett. To make matters worse, Harow, who had once been a loyal aide to Netanyahu, now agreed to serve as a witness for the prosecution to avoid jail time in his own case. And while there was no indication that this was part of the police investigation, some argued that Netanyahu's claims in the recordings that he could get Adelson to change *Yisrael Hayom*'s circulation plans were potential evidence that the vast sums spent on the freesheet could be considered illegal political funding for Netanyahu's benefit.[21]

Much larger corruption investigations were afoot. David Shimron, Netanyahu's attorney of over four decades, was arrested in July 2017 in a case of alleged kickbacks paid by a German shipyard manufacturing submarines and warships for the Israeli navy. Netanyahu wasn't officially a suspect and denied any knowledge of the affair, or of his lawyer also working for the Israeli representatives of the shipyard. But Moshe Yaalon, the former defense minister who had been forced out by Netanyahu a year earlier, suddenly recalled that Bibi had shown a great deal of interest in naval procurement and demanded that Israel buy more submarines.[22]

Another case involved Shaul Alovich, the owner of the telecommunications giant Bezeq, and Shlomo Filber, Netanyahu's former campaign manager, whom he had appointed director-general of the Communications Ministry. Both were arrested in July 2017 on suspicion of colluding in security fraud. In February 2018, Filber, who had served Bibi for two decades, agreed to testify against him. Netanyahu was alleged to have intervened in Alovich's favor in return for positive coverage in a website he owned. Again, Netanyahu denied any knowledge of the actions of one of his closest advisers.[23] A Freedom of Information petition had revealed no less than seven private meetings between Netanyahu and Alovich at the prime minister's residence while he had been communications minister.

Barely a day passed without another development in Netanyahu's legal sagas—associates being hauled in for questioning, billionaires asked to detail the gifts they had showered upon him, former employees of the prime minister's residence suing the couple in court.

Increasingly, Sara became the target as depositions and witness statements were leaked to an insatiable press, which reported on her alleged abrupt orders, obsessive hygiene strictures, and tantrums toward employees at the official residence, as well as her demands for expensive gifts. She began losing cases in the Labor courts as well.

In September 2017, Attorney General Avichai Mandelblit decided to indict her for fraud and breach of trust after a lengthy police investigation into the financial management of the prime minister's official residence raised the charges that she had illegally spent over $100,000 of public funds on private meals by some of the most expensive chefs in Jerusalem, despite the presence of a government-employed cook at the residence.[24] The guests at these meals had been prominent Israeli billionaires.

Bibi and Sara had long had a liking for rich people and a sense of entitlement for the trappings of the high life. When their legal adviser Yaakov Weinroth urged them to write a check for the chefs' bills and avoid an indictment, Sara refused to pay from their own private account.[25]

As the legal troubles accumulated and more of Netanyahu's longtime aides became implicated, the circle of remaining confidants dwindled. He even had to part with his trusted diplomatic emissary Yitzhak Molcho, when he was detained for questioning in the "submarines case." The changing cast of advisers and officials at the prime minister's office joked among themselves about their dispensability, calling themselves "irons" for their anonymity and easy replacement.

As friends and advisers fell away under suspicion, and criminal indictments loomed, a siege mentality pervaded the weekends at the Netanyahus' second home in Caesarea. Ministers who had agreed on policy with him on Thursday found the decisions reversed at the Sunday cabinet meeting, after Bibi had spent a Shabbat with Sara and Yair, their son, who was still unemployed and living at home in his mid-twenties. The weekend after Mandelblit announced his decision to indict Sara, Yair posted a neo-Nazi cartoon on his Facebook page with the faces of his parents' critics, including Ehud Barak, superimposed onto the cartoon. The public backlash forced him to remove it a day later, but not before David Duke and other white supremacists had celebrated it.[26] Yair was becoming a target of media scrutiny, just as his mother had. He and Avner were the only prime ministers' children in Israel's history to have around-the-clock bodyguards and drivers, even though former Shin Bet chief Yoram Cohen insisted there was no security risk. Public criticism intensified when tapes emerged of Yair, during a tour of Tel Aviv sex clubs, with his driver and bodyguards, talking to friends about the services of strippers and prostitutes.

"Nothing will happen, because nothing happened," became Netanyahu's constant response in public to the allegations against them. In Likud rallies organized by his supporters, he launched into long rants against the "leftist fake news media" he said were behind the "unprecedented witch hunt" against him and his family. He made long lists of his achievements, punctuated with the refrain, "That, they don't report!" He was determined not to resign. Even when in February 2018 the police recommended indicting him on multiple charges of bribery and fraud, he vowed to continue serving as prime minister. And even if the media refused to recognize it, Netanyahu was certain the Israeli people knew, just as the world leaders had come to understand, how indispensable his leadership was.

In April 2017, at a gathering of the prime minister's office employees for Passover, Netanyahu described the Israeli media as "an industry of depression." He accused them of "not reflecting the public's feelings":

> Where they see unemployment, I see full employment. Where they see a ruined economy, I see a flourishing economy. Where they see congestion, I see interchanges, trains, bridges. Where they see hesitation and insecurity, I see steadfastness and incredible strength that projects all around us. . . . Where they see a sinking, crumbling nation, I see Israel rising as a global force. I see it all over the world, in all the leaders arriving here every day and in my meetings with them abroad, with the leaders of world powers. That's how they see us—as a global technological power, as a world force in security, in intelligence, in technology. Israel is a wonderful country and from the perspective of decades, certainly from thousands of years, they will truly see a big miracle happened here.[27]

Incapable of recognizing the work of others who built Israel long before he became its leader, and raging against those who won't acknowledge his greatness, Netanyahu is reduced to believing it is a miracle that could never have been achieved without him.

Epilogue
Netanyahu's Israel at Seventy

At the time of this writing, despite all his legal travails, Benjamin Netanyahu is still prime minister of Israel. He reacts with surprise when foreign guests occasionally inquire politely whether he has any retirement plans (Israelis know better than to ask that question). The fact that Netanyahu has been prime minister for over a decade is proof to him that he should remain in office for the foreseeable future. He sees no one capable enough or worthy of replacing him and fails to understand how anyone could contemplate someone else leading Israel.

To be the prime minister of Israel, he believes, one needs a grasp of history, a vision for the future, and the fortitude to withstand unbearable pressures. He knows only one man with these qualities. The idea of one of his long list of political rivals (including all his senior Likud colleagues) occupying his office is not just laughable but a threat to the nation's survival, in his opinion. The Jewish state has existed for seven decades now, but to Netanyahu its existence remains as precarious as that of the Hasmonean dynasty of Judea, constantly at risk from the Roman Empire. One wrong turn and Israelis in the twenty-first century could face a similar fate to the Jews of Europe in the Holocaust.

Netanyahu's unique awareness of imminent destruction is why he believes, despite Israel being a democracy, that any challenge to his leadership is a threat to national security. He brands any legitimate attempt, real or perceived, to topple his government as a "putsch against an elected leader." This is in contradiction to Israel's parliamentary system, whereby the prime minister is elected, and can at any time be deposed, by a majority of the members of the Knesset, especially as Likud under his leadership has never received more than a quarter of the votes in an election.

Indeed, although Netanyahu may soon surpass David Ben-Gurion as Israel's longest-serving prime minister, he has also constantly been the prime minister with the smallest proportion of the national vote. He has ruled for so long only thanks to the splintered Israeli consensus and his knack for inciting certain communities and sections of society against one another. He has built unhappy coalitions of dissatisfied politicians who are convinced, like him, that no matter how much time they spend in power, they are still outsiders facing a mythological elite.

Netanyahu didn't create the divisions in Israeli society. Likud inherited those from Israel's founding fathers. But whereas the party's first leader, Menachem Begin, who was so despised by Bibi and Benzion for his perceived weakness, dedicated his career to trying to bridge those gaps and unify the nation, Netanyahu has prised open every possible crack.

In Netanyahu's Israel, the economy has never been so successful. But he has done nothing to address the growing inequality. Israel's neighbors have never been as weak and the IDF so powerful. But Netanyahu, who inherited the most favorable conditions for peace with the Palestinians, has never tried to grasp the opportunity. The only peace he has been willing to consider is one where Israel bullies the Palestinians into submission. Until that happens, he will continue building walls.

Netanyahu is no warmonger. For all his talk of confronting the Iranian threat, he has been too risk-averse to launch any wars—which is to his credit. He is the prime minister with the lowest casualty rates in Israel's history.[1] But Netanyahu's Israel is living on borrowed time. Even if the Palestinians are too weak to rise up again and the world has ceased to care, the occupation of another nation, nearly of equal size, is eroding Israeli democracy and human rights at an alarming rate. Netanyahu has no plans to deal with that erosion, save for stoking racism and fear.

Netanyahu has no plans because his policies are tailored for his daily political preservation and inspired only by a bleak view of Jewish history. There is nothing in between immediate survival and centuries of jeopardy. Bibi inherited from Benzion a deep disdain for what he sees as an inherent weakness in the Jewish character. Only a strong leader, capable of withstanding unbearable pressure to concede, can safeguard Jewish sovereignty for another generation. But their lack of faith in the Jews runs counter to every intellectual, spiritual, and material achievement of Jews around the world, and of course the foundation and success of Israel long before Bibi came along.

Israel turns seventy in 2018. Netanyahu will be seventy in 2019. He is convinced that no one else but he is qualified to lead the nation into its eighth decade and beyond. But sooner or later, Netanyahu will be forced to leave. He will lose an election, or his rivals will finally muster the courage and a majority to depose him in the Knesset. He may even hang on long enough for the wheels of justice to finally turn him out for incurable corruption. Israel will have other competent leaders, and despite Netanyahu's dire predictions, it will survive without him. They may lack his intellect, powers of analysis, and burning sense of destiny, but they will likely be less suspicious and more conscious of everyday life in the Jewish state.

Perhaps Israel's next leader will be a less safe pair of hands and Netanyahu's sad legacy will have been to pave the way for an even less tolerant and much more dangerous Israel. Hopefully, however, the next leader will embark upon a necessary process of healing and building afresh—because on the day after Benjamin Netanyahu leaves, his ultimate legacy will not be a more secure nation, but a deeply fractured Israeli society, living behind walls.

Jerusalem,
February 2018

Acknowledgments

"Let me tell you my Bibi story"—I can't count the number of times an Israeli, upon hearing I was writing a biography of Benjamin Netanyahu, wanted to tell me his or her recollection of meeting Bibi at some point. It was hardly surprising, considering Israel's small size and the length of time Netanyahu has been involved in its public life. Their story told, they would invariably ask to remain anonymous. Netanyahu is still prime minister, and many of the interviewees for this book were anxious not to incur his displeasure. I thank them all for sharing their experience and insight.

One Israeli who refused to cooperate with this book was Benjamin Netanyahu. My formal and informal requests for interviews were ignored. I did visit him in his office twice during the period of research, in meetings together with senior editors of *The Economist*, a newspaper Bibi much admires. The contents of those meetings were off-record but I will reveal that each time, as we entered his office, Netanyahu turned to my bosses saying, "This is Mr. Pfeffer who's writing a book about me. He doesn't know anything about me. It will be a cartoon." You, dear reader, will be the judge.

Despite Netanyahu's incessant efforts to muzzle it, Israeli journalism remains as defiant and combative as ever. In writing this book, I have continuously been proud, as an Israeli journalist, to encounter the constant reminders of just how thoroughly my colleagues have covered Netanyahu's career. This book would have been impossible without the fruits of their labor, and I am indebted to all those tireless reporters who have spent decades burrowing away, unveiling the truth and safeguarding Israel's increasingly fragile and limited democracy.

I have been fortunate for most of the past two decades to have written for the Haaretz Group. It has been my journalism school, my workplace, and a bastion of all that is best in Israel. I am grateful to our publisher Amos Schocken, without whom this unique institution would not have survived and prospered. My bosses, the editors of *Haaretz*'s English edition, my undying ally Charlotte Hallé, Noa Landau, and Avi Scharf gave me crucial support and the leave to complete this book. Many other *Haaretz* colleagues gave me invaluable insight and information, particularly Aluf Benn, Barak Ravid, Gidi Weitz, and Amir Oren.

For the past three years I have had the privilege of reporting from Israel for *The Economist*. Anton La Guardia, who as Middle East editor hired me, gave me extremely useful advice for writing this book and was good enough to read some of its earlier drafts. Other early readers who helped with advice and encouragement were Lea Rappaport-Geller, Rokhl Kafrissen, and Bret Stephens.

This book would never have even been born without three people in particular. My wonderful agent, Deborah Harris, gave me the first push to write it and has continued faithfully pushing all the way. Jackie and David Landau assured me it was a task within my abilities and continued supporting me. Sadly, David's battle with cancer ended in January 2015. This book is dedicated to his memory. Jackie kindly gifted me David's writing desk and a portion of his library, which have been my constant companions in writing this book. David's research assistant, Shira Philosof, gave me access to David's archives, which were very helpful.

My editor at Basic Books, Dan Gerstle, had faith in this project and was a terrific guide throughout the entire process. He had near-infinite patience with the continuous delays and changes of course until completion.

Thank you to Daniella Peled, without whom I would never have been able to write this. I am nothing without the love and support of my parents, Miryam and David, and my children, Adam, Noam, Tamar, Eitan, and Gilad.

A Note on Sources

FOR ALL THE INTENSE INTEREST IT GENERATES, THERE ARE RELATIVELY FEW GOOD books and biographies on Israeli politics and political figures. Israeli political journalists work daily, feeding the beast and the small Hebrew-speaking audience; the investment of labor in political books is not very rewarding financially.

Thankfully, these political journalists more than make up for the lack of books in their daily output. A great many of them have done enough work to lay the foundations for any serious research in the Netanyahu period. The work of five of these journalists in particular is invaluable to any understanding of this era: *Haaretz*'s Yossi Verter; Nahum Barnea of *Yedioth Ahronoth*; Ben Kaspit of *Maariv*; Channel 10's Raviv Drucker; and Channel 2's Amit Segal. To this must be added the more specialized work of my *Haaretz* colleagues Aluf Benn and Barak Ravid on diplomacy; Gidi Weitz on corruption; Guy Rolnik on the economy; and Amos Harel and Amir Oren on security policy. Outside Israel, the one journalist who best chronicled the eight stormy years of the Netanyahu-Obama relationship is Jeffrey Goldberg of *The Atlantic*.

Of the biographies that have been written during the Netanyahu years, the first two, published in 1997, are very useful—Ronit Vardi's *Bibi—Who Are You Mr. Prime Minister?* (in Hebrew) (Jerusalem: Keter, 1997), and Ben Kaspit and Ilan Kfir's *Netanyahu: The Road to Power* (in Hebrew) (Tel Aviv: Alpha, 1997).

Other useful books on Israeli politics include Dan Margalit's *I Saw Them* (in Hebrew) (Or Yehuda: Kinneret Zmora-Bitan, 1997), and Nahum Barnea's *Netanyahu Days* (in Hebrew) (Or Yehuda: Kinneret Zmora-Bitan, 1999). *The Princes: The Sons and Daughters of the Begin Generation Who Became Leaders* (in Hebrew), by Gil Samsonov (Or Yehuda: Kinneret Zmora-Bitan, 2015), offers a rare insider's view of the evolution of Likud's leadership, and Arieh Eldad's *How Things Are Seen from Here: What Happens to the Leaders of the Right When They Come to Power* (in Hebrew) (Or Yehuda: Kinneret Zmora-Bitan, 2016) is a fascinating right-wing perspective on the failings of Likud prime ministers. *Sayeret Matkal: The Elite Unit of Israel* (in Hebrew) (Jerusalem: Keter, 2000), by Moshe Zonder, is a groundbreaking history of the unit in which the Netanyahu brothers served. Among the Israeli political biographies, David Landau's *Arik: The Life of Ariel Sharon* (New York: Knopf, 2013) is a rare masterpiece.

Important aspects of Israeli politics and Netanyahu's career are covered in *Generals in the Cabinet Room: How the Military Shapes Israeli Policy*, by Yoram Peri (Washington, DC: United States Institute of Peace Press, 2006), and *The Worst Kept Secret: Israel's Bargain with the Bomb*, by Avner Cohen (New York: Columbia University Press, 2010). Of the handful of books written about specific Israeli elections, the two written by Daniel Ben Simon on the 1996 and 1999 campaigns—*Another Land—Victory of the Margins: How the Left Collapsed and the Right Arose* (in Hebrew) (Tel Aviv: Arye Nir, 1997), and *Disenchanted Tribes: Israel Goes to Elections '99* (in Hebrew) (Jerusalem: Carmel, 1999)—are by far the most perceptive and informative.

For an understanding of America's role in Middle East diplomacy and the frequent clashes between Netanyahu and US administrations, Aaron David Miller's *The Much Too Promised Land* (New York: Bantam, 2009) and Dennis Ross's *The Missing Peace* (New York: Farrar, Straus and Giroux, 2004) and *Doomed to Succeed* (New York: Farrar, Straus and Giroux, 2015) are indispensable. Peter Beinart's *The Crisis of Zionism* (New York: Times Books, 2012) makes a start on understanding the growing divide between Netanyahu's Israel and the Jews of the Diaspora.

Adi Armon's research in the early years of Benzion Netanyahu and the ideological struggles that formed his worldview appeared in *Haaretz* and are key to understanding his formative years. Profiles of Netanyahu appearing in the American press over the years that have the rare distinction of withstanding the test of time are David Remnick's "The Outsider" in *The New Yorker*, May 25, 1998, and "Star of Zion," by David Margolick, in *Vanity Fair*, June 1996, along with the chapter on Netanyahu in *Views in Review: Politics and Culture in the State of the Jews* (New York: Farrar, Straus and Giroux, 1998), by Avishai Margalit.

An extremely useful guide for the non-initiated to Israeli politics and the fundamentals of the Israeli-Palestinian conflict is Anton La Guardia's *Holy Land, Unholy War: Israelis and Palestinians* (London: John Murray, 2001). The indispensable books on Israeli and Zionist history during the lives of Bibi and his father and grandfather are Tom Segev's *One Palestine, Complete: Jews and Arabs Under the British Mandate* (New York: Metropolitan Books, 2000); *1949: The First Israelis* (New York: Free Press, 1986); *The Seventh Million: The Israelis and the Holocaust* (New York: Hill and Wang, 1993); and *1967: Israel, the War, and the Year That Transformed the Middle East* (New York: Metropolitan Books, 2007); Avi Shlaim's *The Iron Wall: Israel and the Arab World* (New York: Norton, 2000); Benny Morris's *Righteous Victims: A History of the Zionist-Arab Conflict, 1881–1998* (New York: Knopf, 1999) and *Enemies and Neighbours*, by Ian Black (London: Allen Lane, 2017).

Notes

Where source notes are not included for direct quotations, the material is from my own reporting, including personal interviews on and off the record.

Prologue: Netanyahu's Israel

1. Tal Shalev, "Netanyahu at the Border with Egypt: 'The Impossible Has Been Achieved,'" *Walla*, January 2, 2013.

2. Barak Ravid, "Netanyahu: 'Israel Has No Asylum Seeker Problem, Only Illegal Job Immigrants,'" *Haaretz*, September 30, 2014.

Chapter 1: An Orator of the Highest Grace

1. Benjamin Netanyahu, *A Durable Peace: Israel and Its Place Among the Nations* (New York: Warner Books, 2009), loc. 696, Kindle; first English edition published as *A Place Among the Nations: Israel and the World* (New York: Bantam, 1993).

2. Nathan Mileikowsky, *Orations: A Nation and a Land* (in Hebrew) (Tel Aviv: Miskal, 1994), 18.

3. Ibid., 28.

4. Ibid.

5. Ibid., 179.

6. Netanyahu, YouTube page, "The Personal-National Story of Prime Minister Benjamin Netanyahu" (in Hebrew), February 14, 2015, https://m.youtube.com/watch?v=kgoQfMcA_ek.

Chapter 2: Propaganda, Propaganda, and Propaganda

1. Ze'ev Jabotinsky, "Smol Ha'Yarden" (poem, in Hebrew), *Doar Ha'Yom*, April 11, 1930.

2. Ze'ev Jabotinsky, "Vegan Aizerner Vand (Mir Un DiArbe)—Iron Wall (Us and the Arabs)," handwritten article (Yiddish), 1923, archived at Jabotinsky Institute website, www.infocenters.co.il/jabo/jabo_multimedia/Files/linked/א1%20-7_13.PDF.

3. Anita Shapira, *Ben-Gurion: Father of Modern Israel* (in Hebrew) (Tel Aviv: Am Oved, 2015), 49, 68.

4. Arye Naor, *David Raziel* (in Hebrew) (Tel Aviv: Yedioth Books, 1990), 54.

5. Ari Shavit, "In the Shadow of History," *Haaretz*, May 1, 2012.

6. Benzion Netanyahu, "Towards Ourselves," *Ha'Yarden*, August 5, 1934.

7. Benzion Netanyahu, "Plan for Defeat," *Ha'Yarden*, June 6, 1934.

8. B. Soker (pseudonym), "'Our' University," *Beitar*, November 1943.

9. Adi Armon, "Ben-Zion Netanyahu, the Formative Years," *Haaretz*, November 13, 2016.

10. Ibid.

11. Naor, *David Raziel*, 160.

Chapter 3: On the Sidelines of History

1. Anita Shapira, *Ben-Gurion: Father of Modern Israel* (in Hebrew) (Tel Aviv: Am Oved, 2015), 106.

2. Ofer Grosbard, *Menachem Begin: A Portrait of a Leader* (in Hebrew) (Tel Aviv: Resling, 2006), 82.

Chapter 4: The End of the Great Zionist Dream

1. Ari Shavit, "Ben-Zion Netanyahu in a 1998 Interview: 'There's No Such Thing as a Palestinian People,'" *Haaretz*, April 30, 2012.

2. "Partition Will Not Solve the Palestine Problem!," *New York Times*, September 12, 1947.

3. David Ben-Gurion, *Vision and Way*, vol. 5 (in Hebrew) (Tel Aviv: Ministry of Defense, 1971), 166.

4. Shavit, "Ben-Zion Netanyahu in a 1998 Interview."

Chapter 5: Life Within Sharp Borders

1. Yonathan Shapiro, *Chosen to Command* (in Hebrew) (Tel Aviv: Am Oved, 1989), 82.

2. Jonathan Netanyahu, *Yoni's Letters*, edited by Iddo and Benjamin Netanyahu (in Hebrew) (Tel Aviv: Maariv, 1978), 21.

3. Gadi Blum, "The Power Plan," *Yedioth Ahronoth*, October, 13, 2006.

4. Amos Oz, *A Tale of Love and Darkness* (in Hebrew) (Jerusalem: Keter, 2002), 154.

5. Ibid., 68.

6. Educational Television, Friday Supplement, "Dan Margalit interviews Benzion Netanyahu," April 14, 2005, https://m.youtube.com/watch?v=JmNTOnG3IyM.

Chapter 6: A Terrible Dislocation

1. Channel 20 (Israel), *Generations*, December 17, 2015, https://m.youtube.com/watch?v=zxuL-RF4U2Y.

2. Judith Katzir, *Tzilla* (in Hebrew) (Tel Aviv: New Library, 2013), 79.

3. Michael Bar-Zohar, *Ben Gurion* (in Hebrew) (Tel Aviv: Yedioth Books, 2013), 452. The first two kingdoms are the biblical one and then the Maccabean one; the current state of Israel is sometimes referred to as the third kingdom.

4. Benjamin Netanyahu, *A Durable Peace: Israel and Its Place Among the Nations* (New York: Warner Books, 2009), loc. 2474, Kindle; first English edition published as *A Place Among the Nations: Israel and the World* (New York: Bantam, 1993).

5. Channel 20 (Israel), *Generations*, December 17, 2015, https://m.youtube.com/watch?v=zxuL-RF4U2Y.

Chapter 7: American Ben, Israeli Bibi

1. Jonathan Netanyahu, *Yoni's Letters*, edited by Iddo and Benjamin Netanyahu (in Hebrew) (Tel Aviv: Maariv, 1978), 29.

2. Ibid., 20.

3. Ibid., 21.

4. Ibid., 52.

5. Benjamin Netanyahu, *A Durable Peace: Israel and Its Place Among the Nations* (New York: Warner Books, 2009), loc. 2488, Kindle; first English edition published as *A Place Among the Nations: Israel and the World* (New York: Bantam, 1993).

6. Ibid.

Chapter 8: You Have to Kill Arabs

1. Benjamin Netanyahu, *A Durable Peace: Israel and Its Place Among the Nations* (New York: Warner Books, 2009), loc. 2496, Kindle; first English edition published as *A Place Among the Nations: Israel and the World* (New York: Bantam, 1993).

2. Ibid., loc. 2507.

3. Ibid., loc. 2516.

4. Protocol of meeting of cabinet defense committee, June 15, 1967 (Israel State Archive).

5. Netanyahu, *Durable Peace*, loc. 5841.

6. Ibid., loc. 3274.

7. Jonathan Netanyahu, *Yoni's Letters*, edited by Iddo and Benjamin Netanyahu (in Hebrew) (Tel Aviv: Maariv, 1978), 161.

8. Max Hastings, *Yoni* (in Hebrew) (Jerusalem: Idanim, 1979), 87.

9. J. Netanyahu, *Yoni's Letters*, 166.

10. Ibid., 178.

11. Ibid.

12. Iddo Netanyahu, *Yoni's Last Battle* (in Hebrew) (Tel Aviv: Maariv, 1991), 58.

13. Channel 10 (Israel), *The Source*, interview with Amiram Levin, June 14, 2017, https://m.youtube.com/watch?v=QZ_JawoyBz4.

14. J. Netanyahu, *Yoni's Letters*, 193.

15. Ibid., 163.

16. Ibid., 207.

17. Moshe Zonder, *Sayeret Matkal: The Elite Unit of Israel* (in Hebrew) (Jerusalem: Keter, 2000), 67.

18. Ibid., 72.

19. See photo at the Government Press Office's National Photo Collection, http://gpophotoeng.gov.il/fotoweb/Grid.fwx?search=Sabena#Preview23.

Chapter 9: I've Reached My Target

1. Charles H. Ball, "Professor Recalls Netanyahu's Intense Studies in Three Fields," *MIT News*, June 5, 1996.

2. Ibid.

3. Channel 10 (Israel), "Netanyahu Eulogises His Father," April 30, 2012, https://m.youtube.com/watch?v=QZ_JawoyBz4.

4. Jonathan Netanyahu, *Yoni's Letters*, edited by Iddo and Benjamin Netanyahu (in Hebrew) (Tel Aviv: Maariv, 1978), 222.

5. Ibid.

6. Josef Argaman, *It Was Top Secret* (in Hebrew) (Tel Aviv: Israeli Defense Ministry, 1991), 369.

7. Even though there is no temple, some call the modern state of Israel the third temple.

8. "Yom Kippur War, 40 Years Back: Where Were the Leaders Then," *Walla*, September 13, 2013.

9. J. Netanyahu, *Yoni's Letters*, 239.

10. Barak Ravid, "Netanyahu to Bennett: Don't Lecture Me About Backing the IDF, I Led More Soldiers into Battle Than You," *Haaretz*, March 27, 2016.

11. Channel 2 (Israel), *Yair Lapid* (talk show), January 2, 2006.

12. Benjamin Netanyahu, *A Durable Peace: Israel and Its Place Among the Nations* (New York: Warner Books, 2009), loc. 4555, Kindle; first English edition published as *A Place Among the Nations: Israel and the World* (New York: Bantam, 1993).

13. Quoted in Moshe Zonder, *Sayeret Matkal: The Elite Unit of Israel* (in Hebrew) (Jerusalem: Keter, 2000), 77.

Chapter 10: Trying to Save the State

1. Benjamin Netanyahu, *A Durable Peace: Israel and Its Place Among the Nations* (New York: Warner Books, 2009), loc. 3683, Kindle; first English edition published as *A Place Among the Nations: Israel and the World* (New York: Bantam, 1993).

2. Melvin I. Urofsky, *We Are One! American Jewry and Israel* (Garden City, NY: Anchor Press, 1978), 12.

3. "Notable & Quotable: Martin Luther King Jr. on Israel: Martin Luther King Jr. Speaking to the Annual Convention of the Rabbinical Assembly on March 25, 1968," *Wall Street Journal*, March 31, 2015.

4. Philip Weiss, "How 1967 Changed American Jews," *Mondoweiss*, June 8, 2017.

5. Gil Samsonov, *The Princes: The Sons and Daughters of the Begin Generation Who Became Leaders* (in Hebrew) (Or Yehuda: Kinneret Zmora-Bitan, 2015), 205.

6. Jonathan Netanyahu, *Yoni's Letters*, edited by Iddo and Benjamin Netanyahu (in Hebrew) (Tel Aviv: Maariv, 1978), 265.

7. Ofer Grosbard, *Menachem Begin: A Portrait of a Leader* (in Hebrew) (Tel Aviv: Resling, 2006), 150.

8. Ibid., 164.

9. Yonathan Shapiro, *Chosen to Command* (in Hebrew) (Tel Aviv: Am Oved, 1989), 174.

10. J. Netanyahu, *Yoni's Letters*, 236.

11. Ibid., 239.

12. Grosbard, *Menachem Begin*, 164.

13. J. Netanyahu, *Yoni's Letters*, 218.

14. Anita Shapira, *Ben-Gurion: Father of Modern Israel* (in Hebrew) (Tel Aviv: Am Oved, 2015), 106.

Chapter 11: Stop the World!

1. Benjamin Netanyahu, *A Durable Peace: Israel and Its Place Among the Nations* (New York: Warner Books, 2009), loc. 3649, Kindle; first English edition published as *A Place Among the Nations: Israel and the World* (New York: Bantam, 1993).

2. Saul David, *Operation Thunderbolt* (London: Hodder and Stoughton, 2015), 37.

3. Iddo Netanyahu, *Yoni's Last Battle* (in Hebrew) (Tel Aviv: Maariv, 1991), 15.

4. Jonathan Netanyahu, *Yoni's Letters*, edited by Iddo and Benjamin Netanyahu (in Hebrew) (Tel Aviv: Maariv, 1978), 28.

5. Max Hastings, *Going to the Wars* (London: Macmillan, 2000), loc. 3402, Kindle.

6. Ibid., loc. 3576.

7. Ibid., loc. 3543.

8. Moshe Zonder, "The Select," *Maariv*, August 8, 1994.

9. Shimon Peres, *Go with the Men* (in Hebrew) (Jerusalem: Idanim, 1978), 157.

10. Channel 10 (Israel), *The Source*, Interview with Amiram Levin, June 14, 2017.

11. Laura Blumenfeld, "Brothers in Arms," *Washington Post*, March 9, 1997.

Chapter 12: Why Aren't You in Uniform?

1. Michael Barbaro, "A Friendship Dating to 1976 Resonates in 2012," *New York Times*, April 7, 2012.

2. Ibid.

3. Richard Stengel, "Bibi's Choice: Will He Make War? Can He Make Peace?" *Time*, May 28, 2012.

4. Yehuda Avner, *The Prime Ministers: An Intimate Narrative of Israeli Leadership* (Jerusalem: Toby Press, 2010), 37.

5. WGBH (Boston), "Advocates: Should the United States Support 'Self-Determination' for Palestinians in a Middle East Peace Settlement?," June 6, 1978.

6. Ofer Grosbard, *Menachem Begin: A Portrait of a Leader* (in Hebrew) (Tel Aviv: Resling, 2006), 74.

7. Benjamin Netanyahu, *A Durable Peace: Israel and Its Place Among the Nations* (New York: Warner Books, 2009), loc. 2601, Kindle; first English edition published as *A Place Among the Nations: Israel and the World* (New York: Bantam, 1993).

8. Ari Shavit, "Ben-Zion Netanyahu in a 1998 Interview: 'There's No Such Thing as a Palestinian People,'" *Haaretz*, April 30, 2012.

9. Benjamin Netanyahu, ed., *International Terrorism: Challenge and Response* (Jerusalem: Jonathan Institute, 1981), 39.

Chapter 13: Prime Minister in Ten Years Time

1. David Landau, *Arik: The Life of Ariel Sharon* (New York: Knopf, 2013), 164.

2. Dennis Ross, *Doomed to Succeed* (New York: Farrar, Straus and Giroux, 2015), 180.

3. Richard Reeves, *President Reagan* (New York: Simon and Schuster, 2005), 94.

4. Yehuda Avner, *The Prime Ministers: An Intimate Narrative of Israeli Leadership* (Jerusalem: Toby Press, 2010), 585.

5. Reeves, *President Reagan*, 69.

6. Interview with Moshe Arens, David Landau Archive, Jerusalem.

7. Landau, *Arik*, 196.

8. Interview with Moshe Arens, David Landau Archive.

9. Shimon Shiffer, *Snow Ball* (in Hebrew) (Jerusalem: Idanim, 1984), 112.

10. Seth Anzisk, "Preventable Massacre," *New York Times*, September 16, 2012.

11. Reeves, *President Reagan*, 129.

12. Anzisk, "Preventable Massacre."

13. FAIR (Fairness and Accuracy in Reporting), "Are You on the Nightline Guestlist?," January 1, 1989.

14. Ross, *Doomed to Succeed*, 195.

15. Benjamin Netanyahu, *A Durable Peace: Israel and Its Place Among the Nations* (New York: Warner Books, 2009), loc. 6048, Kindle; first English edition published as *A Place Among the Nations: Israel and the World* (New York: Bantam, 1993).

16. Interview with Benjamin Netanyahu, David Landau Archive.

17. William Safire, "Six Long Months," *New York Times*, March 3, 1983.

Chapter 14: If He Had a Sense of Humor, He'd Be a 10

1. "Shamir: The Sea Is the Same Sea, the Arabs the Same Arabs and Netanyahu the Same Netanyahu," Walla, October 26, 2000.

2. David Margolick, "Star of Zion," *Vanity Fair*, June 5, 1996.

3. Shalom Yerushalmi, *The Crucial Moment* (in Hebrew) (Or Yehuda: Kinneret Zmora-Bitan, 2017), 415.

4. Quoted in Oren Perisko, "Hate from Second Sight," *The Seventh Eye*, March 15, 2016.

5. Eti Hasid, Hanan Kristal, and Ilan Kfir, "Elections 1996," *Hadashot*, December 26, 1986.

6. Dalya Shchori, in *Al Hamishmar*, November 11, 1985.

7. Nurit Brezky, "For Me Television Is an Arena," *Maariv*, August 21, 1987.

8. Benjamin Netanyahu, *A Place Among the Nations* (in Hebrew) (Tel Aviv: Yedioth Books, 2001), 208.

Chapter 15: Prime Minister? Of Course Not

1. Gil Samsonov, *The Princes: The Sons and Daughters of the Begin Generation Who Became Leaders* (in Hebrew) (Or Yehuda: Kinneret Zmora-Bitan, 2015), 208.

2. Shalom Yerushalmi, *The Crucial Moment* (in Hebrew) (Or Yehuda: Kinneret Zmora-Bitan, 2017), 418.

3. Masha Hamilton, "Israeli Quits to Protest Shultz Talks," *Washington Post*, April 1, 1988.

4. Ben Kaspit and Ilan Kfir, *Netanyahu—The Road to Power* (in Hebrew) (Tel Aviv: Alpha, 1997).

5. Thomas L. Friedman, "Baker, in a Middle East Blueprint, Asks Israel to Reach Out to Arabs," *New York Times*, May 23, 1989.

6. Aaron David Miller, *The Much Too Promised Land* (New York: Bantam, 2008), 40.

7. "Robert Gates: The Man Who Would Ban Netanyahu from the White House," *Haaretz*, January 14, 2014.

8. "When You're Serious, Call Us," *Newsweek*, June 24, 1990.

9. Benjamin Netanyahu, *A Durable Peace: Israel and Its Place Among the Nations* (New York: Warner Books, 2009), loc. 2398, Kindle; first English edition published as *A Place Among the Nations: Israel and the World* (New York: Bantam, 1993).

10. Linda Scherzer, "Gas Mask, Time Warp," *Times of Israel*, January 14, 2014.

Chapter 16: A Crime Unprecedented in the History of Democracy

1. Thomas L. Friedman, "Uneasy Debate for Jews in U.S. on Loans Issue," *New York Times*, March 2, 1992.
2. Haim Misgav, *Conversations with Yitzhak Shamir* (in Hebrew) (Tel Aviv: Sifriat Poalim, 1997), 172.
3. Avishai Margalit, *Views in Review* (New York: Farrar, Straus and Giroux, 1998), 321.
4. Israel Television, *Mabat*, January 14, 1993.
5. Yaakov Neeman, *Fear Not My Servant Jacob* (in Hebrew) (Tel Aviv: Yedioth Books, 2017), 219.

Chapter 17: A Political Failure?

1. Yaffa Moskowitz, *Disunity in Unity* (Azur: Cherikover, 2004), 85.
2. Benjamin Netanyahu, *A Durable Peace: Israel and Its Place Among the Nations* (New York: Warner Books, 2009), loc. 2302, Kindle; first English edition published as *A Place Among the Nations: Israel and the World* (New York: Bantam, 1993).
3. Ibid., loc. 2171.
4. Ibid., loc. 4362.
5. Ibid., loc. 5857.
6. Ibid., loc. 6092.
7. Ibid., loc. 2186.
8. Benjamin Netanyahu, "Peace in Our Time?," *New York Times*, September 5, 1993.
9. Zeev Sternhell, "The Faded Stars of the March of Folly," *Haaretz*, September 24, 1993.
10. Nissim Mishal, *Uncensored* (in Hebrew) (Tel Aviv: Yedioth Books, 2011), 98.

Chapter 18: Rabin Is "Not a Traitor"

1. Nahum Barnea, "Over the Balcony," *Yedioth Ahronoth*, July 3, 1994.
2. Nissim Mishal, *Uncensored* (in Hebrew) (Tel Aviv: Yedioth Books, 2011), 61.
3. Israel Television, *Mabat*, October 5, 1995.
4. Knesset Protocol, 13th Knesset, 376th session, October 5, 1995.
5. Ibid.
6. Channel 1 (Israel), *News*, October 5, 1995.
7. Arieh Eldad, *How Things Are Seen from Here: What Happens to the Leaders of the Right When They Come to Power* (in Hebrew) (Or Yehuda: Kinneret Zmora-Bitan, 2016), 424.
8. Mishal, *Uncensored*, 60.
9. Nahum Barnea, "Story of an Alibi," *The Seventh Eye*, May 1, 2000.

10. Mishal, *Uncensored*, 73.

11. Eldad, *How Things Are Seen from Here*, 303.

12. Yitzhak Rabin, "The Last Speech," November 4, 1994, Yitzhak Rabin Center.

Chapter 19: Good for the Jews

1. Ben Kaspit and Ilan Kfir, *Netanyahu—The Road to Power* (in Hebrew) (Tel Aviv: Alpha, 1997), 264.

2. Daniel Ben Simon, *A Different Land* (Tel Aviv: Arye Nir, 1997), 42.

3. Ibid., 59.

4. Ibid., 57.

5. Kaspit and Kfir, *Netanyahu*, 265.

6. Ronit Vardi, *Bibi: Who Are You, Mr Prime Minister?* (in Hebrew) (Jerusalem: Keter, 1997), 302.

7. Laura Blumenfeld, "A Long Bad Dream," *Washington Post*, November 21, 1995.

8. Ben Simon, *Different Land*, 209.

9. Dan Margalit, *I Saw Them* (in Hebrew) (Or Yehuda: Kinneret Zmora-Bitan, 1997), 228.

10. Channel 2 (Israel), "Twenty Years to Netanyahu's First Victory," May 23, 2016.

11. Ibid.

12. Dick Morris, *Behind the Oval Office* (New York: Random House, 1997), 167.

Chapter 20: The Bedrock of Our Existence

1. Aaron David Miller, *The Much Too Promised Land* (New York: Bantam, 2008), 269.

2. Benjamin Netanyahu, Speech to US Congress, July 10, 1996, Israel Ministry of Foreign Affairs archive.

3. Ibid.

4. Steven Erlanger, "In Netanyahu, Congress Sees Familiar Spin," *New York Times*, July 11, 1996.

5. Channel 2 (Israel), "Twenty Years to Netanyahu's First Victory," May 23, 2016.

6. Haim Misgav, *Conversations with Yitzhak Shamir* (in Hebrew) (Tel Aviv: Sifriat Poalim, 1997), 209.

7. Channel 1 (Israel), Conference Call, July 28, 1997.

8. "Israel's Serial Bungler," *The Economist*, October 9, 1997.

Chapter 21: Dragged to Wye

1. Ari Shavit, "Why We Hate Him," *Haaretz*, December 27, 1997.

2. Alex Fishman, "Outrage in the IDF: CGS Silenced by Netanyahu," *Yedioth Ahronoth*, January 15, 1998.

3. Raviv Drucker, *Harakiri: Ehud Barak—The Failure* (in Hebrew) (Tel Aviv: Yedioth Books, 2002), 71.

4. Ibid., 77.

5. Channel 1 (Israel), *News*, July 23, 1997.

6. Amira Segev, "Sharon: I Told the PM, I Don't Know Whether to Help Your Right Hand or Your Left Hand," *Haaretz*, August 13, 1997.

7. Dennis Ross, *The Missing Peace* (New York: Farrar, Straus and Giroux, 2004), 354.

8. Ibid., 370.

9. Ibid., 435.

10. Ibid., 449.

Chapter 22: They. Are. Afraid.

1. Haim Misgav, *Conversations with Yitzhak Shamir* (in Hebrew) (Tel Aviv: Sifriat Poalim 1997), 160.

2. Dennis Ross, *The Missing Peace* (New York: Farrar, Straus and Giroux, 2004), 485.

3. Nahum Barnea, "The Journey of a Coat," *Yedioth Ahronoth*, January 8, 1999.

4. Nissim Mishal, *Uncensored* (in Hebrew) (Tel Aviv: Yedioth Books, 2011), 190.

Chapter 23: A Concerned Citizen

1. "The Netanyahu Report: Full Version," Ynet, September 27, 2000.

2. Ari Shavit, "Ben-Zion Netanyahu in a 1998 Interview: 'There's No Such Thing as a Palestinian People,'" *Haaretz*, April 30, 2012.

3. Lilach Weissman, "Netanyahu Held Tax Haven Bank Account," *Globes*, January 15, 2014.

4. "Ranking of Richest Politicians in Israel," *Forbes Israel*, June 15, 2015.

5. Channel 10 (Israel), *The Source*, "Bibi Uncensored," October 9, 2008.

6. Dennis Ross, *The Missing Peace* (New York: Farrar, Straus and Giroux, 2004), 682.

7. David Landau, *Arik: The Life of Ariel Sharon* (New York: Knopf, 2013), 350–351.

8. Ibid.

9. Channel 1 (Israel), *News*, February 11, 1983.

10. "Netanyahu Is Inciting Against Sharon Like He Incited in Rabin's Time," Walla, March 24, 2002.

11. James Bennet, "A Day of Terror: The Israelis; Spilled Blood Is Seen as Bond That Draws 2 Nations Closer," *New York Times*, September 12, 2001.

12. Benjamin Netanyahu, *Fighting Terrorism: How Democracies Can Defeat the International Terrorist Network* (New York: Farrar, Straus and Giroux, 2001), xix.

13. "Benjamin Netanyahu Testifies About Iraq to Congress," CNN, September 12, 2002.

14. "A Clean Break: A New Strategy for Securing the Realm," Institute for Advanced Strategic and Political Studies, 1996.

15. Arieh Eldad, *How Things Are Seen from Here: What Happens to the Leaders of the Right When They Come to Power* (in Hebrew) (Or Yehuda: Kinneret Zmora-Bitan, 2016), 452.

16. Ari Shavit, *Partition: Disengagement and Beyond* (in Hebrew) (Jerusalem: Keter, 2005), 148.

17. Gideon Alon, "Sharon: Netanyahu Fled for Personal Reasons," *Haaretz*, August 10, 2005.

Chapter 24: My Own Media

1. Gil Samsonov, *The Princes: The Sons and Daughters of the Begin Generation Who Became Leaders* (in Hebrew) (Or Yehuda: Kinneret Zmora-Bitan, 2015), 396.

2. Shahar Ilan, "Ninety Percent of the Knesset Members Supported," *Haaretz*, April 30, 2007.

3. "The Talansky Testimony," *Haaretz*, May 28, 2008.

4. Samsonov, *The Princes*, 402.

Chapter 25: Threats Are What Work

1. Anshel Pfeffer, "Netanyahu Wasn't Surprised by the Election Result," *Haaretz*, February 13, 2009.

2. Merav David, "Talking Unity: Netanyahu and Livni Are Meeting in Jerusalem," NRG, February 22, 2009.

3. Attila Shumpalvi, "Barak After Meeting Netanyahu: 'We Are Going to Opposition,'" Ynet, February 23, 2009.

4. Pinchas Wolf, "Netanyahu's Government Approved by 69 Votes," Walla, March 31, 2009.

Chapter 26: A New Pragmatic Bibi?

1. Ali Abunima, "How Obama Learned to Love Israel," Electronic Intifada, March 4, 2007.

2. Jeff Zeleny, "Obama Meets with Israeli and Palestinian Leaders," *New York Times*, July 24, 2008.

3. Glenn Kessler, "Obama's Signals on Middle East Scrutinized by All Sides," *Washington Post*, January 23, 2009.

4. Anshel Pfeffer, "Hoenlein: Obama's Spirit of Change Could Harm Israel," *Haaretz*, February 13, 2008.

5. Max Boot, "More 'Daylight' Between Netanyahu's Israel and the U.S.—Is That What Obama Wants?," *Los Angeles Times*, March 19, 2015.

6. Roni Sofer, "Netanyahu: A Demilitarized Palestinian State by Our Side," Ynet, June 14, 2009.

7. Ibid.

8. Ibid.

9. Jonathan Allen, "Netanyahu Wows Congress," *Politico*, May 24, 2011.

10. "The President's Speech in Cairo: A New Beginning," Obama White House Archives, June 4, 2009, https://obamawhitehouse.archives.gov/issues /foreign-policy/presidents-speech-cairo-a-new-beginning.

11. "Obama Says Egyptian Transition 'Must Begin Now,'" CNN, February 2, 2011.

12. Benjamin Netanyahu, *A Place Among the Nations* (in Hebrew) (Tel Aviv: Yedioth Books, 2001), 209.

Chapter 27: Your Father Wrote History.
You Are Making History.

1. "Netanyahu: I Congratulated Olmert on the Attack in Syria," *NRG-Maariv*, September 19, 2007.

2. Benjamin Netanyahu, *A Durable Peace: Israel and Its Place Among the Nations* (New York: Warner Books, 2009), loc. 5173, Kindle; first English edition published as *A Place Among the Nations: Israel and the World* (New York: Bantam, 1993).

3. Ibid., loc. 5581.

4. Ibid., loc. 75.

5. Peter Hirschberg, "Netanyahu: It's 1938 and Iran Is Germany," *Haaretz*, November 14, 2006.

6. Helene Cooper, "Obama Condemns Iranian Crackdown," *New York Times*, June 23, 2009.

7. Allyn Fisher-Ilan, "Israel Defense Chief: Iran Not an Existential Threat," Reuters, September 17, 2009.

8. David E. Sanger, "Obama Ordered Sped Up Wave of Cyberattacks Against Iran," *New York Times*, June 1, 2012.

9. Channel 2 (Israel), *Uvda*, "The Iranian File Is Opened," November 4, 2012.

10. Nahum Barnea, "Why Didn't We Bomb Iran," *Yedioth Ahronoth*, April 27, 2017.

11. Channel 2 (Israel), *Uvda*, "Meir Dagan's Last Interview," May 6, 2016.

12. Ibid.

13. Eli Berdenstein, "Meir Dagan: Iran Won't Have a Nuclear Weapon Until 2015," *NRG-Maariv*, January 6, 2011.

14. Elisabeth Bumiller, "Iran Raid Seen as Complex Task for Israeli Military," *New York Times*, February 19, 2012.

15. Channel 2 (Israel), "Benzion Netanyahu's Last Interview," April 30, 2012.

16. Channel 2 (Israel), "Benzion and Benjamin Netanyahu in a Joint Interview," February 7, 2009.

17. "Proud to Be Your Son, Father," *Yisrael Hayom*, May 1, 2012.

18. Ibid.

19. Richard Stengel, "Bibi's Choice," *Time*, May 28, 2012.

20. Ari Shavit, "The Decision-maker Warns: We Can't Rely on the US to Attack Iran in Time," *Haaretz*, August 10, 2012.

21. Attila Shumpalvi, "Netanyahu's Aides Against Peres: He Was Wrong About the Iraqi Reactor as Well," Ynet, August 16, 2012.

22. Ibid.

23. Ben Kaspit, "Strong in Tehran, Weak at Home," *Maariv*, August 1, 2012.

24. "Key Portions of Israeli PM Netanyahu's U.N. Speech on Iran," Reuters, September 27, 2012, https://www.reuters.com/article/us-un-assembly -israel-text/key-portions-of-israeli-pm-netanyahus-u-n-speech-on-iran-id USBRE88Q1RR20120927.

25. Natasha Mozgovay, "Netanyahu Bomb Cartoon at UN Sparks Media Frenzy," *Haaretz*, September 28, 2012.

26. Barnea, "Why Didn't We Bomb Iran."

Chapter 28: The Arab Voters Are Moving in Droves

1. Jeffrey Goldberg, "The Crisis in US-Israel Relations Is Officially Here," *The Atlantic*, October 28, 2014.

2. James Ball, "Obama Issues Syria a 'Red Line' Warning on Chemical Weapons," *Washington Post*, August 20, 2013.

3. "Two Scenes from the Grand Synagogue of Paris," *Tablet*, January 11, 2015.

4. Barak Ravid, "Netanyahu: I Will Go to Congress Like I Went to Paris— to Speak for All Jews," *Haaretz*, February 9, 2015.

5. Jennifer Epstein, "Bibi: Israel Can't Wait Long on Iran," *Politico*, March 5, 2012.

6. "Netanyahu: Hitler Didn't Want to Exterminate the Jews," *Haaretz*, October 21, 2015.

7. Jonathan Liss, "Netanyahu Fired Ministers Lapid and Livni: 'I Won't Suffer Opposition Within the Government," *Haaretz*, December 2, 2014.

8. Batsheva Sobelman, "Israeli Officials Blast Deal with Iran as 'Self-Delusional,'" *Los Angeles Times*, November 23, 2013.

9. Ravid, "Netanyahu: I Will Go to Congress."

10. "PM Netanyahu's Speech to a Joint Session of the US Congress," Israel Ministry of Foreign Affairs, March 3, 2015.

11. Comedy Central, *The Daily Show*, March 3, 2015.

12. Moran Azulay, "Netanyahu After Housing Report: Our Biggest Challenge is Iran," Ynet, February 26, 2015.

13. Channel 2 (Israel), "Dagan in Tel Aviv Rally: Fearful of Our Leadership," March 7, 2015.

14. Channel 2 (Israel), "How Netanyahu Won the Election," January 25, 2016.

15. Ariel Kahana, "Prime Minister: If I'm Elected There Won't Be a Palestinian State," *Makor Rishon*, March 16, 2015.

16. Anshel Pfeffer, "Netanyahu, Herzog Fight Election Day Battle of the Gap," *Haaretz*, March 13, 2015.

17. Amit Segal, "Special: How Netanyahu Won the Elections," Channel 2 (Israel), January 25, 2016.

Chapter 29: A Bad Mistake of Historic Proportions

1. Barak Ravid, "Netanyahu: Iran Nuclear Deal Makes World Much More Dangerous," *Haaretz*, July 14, 2015.

2. Jeremy Stahl, "Benjamin Netanyahu Still Hates the Iran Deal But Is Starting to Concede It Could Work," *Slate*, October 1, 2015.

3. Jessica Elgot, "Huffington Post Meets President Barack Obama," *Huffington Post*, March 21, 2015.

4. Yossi Verter, "Netanyahu Remains a Small Politician, Just Like in 1994," *Haaretz*, January 3, 2016.

5. Rotem Elizera, "The CGS' Scissors Speech," Ynet, February 18, 2016.

6. Barak Ravid, "Pardo: The Conflict with the Palestinians Is the Main Threat on Israel," *Haaretz*, July 6, 2014.

7. Channel 2 (Israel), *Uvda*, "What's Happening in the Prime Minister's Office?," November 7, 2016.

8. John Hudson, "Is the New York Times Israel's Greatest Enemy?," *The Atlantic*, January 19, 2012.

9. Anshel Pfeffer, "Top Israeli Journalist Reads Out Netanyahu Manifesto Against Her on Live TV," *Haaretz*, November 8, 2016.

10. "Sarkozy Tells Obama Netanyahu Is a 'Liar,'" Reuters, November 8, 2011.

11. Amir Tibon, "The Secret Back Channel That Doomed the Israel-Palestine Negotiations," *New Republic*, November 26, 2014.

12. Barak Ravid, "Kerry Places Blame on Israel for Crisis in Peace Talks," *Haaretz*, April 8, 2014.

13. Nahal Toosi, "Netanyahu Slams Obama for 'Gang Up' with U.N. Resolution," *Politico*, December 23, 2016.

14. Anshel Pfeffer, "Shimon Peres' Unfinished Business Hangs over His Funeral," *Haaretz*, September 30, 2016.

Chapter 30: Nothing Will Happen, Because Nothing Happened

1. "Fmr. Sec. Hillary Clinton to Fareed Zakaria: Putin Indirectly Responsible for MH17," CNN, July 27, 2014, http://cnnpressroom.blogs.cnn.com/2014/07/27/fmr-sec-hillary-clinton-to-fareed-zakaria-putin-indirectly-responsible-for-mh17.

2. Anshel Pfeffer, "The Collapsing Political Triangle Linking Adelson, Netanyahu and Trump," *Haaretz*, November 8, 2016.

3. Larry Solov, "Breitbart News Network: Born in the USA, Conceived in Israel," *Breitbart*, November 17, 2015.

4. Joshua Green, *Devil's Bargain: Steve Bannon, Donald Trump, and the Storming of the Presidency* (New York: Penguin Press, 2017), 51.

5. Twitter, @amit_segal, December 12, 2016.

6. Monica Langley, "Trump in Exclusive Interview Tells WSJ He Is Willing to Keep Parts of Obama Health Law," *Wall Street Journal*, November 11, 2016.

7. Barak Ravid, "Trump Declines to Endorse Two-State Solution, Calls on Netanyahu to Hold Back on Settlements," *Haaretz*, February 16, 2017.

8. Chaim Levinson, "Is Netanyahu Responsible for Rise in Settlers Numbers?," *Haaretz*, October 14, 2015.

9. Amir Tibon, "Israeli Ambassador: For First Time in Many Years, 'No Daylight' Between Israel, U.S.," *Haaretz*, March 26, 2017.

10. Jack Moore, "Mrs. Netanyahu Tells Melania Trump: 'The Media Hates Us. Like You,'" *Newsweek*, May 22, 2017.

11. "Statements by PM Netanyahu and US President Donald Trump," Israel Ministry of Foreign Affairs, May 22, 2017.

12. Channel 2 (Israel), "Abbas: Doubt if Trump Can Move Talks," August 20, 2017.

13. Ido Ben Porat, "Netanyahu in Samaria: In Eretz Yisrael Settlements Will Not Be Uprooted," *Arutz Sheva*, August 28, 2017.

14. Anne Barnard, "Iran Confirms Israeli Airstrike in Southern Syria Killed One of Its Generals," *New York Times*, January 19, 2015, https://www.nytimes.com/2015/01/20/world/middleeast/iran-says-one-of-its-generals-was-killed-in-israeli-strike-in-syria.html.

15. Nick Robinson, *Election Notebook: The Inside Story of the Battle over Britain's Future* (London: Bantam, 2015), 68.

16. Lally Weymouth, "Egyptian President Abdel Fatah al-Sissi, Who Talks to Netanyahu 'a Lot,' Says His Country Is in Danger of Collapse," *Washington Post*, March 12, 2015.

17. See, for example, Yonah Jeremy Bob, "Analysis: Bibi Tours Gone in the Blink of an Eye," *Jerusalem Post*, January 4, 2017.

18. Yaniv Kubovich, "Netanyahu Questioned by Police over Gifts," *Haaretz*, January 3, 2017.

19. Gidi Weitz, "Details of Bribery Deal Netanyahu Negotiated with Media Mogul Revealed," *Haaretz*, January 11, 2017.

20. Revital Hovel, "Forced to Divulge Phone Records, Netanyahu Says He Spoke to Adelson 40 Times a Year," *Haaretz*, August 31, 2017.

21. Revital Hovel, "Former Netanyahu Aide Ari Harow Reaches Deal to Become State's Witness," *Haaretz*, August 4, 2017.

22. "Netanyahu Was Directly Involved in German Submarine Deal Ya'alon Reportedly Tells Police," *Haaretz*, January 29, 2017.

23. Shelly Appelberg, "Israel Cracks Down on Largest Telecom Firm Bezeq; CEO, Two Netanyahu Allies Arrested," *Haaretz*, July 13, 2017.

24. Revital Hovel, "Attorney General Announces Sara Netanyahu Will Be Indicted for Fraud," *Haaretz*, September 8, 2017.

25. Channel 12 (Israel), Interview with Yaakov Weinroth, *Uvda*, November 9, 2017.

26. "Netanyahu's Son Celebrated on Neo-Nazi Website After He Posted Anti-Semitic Meme," *Haaretz*, September 12, 2017.

27. Itamar Eichner, "Netanyahu on the Media: They See Congestion, I See Interchanges," Ynet, April 3, 2017.

Epilogue: Netanyahu's Israel at Seventy

1. According to a study carried out for this book by data-analyst Nehemia Gershuni-Aylho, Netanyahu has had by far the lowest number of deaths annually from warfare and terrorist attacks, on average, during his premiership than any other elected Israeli prime minister.

Index

YARDEN GABBAY

ANSHEL PFEFFER has covered Israeli politics and global affairs for two decades. He is a senior correspondent and columnist for *Haaretz* and Israel correspondent for *The Economist*. He lives in Jerusalem.